V OTHER PUBLIC INSTITUTIONS

VI DEMOCRACY IN BRITAIN

Preface

This book is a general introduction to British politics. It is an attempt to convey clear information about every significant aspect of the subject and to facilitate an adequate understanding of the British political system. Within the compass of a brief introductory text it is not possible to provide a detailed description or analysis of all the topics covered. Readers who wish to delve more deeply into any particular aspect should refer to the suggestions for further reading at the end of each chapter.

Part I deals with the political and electoral context within which the process of British politics takes place. Chapter 1 considers British political culture, which is defined as the historical, cultural and attitudinal setting within which our political institutions have to operate. Chapter 2 discusses the living constitution by describing the key characteristics and analysing some of the leading interpretations of constitutional developments in Britain. Chapter 3 describes the electoral system and assesses its strengths and weaknesses in the eyes of academics and politicians alike. Chapter 4 deals with voting behaviour by identifying the most significant groups in the electorate, the main influences upon voting and some continuing uncertainties about the future.

Part II considers the sources of power, pressure and opinion within the British political system. Chapter 5 deals principally with the two main political parties by considering their ideological principles, political functions, national organisation and constituency activities. Chapter 6 reviews the main functions, organisation and power of pressure groups, and analyses the nature and extent of their involvement in the political process. Chapter 7 looks at the important role of the media, and assesses the nature and extent of their influence within the political system. Chapter 8 considers public opinion by seeking to clarify its composition, the process by which it is formed and its effects upon British politics.

Part III describes the activity and significance of the three traditional institutions which constitute Parliament in Britain. Chapter 9 reviews the powers and functions of the Monarchy, and assesses its special relationship with the British public. Chapter 10 on the House of Lords describes the composition, powers and functions of that ancient institution, and reviews briefly the various proposals for its reform. Similarly Chapter 11 describes the composition, powers and functions of the House of Commons and then reviews briefly the prospects for its reform.

Part IV deals with the main components of central government in Britain. Chapter 12 describes the machinery of Cabinet government, and goes on to consider the power of the Prime Minister and the role of the Cabinet. Chapter 13 describes the work of central government Departments, considers the role of Ministers and reviews some of the key problems which arise in Whitehall. Chapter 14 deals with the civil service, describes its composition and functions, and considers the various methods of controlling the bureaucracy. Chapter 15 looks at policy and decision making in British central government by identifying the main stages in the process and analysing some of the key aspects and possible improvements.

Part V is concerned with the other public institutions in the British political system. Chapter 16 describes the structure and composition, powers and functions of local government, before going on to consider its relations with central government and the various attempts by the latter to achieve greater control. It also discusses some of the ways in which the balance between central power and local autonomy changed in the 1980s. Chapter 17 deals with the public sector, notably the problems posed by public corporations and the continuing argument about how best to control them. It also reviews the wide-ranging debate on privatisation and the issues raised by the residual public sector. Chapter 18 considers the legal system by dealing briefly with the structure of criminal and civil justice before examining issues of law and order, civil rights and the reform of legal services in this country.

Part VI considers some more philosophical issues about the nature and limits of democracy in Britain. Chapter 19 looks at the impact of the European Community upon the process of politics in Britain. Chapter 20 concludes the book with a few synoptic observations about the essence of British parliamentary democracy.

Many people have helped in the preparation and development of this book. I would particularly like to thank Robert Marshall for his invaluable help in up-dating and checking many of the facts and figures for the second edition, Keith Povey and Tony Waterman for their editorial services, and Jane Wightwick for her constant encouragement and support. I must also record my thanks to the following for having read and commented upon various parts of the first edition: Sir Clifford Boulton, Sir Kenneth Bradshaw, Keith Britto, Dr David Butler, Rt Hon. Lord Callaghan, John Cole, Professor Ivor Crewe, Bryan Davies, the late Charles Douglas-Home, Frank Field MP, Robin Grove-White, John Hanvey, Rt Hon. Edward Heath MP, Hon. Douglas Hogg MP, Lord Hunt of Tanworth, Peter Kellner, David Lipsey, Dr Edmund Marshall, Peter McGregor, Dr David Menhennet, Dr Janet Morgan, Professor Roger Morgan, Rt Hon. Chris Patten MP, William Plowden, Rt Hon. Enoch Powell, John Roper, Sir John Sainty, Jack Straw MP, Alan Taylor and David Walter. In the Library of the House of Commons Dermot Englefield, Geoffrey Lock and John Palmer were also very courteous and helpful, as were all the staff of that excellent institution.

Any insights achieved in this book owe a great deal to those already mentioned and to many others at Essex University and elsewhere with whom I have discussed aspects of British politics over the years. Any errors of fact or opinion are, of course, entirely my own responsibility.

London, December 1990

F.N. FORMAN

⬡ List of Figures

Part I
The political and electoral context

1 British political culture

Any book on British politics has to begin with a chapter on British political culture, since this is the context within which our politics take place. The term 'political culture' is taken to mean the historical, cultural and attitudinal setting within which our political institutions have to function.[1] It is not easy to generalise about political culture, but it is possible to identify some key characteristics which influence both the process and the outcome of politics in Britain.

1.1 Key Characteristics

The key characteristics of British political culture can be stated quite simply, but they need to be qualified and refined if they are to be useful to students of British politics. It has often been stated that politics in this country are influenced by the notable continuity of our national history, the unitary nature of the state, the underlying cohesion of our society and the degree of political agreement on fundamental issues. Traditionally there has been considerable moderation in the policies pursued by successive governments and this has been matched by a considerable degree of public detachment from the process of politics except, of course, at election times. General statements of this kind have often been made and sometimes in a rather complacent tone. Yet it would be unwise to accept them at face value and we would do well to examine the extent to which they now accord with the evidence available to us today.

Historical Continuity

There has been notable continuity in our national history and this country is one of the oldest nation states in Europe. Such continuity is symbolised by some of our national institutions, such as the Monarchy and Parliament, which date back at least to medieval times. Although there have also been some notable discontinuities in our national history, such as the Civil War and the Interregnum in the mid-seventeenth century, this country has not been invaded successfully against the popular will since 1066 and the only successful revolution since the Civil War was the peaceful *coup* of 1688 when James II fled the throne and William and Mary were invited by Parliament to take his place.

This continuity applies to a greater or lesser extent to all parts of the United Kingdom. In the case of *Wales*, the Welsh have been living in the same kingdom as the English since the fourteenth-century English conquests. The link was later reinforced and personified by the victory of Henry Tudor (a Welshman) at Bosworth Field in 1485 and subsequently ratified by Act of Parliament in 1536 at the behest of his son Henry VIII.

In the case of *Scotland*, the constitutional bond between the Scots and the English was first established in 1603 when James VI of Scotland succeeded Elizabeth I and so became James I of England. The bond was later sealed by the

Act of Union in 1707, although what was by then the Hanoverian succession to
the throne of the United Kingdom was not really secure until the defeat of the
Young Pretender in 1745.

In the case of *Ireland*, the troubled relationship between the Irish and the
English can be traced back at least to the Anglo-Norman invasion of Ireland in
1169–71. The Act of Union in 1800, which marked the constitutional unification
of the two countries in one kingdom, was later ruptured by the 1916 Irish national
uprising which led to the partition of Ireland in 1921 and the creation of Northern
Ireland in 1922 as the last remaining part of the United Kingdom on the island of
Ireland.

The result of this chequered history is that we now live in what is known
officially as the United Kingdom of Great Britain and Northern Ireland, although
it will be convenient for us to use the more colloquial term 'Britain' throughout
the rest of this book. Figure 1.1 is a map of the British Isles showing the
boundaries of England, Wales, Scotland and Northern Ireland, as well as the
location of some of the principal cities.

Figure 1.1 Map of the British Isles

Unitary State

One important consequence of this national history is that we live in a unitary state. This means essentially that the laws passed by Parliament at Westminster apply normally to the entire country and that in all important matters it is correct to speak of the country being governed from London. Of course there is a well-established structure of local government which can also claim a degree of democratic legitimacy, since its councillors are directly elected by the people in their localities. Yet, as we shall see in Chapter 16, the powers and functions of local government in this country are determined essentially by Parliament at Westminster.

Unlike the situation in the United States or the Federal Republic of Germany, where there are written constitutions which define the legal rights and status of the various levels of government, in the United Kingdom it is Parliament which is legally and constitutionally supreme (except now in those matters where European Community law prevails) and its writ runs throughout the country. Of course, as we shall see in Chapters 18 and 19, the law of the land is often interpreted, and hence modified, by judicial decisions in the courts and increasingly by the European Court in Luxembourg as well. Yet in this country it is still difficult to get away from the principle that no institution has traditionally been considered on a par with Parliament and it is this which has given force to the idea that we live in a unitary state.

Cultural Cohesion

There has been in this country for a long time considerable cultural cohesion which has been reinforced by the fact that about four-fifths of the total population of the United Kingdom are English and about four-fifths live in urban or suburban areas. This means that in many respects the great majority of the British people live similar lives and hold a range of common attitudes based upon common experiences. They purchase mass-manufactured goods, they use common public services, they earn their living in a number of recognisably standard ways, they spend their leisure time in a range of common pursuits, and they share broadly similar aspirations for themselves and their families. Above all, they are subjected every day to the standardising influences of the mass media which now do more than anything else to create a sense of shared national experience.

On the other hand, there are some significant cultural variations which derive from a wide range of economic, social, geographical and ethnic factors. For example, the more traditional industrial structure in the north and west of the country has been significantly different (until recent times) from the more modern technological structure in the south and east of the country (at any rate outside London). Yet this is now changing as old industries decline and a new, predominantly service, economy grows to a greater or lesser extent in all parts of the country under the spreading influence of information technology. Equally, while in the nation as a whole the ethnic minorities make up no more than one-twentieth of the entire population, there are some parts of our large cities – for example, in London, Leicester or Bradford – where coloured people account for more than one-fifth and sometimes as much as one-third of the local population. In recent times these demographic developments have led some spokesmen for the Moslem community in Britain actually to call for legal and institutional arrangements designed to give them a special status and a real degree of cultural and religious autonomy *within* the United Kingdom.

In all parts of the country British society still divides on class lines, although many of the traditional class distinctions based upon occupation have had their sharper edges blurred by the upwardly mobile and by the convergence of life-styles referred to above.[2] From one point of view it seems that, as people in all classes become more similar in their habits and aspirations, the tendency towards social uniformity may even increase. Yet from another point of view this looks less likely in view of the widening disparities of income and wealth between the poorest and the richest sections of society – notably, between the majority in well paid, full-time employment and the minority who are either peripherally employed in part-time jobs or not employed at all.

In future much will depend upon the extent to which common economic and social aspirations are fulfilled or thwarted by the distribution of the available opportunities between different social groups and different parts of the country. It will also depend upon the extent to which nationalist impulses are stoked up or dampened down by the economic and political experience of people living in the outlying and ethnically distinct parts of the United Kingdom. For example, a small minority of the Welsh are Welsh-speaking and hence attracted by the cause of Plaid Cymru, the Welsh Nationalist party, and their number could grow in future if the Principality appeared to languish or be seriously disadvantaged by London rule. As it happens, recent evidence seems to suggest that the Welsh economy has been growing faster than its English counterpart.

A somewhat larger minority of the Scots identify with the cause of the Scottish National party, which aspires to full Scottish independence within the European Community. However, mainstream opinion north of the border seems more disposed to the idea of devolution to a Scottish National Assembly, as was evident from the success of the multi-party campaign (not including the Conservatives or the SNP) for a Scottish Constitutional Convention.[3]

In Northern Ireland, political circumstances are even more peculiar in that opinion is divided on religious and constitutional lines according to the contrasting attitudes of the Protestant and Catholic communities towards the idea of Irish unity. The hard-line Unionists wrap themselves in the Union Jack, but would probably prefer to govern their part of Ireland free from Westminster tutelage, as they did from 1922 to 1972. The hard-line Nationalists, who support Provisional Sinn Fein, the political wing of the IRA in the north, are prepared to use both the bullet and the ballot in their struggle for unification with the rest of Ireland. Due allowance must therefore be made for all these centrifugal forces in the United Kingdom.

Two Kinds of Consensus

There is an underlying political consensus in this country, but it needs to be carefully defined if the reader is not to get the wrong ideas about it. A clear distinction has to be drawn between consensus on matters of policy and consensus on matters of procedure. We shall therefore deal briefly with each in turn.

Consensus on matters of policy was most marked during the Second World War, when there was a strong national commitment to a united war effort both at home and abroad. In the spheres of economic and social policy this was reflected in the general support given to the goals of the 1942 Beveridge Report which foreshadowed the principal elements in the postwar Welfare State and the 1944 Keynesian White Paper which established the postwar objective of full employment. Such an approach was adhered to in broad terms by successive postwar governments, whether Labour or Conservative, for the following 25 years or so. However in the late 1960s this consensus began to be called into question during the period of the second Wilson Labour Administration and it was all but abandoned in the early 1970s during the first two years of the Heath Conservative Administration. Since the late 1970s this kind of policy consensus has been out of fashion, at least among the dominant elements in the two major parties.

It should be added, however, that there are many politicians and political commentators who argue that a new policy consensus based upon market principles was formed under Mrs Thatcher in the 1980s which will influence, if not determine, the policy choices of governments in the 1990s. According to this argument, the postwar consensus effectively collapsed under the stresses and strains of high inflation and unemployment in the 1970s and early 1980s, only to be gradually replaced by the so-called 'new realism' of the late 1980s and beyond. It is too soon to be sure about this, but there is certainly some evidence that several Thatcherite ideas will outlast Mrs Thatcher – for example, the diminished power of the trade unions, the massive extension of home ownership, and the shrinking of the state industrial sector.

Consensus on matters of procedure, on the other hand, seems to have survived intact in its traditional form for a much longer period. Ever since the successive extensions of the franchise in the nineteenth and early twentieth centuries, this kind of consensus has been signified by widespread agreement upon the desirability of using parliamentary channels for the implementation of political change. However certain powerful pressure groups and minority sections of public opinion have occasionally challenged this view – for example, those in Scotland and elsewhere who have backed popular campaigns for non-payment of the 'Poll Tax'. It has included widespread acceptance of the view that General Election results should be regarded as decisive, provided, of course, the electoral system produces a clear majority in the House of Commons for the victorious party. It has also included broad agreement upon the undesirability of making extensive constitutional changes unless backed by overwhelming all-party support. However this last point did not inhibit the Thatcher Government's sustained assault upon the alleged overspending and other shortcomings of local government which had constitutional consequences of the first importance, including a degree of political centralisation not seen in Britain since the time of the postwar Labour Government.

It should be noted that all such examples of procedural consensus need to be seen against the background of the constitutional controversies which have been pursued at least since the mid-1970s, when there was much spoken and written about the alleged 'ungovernability' of this country. Since that time there has been a long-running argument about devolution to Scotland and Wales, reform of the House of Lords, the use of referenda to determine particularly difficult constitutional questions, and the introduction of proportional representation in the name of achieving a fairer electoral system. More recently, in the late 1980s, there were fierce debates about the reform of the official secrecy law and the Labour Policy Review included a wide range of far-reaching constitutional reforms, including a plan for the introduction of regional assemblies in England. In other words, there now seems to be less consensus than there used to be on the rules of the game in British politics.

1.2 **Other Significant Features**

There are a number of other significant features in British political culture which are worthy of mention at this stage. They are characteristics more associated with the period from 1945 to 1979 than with more recent times, but it seems likely that they have not been expunged by the more radical and polarised positions of the two main parties in the 1980s. Indeed since then there has been a growing body of evidence that some of the more traditional features of British political culture are being reasserted.

Moderation of Governments

It has been traditional to argue that a significant feature of British political culture is the moderation and restraint shown by all governments.[4] This has been reflected in the fact that, whereas all modern British governments with a working majority in the House of Commons have had almost unfettered powers of legislative and political decision, they have usually exercised such power in a relatively moderate and restrained way. Of course such an assertion always seems more credible to the supporters rather than the opponents of any government, but there are nevertheless some compelling reasons why it has often been borne out in practice, notwithstanding the noticeably more ideological tone and actions of central government in the mid-1970s and most of the 1980s.

Such moderation should not be confused with what were identified as middle-of-the-road policies of the kind pursued with conviction and continuity by Labour and Conservative governments in the 25 years or so after the Second World War. Rather it should be defined as a clear recognition by nearly all politicians in office that the vast majority of the British people greatly prefer an atmosphere of comfortable co-operation to unsettling conflict and are more than likely to cast their votes at elections under the influence of that preference. An even more fundamental reason for such moderation and restraint is that the economic and political realities of the modern world impose such cautious behaviour upon all governments, no matter how abrasive or exhilarating the rhetoric may be. In the complex conditions of the interdependent world in which we live and with the growing realisation of our common ecological as well as economic predicament, every government soon discovers that it can wield relatively little effective power, except on the surface or in the margin of events. Both at home and abroad there are many other influential participants in the political process to prevent any government from being able to achieve much more than that. It is in this sense of impaired capacity for taking truly independent and autonomous action that any modern government simply has to be moderate and restrained in what it attempts to do.

Public Detachment from Politics

It has also been said of British political culture that the people of this country are relatively detached from the process of party politics, put a high value upon the maintenance of political stability and are not usually keen to face up to the need for radical change, especially when it affects them directly.[5] This view is reflected in the typically low turn-out at local elections; the continuing support for some of our most familiar and reassuring institutions, such as the Monarchy or the National Health Service; and the strength of parochial opposition to any larger developments which may be in the wider public interest, but which threaten to disturb 'my back yard'. It is also reflected in the widespread public preference for the quiet life and for 'cultivating one's garden' which finds expression in various social institutions from pubs to fishing clubs which absorb so much of the time and energy of the British people. In such circumstances the idea of active or continuous participation in the process of politics appeals to no more than a small and unusual minority of the population.

It should not be assumed, however, that this relatively benign, and often cynical, neglect of the political process by the vast majority of the British people means that they are not in the habit of joining a myriad of voluntary organisations according to taste and experience. Indeed, in this sense, the British are some of the foremost 'joiners' in all the advanced industrial countries. Whether individual citizens are members of the National Trust or the Consumers' Association, the MCC or the RSPCA, they find themselves involved in the process of politics from time to time, even if only in connection with a single issue at a particular time. The point is that most ordinary citizens are not very sanguine about the role or capacity of government – hence the familiar joke, 'I'm from the Government and I'm here to help you'. The result is that many people have concluded that it is not very sensible to hold high expectations of government or other public agencies and this has led them to be wary of the promises made by politicians at election time. Yet paradoxically such scepticism and even mistrust of government and bureaucracy does not prevent many of the same people, notably those employed in the public sector, from looking to government and other public agencies for material reward or redress of grievances.

As Paul Barker has written, there has been 'an undoubted retreat into the shell of self (or perhaps self plus family)'.[6] Concern with relative advantage or deprivation within narrowly defined reference groups and a determination to protect the local environment have been more evident than the general interest (except when artificially prompted by opinion pollsters) in the competitive performance of the economy or the transcendent issues of war and peace, ecological survival or disaster. The struggle for material satisfaction, or in some cases simply survival, is so all-absorbing for most people that few have either the time or the inclination to involve themselves directly in the formal process of politics. In these circumstances the idea of a conscious political culture has little meaning or resonance for anyone but practising politicians, pressure group activists, and media or academic pundits.

1.3 Conclusion

When we consider British political culture, the main need is to distinguish between the cluster of dated myths and stereotypes which still appears in some accounts and the changing social realities which must qualify such simple notions. If we wish to have an up-to-date understanding, we need to realise that many of the traditional values and assumptions of British politics have been called into question by recent developments in our society. For example, when the economy grew strongly during most of the 1980s, there was little evidence of the values of civic culture which had been identified and admired by American academics visiting this country in the 1950s and 1960s. A spirit of tolerance and a disposition to compromise were hardly the hallmarks of either the Thatcher Administration or its fiercest political opponents. In many ways British society became coarser in the 1980s as the British economy grew faster and a larger number of people than ever before began to prosper as a result of their own efforts.

The outlook for the 1990s is as yet uncertain, since much will depend upon whether the Conservatives under a new leader can achieve an unprecedented fourth term of office. All that can safely be said is that our political culture can change significantly from one time to another and that our basic assumptions have frequently to be re-examined in the light of changing political circumstances.

Suggested Questions

1. What are the key characteristics of British political culture and how have these changed over the years?
2. Is the nature of British society conducive to the practice of democratic politics?

Notes

1. See D. Kavanagh, 'Political culture in Great Britain, the decline of the civic culture', in G. Almond and S. Verba (eds), *The Civic Culture Revisited* (Boston: Little, Brown, 1980) pp. 136–62.
2. For example, 78 per cent of white collar and 46 per cent of blue collar trade union members had become owner–occupiers by 1980, according to a MORI poll in *The Sunday Times* on 31 August 1980. The proportions have grown since then, reflecting the growth of owner–occupation in general from 55 per cent of housing tenure in 1980 to 68 per cent in 1990.
3. This campaign culminated in the so-called 'Claim of Right' which was signed by representatives of all the parties in Scotland (except the Conservatives and the SNP) in Edinburgh at the end of March 1989. It reflected the fact that according to opinion polls about 80 per cent of Scots would like to have some sort of Parliament of their own with powers over legislation and administration.
4. See R. M. Punnett, *British Government and Politics*, 5th edn (London: Heinemann, 1987).
5. See A. H. Birch, *The British System of Government*, 8th edn (London: Allen & Unwin, 1990).
6. *New Society*, 29 November 1979.

Further Reading

Almond, G. A. and Verba, S. (eds), *The Civic Culture Revisited* (Boston: Little, Brown, 1980).
Butler, D. E. and Sloman, A., *British Political Facts*, 6th edn (London: Macmillan, 1986).
Catterall, P. (ed.), *Contemporary Britain* (Oxford: Basil Blackwell, 1990).
Dahrendorf, R., *On Britain* (London: BBC, 1982).
Marwick, A., *British Society Since 1945* (Harmondsworth: Penguin, 1982).
Paxman, J., *Friends in High Places: who runs Britain?* (London: Michael Joseph, 1990).
Sampson, A., *The Changing Anatomy of Britain* (London: Hodder & Stoughton, 1982).
Social Trends 20 (London: HMSO, 1990).

2 The living constitution

A constitution is usually defined as a body of fundamental principles, rules and conventions according to which a state or other organisation is governed. According to such a definition, Britain has a constitution. Yet, as we shall see, it is notably different from the constitutions of most other democratic countries.

2.1 Key Characteristics

Although the key characteristics of the British constitution can be stated quite simply, they contain some powerful paradoxes and internal contradictions. This is mainly because it is a living constitution which is changing and developing all the time. At one time some characteristics may be particularly significant, at another time others and so on. This makes it an interesting subject to study, but one which is hard to describe in a definitive way.

No Codification

The British constitution is unusual in that it is uncodified and has not been assembled at any time into one consolidated document. This makes it very different from the American constitution or those of many Commonwealth countries which were granted constitutional independence by Britain. Indeed, of all the democratic countries in the world, only Israel, Australia and New Zealand are comparable to Britain in having no single consolidated document codifying the way in which their political institutions are supposed to operate and setting out the basic rights and duties of their citizens.

Yet, in the absence of a basic constitutional text, it should not be assumed that we have no constitutional documents from which guidance can be derived when we need to elucidate the laws and conventions which govern British politics. For example, Magna Carta, which was signed by King John at the behest of the barons in 1215, is perhaps our best known constitutional document. It provided in 61 clauses a clear statement of feudal law and custom. Many other documents of equal or greater constitutional significance have been produced since then.

The Bill of Rights in 1689 put the stamp of parliamentary approval on the succession of William and Mary to the throne deserted by James II and extended the powers of Parliament at the expense of the Crown. The Act of Settlement in 1701 was described in its preamble as 'an Act for the further limitation of the Crown and the better securing of the rights and liberties of the subject'. The Act of Union with Scotland in 1707 declared in Article 3 that 'the United Kingdom of Great Britain be represented by one and the same Parliament to be styled the Parliament of Great Britain'. The Act of Union with Ireland in 1800 brought about the formation of the United Kingdom of Great Britain and Ireland, later to be amended to 'Northern Ireland' following Irish partition in 1921.

The Reform Act in 1832 was the first of a series of statutes over the period from then until modern times which were designed to extend the franchise at parliamentary elections. The Ballot Act in 1872 introduced secret ballots for all elections to Parliament and all contested municipal elections. The Local Government Act in 1888 established elected County Councils for the first time in new administrative Counties. The Parliament Act in 1911 regulated the relations between the two Houses of Parliament and confirmed the legislative supremacy of the Commons, while reducing the maximum span of a Parliament from seven to five years. The Redistribution of Seats Act in 1944 established independent Parliamentary Boundary Commissions to demarcate the constituencies on a fair and regular basis. The Representation of the People Act in 1969 lowered the voting age from 21 to 18. It is worth noting that, except for Magna Carta, which predated the founding of Parliament in 1265, all the examples given are drawn from statute law, in other words Acts of Parliament.

There are, however, many other important documents which clarify our constitution by setting out the rights and duties which we now take for granted. For example, there are the judicial proceedings which have served to clarify and confirm the rights and duties of British citizens over the centuries. In Bushell's case of 1670, Lord Chief Justice Vaughan established the independence of juries. In Sommersett's case of 1772, Lord Mansfield recognised the freedom of a former slave from the American colonies on the grounds of his residence in England and argued that slavery was 'so odious that nothing can be suffered to support it but positive law'. In *Beatty* v. *Gillbanks* of 1882, Justice Field established the principle that a man may not be convicted for a lawful act, even if he knows that it may cause another to commit an unlawful act.

Other documentary sources for our uncodified constitution include Erskine May, the classic and constantly up-dated guide to the procedures and privileges of Parliament; and certain learned works written by leading constitutional theorists down the ages, such as Blackstone and Bagehot.[1]

Considerable Flexibility

Another key characteristic of the British constitution is its considerable flexibility. This derives partly from the absence of neat, constitutional formulae consolidated in a single authoritative document, as is the case, for example, in the constitution of the Fifth Republic in France. However it is essentially because no Parliament can bind its successors and any Parliament can undo the legislation of its predecessors that it is difficult to achieve formal methods of constitutional limitation in Britain.

It soon becomes apparent from even a cursory study of British history that the flexibility of our constitution stems essentially from the way in which the theoretically absolute and unlimited power of Parliament has been severely modified and limited in practice by political tradition and precedent, the influence of constitutional conventions and the well-established commitment to the rule of law. All these intuitive and practical constraints upon the theoretical supremacy of Parliament are trumped by the political supremacy of the electorate at periodic General Elections. Yet the former constraints remain vital moderating influences which help to preserve a constitutional balance without recourse to any formal separation of powers, as in the United States.

Importance of Conventions

Another key characteristic of the British constitution is the importance of conventions, in other words established custom and practice. The conventions which have been so powerful in their influence upon constitutional developments in Britain are the product of organic growth over the centuries. They include, for example, the convention that the Monarch should send first for the leader of the largest single party in the House of Commons to form a new government following a General Election or the demise of a Prime Minister in office, and the convention that Ministers are responsible and can be held to account by Parliament for what does or does not happen in their Departments.

This helps to explain why certain principles not declared in law, such as the royal prerogative or ministerial responsibility, have developed so fully over the years. It also suggests why there are such formidable obstacles to the achievement of deliberate constitutional reform in Britain. We discover a paradoxical quality in our constitutional arrangements which can best be understood only after close study of the way our political institutions have evolved over the centuries rather than by reference to any basic texts of the constitution. This is why we must refer to our living constitution which has been part of the more general development of British politics and society over the centuries.

2.2 Views of the Constitution

For schematic purposes we can say that there are really three different views of the constitution in Britain. There is the classic liberal view, which is based upon nostalgia for the period when Parliament really did hold sway over the Executive. There is the governmental view, which is based upon the assumption that the Executive should consider itself answerable not so much to Parliament as to the electorate every four or five years at General Elections. There is the empirical view, which seeks to take account both of the weakness of Parliament in relation to the Executive and of the government of the day in relation to all the other limiting forces in the real world both within this country and abroad. We shall therefore consider each of these views in turn.

Classic Liberal View

Of the various interpretations of the British constitution which have been put forward over the years, perhaps the best known is the classic liberal view which is associated with the nineteenth-century writings of Bagehot and Dicey.[2] This view holds that the House of Commons is the supreme political institution with the power to make and unmake governments, pass any laws and resolve the great political issues of the day. It accords only subsidiary constitutional significance to the Monarchy and the House of Lords. It takes little account of the political parties, pressure groups, the civil service, the media or public opinion. As R.H.S. Crossman pointed out, such a view could only have been valid for the period before any significant extension of the franchise, before the establishment of disciplined party organisations and before the development of the modern civil service.[3]

This classic liberal view applied only during a brief era, 1832–67, when the House of Commons really did reign supreme. During that atypical period no fewer than 10 administrations fell because the Commons withdrew their support. By about 1885 the main principles propounded by Bagehot and Dicey were already being eroded or overtaken by new political realities which became steadily more significant during the last quarter of the nineteenth century. For example, the legislative supremacy of Parliament was gradually overcome by the growing political power of the political parties as they sought to appeal to a wider electorate which was extended in successive Reform Bills. The rule of law, which Dicey had identified as the fundamental principle of the constitution, was not necessarily the paramount consideration for all participants in the political process, at any rate for the disadvantaged sections of the community which often appealed to superior notions of natural justice. The importance of conventions meant little to all those who were outside the charmed circle of parliamentary politics.

In modern times students of the British constitution need to make sense of a much more complex and bureaucratic form of democracy in which parliamentary supremacy is only one important principle among many. The classic liberal view, although still regarded with respect and firmly established among the received ideas of British politics, is no longer particularly instructive as a guide to contemporary politics. It has been rendered rather obsolete by the enormously increased scope of modern government and by the growing power of political parties, pressure groups, the media and public opinion. The elitist parliamentary ideas of the mid-nineteenth century have had to give way to the claims of a more pluralist and populist democracy in the late twentieth century. The classic liberal view is shown diagrammatically in Figure 2.1.

Figure 2.1 Classic liberal view of the constitution

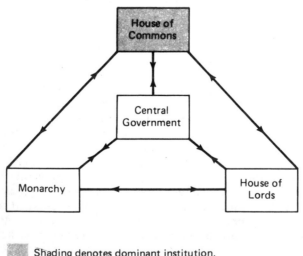

Shading denotes dominant institution.
Arrows denote lines of contact.

Governmental View

Another well-known interpretation of the British constitution may be called the governmental view. This holds that the former power of the Monarch has been passed not to Parliament but to the Prime Minister and Cabinet, subject only to criticism in Parliament and periodic confirmation or rejection by the mass electorate at General Elections. It is a view usually associated with the writings of L.S. Amery and Herbert Morrison.[4] It maintains that the Government has a clear responsibility to govern and that the essential form of political accountability is the responsibility of the governing party to the electorate. Accordingly the role of back-bench MPs and pressure groups is to act essentially as filters or megaphones between the Government and the electorate. L.S. Amery was succinct when he wrote that 'the combination of responsible leadership by Government with responsible criticism in Parliament is the essence of our constitution'.[5]

Although this view, too, has to be qualified if we are to form an accurate impression of the way the British constitution really works, it has more validity than the classic liberal view which is now characterised by sentimentality towards a vanished era of truly parliamentary government. In the administrative and legal spheres at any rate modern British governments have had virtually unlimited power, provided they have had an overall working majority in the House of Commons and as long as they have been careful to keep their parliamentary supporters united behind them. Under the terms of the 1911 Parliament Act a government can retain this power for a maximum term of five years before it is obliged to seek a fresh mandate from the electorate. In view of the notable imbalance of political resources between government and opposition, there is some truth in Lord Hailsham's allegation that we live in 'an elective dictatorship' tempered only by the minimal restraints of our constitutional conventions and the governing party's normal desire to get re-elected.[6] The governmental view is shown diagrammatically in Figure 2.2 overleaf.

Empirical View

More accurate still in modern conditions is the empirical view of the constitution which emphasises both the weakness of Parliament in relation to the government of the day and the weakness of the Executive in relation to pressure groups, the media, public opinion and other actors on the domestic and international scene. It emphasises the way in which a deliberate extension of constitutional power can lead to a decline of effective power, no matter how great the parliamentary majority or the political momentum of the party in office. This is essentially because, if a government becomes over-extended in its ambitions or overloaded in its commitments, it is likely to encounter so many real-world obstacles and to create so many political enemies that it is unable to achieve its objectives.

Indeed a dispassionate reading of British constitutional history leads to the important conclusion that the most abiding political problem has been the gaining and retaining of public consent for the actions of government. Stage by stage, from the thirteenth century to the present time, governments in Britain, whether monarchical or parliamentary, have had to cede and share power with the other great interests in the land – and nowadays most notably with our partners in the European Community. Effective government has been possible only with the

Figure 2.2 Governmental view of the constitution

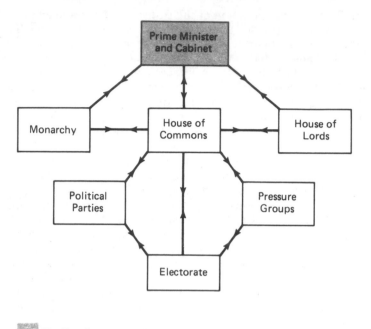

Shading denotes dominant institution.
→ Arrows denote lines of contact.

consent, or at least the tacit acquiescence, of those most directly affected by it or involved with it. Against this background it makes sense to regard successive British governments as stable rather than strong and to avoid confusing the concentration of responsibility with the concentration of power. Today administrative convenience, public opinion and European Community law are just a few of the powerful forces which condition and limit the exercise of power by any British government.

Thus the contemporary British constitution is based upon two key paradoxes. The first is the limited power of a theoretically supreme Parliament, which reflects the fact that, while Parliament is theoretically capable of passing any law, it is politically capable only of criticising and partially controlling the government of the day. The second is the limited power of the allegedly all-powerful Executive, which reflects the fact that, while a government with a working majority in the Commons can invariably get its way in Whitehall and Westminster, little is achieved if its freedom of manoeuvre is unduly circumscribed by administrative constraints, media influence, interest group pressure, or the framework of European Community law. Thus a complicated network of informal checks and balances ensures that the living constitution continues to develop organically, but makes it ill-suited for rapid adjustment to new challenges or effective response to those who do not recognise the rules of the game. For a diagrammatic representation of this view see Figure 2.3.

Figure 2.3 Empirical view of the constitution

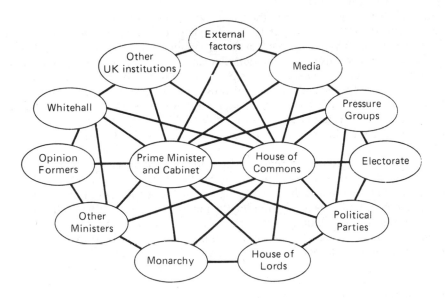

N.B. No dominant institution.
Everything influences and is influenced by everything else.

2.3 **The Scope for Change**

Over the years constitutional changes have occurred piecemeal, even haphazardly, in response to the needs of public policy or the dictates of political necessity. No coherent pattern seems to have emerged and there has been no real attempt to co-ordinate the various initiatives which have been taken. Some have argued that there is an emerging constitutional crisis caused notably by two factors: the ever-widening gap between the received ideas about Britain's 'unwritten constitution' and contemporary political realities; and the challenge to British parliamentary supremacy posed by the encroachment of European Community law. We shall look briefly at each of these matters later in this chapter, but first we must consider the threat to parliamentary government posed by the idea of referenda.

The Use of Referenda

The use of referenda in two celebrated instances in the 1970s was probably one of the most notable constitutional developments of modern times.[7] Any referendum is still an alien device in the British political system which has been dominated for so long by the assumptions and practices of parliamentary democracy. It sits uneasily with our traditional constitutional arrangements, although its apparently satisfactory use on two important occasions in the 1970s testified to the flexibility of the British constitution.

In 1975 British membership of the European Community, for which Parliament had legislated in 1972, was put to a national referendum by the then Labour Government, mainly because each of the two main parties was still deeply divided on the issue and because it was thought that this device would settle the issue once and for all. Indeed the Wilson Government was so seriously split on the issue that it was necessary to suspend the normal convention of collective responsibility for the duration of the referendum campaign, so that Cabinet Ministers could argue freely against each other in public – something which had not happened since the open agreement to differ in the National Government in 1931 on the issue of tariff reform.

In 1979 the legislation proposed by the Callaghan Government for the devolution of certain legislative powers to Scotland and Wales also had to be put to separate referenda in each of these parts of the United Kingdom, because there seemed to be no other way of trumping the persistent and effective parliamentary opposition to the legislation from both sides of the House. As it happened, the House of Commons had passed an amendment to the legislation which insisted that, unless at least 40 per cent of those entitled to vote in each relevant part of the country supported the policy, the provisions of the legislation could not be put into effect. In the event this proved to be a sufficient obstacle to the implementation of the legislation, since in neither Scotland nor Wales did as many as 40 per cent vote 'Yes'.

These two special cases have been seen by some people as valid precedents for the use of referenda on other issues, especially when the position taken by the majority in the House of Commons is at odds with the majority view of public opinion as, for example, on the emotive issue of capital punishment. The pressure for the use of referenda in such cases reflects public impatience with the fastidious views of many MPs in all parties. It is also testimony to the diminished status and authority of Parliament in the eyes of the public. The calls for referenda are therefore largely the result of public cynicism and impatience with the traditional ways of representative democracy in this country.

Other Pressures for Change

These and other constitutional developments may have been misinterpreted or even misrepresented in some cases. Yet they have encouraged some searching reconsideration of many of our basic constitutional assumptions and strengthened demands for procedural, electoral and constitutional reform.

The advocates of parliamentary reform have argued for further procedural changes at Westminster which would strengthen the role of Select Committees and make more effective the rather antiquated procedures of financial control in the Commons. The Liberal Democrats, and a few others in each of the main parties, have campaigned for electoral reform – specifically the introduction of various forms of proportional representation. The Labour party has renewed its commitment to abolish, or at any rate recast, the House of Lords in order to accommodate representatives from the new regional assemblies which it has proposed. Notable legal figures, such as Lord Scarman and other signatories of Charter 88, have argued the case for a new constitutional settlement based upon a

Bill of Rights and a codified constitution which would be interpreted and protected by a powerful Supreme Court.[8]

The Conservative Government under Mrs Thatcher secured parliamentary approval for a wide range of legislative measures which, while not deliberate constitutional changes, have had significant constitutional implications.[9] The 1979–83 Conservative Government introduced legislation to restrict the already limited autonomy of local government. The 1983–7 Conservative Government introduced further legislation to curb high-spending local authorities and to abolish the Greater London Council and the other Metropolitan Councils. The 1987–90 Thatcher Administration secured parliamentary approval for legislation which introduced the highly controversial Community Charge (Poll Tax) into Scotland in 1989 and into England and Wales (but not Northern Ireland) in 1990, along with the Uniform Business Rate which is being phased in over a number of years. It also introduced a radical reform of the legal profession which may change English legal practice in significant ways.

Since the 1987 General Election two constitutional issues have been illuminated in a sharper light. Firstly, there is the political problem posed by the ever widening gap between the received ideas about Britain's 'unwritten constitution' and the contemporary political realities. One manifestation of this has been the all-party and non-party campaign under the banner of Charter 88 for comprehensive constitutional change. This campaign has been based upon a 10-point programme which has called, among other things, for a new Bill of Rights, an independent and reformed judiciary, and proportional representation.[10] Another manifestation of a more party-political character has been the extent of Scottish disgust with all things Conservative and English, which has been especially evident since the dramatic SNP victory at the Glasgow Govan by-election in November 1988. In the eyes of many Scots this was a clear protest against both English Conservatism and the ineffectiveness of the Scottish Labour party at Westminster. A good deal of renewed momentum has been achieved by the Scottish National party in recent years and from time to time it has commanded strong support in opinion polls north of the border.[11] It has also given a new sense of urgency to those who have campaigned for the establishment of a Scottish Assembly and it galvanised most of the other parties into supporting a 'Claim of Right' for Scotland at the multi-party Constitutional Convention which was held in Edinburgh in March 1989.

The other issue, with even more far-reaching implications, which has arisen especially in the late 1980s is the challenge to British parliamentary supremacy posed by the encroachment of European Community law. This is something which has been highlighted by those in all parties who have opposed British membership of the European Community, just as it has tended to be played down by those who have favoured British membership. Now that Britain has been a member of the European Community for nearly two decades, virtually no one is seriously arguing the case for British withdrawal. Yet a growing minority of politicians in all parties (especially on the parochial wing of the Conservative party) are now arguing for a redefinition of Britain's relations with her Community partners along more international rather than supranational lines. It seems that such people have belatedly woken up to the fact that, under the terms of Section 2 of the 1972 European Communities Act, Community law must take precedence over British law in those areas of activity where there is a clear Treaty basis for it. In so far as sectional interests in the United Kingdom or politicians at Westminster may choose to ignore or challenge this fact of Community life, they will find themselves or their Government before the European Court defending cases brought by the European Commission, other member states or private litigants. As long as Britain remains within the European Community, the inevitable result will be that British parliamentary supremacy will become increasingly attenuated as the scope of Community law is extended into more areas of our national life. More decisions of political importance will be taken at Community level by the Community institutions and more of the decisions in the Council of Ministers will be taken by qualified majority vote under the aegis of the 1986 Single European Act. The so-called 'democratic deficit' which these developments have revealed is unlikely to be closed at Westminster and the other national Parliaments, but rather by the European Parliament with its growing powers of co-decision with the Council of Ministers. Admittedly, British Ministers have forcefully put the case for the doctrine of 'subsidiarity', which implies that no decision should be taken at Community level which could more appropriately be taken at national level (and, incidentally, that no decision should be taken at national level which could more appropriately be taken at sub-national level). Yet it is not at all clear that our Community partners see things in the same way or are as determined to safeguard theoretical national sovereignty and actual national competence. Whatever the outcome of this political struggle, it is clear that it already makes no sense to consider British politics in an exclusively national context.

2.4 Conclusion

Some years ago Nevil Johnson argued that 'the gap between the theory and the reality of British political institutions and procedures has assumed serious dimensions' and that 'the root of the political difficulty is to be found in a refusal to recognise that much of the traditional language of the British constitution . . . has lost its vitality'.[12] It is a tenable point of view, which has become all the more credible as the British nation-state has been challenged by the European Community from above and by local loyalties from below. In such dynamic circumstances the preservation of the constitutional *status quo* will become increasingly unrealistic and various forms of constitutional change will become even more pressing.

The clear conclusion is that constitutional change is nearly always on the agenda of British politics. Sometimes it is there explicitly, because the politicians in office wish to change the constitutional arrangements. Sometimes it is there implicitly, because the policies of a radical government may have important constitutional implications. Sometimes it is forced onto the political agenda by nationalist movements within the United Kingdom or supranational developments within the European Community. In any event it should remind us that change is constant, if not always welcome, in our living constitution.

Suggested Questions

1. What are the key features of the British constitution?
2. Which view of the British constitution accords best with contemporary political circumstances?
3. How great is the scope for change in British constitutional arrangements?

Notes

1. William Blackstone, who was Professor of Common Law at Oxford University, published his famous *Commentaries upon the Laws of England* between 1765 and 1769. In that work he presented a clear and systematic description of English law in the mid-eighteenth century. Walter Bagehot was equally famous in the nineteenth century for his great work *The English Constitution* which was published in 1867. This set out what he saw as the principles of British parliamentary democracy at that time.
2. See W. Bagehot, *The English Constitution* (London: Fontana, 1978) and A. V. Dicey, *The Law of the Constitution* (London: Macmillan, 1959).
3. See R. H. S. Crossman's 'Introduction' to W. Bagehot, *The English Constitution*, p. 35.
4. See L. S. Amery, *Thoughts on the Constitution* (London: OUP, 1947) and H. Morrison, *Government and Parliament* (London: OUP, 1959).
5. L. S. Amery, *Thoughts on the Constitution*, p. 32.
6. See Q. Hailsham, *The Dilemma of Democracy* (London: Collins, 1978) for an exposition of this argument.
7. 'Referendum' is defined in the Concise Oxford Dictionary (6th edition) as 'the referring of political questions to the electorate for direct decision by general vote'. For a fuller discussion of this subject see D. E. Butler and A. Ranney (eds), *Referendums: a comparative study of practice and theory* (Washington D. C.: American Enterprise Institute, 1978) and V. Bogdanor, *The People and the Party System* (London: CUP, 1981), pp. 11–93.
8. *Charter 88* is the name for a non-party movement launched by 230 prominent public figures in London in November 1988. It believes that fundamental liberties are insufficiently protected under the British constitution, since liberty in Britain is not so much a set of rules as a state of mind. It has called for a written constitution, electoral reform, a Bill of Rights, reform of the House of Lords and the judiciary, and equitable power sharing between central and local government.
9. See C. Graham and T. Prosser (eds), *Waiving the Rules: the constitution under Thatcherism* (Milton Keynes: Open University Press, 1988) for a fuller exposition of this argument.
10. The other seven points called for in *Charter 88* were: the subjection of executive and prerogative power to the rule of law; the establishment of freedom of information and open government; the creation of a democratic, non-hereditary second chamber; the placing of the executive under the control of a democratically renewed Parliament; the provision of legal remedies against the abuse of power by central or local government; an equitable distribution of power between the different levels of government; and a written constitution anchored in the idea of universal citizenship.
11. See, for example, the System Three poll in March 1989 which showed that 52 per cent of those questioned supported the SNP policy of Scottish independence within the European Community, while 67 per cent did not believe that the campaign for a Scottish Assembly would succeed in changing the mind of the Conservative Government on the way in which Scotland ought to be governed. The same poll also recorded a doubling of support for the SNP to 27 per cent compared with its 14 per cent rating at the 1987 General Election.
12. N. Johnson, *In Search of the Constitution* (London: Methuen, 1980), p. 26.

Further Reading

Birch, A. H., *Representative and Responsible Government* (London: Allen & Unwin, 1964).

Bogdanor, V., *The People and the Party System* (Cambridge University Press, 1981).

Bromhead, P., *Britain's Developing Constitution* (London: Allen & Unwin, 1974).

Finer, S. E. (ed.), *Five Constitutions* (Harmondsworth: Penguin, 1979).

Graham, C. and Prosser, T. (eds), *Waiving the Rules: the constitution under Thatcherism* (Milton Keynes: Open University Press, 1988).

Johnson, N., *In Search of the Constitution* (London: Methuen, 1980).

Marshall, G, *Constitutional Conventions* (Oxford: Clarendon Press, 1986).

Miliband, R., *Capitalist Democracy in Britain* (Oxford University Press, 1984).

Norton, P., *The British Constitution in Flux* (Oxford: Martin Robertson, 1982).

Ranney, A. (ed.), *The Referendum Device* (Washington, DC: American Enterprise Institute, 1981).

3 The electoral system

The electoral system in Britain is the product of centuries of development. It began to be put on a democratic basis at the time of the 1832 Reform Act. Subsequent Acts in 1867, 1884, 1918, 1928, 1948, 1969 and 1985 have carried forward the process of modernisation. The result is that today we have a system of universal adult suffrage in which everyone aged 18 and over has the right to vote (including those living overseas and those temporarily on holiday abroad) with the exception of convicted felons, certified lunatics and peers of the realm.

3.1 The System Today

At the 1987 General Election, 2325 candidates stood for election to Parliament and 43 181 321 people were eligible to vote. The 650 constituencies vary considerably in population and geographical area, but the average electorate in each constituency was about 67 000 in 1987. For example, the Western Isles with the smallest electorate of about 23 000 was one of the largest in geographical area, whereas the Isle of Wight, with the largest electorate of about 94 000, was geographically confined to quite a small area. These discrepancies derive mainly from the fact that the population has expanded in some parts of the country – for example, East Anglia and the South-West of England – while it has contracted in other parts, such as the inner city areas of London, Birmingham and Liverpool. The Boundary Commissions, which are strictly independent bodies, attempt every 10 to 15 years to rectify the most glaring anomalies and the next review of constituency boundaries is due in the mid-1990s. Yet usually they do not quite keep pace with the movements of population over the intervening periods.

Electoral Mechanisms

On election day voters go to the polls to cast their votes in secret by putting an 'X' against one name on the ballot paper. Any other mark produces a spoiled vote which is usually judged invalid at the end of the count. The marked ballot papers are folded and deposited by the voters in locked ballot boxes where they remain until the polling stations close at 10.00 p.m. The ballot boxes are then transported to a central point in the constituency (often a Town Hall) where the counting of the votes takes place under the supervision of the Acting Returning Officer (normally the Chief Executive of the local authority concerned). The results are declared at varying times depending upon the nature and size of the constituency, usually not less than about three hours after the closing of the polls but sometimes not until the following day.

Since 1948 it has also been permissible to cast postal votes if the voters concerned apply to be put on their constituency postal registers at least two weeks before polling day. Those who qualify for postal votes include people prevented by the nature of their job from voting in person (for example, merchant seamen or long-distance lorry drivers), people who are too sick or handicapped to vote in person, and those who have moved out of the constituency but are still on the electoral register where they used to live, including those living overseas, provided they have not been away for more than five years. People away on holiday on polling day also qualify for postal votes or can get a friend or relative to cast a proxy vote for them, provided they complete in advance the necessary formalities specified in the 1985 Representation of the People Act. Traditionally postal votes have accounted for about 2 per cent of the votes cast, but this has probably increased in recent years. Postal voting is generally reckoned to favour the Conservatives because of their traditionally superior organisation on polling day and immediately before. Yet it can only make a decisive difference to the result in very marginal constituencies.

Any British citizen, who is resident in this country and who will be at least 21 years old when a new Parliament meets, is legally entitled to stand for election to the House of Commons. The only provisos are that he or she must get 10 qualified voters in the constituency to sign the nomination papers and must deposit a sum of £500 with the Returning Officer, to be refunded after the election if the candidate concerned gets more than 5 per cent of the votes cast. There is no requirement that candidates should reside in the constituency which they seek to represent and only a few limited categories of people are automatically disqualified from standing for Parliament.[1] Since 1970 candidates have been allowed to put on the ballot papers not only their names (in alphabetical order), but also a description of their party or political position in not more than six words – for example, 'Conservative', 'Labour party candidate', 'Scottish Nationalist', 'Monster Raving Loony party'.

Each candidate is restricted by law to a maximum expenditure during the three to five weeks campaign of £2700 plus 3.1p for every voter in a rural constituency and £2700 plus 2.3p for every voter in an urban constituency. This allows a maximum expenditure of about £5800 in a rural seat and about £5400 in an urban seat, although most candidates report expenses of about two-thirds the legal maxima. The main reason why parliamentary elections appear to be fought on the cheap in Britain as compared with other countries is that the serious money is spent by the parties centrally – about £15 million in 1987 compared with £7.6 million in 1983. Even so, these are not enormous figures for a country with an electorate of more than 43 million. The real explanation is that neither the parties nor the candidates have to spend large sums of money on buying television time, as in the United States, or on buying votes, as in Japan.

Each candidate has to have a designated agent who is legally responsible for seeing that all aspects of election law are observed and who, in an extreme case, could be sent to prison if found guilty of electoral malpractice by a court. The agent also serves in most cases as the local campaign manager for the candidate, although this is not part of his legal duties. The bulk of the work in every election campaign is done by voluntary workers who are usually paid-up members of the party, but who may simply be sympathisers with the party cause.

First-past-the-post

The British electoral system is commonly described as 'first-past-the-post'. This means that in each constituency the candidate with the largest number of votes wins the seat. Usually this has the effect of turning the largest single minority of votes cast in the nation into a clear majority of seats in the House of Commons for the largest single party. In this way the system has benefited the two leading parties and discriminated against the political fortunes of all other parties, unless their votes are geographically concentrated in a particular part of the country.

This pattern of discrimination has been discernible for years in the British electoral system. At the 13 General Elections since the Second World War no party has ever won more than half the votes cast, although individual candidates often achieve this in safe seats. Yet the winning party has seldom won fewer than half the seats in the House of Commons, except notably in February 1974 when the Labour party won power with fewer popular votes than the Conservative party, but votes which produced a larger number of seats in the House of Commons. This occurred because the votes of the Labour party in that election happened to be more effectively concentrated in a number of marginal constituencies, thus giving it an edge over the Conservative party in Parliament.[2]

In normal circumstances the two leading parties have benefited from this multiplier effect which can produce a sizeable majority of parliamentary seats on the basis of a minority of the popular votes cast.[3] For example, the Labour party enjoyed a positive differential (that is, between the percentage of seats won and votes cast) of 14 per cent in 1945 and 11 per cent in October 1974, while the Conservative party enjoyed a positive differential of 8 per cent in 1959, 9 per cent in 1979 and 15 per cent in 1987. On the other hand, the Liberal party has been the most notable victim of the system during the period since 1945. From 1945 to 1979 the Liberal share of the popular vote ranged from 2 per cent in 1951 to 19 per cent in February 1974. Yet the system prevented the Liberals from winning more than 2 per cent of the seats in the Commons even in their most successful attempt, in February 1974. In the 1983 General Election this multiplier effect worked even more dramatically against the interest of the Alliance of Liberals and Social Democrats, which won 25 per cent of the votes cast but only 3 per cent of the seats in the House of Commons. In the 1987 General Election it was virtually the same story with the Alliance winning about 23 per cent of the votes cast, but still getting only 3 per cent of the seats in the Commons.

Plainly the number of seats won is in no way proportional to the number of votes cast by the electorate. Yet the system has never been arithmetically fair to all parties and it has always had a bias against second or third parties whose votes are not socially or regionally concentrated. Its political merits lie elsewhere, namely in the tendency for most General Elections to produce effective parliamentary majorities for single-party governments. This has enabled the electorate to hold the governing party to account for what happens, or fails to happen, during a particular Parliament. Figure 3.1 demonstrates the multiplier effect at the 1987 General Election.

Proportional Representation

The characteristics of the British electoral system have led many people, especially supporters of the smaller parties, to argue strongly for the introduction of a system based upon proportional representation.[4] There are a number of variants of the basic idea.

The proposal which has found the most favour over the years is for proportional representation on the basis of a single transferable vote in large multi-member constituencies. This would allow the electorate to vote in each constituency for

Figure 3.1 Voting by party in June 1987

	Number of votes	Votes as % of electorate (a)	Votes as % of votes cast (b)	% of seats won
Conservative	13 763 066	31.8	42.3	57.8
Labour	10 029 778	23.2	30.8	35.2
Alliance	7 341 290	17.0	22.6	3.4
SNP	416 873	1.0	1.3	0.5
Plaid Cymru	123 589	0.3	0.4	0.5
OUP	276 230	0.6	0.8	1.4
DUP	85 642	0.2	0.3	0.5
SDLP	154 087	0.4	0.5	0.5
PSF	83 389	0.2	0.3	0.2
All NI	72 671	0.2	0.2	–
Others	58 133	0.1	0.2	0.2
TOTAL	32 529 423	75.3	100	100

(a) Estimated electorate at 11 June 1987: 43 181 321
(b) Excluding spoiled or rejected ballot papers

individual candidates in order of preference. To get elected a candidate would need a certain quota of votes (established by dividing the number of valid votes cast by the number of elected representatives for the constituency, plus one). Thus in a five-member constituency in which 100 000 votes were cast the number of votes required for the quota (and hence election on the basis of first preferences) would be 20 001. The leading candidate's votes surplus to the quota and the votes for all the other candidates in order of preference would then be redistributed among the other candidates according to the voters' second and subsequent preferences until the requisite number of candidates (in this case five) had qualified for election. Thus every elected candidate could be said to have sufficient votes from the electorate (at least on the basis of second and subsequent preferences) and it would be possible for the voters to plump for individual candidates within the ideological range of any large party. For example, in a safe Conservative constituency the voters might choose two hard-line Conservatives, one 'wet' Tory, one Liberal and one moderate Labour. In a safe Labour seat they might equally choose two mainstream Kinnockites, one Labour right-winger, one Liberal and one moderate Tory.

This system of proportional representation was recommended by a Speaker's Conference in 1917. It was actually used in some of the multi-member University seats between 1918 and 1948; it was advocated by the Kilbrandon Commission in 1973 as part of the proposals for devolved Assemblies in Scotland and Wales; and it is now used for parliamentary elections in the Irish Republic and local government elections in Northern Ireland.

Another variant of proportional representation which has been advocated is based upon the additional member principle. In this system, which is used in the Federal Republic of Germany, half of the *Bundestag* members are elected by plurality in single-member constituencies and the other half from party lists drawn up within each *Land*. The voter has two votes: one for a constituency candidate and the other for a party list. The former enables him to express his first preference and, if it is in a good area for his party, to secure his real choice for Parliament by direct election. The latter enables him to express what amounts to his second preference, usually by voting for the party list of one of the smaller parties in an attempt to ensure that the major opponent of his real first preference does not get elected. In other words, he casts his second vote for the party which he dislikes least in an attempt to exclude the party which he dislikes most. The system therefore improves the parliamentary prospects for the smaller parties (such as the Free Democrats or the Greens) which might not otherwise have enough concentrated voting strength to get any of their candidates elected on a basis of first-past-the-post. It is also qualified by the so-called 5 per cent rule which prevents parties with less than 5 per cent of the popular vote or three outright victories on the basis of first-past-the-post from securing any representation at all in the *Bundestag*.

Yet another variant which might well attract all-party support in Britain is based upon the two-ballot system used in France. This uses single-member constituencies, but requires a candidate to win over half the votes cast in order to be elected on the first ballot. Failure to do this triggers a second ballot in which the result is decided by simple plurality, that is to say first-past-the-post. To go forward to the second ballot (if there is no outright winner on the first ballot), a candidate requires at least 12.5 per cent of the votes cast in the first ballot. This eliminates a great number of candidates from smaller parties or political splinter groups and automatically clarifies the voters' choice at the second ballot. The great advantage of the system is that it ensures real democratic legitimacy at least for those elected outright on the first ballot. The most commonly recognised disadvantage is that it is capable of producing bipolarised distortions which make it possible for a candidate who came third on the first ballot to triumph on the second ballot, because both his own supporters and some of the supporters of each of his stronger opponents find him the least unacceptable of the candidates in the second round. In other words, at the first ballot the voter chooses, whereas at the second he eliminates.

Nearly all the MPs in the minor parties and some MPs in the large parties favour a change to proportional representation in Britain. Yet on present evidence it does not seem likely to be introduced, because the great majority of MPs in both large parties share a strong vested interest in the present electoral system and therefore oppose any such change in electoral law. Thus electoral reform is unlikely to occur in Britain, unless it is forced upon one or other of the large parties by the imperatives of political bargaining in a future 'hung Parliament', that is to say one in which no single party has an overall majority in the House of Commons.[5]

3.2 Criteria of Assessment

In a celebrated text written more than 30 years ago W. J. M. Mackenzie suggested four criteria by which an electoral system could be assessed. These were the quality of those elected, the effectiveness of the legislature, the fairness of the electoral results, and the degree of public confidence inspired.[6] It may therefore be convenient to consider the British electoral system in the light of these four, admittedly rather ideal, criteria.

The Quality of the MPs

Members of Parliament in Britain are not strictly representative of the general public in that they are usually better educated and more economically privileged than the electorate as a whole. Of course these general observations should come as no real surprise, since similar statements could be made about every national assembly throughout the world, including those in Communist or former Communist countries. Yet there remains a utopian bias in some quarters in favour of achieving a more 'representative' House of Commons, by which people mean one composed of those more like you and me!

Taking the House of Commons which was elected in June 1987, we find that 99 per cent of the Conservative MPs and 70 per cent of the Labour MPs came from middle-class or professional occupations. Of all the MPs, 80 per cent had benefited from higher or further education and 34 per cent had been to university at Oxford or Cambridge. Of the Conservative MPs, 23 per cent had been educated at one of the old public schools, as had 3 per cent of Labour MPs. The 46 MPs from the minor parties came overwhelmingly from middle-class or professional occupations (93 per cent of them to be exact), but none of them had been educated at an old public school and only 13 per cent of them had been to university at Oxford or Cambridge. It is therefore clear that Conservative MPs still tend to come from more privileged backgrounds than other MPs, although this socioeconomic differential has narrowed noticeably in recent years.

Of course these characteristics are not necessarily signs of quality and in any case the standard of MPs could always be higher. Yet quality is not really a function of the electoral system. It derives much more from the intermittent nature of parliamentary work, the frustrations of life on the back benches, the unwillingness of many employers to encourage their employees to stand for Parliament, and the relatively low esteem in which politicians are held by the vast majority of the British people. All these factors may discourage many able people from standing for Parliament or even from entering active politics in the first place. Furthermore, in our front-bench dominated political system, no more than about 90 MPs are paid members of any government and no more than about another 90 are involved in the tasks of front-bench opposition. Thus the vast majority of MPs in the House of Commons at any time are obliged to busy themselves with other forms of political activity, such as liaising with outside interests or welfare work on behalf of their constituents. This may be appreciated by their contacts and expected by their constituents, but it does not necessarily attract the most talented people into Parliament.

Effectiveness of the Legislature

It is hard to see why any shortcomings in the legislature should necessarily be attributed to the working of the electoral system. Quite the contrary, since one of the familiar charges against our system is that it makes it all too easy for one or other of the parties to win an overall majority in the Commons which can then be used to push through its partisan legislation, often against rather ineffective parliamentary opposition and sometimes in defiance of the expressed wishes of the general public.

According to this argument, Parliament is actually too effective at churning out partisan, ill-considered legislation and too ineffective at controlling the actions of the government of the day. If this is so, it is essentially because all MPs not in the Government have little involvement and no responsibility in the formative stages of policy and decision making. It is also because government back-benchers are inhibited by party loyalty and political self-interest from pursuing continuous public criticism of their own Ministers. Parliamentary control is therefore left largely in the hands of the Opposition, which is usually unable to do more than kick up a fuss about controversial government decisions or delay the contentious elements in the government's legislative programme.

Fairness of the Results

It is here that we enter the area of greatest controversy about our electoral system. While it enables the electorate to choose what is normally a single-party government every four or five years at General Election time, it does not produce a House of Commons which is anything like an exact reflection of the votes cast for each party. Essentially, it is a system which enables the largest single minority of voters in the national electorate to bring about the return of a single-party government with an overall majority in the House of Commons. There is, in fact, a threshold of between 35 per cent and 40 per cent of the votes cast above which (especially in marginal seats with three or more candidates) a party has a good chance of capturing seats, but below which it is likely to fail to form the Government.

This situation arises because most General Elections in Britain tend to be contests between at least three parties in which the second- and third-ranking parties frequently split the losing vote between them, thus ensuring that neither has a real chance of defeating the leading party. Obviously there is always the possibility of tactical voting by the supporters of one or other of the losing parties, yet on the whole this has not made much difference to the results (except occasionally at by-elections), since none of the parties can be sure of delivering enough of its supporters to guarantee such an outcome. The same flaw affects the idea of an electoral pact between the various opposition parties in which all but one of them would stand down in individual constituencies in favour of the party with the best chance of defeating the incumbent.

In the General Election of February 1974 the third party (the Liberals) received more than six million votes, but won only 14 seats in the House of Commons. Conversely the party which won the election (Labour) did so with fewer popular votes than the party which came second in parliamentary terms (the Conservatives), since Labour votes were distributed more effectively than Conservative votes in the marginal seats. In the 1983 General Election the discrepancy between votes and seats was even more striking in the case of the Alliance parties, which together received more than seven million votes, but won only 23 seats in the House of Commons. The same was true of the 1987 General Election when the Alliance again won over seven million votes, but had to be satisfied with only 22 seats.

Of course the results could be very different if the potential supporters of third parties, those who abstain from voting and those who are deterred from supporting their first preference for fear of casting wasted votes, were all to vote in accordance with their real political preferences. In that case there would be a possibility of third parties coming first in many parts of the country.

The most sensible conclusion is that the British electoral system is likely to remain unfair to third parties, but it is by no means clear that a particular party will always come third. In this scheme of things fairness is not the prime consideration. The overriding purpose is to elect to government a single party with a sufficient parliamentary majority to ensure its authority to govern throughout the period of a normal four- or five-year Parliament.

Public Confidence Inspired

It is difficult to produce reliable measures of public confidence in something as abstract as an electoral system. One way of assessing it is to note the degree of popular support for electoral reform as measured by opinion polls. This has been consistently strong among Liberal and Social Democratic voters, but it has also proved attractive to representative samples of the electorate as a whole.[7]

Another way of assessing public confidence in the electoral system is to log the performance of the two large parties at successive General Elections. In view of the fact that they are so clearly associated in the public mind with adherence to the existing electoral system, a high level of support for both of them together could also be interpreted as support for the existing rules of the game. We find that the proportion of the electorate voting for the Conservative and Labour parties taken together fell consistently from 79 per cent in 1951 to 56 per cent in October 1974. It rose to 62 per cent in 1979, fell back to 51 per cent in 1983, but rose again to 55 per cent in 1987.[8] Furthermore the Conservatives won the 1987 General Election with the support of only 32 per cent of the total electorate, while Labour theoretically came third with 23 per cent behind the 25 per cent of the electorate who did not bother to vote at all. In so far as any valid or lasting conclusion can be drawn from this evidence, it can hardly be that the British public has given a massive vote of confidence to the electoral system.

3.3 **Conclusion**

The British electoral system has come a long way since Queen Victoria confided to her diary that 'it seems to me a defect in our much famed constitution to have to part with an admirable Government . . . merely on account of the number of votes'.[9] Nowadays a General Election is usually seen as a public verdict upon the record of the party in government and the competing attractions of the various opposition parties. Yet the mass electorate is politically sovereign only on condition that it exercises its sovereignty when invited to do so by the Prime Minister of the day and within the limits of political choice offered by the political parties.

Modern British politics is essentially about the struggle for power between the political parties. Of course there has always been some ideology in the political rhetoric and the party manifestos. Yet for most of those who reach the top of the political tree the ideological content has often been little more than a necessary part of the political ritual, the tribute which party leaders and others have had to pay to their more zealous followers and supporters, especially when in opposition. Some would argue that this changed when Margaret Thatcher was Leader of the Conservative party from 1975 to 1990. Yet the appeal of pragmatism usually trumps ideology if the latter is seen as a threat to a party's chances of gaining or retaining power.

In short, the conduct of elections and the parliamentary results which ensue are seldom more important than the actual behaviour of the parties either when elected into government or when released from the responsibilities of public office. While free elections on the basis of universal adult suffrage are an indispensable foundation for our electoral system, it is the quality of party politics between elections and the conduct of every government in office which is vital to the future of our democracy.

Suggested Questions

1. Describe the working of the British electoral system.
2. To what extent does the British electoral system satisfy the four criteria suggested by W. J. M. Mackenzie?
3. Analyse the arguments for and against a change to proportional representation in Britain.

Notes

1. Those disqualified from standing for Parliament are: certified lunatics; deaf mutes; English and Scottish peers; people serving in the civil service, the armed forces and the police; and ordained clergymen in the Church of England, the Church of Ireland, the Church of Scotland and the Roman Catholic Church. Since the Bobby Sands case in Northern Ireland in 1981, convicted offenders detained for more than one year have also been disqualified for the duration of their sentences under the 1981 Representation of the People Act.
2. Following the 1987 General Election in which Labour did really well only in its safest seats, the Conservative vote has been the more effectively distributed of the two main parties. Yet this has not prevented both Labour and the Liberal Democrats from doing very well in certain by-elections, notably mid-Staffordshire in March 1990 and Eastbourne in October 1990.
3. The evidence for the multiplier effect in British politics can be derived from successive Nuffield Election Studies since 1950. However, the effect has diminished somewhat in recent years as a larger proportion of the seats have become 'safe' for one or other of the main parties.
4. See V. Bogdanor, *The People and the Party System* (London: CUP, 1981), pp. 97–258 for a fuller discussion of proportional representation.
5. From time to time there has been some discussion of a possible electoral pact between the opposition parties in order to facilitate the defeat of the Conservatives. Yet with Labour having done better in the opinion polls since mid-1989, it seems unlikely that such a pact will actually be concluded.
6. See W. J. M. Mackenzie, *Free Elections* (London: Allen & Unwin, 1958), pp. 69–71.
7. For example, a poll by Opinion Research and Communication published in *The Times* on 17 January 1980 showed that 72 per cent of those questioned approved of an electoral system based upon the principle of proportionality.
8. The statistics on turn-out at General Elections depend very much upon the accuracy of the Electoral Register. On average it has been little more than 90 per cent accurate and even less so in inner city areas where the population is very mobile.
9. Quoted in E. Longford, *Victoria R.I.* (London: Weidenfeld & Nicolson, 1964), p. 518.

Further Reading

Alderman, G., *British Elections, Myth and Reality* (London: Batsford, 1978).
Bogdanor, V., *The People and the Party System* (Cambridge University Press, 1981).

Butler, D. E. and Kavanagh, D., *The British General Election of 1987* (London: Macmillan, 1988).

Finer, S. E. (ed.), *Adversary Politics and Electoral Reform* (London: Anthony Wigram, 1975).

Harrop, M. and Miller, W. L., *Elections and Voters* (London: Macmillan, 1987).

Johnston, R. J., *Money and Votes: constituency campaign spending and election results* (Beckenham: Croom Helm, 1987).

Lakeman, E., *Power to Elect: the case for proportional representation* (London: Heinemann, 1982).

Lodge, J. (ed.), *Direct Elections to the European Parliament 1984* (London: Macmillan, 1986).

McLean, I. *Elections*, 2nd edn (London: Longman, 1980).

Pulzer, P., *Political Representation and Elections in Britain*, 2nd edn (London: Allen & Unwin, 1975).

4 Voting behaviour

Voting behaviour in Britain since the Second World War has been characterised mainly by the tendency of the electorate at General Elections to divide between the two main parties. There was a period in the 1980s when the formation of a three-party system seemed to be imminent, but since the 1987 General Election the traditional two-party model seems to have been reasserted. This is not altogether surprising, since the dominance of two main parties (not always the same) has clear antecedents in British political history.

In the late eighteenth and early nineteenth centuries there was a struggle for power between the Whigs and the Tories. In the late nineteenth and early twentieth centuries there was a struggle between the Liberals and the Conservatives. During the first few decades of this century it was uncertain whether or not Labour would displace the Liberals as the main opponent of the Conservatives. However, since the end of the Second World War, the effective choice at all General Elections has been between the Conservative and Labour parties.

Of course the formation in 1981 of the Alliance between the Liberals and the newly formed Social Democrats and its impressive performance in terms of the popular vote at the 1983 and 1987 General Elections might have presaged a decisive change in the balance of British political forces, but in the event this was not to be. The Alliance split asunder in the wake of the 1987 General Election, when David Owen and some Social Democrats refused to join the newly formed Liberal Democratic party, and the leadership of the Labour party rediscovered the path of political moderation and common sense.

4.1 Groups in the Electorate

It is possible to identify many different groups in the British electorate. The lines of political cleavage can be drawn in a number of different directions, according to various criteria. In this section we shall summarise the position according to the most widespread and familiar definitions.

Party Loyalists

At General Elections since the Second World War the Conservative and Labour parties have each usually been able to count upon the loyal support of at least 7 500 000 voters, most of whom have voted consistently for one or other of the main parties at every General Election. Since 1964 there have also been at least 600 000 voters who have consistently supported the Liberal party at General Elections, although before that, during the 13 years of Conservative rule from 1951 to 1964, the number of Liberal loyalists had been considerably smaller.

In Scotland and Wales there have been smaller sections of the electorate which have voted for the nationalist parties; the Scottish National party and Plaid

Cymru. It is hard to ascertain how many of these voters have been 'loyalists', since such parties have always attracted substantial and varying protest votes and their electoral fortunes have fluctuated accordingly. At the 1987 General Election they collected together about 540 000 votes, or just under 2 per cent of the total vote in the United Kingdom.

In Northern Ireland there have been about 730 000 voters, of whom about two-thirds have habitually voted for an assortment of Protestant and Unionist candidates, while the votes of the other one-third have traditionally gone mostly to the Catholic Social Democratic and Labour party (SDLP). However, at the 1987 General Election, the Provisional Sinn Fein, the political wing of the Irish Republican movement in Northern Ireland, attracted about 83 000 votes or just over 11 per cent of the total vote in the six counties, slightly down on the 13 per cent which it received in 1983.

Floaters and Abstainers

The vital group of floating voters has varied in number and in composition at each General Election since the Second World War. This volatile section of the electorate, which by definition is never made up of exactly the same people from one General Election to the next, seems to have grown in size over the years. Over the period 1959–79 about half the electorate changed its voting behaviour at least once, if we include moves to and from abstention.[1] Over one-third of those who voted Labour in 1979 deserted the party in 1983, as did nearly one-quarter of those who had voted Conservative, thus effectively determining the outcome of the 1983 election. At the 1987 General Election it was the Alliance of Liberals and Social Democrats which suffered most from the floating vote, losing nearly one-third of its 1983 vote to other parties or to non-voting. Each of the main parties too suffered from defectors, with the Conservatives losing 23 per cent of their 1983 vote to other parties and abstention and Labour losing 25 per cent in the same way. Such floating voters therefore provide the key to electoral victory or defeat at every General Election.

In particular, the floating voters determine the electoral fortunes of the minor parties, since without the benefit of desertions from both main parties it would be difficult for them to collect many extra votes. Of course there is always the possibility that a third party can become one of the two leading parties in Parliament, provided it manages to break through a threshold of about 35 per cent of the votes cast, above which it is likely to win a substantial number of seats in the House of Commons but below which it is likely to languish in frustrating parliamentary weakness. After all it was in just such a manner that the Labour party gradually displaced the Liberals during the first half of this century.

As for those who do not vote, for whatever reason, we discover that such people have accounted for between 16 per cent and 28 per cent of the total electorate at General Elections since the Second World War.[2] Since voting is voluntary in Britain, such non-voters can have a decisive influence upon the electoral outcome. For example, it has been estimated that differential non-voting had a vital influence upon the results of the 1951 and both the 1974 General Elections. It could have a similarly decisive influence upon the next election.

Social Class as a Basis for Voting

The most significant cleavages in the British electorate are still based upon class factors of one kind or another. Yet the meaning of social class is changing and its correlation with voting behaviour changes accordingly.

At General Elections since the Second World War the Conservative vote has usually consisted of perhaps two-thirds of the total middle-class vote and about one-third of the total working-class vote, according to the broadest definitions. The Labour vote has usually been made up of perhaps one-quarter of the total middle-class vote and more than half of the total working-class vote, according to the same broad definitions. The minor party votes in England have tended to be even less class-based (which has been part of their electoral problem), and in the other parts of the United Kingdom there has been no overwhelming class bias in the votes of the nationalist parties.

There has always been a significant number of people whose voting behaviour could not easily be explained or predicted on traditional class lines. The most notable example has been that of the working-class Conservatives.[3] Typically, more than one-third of all Conservative votes at General Elections since the war have come from working-class people. This means, for example, that at the 1983 General Election there must have been at least four million working-class people who voted Conservative, while at the 1987 General Election the party is estimated to have received as much as 36 per cent of the manual workers' vote – its best achievement among this group at any election since the Second World War. In view of the bottom-heavy shape of the social structure in Britain, it is evident that the Conservative party could never be elected to office if it did not manage to attract a sufficient proportion of the working-class vote. Equally it is clear that the Labour party was badly damaged by the steady erosion of its working-class base in the 1980s.

In general, class-based voting of the traditional kind has weakened steadily in Britain over the years since the 1960s, notably within the changing working class. In 1959 Labour's share of the vote of manual workers and their families was 40 per cent larger than its share of the vote of white-collar workers and their families. By 1983 the gap had narrowed to 21 per cent and by 1987 it had narrowed still further to 16 per cent. For a considerable period in the 1970s and 1980s the Labour party lost working-class votes to the Conservatives. For example, at the 1983 General Election there was a swing from Labour to the Conservatives of 2 per cent among skilled manual workers and 4 per cent among semi-skilled and unskilled workers. At the 1987 General Election Labour concentrated upon trying to recover the working-class support which it had lost in 1983 and to some extent it was successful in doing so. It increased its vote among the semi-skilled and unskilled manual workers and their families by 6 per cent, but it continued to lose the votes of skilled workers and their families, where the swing to the Conservatives was more than 2 per cent compared with 1983.[4]

At the 1983 General Election it was the Alliance which was the main beneficiary of working-class desertions from Labour, since it gathered three times as many such votes as the Conservatives. Yet at the 1987 General Election Labour's fortunes varied as between the traditional and the new working class. It did well among the traditional unskilled manual class at the expense of the Alliance, whereas among the new skilled working class both Labour and the Alliance lost votes to the Conservatives. While at the 1959 General Election 62 per cent of all manual workers and their families had voted Labour, by 1983 Labour support from this quarter had fallen to 38 per cent. This was probably the low point for Labour among this section of the electorate, since at the 1987 General Election its support from this quarter had recovered to a respectable 50 per cent, largely at the expense of the Alliance. Since the Alliance has now disintegrated and since the Liberal Democrats have been languishing in the opinion polls, it seems likely that the Labour party will be able to hold, and probably increase, its working-class support at the next General Election.

In any event such a transformation of working-class voting behaviour has been rightly described by Ivor Crewe as 'the most significant post-war change in the social basis of British politics'.[5] This decline of traditional class-based voting in Britain could be attributed partly to the changing nature of the working class and partly to the desertion from Labour of the new skilled working class, especially those in this group who were owner–occupiers living in the south of England. A Gallup survey conducted at the time of the 1983 General Election showed that Labour trailed the Conservatives by 22 per cent among working-class owner–occupiers and by 16 per cent among working-class voters living in the south of England.[6] At the 1987 General Election Labour managed once again to achieve a strong position for itself among the traditional working class (especially those who were trade union members living in Scotland or the north of England), whereas among the new skilled working class it continued to lose support to the Conservatives. Thus Disraeli's 'two nations' are not only to be found in different classes and different parts of the country, but also within the working class itself.

Gender and Age Differences in Voting

Two further ways of categorising the electorate are by gender and age.[7] With regard to *gender differences in voting*, Labour has traditionally had a clear lead among male voters at General Elections since the Second World War, scoring a notable 19 per cent advantage over the Conservatives in 1945 and 1966. On the other hand, the Conservatives have traditionally had a clear lead among the female voters, scoring an almost as impressive 12 per cent and 13 per cent advantage over Labour in 1951 and 1955 respectively. At the 1979 General Election the Conservatives managed to maintain their strength among female voters with a 9 per cent lead over Labour, but, since it was such a good result for the Conservatives, they also scored a 5 per cent lead over Labour among male voters. At the 1983 General Election this trend was reversed and, unusually, the Conservatives drew more of their support from men than from women. This was mainly because the Alliance made such inroads into the female vote, gaining 28 per cent of female support as compared with the 14 per cent achieved by the Liberals on their own in 1979. At the 1987 General Election all the parties drew their support about equally from men and women.[8]

With regard to *age-related differences in voting behaviour*, Labour has traditionally done particularly well among voters under the age of 30, scoring a 28 per cent lead over the Conservatives in 1945, a 17 per cent lead in 1966 and a 16 per cent lead in October 1974. On the other hand, the Conservatives have traditionally done rather well among those in late middle age (50–64), scoring an 18 per cent lead over Labour in 1951, a 14 per cent lead in 1955 and a 13 per cent lead in 1959. The fortunes of the two main parties in the other age groups (30–49 and 65 and over) have been more evenly balanced. Whereas Labour did well among the 30–49 age group in 1945 and 1966 with leads over the Conservatives of 16 per cent and 13 per cent respectively, the Conservatives did well among those over 65 in 1955, 1970 and February 1974 with leads over Labour of 9 per cent, 9 per cent and 14 per cent respectively. In 1979 Labour was able to retain a small lead of 1 per cent over the Conservatives among the 18–24 age group, notwithstanding the fact that it trailed the Conservatives by 7 per cent among voters of all ages and by 10 per cent among those aged 35 and over.

At the 1983 General Election Conservative voting support increased steadily with age, but on a gentler gradient than before. The largest Conservative lead was 20 per cent over Labour in the 35–44 age group, while the smallest was 11 per cent over the Alliance in the 18–22 age group. The Conservatives retained their lead over Labour among those over 65 and did surprisingly well among first-time voters by taking 41 per cent of those who voted in that age group, as compared with 30 per cent for the Alliance and 29 per cent for Labour.

At the 1987 General Election Conservative voting support once again increased steadily with age, rising from 37 per cent of the 18–24 age group to 46 per cent of those over 55 years of age. Labour did best among voters in the 18–24 age group, where it secured the support of 40 per cent.[9] The relative importance of younger voters is likely to increase at the next General Election, since by that time there will be a considerable section of the electorate too young to have any adult memories of the last Labour Government. Indeed, 38 per cent of those interviewed in a 1989 opinion poll could remember nothing at all about the Wilson and Callaghan Labour Governments in the 1970s.[10]

Other Sectional Cleavages

There are, of course, other sectional cleavages in voting behaviour in Britain. In many ways these have become increasingly important over the years as the voters have become more volatile and instrumental in their voting behaviour.

Firstly, there are the *geographical variations in voting behaviour*. At the 1979 General Election the Midlands and the south of England voted strongly for the Conservatives, especially in the new towns and the more prosperous working-class suburbs. On the other hand, South Wales, the north of England and much of Scotland remained largely loyal to the Labour party.[11] At the 1983 General Election the Conservatives had a 16 per cent lead over Labour among working-class voters in the south of England, while Labour had a 10 per cent lead over the Conservatives among the same group in the north of England and in Scotland. At the 1987 General Election there were further sharp variations in voting behaviour as between different regions. In north and west Britain Labour polled particularly strongly, increasing its vote by more than 6 per cent as compared with 1983. In south and east Britain the Conservatives increased their vote by more than 1 per cent, in spite of the fact that their overall vote was fractionally down compared with 1983. It was almost as if there were two elections taking place simultaneously: in the south and east former Alliance supporters switched in similar proportions to Conservative and Labour, whereas in the north and west they switched disproportionately to Labour. Indeed the Alliance was the victim of a two-party squeeze. As Curtice and Steed have written, it 'emerged from the election with the pre-1981 Liberal party's dependence upon a rural, peripheral and middle-class base'.[12]

The consequences of this 'denationalisation' of British politics are quite striking. Although the Labour vote in 1987 rose slightly and fairly evenly across the whole of the south and east of Britain, the party only managed to win three seats outside Greater London (Norwich South, Oxford East and Bristol South) south and east of a line from the Severn Estuary to the Wash. On the other hand, the Conservatives won no seats in the great northern cities of Liverpool, Manchester and Newcastle, only two in Edinburgh and none in Glasgow. Perhaps the most marked and interesting sub-regional effect was the strong attraction of Thatcherite Conservatism for voters in the outer metropolitan area immediately surrounding Greater London. In these constituencies, especially in the north-east and north-west commuter belts of Greater London, the Conservative vote rose by more than 5 per cent in several cases.

Secondly, there are the *sociological differences in voting behaviour*, of which perhaps the most remarkable in recent years has been the cleavage between the traditional and the new working class. As a stereotype, the former group could be described as those who live in Scotland or the north of England, are council tenants, trade union members and work in the public sector. Equally, the latter group could be described as those who live in the south and east of England, are owner–occupiers, non-trade union members and work in the private sector, very often in a self-employed capacity.

At the 1983 General Election Labour led the Alliance by 33 per cent and the Conservatives by 38 per cent among voters who were council tenants, while the Conservatives had a 19 per cent lead over the Alliance among new working-class owner–occupiers and a 22 per cent lead over Labour in the same category. Among trade unionist voters the Conservatives improved their position and came second to Labour with 32 per cent as compared with 39 per cent in that category. Yet the defection of trade unionist voters was responsible for the biggest drop in any single category of the Labour vote (down by 14 per cent to 39 per cent), while the Alliance increased its support among trade unionist voters by 12 per cent in line with its general performance in the electorate. Labour's strongest position was among those of the unemployed who decided to vote, among whom it had a 15 per cent lead over the Conservatives. Yet only the Alliance actually increased its support in that group, from 15 per cent to 26 per cent of the total electorate.

At the 1987 General Election Labour led the Conservatives by 32 per cent and the Alliance by 39 per cent among voters who were council tenants, while the Conservatives had a 12 per cent lead over Labour and a 20 per cent lead over the Alliance among owner–occupiers in the new working class. Among trade unionist voters Labour improved its position compared with 1983 by establishing an 18 per cent lead over the Conservatives and a 26 per cent lead over the Alliance. As for the cleavage between public- and private-sector workers, it is interesting that Labour did better than the Conservatives in both groups (17 per cent better among the former and 1 per cent better among the latter) and dramatically better than the Alliance, which only got 19 per cent and 23 per cent from each group respectively.[13] Conservative support increased most significantly in the two lowest socioeconomic groups, with the result that the party got 36 per cent of those voters, its largest share since the Second World War. On the other hand, the Conservatives polled quite poorly among the middle-class, public-sector salariat at 44 per cent and even worse among the university-educated middle class with 34 per cent, compared with an impressive 36 per cent for the Alliance in that category. Education more than class was a decisive determinant of Alliance voting.

In short, the British electorate no longer divides neatly into two traditional, class-based voting groups, essentially because British society is no longer like that. The voters have become less easy to categorise in sociological terms and less inclined to adhere to their traditional voting allegiances. In such circumstances predictions of voting behaviour along traditional lines on the basis of a simple split between middle class and working class are increasingly unlikely to be accurate in modern conditions. Greater account has now to be taken of the social mobility and the electoral volatility of modern British society. Profiles of some typical voters are shown in schematic form in Figure 4.1.

Figure 4.1 Profiles of some typical voters

* *Conservative loyalist*: Man or woman of more than 55,
    middle class, owner–occupier, living in the south
    of England and often self-employed.

* *Labour loyalist*: Man or woman of less than 24, manual
    worker, council tenant, living in the north of England,
    Scotland or Wales, working in the public sector
    and a member of a trade union.

* *Alliance voter*: Man or woman of 25 to 34,
    middle class, owner–occupier,
    living in any part of Britain and working
    in a white collar job in the
    private or public sector.

4.2 Main Influences on Voting

Traditionally it has been argued that there are three main influences on voting behaviour in Britain – political inheritance, self-interest and the performance of the party in office.[14] Of course, there are other important influences on voting behaviour which cannot be ignored, such as policy and sentiment, image and technique. As we have already observed, other social factors, such as occupation, housing tenure, educational attainment and neighbourhood or peer group pressures, also have an impact. We must therefore take account of a wide variety of influences.

Political Inheritance

The influence of political inheritance means the political attitudes and loyalties which voters derive from their parents and families. On the basis of surveys conducted in the 1960s Butler and Stokes were able to show a high correlation (typically over 75 per cent) between the voting behaviour of one generation and the next within family households.[15] This was not surprising at the time, in view of the well-established fact that the opinions of young people on most issues, whether political or not, tended to accord with those of their parents. Indeed there is still considerable inertia in the party political loyalties of many voters at General Elections, which in most cases reflects the voting habits derived from family inheritance and social surroundings. We see this most clearly in the few remaining tight-knit communities, such as the valleys in South Wales, where there is still effectively a one-party voting tradition (in this case for the Labour party) in spite of the fact that modern social and geographical mobility has begun to erode it at the edges.

The key point at recent General Elections has been that it has not always been possible for either of the main parties to turn such traditional loyalties fully into a level of voting support commensurate with their party identifiers in opinion polls. For example, at the 1987 General Election 35 per cent of the electorate claimed to regard themselves as essentially Labour supporters, but only 31 per cent of those who voted actually supported Labour candidates, which was the equivalent of only 23 per cent of the electorate.[16]

Self-interest

The influence of self-interest derives very largely from the personal experience, favourable or unfavourable, consistent or contradictory, of millions of individual voters. For example, there is a fortunate minority of people in Britain who are born into well-off families, benefit from a good education and manage to lead happy and successful lives. In the majority of cases such people have tended to vote Conservative. Equally there is a large section of the public (typically several million) for whom life is a constant struggle against adverse material conditions. Their lives are characterised by financial insecurity, dependence upon the state and its agencies, and impoverished expectations. In the majority of cases such people have tended to vote Labour, if they have decided to vote at all.

Certainly the 59 per cent of the professional and managerial class and the 52 per cent of the office and clerical class who voted for the Conservatives at the 1987 General Election are likely to have done so principally for reasons of self-interest, although they often describe their reasons for voting in terms of their conception of the national interest. The minority of those groups who voted Labour or Alliance were more likely to have done so for ideological or altruistic reasons. Indeed it is worth noting in this context that at each of the last two General Elections the Labour and Alliance parties made considerable headway among the growing middle-class electorate and that the Alliance actually found its social base among the well-educated middle class. This suggests that self-interest is not always a dominant influence upon voting behaviour. Other factors, such as ideology and altruism, apathy and disillusion, play an important part as well.

Government Performance

The performance of the party in office might seem to be an influence on voting behaviour too obvious to be worth stating, if it were not for the fact that it emphasises the importance of the growing tendency for many people to vote *instrumentally*. This is the technical term to describe what happens when millions of floating voters effectively strike a bargain with the politicians, whereby they reward the party in office with re-election or punish it with electoral defeat according to their assessment of its period in government.[17]

This is certainly a view of voting behaviour which is widely held by practising politicians in Britain. It is also supported by the well-established axiom that parties in government are more likely to lose an election than parties in opposition are to win one. Equally it is clear from the three successive Conservative victories in 1979, 1983 and 1987 that it was possible for a large British political party to suffer a small, but significant decline in its share of the votes cast and still win each election handsomely, thanks largely to the fragmentation of the non-Conservative vote. Paradoxically it was possible for a governing party to lose voting support and still win successive General Elections, just as it was possible for one or more of the opposition parties to gain voting support and still lose quite heavily.

Policy and Sentiment

In recent years policy and sentiment have been increasingly important influences upon voting behaviour in Britain. As the voters have become more volatile and instrumental in their attitudes, such factors have begun to weigh at least as heavily as traditional social allegiances.

With regard to policy-based voting, Sarlvik and Crewe have shown that more than two-thirds of the votes cast for the three national parties at the 1979 General Election could have been predicted correctly on the basis of the view held by the voters on certain salient policy issues; and the correlation was over 90 per cent for Conservative and Labour voters.[18] They argued that this was a reflection of the fact that over the period 1964–79 there had been a dramatic decline in the level of popular support for three key Labour policies – further nationalisation, the reinforcement of trade union power, and higher tax-financed spending upon the Welfare State. These policies, which had commanded majority support in 1964 (at any rate among those voters who identified with the Labour party), received less than 25 per cent support among Labour voters in 1979. Labour had therefore lost a great deal of its earlier policy-based appeal.

Yet nothing remains exactly the same in this area of analysis. After a period in the 1970s and early 1980s when many of Labour's most salient policies were not popular with the electorate (for example, the commitment to higher direct taxation or support for unilateral nuclear disarmament), the party emerged from a period of comprehensive policy review with a range of more moderate and pragmatic policies which seem to have proved attractive to the electorate at least on the basis of answers to opinion polls. The present Labour leadership has adjusted at least the presentation of its policies and in so doing has demonstrated the importance of policy and its bearing upon the voting behaviour of many voters.

This should remind us that all voters are less inclined than they used to be to vote in accordance with traditional class or family loyalties, and more inclined to vote in the light of which party most closely reflects their own interests and policy preferences. Indeed evidence adduced by Sarlvik and Crewe suggested that voters' opinions on the policies and performances of each party are twice as likely to explain their voting behaviour as all their social and economic characteristics taken together.[19] A Gallup survey conducted for the BBC at the time of the 1983 General Election also showed that, when the voters preferred the policies of one party and the leader of another, they decided in favour of the former by about four to one, a tendency which on that occasion worked principally to the advantage of the Conservatives.[20]

Yet in weighing the influence of policy on voting behaviour, it is important to distinguish between those policies which the voters, when questioned by opinion pollsters, may consider to be the best in the abstract or for the sake of the country, and those for which they actually vote in the privacy of the polling booth. At the 1983 General Election the former outweighed the latter by nearly three to one. At the 1987 General Election the Labour party would have won if the voters had cast their votes in accordance with their altruistic policy preferences as expressed in answer to opinion polls at the time. The explanation for this has been provided by Ivor Crewe, who has pointed out that, when answering opinion pollsters, the voters respond altruistically and in the abstract, whereas when actually voting they tend to think much more instrumentally of their personal and family interests.[21]

With regard to capricious sentiment as an influence upon voting behaviour, Hilde Himmelweit and others have shown that, 'although in practice both consistency [that is, party loyalty] and ideological thinking [that is, policy considerations] influence the decision to vote, each election is like a new shopping expedition in a situation where new as well as familiar goods are on offer'.[22] This means that evidence from recent General Elections can be interpreted and explained by using a consumer model of voting behaviour. Of course a great deal depends upon how the voters feel during the period just before and during an election campaign and upon whether the public eventually decides to vote for positive or negative reasons or indeed to vote at all.

At the 1987 General Election, for example, the Conservative party achieved a landslide majority in Parliament with almost the same share of the votes cast as in 1983. This was because the votes cast for the other national parties were fairly evenly divided between Labour and the Alliance, but even more because more than two-thirds of those who (according to opinion polls at the outset of the campaign) had seriously considered voting for the Alliance eventually did *not* do so on polling day, because they came to the conclusion that such action might give victory to whichever of the two main parties they disliked the most. As Ivor Crewe has observed, 'once again the Alliance was doubly penalised by the electoral system: unable to convert votes into seats, it was unable to convert support into votes'.[23]

Image and Technique

Party images and campaign techniques are some of the other significant influences upon voting behaviour in this age of modern mass media. They have been identified by the political communications specialists of all the parties as crucial to electoral success in the modern age.

Party images have been formed in the public mind by the party leaders themselves – for example, the association of classlessness and geniality with John Major or of sympathy and good humour with Neil Kinnock – and by the performance and behaviour of the parties whether in government or opposition. The party leaders and their media advisers work hard to preserve or improve their respective images. Indeed, the presentation of policy, if not policy itself, is usually influenced by professional assessments of the image it is likely to convey. Above all, the parties are careful to foster an image of unity if they can, since the appearance of disunity is invariably damaging to their electoral prospects.

Party images are formed incrementally, even subliminally, over many years by what the parties do or fail to do when in government and by the way they behave when in opposition. For example, the Conservative party undoubtedly benefited at the 1987 General Election from Margaret Thatcher's acknowledged experience in high office and her resolute public image as someone who stuck to her guns when the going got rough – for instance, at the depth of the recession in the early 1980s or during the Westland crisis in 1986. Equally the Labour party then suffered in the eyes of many people from a poor image which was the product of several years of unconvincing leadership under Michael Foot, party in-fighting and internecine ideological struggles. By the time the campaign began there was not much that either party could do to improve its image, which in each case had taken years to crystallise. However the Labour party strove very hard and quite effectively to present Neil Kinnock and his wife in a favourable 'presidential' light and this impressed many media professionals and party workers.

Campaign techniques can also have an important influence upon voting behaviour, especially since many of the floating voters do not make up their minds until the final stages of the campaign. The parties therefore make every effort during the campaign to get as much good media coverage as possible and to present both their leaders and their policies in the most favourable light. Yet, in spite of these often expensive efforts, the actual conduct of the campaign seldom makes a decisive difference to the electoral outcome. For example, although it was widely agreed that the Labour leadership fought a brilliant media campaign in 1987, it seems clear that this had little or no effect upon the battle with the Conservatives for first place, but a considerable effect upon the battle with the Alliance for second place. In the case of the minor parties, which in normal times do not get much media attention, effective campaign techniques can be more significant in drawing helpful attention both to their leaders and to their policies.

Other Influences on Voting

In one of the most authoritative studies of voting behaviour in Britain, Heath, Jowell and Curtice have demonstrated the advantages of drawing multi-dimensional maps of the electorate.[24] Using this technique it is possible to take full account of all the various cleavages in the electorate and go beyond the familiar criteria of social class and geography. A modern list of the other variables should include the influence of neighbourhood, occupation, housing tenure, educational attainment and racial identity. On the last point, for example, it appears that Afro-Americans are more dissatisfied with their lives in Britain than Asians. This has provided a political opportunity for Labour among the former group, which led the party to select a number of candidates from the black community in a deliberate and partially successful attempt to win more seats at the 1987 General Election.

In short, there is a wide variety of influences upon voting behaviour in Britain. The traditional influences – that is, political inheritance, self-interest and the performance of the party in office – are still of fundamental importance. Yet the more ephemeral influences (for instance, policy and sentiment, image and technique) have made themselves increasingly felt in recent years and have assumed a growing importance as the voters have shown more volatility in their voting behaviour and as General Election campaigns have become more presidential both in style and in content. The use of such modern techniques emphasises the manipulative aspects of modern party politics and reminds us of the extent to which our election practices have been influenced by the United States. Yet in spite of such new developments it is clear that our electoral politics have not been completely Americanised, not least because of the tight legal limits upon the amount which each parliamentary candidate may spend on election expenses during the rather brief General Election campaigns in Britain.

4.3 **Continuing Uncertainties**

There are some continuing uncertainties which are likely to have a significant influence upon the outcome of future General Elections in Britain. Will the voters be more or less concerned with issues of policy? Will the Conservative vote grow or decline among the new working class? Will a substantial part of the middle class continue to vote Labour or Liberal Democrat? Will men and women come to have less differentiated political leanings? Will the electorate become more or less volatile in its voting behaviour? Will the minor parties recover their combined share of the vote in 1987 or will they suffer significant defections? Will voting turn-out at General Elections grow or decline? To what extent will there be signs of political alienation? Whatever the difficulties, it is worth exploring some of these important questions.

Instrumental or Expressive Voting

There was a time in the late 1950s and early 1960s when some observers proclaimed the end of ideology in Britain and other advanced Western countries.[25] In more recent times it has seemed that ideology and policy considerations have become once again a significant influence upon voting behaviour. This is consistent with the evidence for so-called instrumental voting, whereby voters assess the policies, attitudes and images of the various parties and then cast their votes in the light of such an assessment.

Throughout the 1980s it seemed that the positions taken by the different parties on the main issues of policy had a significant effect upon voting behaviour at General Elections. This was brought about partly by the continuing fragmentation of the traditional working class, which created a rootless, upwardly mobile group whose voting behaviour was particularly susceptible to instrumental appeals from the politicians to their particular interests. It was also a reflection of the increasing sophistication of all those voters who regard their decisions at General Elections as really another form of consumer choice. For such people, as long as there appears to be an attractive political product on offer, a significant number of them will measure its claims against not only their own policy preferences but also their assessment of their own interests. In such a political beauty contest between the parties, the voters' perceptions of political issues and of their own interests in relation to party policies are likely to have a significant effect upon election results.

On the other hand, there is considerable evidence in support of the so-called expressive interpretation of voting – that is to say, the tendency of many in the electorate to vote in accordance with the norms and values of the principal social group to which they belong. According to this theory of voting behaviour, many of the preferences which are justified in opinion polls by reference to voter predilections for particular party policies are actually little more than rationalisations of more basic interests or a cover for a dominant social identification. In other words, if voting behaviour is determined principally by social identity, then we need only look at the changing class proportions within society to be able to forecast likely electoral outcomes.

Conservatives and the Fragmented Working Class

It is reasonable to assume that, as long as the Conservative party can preside over a period of buoyant prosperity, it will retain the support of a significant number of working-class voters. Such support will also depend upon the image of the party in the eyes of the so-called authoritarian working class – that is, those working-class voters who are attracted by whichever party takes the toughest line on issues such as law and order, immigration and trade union behaviour.

Unless the Conservative party forfeits all its claims to experience and competence in office and fails to deliver a general sense of economic well-being by the time of the next election, it is likely that the self-interest of at least some of the working class (notably those whom Brian Walden has described as 'strivers') will deliver to the party a substantial vote. In 1983 the Conservatives benefited from the patriotic appeal of victory in the Falklands and from a divided Opposition. In 1987 they benefited from a rising tide of prosperity and a divided Opposition. It is hard to see how they will be quite so lucky in future elections, but in order to be sure of winning they will need to retain a good part of the working-class vote which they won in 1983 and 1987.

Labour and the Fragmented Middle Class

It is worth noting that, over the last decade and more, even when the Labour party has fared badly at General Elections, its middle-class voting support has held up rather well. There is no complete explanation for this and no certainty that it will continue to be true in future. It may partly be explained by Labour's strong support among white-collar workers in the public sector – for example, teachers and health service workers. It could even be strengthened if Labour managed to broaden its appeal to encompass more issues of concern to the growing middle-class electorate, such as the quality of public services, protection of the environment and greater economic opportunities for women. In recent times there has been some evidence of Labour's ability to do this.

Of course another explanation for this phenomenon is simply that, as the electorate as a whole becomes more middle-class, so Labour voters are likely to become more middle-class as they move up the economic and social ladder. Even though their improved material circumstances and middle-class life-style might be thought to be more consistent with voting Conservative, such voters remain loyal to their social origins and Labour principles.

Gender Differences in Voting

In so far as women usually live longer than men and Conservative voting behaviour is usually more prevalent later in life, it is likely that many women will have a tendency to vote Conservative. Yet recent evidence on this issue now points to virtual equality of voting preferences between the sexes for each of the large political parties.

On the one hand, the traditional model of family life, with the wife and mother staying at home at least while the children are young, suggests that many women are likely to remain relatively insulated from the pro-Labour voting pressures which have been characteristic of at least the highly unionised sectors of employment. Even when married women return to work, many of them take part-time employment in the service sector, so that their jobs can be compatible with their continuing family responsibilities. Once again this does not make it very likely that they will develop Labour voting habits.

On the other hand, at the 1987 General Election the Conservative party got the same proportion of its votes from men as from women, a result which flew in the face of the traditional assumption that the party does better among female voters. There are a number of plausible explanations for what could be a new trend. One is that some women did not like Mrs Thatcher's forceful style of politics. Another is that on several key issues of the campaign – for example, unemployment, the health service and the quality of education – many women found the Conservative party unconvincing, unattractive or both. Another is that women of all ages, especially middle-class women of child-bearing age, were often attracted by the style and approach of the minor party leaders, David Owen and David Steel. Perhaps the most obvious explanation is that 'Thatcherism' had a strong appeal to many male voters, especially those in the upwardly mobile working class. It remains to be seen whether these factors will influence future General Elections, but it seems that the Conservative party no longer enjoys a natural advantage among women voters.

Electoral Volatility

There is no way of knowing for certain whether or not the British electorate will become more volatile in future. However there have been signs of considerable volatility over the past two decades and it seems likely that the trend will continue in future.

At the 1987 General Election there was further evidence of electoral volatility, since all parties suffered from significant desertions by the voters and none more so than the Alliance, which was caught in a predictable squeeze between the two main parties. The Labour party lost 25 per cent of the vote which it had obtained in 1983, with 11 per cent going to the Alliance, 4 per cent to the Conservatives and the rest split between the other small parties and non-voting. The Conservative party lost 23 per cent of the vote which it had obtained in 1983, with 12 per cent going to the Alliance, 5 per cent to Labour and 6 per cent staying at home. The Alliance lost 30 per cent of the vote which it had obtained in 1983, with 10 per cent going to the Conservatives, 12 per cent to Labour and 8 per cent staying at home. Once again it was the Alliance which suffered most from the effects of electoral volatility. More than two-thirds of potential Alliance voters explained their eventual decision to vote differently in terms of their wish not to cast a wasted vote which might have facilitated victory for whichever main party they disliked most.[26] In such circumstances the Alliance actually lost more votes than it won from those in the electorate who indulged in tactical voting.

In future the impact of electoral volatility will depend upon the net effect of a number of different factors. It is likely that increased volatility will be encouraged by the relative weakening of traditional associations between class and party, the growing tendency for voters to cast their votes instrumentally, the advent of capricious 'consumer' voting, and the unsettling influence of the media on the opinion polls. On the other hand, volatility could decrease if there were to be a general recognition of the futility of casting wasted votes for any of the smaller parties, except of course the nationalists in Scotland and Wales. The outcome is therefore uncertain. All that can be said at this stage is that the Conservatives will have to lose a significant proportion of their 1987 vote if Labour is to win the next General Election.

Participation or Alienation

If political participation is measured simply in terms of the turn-out at General Elections since the Second World War, we can see that it has fluctuated between a high point of 84 per cent in 1950 and a low point of 72 per cent in 1970, with an average of 76 per cent over the entire period. In 1970 and 1983 for seasonal reasons (both elections held in June, when many people were on holiday) and in October 1974 for reasons directly connected with public alienation from the political process (two General Elections in one year) the number of those not voting rivalled or exceeded the number of those who voted for the party which came second. Given that the two-party struggle has been a dominant characteristic of the British political system since the war, these facts could be interpreted as signs of real alienation from the political process.

It is also reasonable to argue that such signs of disenchantment with the two large parties are not necessarily signs of dissatisfaction with the electoral system or alienation from the entire political process. Indeed it is worth remembering that many party candidates regularly get more than 50 per cent of the votes cast in their own constituencies. Yet there can be no escape from the fact that the struggle for power between the two leading parties has been the dominant characteristic of the British political system since the Second World War, so perhaps the conclusion is justified.

The secular trend away from the two large parties was halted and slightly reversed in 1987, when the Conservatives and Labour together polled 3 per cent more than they had done in 1983. It remains to be seen whether this reassertion of the traditional duopoly will continue or even grow at the expense of the smaller parties. On the evidence from local elections and opinion polls at the time of writing, it seems likely that it will and that much of the benefit of this process will go to Labour.

4.4 Conclusion

In conclusion, we can say that the main influences upon voting behaviour in Britain are political inheritance, self-interest and the performance of the party in office. Nevertheless these are often subjective influences which can depend upon the conclusions which individual voters draw from their own experience and observation of the political scene. From a more objective point of view, it seems clear that social class, economic occupation, housing tenure, educational attainment and geographical location are among the most important influences upon the way people cast their votes at General Elections. Furthermore the voters do not cast their votes in a vacuum. They go to the polls (or decide not to bother) after weeks and months of verbal bombardment by the politicians and the media as well as assiduous attention from the opinion pollsters. All these various forces help to form the views of the voters, whose voting behaviour has become more volatile and even capricious in consequence.

It is probably still right to agree with Jean Blondel, who wrote years ago that 'the simple division between working and middle class . . . contributes to the clearest cleavage in British political attitudes and voting behaviour'.[27] Yet such a statement no longer tells us all we need to know about voting behaviour in Britain in the 1990s. This is because the traditional working class has become significantly smaller while the middle class has grown, in each case as a function of changing patterns of employment. Such social changes ought to favour the Conservatives, although current opinion poll evidence (in 1990) suggests that the Labour party will do well in spite of its structural handicap. Whatever happens, it is well to remember that there are no certainties in voting behaviour.

Suggested Questions

1. What are the main divisions in the British electorate?
2. Which are the most significant influences upon voting behaviour in Britain?
3. Is social class still a decisive factor in determining the outcome of elections in Britain?

Notes

1. B. Sarlvik and I. Crewe, *Decade of Dealignment* (London: CUP, 1983), p. 66.
2. Since about 6 per cent of the names on the Electoral Register are redundant (i.e. dead, double-counted, emigrated etc.), the true level of non-voting is somewhat lower than the usual figures suggest.
3. For a fuller discussion of this subject see R. T. McKenzie and A. Silver, *Angels in Marble* (London: Heinemann, 1968) and J. H. Goldthorpe, *Social Mobility and Class Structure in Modern Britain* (Oxford: Clarendon Press, 1980).
4. See I. Crewe, 'A new class of politics', in *The Guardian*, 15 June 1987.
5. *The Guardian*, 13 June 1983.
6. Ibid.
7. The evidence on differences in voting behaviour by gender and age has been written up in successive Nuffield Election Studies since 1950. The figures given here are derived from those studies.
8. See the Gallup Survey commissioned by the BBC and published in *The Guardian*, 15 June 1987.
9. Ibid.
10. See Gallup Poll in *The Daily Telegraph*, 7 April 1989.
11. For a detailed breakdown of regional variations in voting behaviour see successive *Times Guides to the House of Commons* which are published after each General Election.
12. See J. Curtice and M. Steed's analysis of voting behaviour in Appendix 2 of D. E. Butler and D. Kavanagh, *The British General Election of 1987* (London: Macmillan, 1988), p. 332.
13. See Ivor Crewe in *The Guardian*, 15 June 1987.
14. See, for example, A. H. Birch, *The British System of Government*, 8th edn (London: Allen & Unwin, 1990), pp. 78–82.
15. See D. E. Butler and D. Stokes, *Political Change in Britain*, 2nd edn (London: Macmillan, 1974), pp. 48–66.
16. *The Guardian*, 16 June 1987.
17. See A. Heath *et al.*, *How Britain Votes* (Oxford: Pergamon Press, 1985).
18. See B. Sarlvik and I. Crewe, *Decade of Dealignment*, pp. 247–344.
19. Ibid., p. 113.
20. *The Guardian*, 14 June 1983.
21. *The Guardian*, 16 June 1987.
22. H. T. Himmelweit *et al.*, *How Voters Decide* (London: Academic Press, 1981), p. 14.
23. *The Guardian*, 16 June 1987.
24. See A. Heath *et al.*, *How Britain Votes*, pp. 170–5.

25. See, for example, D. Bell, *The End of Ideology*, revised edition (London: Collier Macmillan, 1965).
26. *The Guardian* 16 June 1987.
27. J. Blondel, *Voters, Parties and Leaders* (Harmondsworth: Penguin, 1974), p. 86.

Further Reading

Butler, D. E. and Jowett, P., *Party Strategies in Britain: a study of the 1984 European elections* (London: Macmillan, 1985).
Butler, D. E. and Kavanagh, D., *The British General Election of 1987* (London: Macmillan, 1988).
Goldthorpe, J. H., *Social Mobility and Class Structure in Modern Britain* (Oxford: Clarendon Press, 1980).
Heath, A. *et al.*, *How Britain Votes* (Oxford: Pergamon Press, 1985).
Himmelweit, H. T. *et al.*, *How Voters Decide* (London: Academic Press, 1981).
Miller, W. L. *et al.*, *How Voters Change* (Oxford: Clarendon Press, 1990).
Robertson, D., *Class and the British Electorate* (Oxford: Martin Robertson, 1983).
Sarlvik, B. and Crewe I., *Decade of Dealignment* (Cambridge University Press, 1983).
Scarbrough, E., *Political Ideology and Voting* (Oxford: Clarendon Press, 1984).

Part II
Sources of power, pressure and opinion

5) The political parties

British politics is party politics which takes place in what is fundamentally a two-party system. In this chapter, therefore, we shall focus principally upon the Conservative and Labour parties, as they have been the two most significant political forces, at any rate since the Second World War. Beyond them we shall look at the smaller parties, whether those with a national aspiration – such as the Liberal Democratic party – or those with a more geographically limited vocation, such as the nationalist parties in Scotland and Wales. We shall also consider briefly the parties in Northern Ireland and the fringe parties in the rest of the United Kingdom – the Greens, the National Front and so on.

At the outset it is worth trying to offer a common definition which can be applied to every political party to a greater or lesser extent. In the British case this might be: 'an organised and relatively disciplined group of people who freely combine to advance a set of political attitudes or beliefs with a view to translating them via success at elections into administrative decisions or legislation'. In other words, all parties try to influence, and a few aspire to win, the democratic power of government.

5.1 Ideological Principles

Since the Second World War it has been the Conservative and Labour parties which have dominated the British political scene. They have brought to British politics two distinct ideological traditions within which their respective political principles have been advanced in the light of circumstances prevailing at the time.

The Conservative Party

The Conservative tradition stresses the importance of strong government, in the sense that Conservatives believe that a government should act with determination and self-confidence based upon the democratic legitimacy which it derives from its parliamentary majority in the House of Commons. Conservatives have traditionally been suspicious of political ideology of an imperative or all-embracing kind, although when Margaret Thatcher became the leader in 1975 many observers began to doubt whether such a proposition was any longer valid. In the opinion of Samuel Beer, the ideas of independent authority for the executive, class rule by those deemed best equipped to govern, pragmatic decisions of a non-ideological character and strong determined government were all discernible in Conservative political thought for a long time.[1]

Occasionally in the course of its long history the Conservative party has been swept along on the wave of some particular ideology, but such periods have not usually lasted or brought enduring political success. Joseph Chamberlain, a refugee from the Liberal party, did not get very far with his campaign for tariff reform during the early years of this century. Edward Heath felt obliged to reverse the radical free market policies on which he and his colleagues had entered office in 1970. Yet, even though a conscious political ideology does not seem to belong in the Conservative tradition, the party appeared much more ideological in the 1980s – certainly in its free market rhetoric and occasionally in its actions. This reflected the influence of the New Right upon Conservative thinking. Pressure groups outside Parliament, such as the Institute of Economic Affairs and the Adam Smith Institute, and factions within Parliament, such as the self-styled No Turning Back Group of radical Conservative back-benchers, combined to push the party's policy and decision making in a markedly more right-wing direction and to give extra political impetus to the Thatcherite revolution.

In present circumstances the Conservative party stands for a free economy and a strong state.[2] This implies the maintenance of sound money (sometimes called 'monetarism'); the control of public expenditure; the diminution of the public sector via the policy of privatisation; the reduction of tax rates on income; the pursuit of a range of 'supply side' reforms, such as legislative curbs on trade union power, council house sales to sitting tenants and various forms of economic deregulation; greater freedom of choice for consumers, parents and patients; a more selective approach towards social security and unemployment benefit; the reform and deliberate weakening of local government; the reduction and reform of the civil service; a tougher approach towards law and order; a stricter control of immigration; the maintenance of the nation's defences against terrorism and external military threats; and an unsentimental, but constructive, attitude towards British membership of the European Community.

The party has also made a point, even a fetish, of preserving party unity (or at least the appearance of unity) since it is well aware of the political disadvantages of obvious disunity. In the early 1980s this did not prevent the conduct of a bitter, often coded argument between the Thatcherites and the non-Thatcherites, or what the media called the 'Dries' and the 'Wets'. However this argument was largely resolved in favour of the Thatcherites, since all the prominent Wets were sacked or retired from the Cabinet and the rest of the party came to recognise the force of three General Election victories.

During Margaret Thatcher's period as Leader of the party, the emphasis in Conservative rhetoric was put increasingly on the paramount importance of individual attitudes and behaviour in response to material incentives and legislative penalties. Leading party spokesmen were at pains to emphasise the comparatively limited role of the state and other public agencies, but equally to stress that the law should be clearly defined and strongly enforced in those areas in which state power could legitimately be exercised. There were also sustained attempts to reward individual success and to penalise failure, whether in education, work or life in general. Above all, the Conservatives sought to persuade people not to look to the Government for salvation, but to take responsibility for themselves and their families.[3]

The Labour Party

The Labour tradition has been based upon a commitment to the ideology of Socialism ever since the party constitution was adopted in 1918. Yet from the beginning the importance of ideology was balanced to some extent by the more pragmatic outlook of the Fabians and Christian Socialists. It was also tempered by trade union scepticism towards some Socialist principles. Nevertheless, as Samuel Beer observed, 'if the implication of sudden and violent change is extracted . . . it is correct to say that the meaning of Socialism to the Labour party was a commitment to ultimate social revolution'.[4] To the Labour party this has always meant more than a commitment to the public ownership of the means of production, distribution and exchange, as laid down originally in Clause IV of the party constitution. It has also meant a commitment to a form of moral collectivism which has drawn upon the reserves of fellowship and fraternity traditionally associated with the trade union movement.

The Socialist tradition has continued in the modern Labour party. For example, the October 1974 Labour Manifesto contained a clear commitment to 'an irreversible shift in the balance of wealth and power' in favour of working people. The fact that the Labour party, when in office, has not always acted in a particularly Socialist way has merely engendered disillusion and recrimination among its more zealous members. Many activists in the constituency Labour parties gave strong support in the early 1980s to the campaign of Tony Benn and others on the Left of the party in favour of constitutional changes within the Labour movement designed to make Labour MPs more accountable to the ideological elements in the constituency parties and to diminish the more cautious influence of the parliamentary leadership upon Labour policy. The two main changes which were pushed through by the Labour Left after 1979 were mandatory reselection of sitting MPs and election of the Leader and Deputy Leader of the party by an electoral college made up of the trade unions (40 per cent), the Parliamentary Labour party (PLP) (30 per cent) and the constituency parties (30 per cent). However, the further attempt by the Hard Left to alter the 1918 constitutional arrangement whereby the parliamentary leadership and the National Executive Committee (NEC) jointly prepare the Manifesto and to vest sole authority for this in the NEC was rejected by the party at the Wembley Conference in 1980.

In view of the dynamics of policy development within the Labour party in the late 1980s it is difficult to give a definitive description of where the party stands at the time of writing on the main political issues, since there is no certainty that Neil Kinnock's new revisionism contained in the 1989 Policy Review has been accepted by all parts of the Labour movement. Indeed there are some doubts in the minds of media commentators and Labour's political opponents as to whether Mr Kinnock's apparent conversion to a more pragmatic form of Socialism would long outlast his arrival at 10 Downing Street.

In general, however, it would seem that the Labour party favours the return to public ownership or greater public control of some of the industries privatised by the Conservatives; the use of the tax and social security systems for more significant redistribution of income and wealth from the better off to the poor; higher public spending upon the National Health Service, pensions, education and social security; more purposeful intervention in industrial and regional policy by a strengthened Department of Trade and Industry; the repeal of some of the Conservative trade union legislation and its replacement with a new charter of workers' rights; the reversal or alteration of many of the Conservative education reforms, for example by restoring to local authority control 'opted out' schools and City Technology Colleges; the strengthening of the Scottish and Welsh economies by the establishment of elected Assemblies in each of those parts of the United Kingdom, matched eventually by the creation of new English regional assemblies; the abolition of the House of Lords and its replacement with an elected Senate; closer co-operation with Britain's partners in the European Community in supporting positive and interventionist policies; and a paradoxical willingness to retain Britain's nuclear deterrent but eschew any threat to use it.

Following Labour's defeat at the 1987 General Election, there is a significant shift towards a more moderate and pragmatic policy stance, at any rate at the level of Neil Kinnock and his closest colleagues in the parliamentary leadership. The Labour front-benchers have been determined to maximise their chances of returning to power and they believe that this cannot be done on the basis of an old-style Socialist appeal to the public. Their willingness to accept some of the economic and social changes made during the 1980s by the Conservatives is somewhat reminiscent of the Conservative willingness to accept many of the changes made by the postwar Labour Government when they returned to power in the early 1950s. In each case it amounts to a recognition that there has been a sea-change in the conventional wisdom and assumptions of British politics.

The Labour party's shift towards pragmatism has been particularly noticeable on some sensitive and important issues, such as trade union reform and wider home ownership, but it has become increasingly evident right across the board. For example, mainstream Labour attitudes on public ownership, taxation and consumer rights have become more cautious and less doctrinaire than they used to be. It even seems that the party leadership will try to present Labour defence policy as responsibly multilateralist on the symbolically sensitive issue of nuclear disarmament, something which would have been inconceivable for the Labour party just a few years ago. In short, Mr Kinnock and the current Labour leadership seem determined to let no ideological shibboleths stand in the way of their possible return to power on a modern and pragmatic platform after the next General Election.

The Centre Parties

The ideological principles of the centre parties have been less important in postwar British politics. Indeed they have usually based a good deal of their appeal on the idea that they are relatively 'non-ideological' compared with either of the two main parties. For some time the Liberal party sought to occupy the central ground of British politics by consciously distancing itself from what it portrayed as the dogma and polarised ideology of each of the larger parties. In the early 1980s it was joined on that ground by the newly formed Social Democratic party, whose leading members had broken away from the Labour party in the belief that the latter had been irretrievably captured by the Hard Left. Together these two parties had a strong interest in defining their centrist position in clear contrast to each of the two main parties. This meant that they stood for a political middle way which differentiated them most sharply from the right wing of the Conservative party and the left wing of the Labour party, but not necessarily from the moderates in either main party.[5]

Thus the centre parties have favoured the preservation of a mixed economy and they have seen distinctive and complementary roles for both the public and private sectors. Their approach to industrial relations has put the emphasis upon greater employee participation and on the encouragement of co-operative models. They have recognised the need for some sort of incomes policy, although there have been real differences between them on how it should be implemented and enforced. They have favoured a very positive approach towards Britain's membership of the European Community and adequate defence spending in support of Britain's NATO commitments. Although they were opposed to the Conservative decision to purchase the Trident missile system as a replacement for Polaris, their position seems unclear in relation to the time when the new system is introduced. They have strongly advocated the introduction of proportional representation (PR) for elections to Parliament at Westminster, although there has been some dispute about how to do this (that is, before or after a referendum) and about which version of PR to use. Above all, they stand for a less divisive, less ideological and more decentralised approach to solving the continuing problems of British politics.

The Nationalist Parties

The Scottish National party has been motivated principally by the quest for Scottish independence and has therefore been able to encompass a broad ideological spectrum of opinion on nearly all other issues. In recent times most of the party has been able to unite on the basis of left-of-centre opposition to English, Conservative rule from London and Edinburgh, and the aspiration for an independent Scotland within the European Community.

Plaid Cymru, the Welsh Nationalist party, has an ideology which is based upon its determination to preserve the Welsh language and culture as the foundation of a distinctive Welsh identity within the United Kingdom. The party has both a radical and a moderate wing, with the former being in favour of certain forms of direct action in protest against the English dominance of Wales (for instance on the issues of Welsh water for English cities or English second homes in Wales) and the latter seeming more content to use the traditional channels of parliamentary influence to advance the Welsh nationalist cause.

Northern Ireland Parties

In Northern Ireland the majority Protestant community is represented at Westminster by various factions of the Unionist party. All of them stand, to a greater or lesser extent, for continued Protestant supremacy and the maintenance of Northern Ireland as an integral part of the United Kingdom. The minority Catholic community is represented mainly by the Social Democratic and Labour party (SDLP) which has campaigned to improve the economic and social conditions of its supporters and which favours closer links between Northern Ireland and the Irish Republic as a step towards eventual Irish unity by consent. A smaller part of the Catholic community gives its support to the much more radical Provisional Sinn Fein, the political wing of the Irish Republican movement in the north, which campaigns openly for the withdrawal of British troops from Northern Ireland and the subsequent establishment of a united Ireland, if necessary by force.

There have been signs that the politics of Northern Ireland are becoming even more polarised between the hard-liners in the Unionist and Nationalist camps. Many of the Unionists seem to have adopted an increasingly 'garrison' mentality, especially since they felt that the constitutional position of Northern Ireland had been placed in jeopardy by the 1982 initiative of the Conservative Government for the creation of a Northern Ireland Assembly and by the conclusion in 1985 of the Anglo-Irish Agreement with the Government in Dublin.[6] Many of the Nationalists seem to have become more radical and uncompromising in their demands, notably since the ill-fated H-Block hunger strike in 1981, when Bobby Sands and a number of other Republican prisoners starved themselves to death in a fruitless quest for the restoration of 'political status' for Irish Republican Army (IRA) prisoners. Furthermore it seems quite clear that, as long as the Conservatives remain in office in London, no significant concessions will be made to the Republican nationalists in Northern Ireland, not least because of the appalling bombing of the Grand Hotel in Brighton in 1984 and the mortar attack upon 10 Downing Street in February 1991.

The Fringe Parties

There are many fringe parties in British politics and some of the smallest wax and wane with bewildering frequency. On the extreme Right, the National Front is based upon a white racialist ideology which is heavily tinged with xenophobia and impatience with the democratic methods of parliamentary politics. On the extreme Left, the Communist Party of Great Britain has been one of the most unreconstructed and Stalinist parties in the whole of Western Europe, since it has strongly opposed any firm Western response to the Soviet military threat and any liberalising tendencies in the Soviet Union or Eastern Europe. Also on the extreme Left are the Socialist Workers' Party and the Workers' Revolutionary Party which have been distinguishable from the Communist party mainly by their attachment to the idea of workers' control in industry and commerce and by their more favourable attitude towards reform in the Soviet Union. In a different category altogether there is the Green Party which stands for an ecological approach to all political issues and which is now the party-political expression of the buoyant environmental movement in this country and abroad. It has already had a noticeable influence upon the policy of all the other parties and seems likely to make a continuing impact upon British politics over the year to come.

5.2 Political Functions

The political parties in Britain perform a range of political functions. Essentially these can be reduced to one primary function and a number of subsidiary functions, all of which contribute to the working of the British political system.

Primary Function

The primary function of the main political parties in Britain, as Robert McKenzie made clear a long time ago, is to sustain competing teams of potential leaders in the House of Commons in order that the electorate as a whole may choose between them at periodic General Elections.[7] Indeed any attempt by the parties to play a more prominent role in their own right would cut across the chain of responsibility from Cabinet to Parliament to electorate which is fundamental to the British system of parliamentary democracy. In the British political system constitutional power resides essentially with the Prime Minister and Cabinet, supported by a working majority in the House of Commons. In these circumstances the supreme function of the parties is bound to be the gaining and retaining of public consent for the exercise of such power. Any other conception of their paramount task would be inaccurate and improper, according to the conventional wisdom.

Subsidiary Functions

All the parties perform similar subsidiary functions which vary in importance depending upon the particular circumstances of the time. Firstly, they encourage public interest and participation in the process of politics. In other words, they provide permanent structures within which individuals and groups can act if they wish to play a part in politics at local or national level.

Secondly, the parties reflect, moderate and direct into constitutional channels the views and interests of a wide range of sectional groups. Of course, pressure groups have a powerful independent existence in their own right within the political system. Yet the existence of the parties enables and encourages all sectional groups to act in a constitutional manner and leads them to pay more attention to Parliament than might otherwise be the case.

Thirdly, they provide legitimate frameworks for the ventilation, discussion and criticism of political issues. This function has been more prominent in the Labour and centre parties than in the Conservative party, because the former believe in the virtues of considerable grass roots influence upon the process of policy making, whereas the latter has traditionally allowed only a very limited role for its party activists in this sphere. However in the 1980s this contrast became somewhat less marked, since Conservative activists felt encouraged by Margaret Thatcher and her like-minded parliamentary colleagues to make more forcefully known their support for radical policies, especially when such developments appeared to be blocked or delayed by some of the more traditional figures in the parliamentary party. On the other hand, although the annual Conference is theoretically the supreme policy-making body within the Labour movement, its 'decisions' can be heavily influenced and even manipulated by the parliamentary leadership acting in conjunction with the most powerful affiliated trade unions.

Lastly, and by no means least important, the political parties exist to build up membership, raise money, select candidates and organise political campaigns at local, national and European levels. In the Labour party the greater part of the money and (nominally at least) the vast majority of the membership comes from the affiliated trade unions, although there are signs that a growing number of influential figures would like to move the party towards the more democratic principle of one member one vote. In individual constituencies the local trade union branches contribute much of the income for the constituency parties (although on average less than half), while at the national level about 80 per cent of the party's income comes from the trade unions which affiliate to the party varying proportions of their membership. In the Conservative party, on the other hand, a great part of the money comes from donations made by industry and commerce, although in the constituencies the Conservatives (like Labour) usually manage to raise considerable sums of money through the efforts of their voluntary party workers. The smaller centre parties have sought to raise money both locally and nationally in broadly similar ways, except for the fact that they do not rely on official trade union support and their support from business is usually more concentrated in certain quarters.

In modern political conditions all parties find it increasingly difficult to keep going financially at a time when the costs of political activity are rising and the membership of political parties is dwindling in a disturbing way. For example, it has been estimated that the 1987 General Election campaign cost the parties centrally about £15 million, a real increase of about two-thirds compared with 1983. Since the publication of the Houghton Report in 1976, there has been the additional possibility for the parties to receive financial support from public funds in proportion to the votes which they secured at the previous General Election.[8] In theory, this could go a long way towards alleviating the financial problems of the parties, as it has done on the Continent, where a similar approach applies. In practice, it has proved impossible so far to get the necessary all-party agreement to anything more than token financial support for the Leader of the Opposition and a few other senior opposition figures. This is mainly because the Conservative party is ideologically opposed to state aid to political parties, does not wish to discourage the fund-raising efforts of its own voluntary workers and seeks to retain the comparative advantage which it derives from the present voluntary arrangements.

5.3 National Organisation

In matters of national party organisation there is a notable contrast between the Conservative party, which was created from the centre and the top down, and the Labour party which was created from the grass roots up. The Conservative organisation was originally intended to act as the handmaid of the parliamentary party, whereas the Labour organisation was conceived as the servant of the National Executive Committee and ultimately the annual party Conference. Such contrasting origins and traditions have left their mark upon the way in which each of the main parties is organised today. However Neil Kinnock has made significant organisational changes in the Labour party which have brought it more under the sway of the Parliamentary leadership.

The Conservative Party

The Conservative party organisation is under the control of the party Chairman who is appointed by and responsible to the Leader of the party. The party Chairman is normally a trusted colleague of the party Leader with a seat in the Commons or the Lords and usually a place in the Cabinet as well. It is rare for the Chairman to be at odds with the Leader, but, if that happens, it is the Chairman who has to go.

Conservative Central Office exists to carry out the wishes of the Leader of the party and to meet the various organisational needs of the party at every level. It is also the head office and central point of co-ordination for the party organisation in the different parts of the country (although the Scottish Conservative party has its own organisational structure) and thus provides support, material and advice for the constituency associations. It includes the Conservative Research Department, which acts as a briefing organisation for the party and a miniature civil service for the Parliamentary leadership when the party is in opposition.

The party Conference is organised by the National Union of Conservative Associations, but with the guidance of the party Chairman and key officials at Central Office. The Conference provides an annual occasion not so much for policy making as for the activists from constituencies all over the country (at least 5000 people in all) to come together for a mixture of social and political purposes,

Figure 5.1 Conservative party organisation

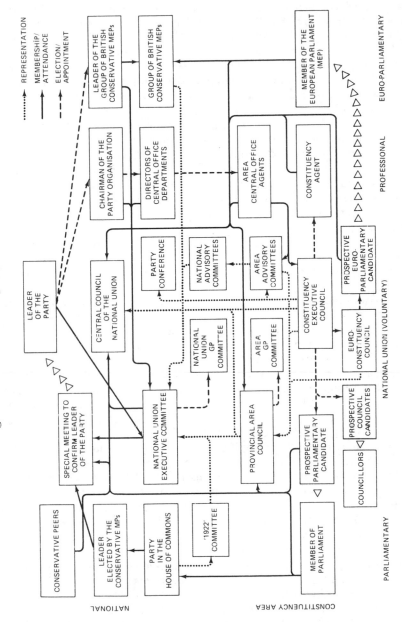

including habitual adulation of the party Leader on the final day. However, with the decline of deference in British politics, it is no longer wise or easy for the party leadership to ignore the views of the party rank and file. As Richard Kelly has observed in commenting on the modern Tory Conference, 'its bourgeois participants feel sure that they convey the new *vox populi* and are naturally impatient with any leaders who do not listen'.[9]

Between annual Conferences (held every autumn) the National Union continues to function on behalf of the party in the country and helps to maintain cohesion and morale in the constituency associations. The governing body of the National Union is called the Central Council. Since this consists of about 4000 people and meets only once a year in the spring, it is really a slightly smaller-scale party Conference. It has an Executive Committee of about 200 people representing all sections of the party which meets five times a year. This in turn elects a General Purposes Committee of about 60 people which makes most of the day-to-day decisions of the National Union, including those related to the agenda and arrangements of the annual party Conference.

Within the framework of the National Union there are various advisory committees at national level which are often replicated at area and constituency levels as well. These include the Women's National Committee, the Local Government Advisory Committee, the Trade Union Advisory Committee, the Young Conservative National Committee, the Conservative Political Centre National Committee and so on. Yet none of these bodies is much more than a sounding-board for a particular section of party opinion. Nearly all those who are prominent in these hierarchies have to be elected by those below them, although some are co-opted on the basis of their special knowledge or personal contacts. They provide useful frameworks for political discussion within the party (especially the Conservative Political Centre (CPC), which was designed for this), although there is usually no likelihood of deflecting the party leadership from a particular course of action to which it is strongly committed.

Just occasionally one or other of these bodies within the party has been known to go astray and cause the party leadership considerable embarrassment. One example was the Federation of Conservative Students which was infiltrated by the extreme Right during the early 1980s and as a result became such an embarrassment to the party that it had to be wound up and replaced by the more docile and amenable Conservative Collegiate Forum which is organised and controlled from Central Office. Furthermore there has been some pressure within the party since about the mid-1970s for the party Chairman to be an elected and not an appointed position. This pressure has been associated with the so-called Charter Movement which got going following the Chelmer Report, which made recommendations for the reorganisation of the voluntary party along more democratic lines in the mid-1970s.

In the House of Commons the party is organised within a framework capped by the 1922 Committee, which was named after a famous meeting of Conservative back-benchers held at the Carlton Club in that year. The Committee is led by its Chairman, who is a senior back-bencher elected annually by his back-bench colleagues. It has an influential Executive Committee made up of other senior back-benchers also elected annually by their colleagues. Under its auspices there is a considerable sub-structure of party back-bench committees each covering an area of policy – finance, industry, agriculture, employment, environment, education, defence, foreign affairs and so on – and each with a slate of officers elected annually by their colleagues. In the House of Lords the party is more loosely organised in the Committee of Conservative and Unionist Peers.

When the party is in government, such committees can have an influence on policy via the subtle process of the politics of anticipated reaction, that is, when Ministers adjust their intended actions in the light of expected or actual responses from the relevant back-bench committees. When the party is in opposition, such committees are probably more influential and they are certainly busier, since the various shadow spokesmen are appointed chairmen of the relevant committees and their fellow officers from the back-benches can have considerable influence upon the process of party policy making. In opposition there has also been a so-called Business Committee which is made up of the officers of the 1922 Committee and the officers of all the various back-bench committees under its rubric. This has served as a broader institutional link between the Shadow Cabinet and the various back-bench subject committees.

As for the position of the party Leader, before 1965 such a person was said to 'emerge' from a process of informal soundings and consultations within all sections of the party, but principally in the Commons. Since 1965 the choice of party Leader has resulted from a process of election by all members of the parliamentary party in the Commons, who are expected to consult each other informally and take account of the views of the party in the Lords, the European Parliament and the country as well. Such elections can take place every year in the autumn. Yet, as long as the Leader maintains the confidence of the parliamentary party, the contest is merely an annual formality with only one nomination.[10]

The Labour Party

The Labour party organisation is under the control of the General Secretary, who is the senior paid official responsible to the National Executive Committee, which is accountable in its turn to the annual party Conference. In view of the dual hierarchy in the party, the Leader of the party and his senior parliamentary colleagues can be at odds over matters of policy and procedure with prominent members of the National Executive Committee, who are often back-bench MPs of a more radical disposition elected to the NEC by the constituency Labour parties. However, since Neil Kinnock became leader of the party in 1983, and especially after Labour's third consecutive defeat in 1987, serious efforts have been made by the parliamentary leadership to regain effective control of the NEC and of the party organisation which serves it. This has meant much greater emphasis upon attractive presentation of united Labour policy and much greater influence from the centre than was formerly the case in the Labour movement.

The staff at Labour party headquarters, including the Research Department, are responsible to the General Secretary. They perform a range of support functions similar to those performed by Conservative Central Office. The party Chairman, who normally holds office for one year only, is usually the member of the NEC with the longest continuous membership of that body. He is responsible to the party as a whole rather than to the Leader of the party.

The Labour party Conference has always been a much more powerful gathering than its Conservative counterpart. Its claim to a real political role is based upon the fact that it is constitutionally and formally the policy-making body of the party, while the party in Parliament is theoretically little more than the parliamentary arm of the entire Labour movement.[11] The Conference is presided over by the Chairman of the party, who is assisted by a Conference Arrangements Committee composed of representatives of all the main sections of the Labour movement. Out of a total national party membership of about 7.2 million, a few of the largest affiliated trade unions have enormous block votes at Conference. For example, the Transport and General Workers Union has a block vote of about 1.2 million and the Amalgamated Engineering Union has one of about 840 000 votes. By comparison neither the smaller trade unions nor the constituency parties have much voting power at Conference, although they can make their influence felt with extra militancy. The Conference is composed of mandated delegations which are expected to vote in accordance with the decisions previously taken by the organisations which they represent. Members of Parliament can attend, but, unless they are members of the NEC, they do not usually play a prominent part in the proceedings.

The NEC is the powerful body which claims to act in the name of the entire Labour movement between annual Conferences. It includes representatives of the affiliated trade unions, the constituency parties, the Women's Section, the Young Socialists, other affiliated Socialist societies, together with automatic representation for the Leader, the Deputy Leader and the party Treasurer. It acts in the name of the Conference and carries on the business of the party from one year to the next. It also has a constitutional claim to a major role in party policy-making and to participation with the Cabinet or Shadow Cabinet in the preparation of the party Manifesto. There is therefore an inherent tension between it and the leadership of the parliamentary party, although under Neil Kinnock's leadership most of the disputes have been settled on terms acceptable to the parliamentary leadership. This is because what used to be called the Soft Left has come to wield an increasing influence over every aspect of the party's activity as Neil Kinnock and his closest colleagues (including notably Larry Whitty, the General Secretary, and Peter Mandelson, when Director of Communications) have sought to take control away from the Hard Left by acting in concert with sympathetic trade union leaders.

In the House of Commons the Parliamentary Labour Party (PLP) is led by the Leader, who chairs the Parliamentary Committee (Shadow Cabinet) which is the executive committee of the party in Parliament. Since 1970 the weekly meetings of the entire PLP have been chaired by an elected Chairman who is usually a senior back-bencher. As in the Conservative party, back-benchers involve themselves with various subject groups, depending upon their particular policy or constituency interests. In both cases, however, they have relatively little formative influence over the process of policy making.[12]

In opposition, the members of the PLP vote every year for those of their colleagues who aspire to places in the Shadow Cabinet. The top 15 are elected and the Leader is then free to distribute the portfolios as he sees fit. The junior shadow spokesmen are appointed by the leader according to the usual criteria of political clout, personal merit and regional or ideological balance. In government, the party Leader is, of course, Prime Minister and therefore free to allocate the real ministerial responsibilities as he sees fit, subject to the usual political considerations of ideological and regional balance within the party. However, since the early 1980s, Tony Benn and others on the Hard Left of the party have urged that there should be provision for the members of a Labour Cabinet to be elected by the PLP, rather than appointed by the Prime Minister of the day.[13] In partial response to this pressure provision is now made for all the elected

Figure 5.2 Labour party organisation

Annual Conference
Elected delegates from Constituency Labour Parties, national trade unions and affiliated organisations; ex officio Labour MPs, peers and European MPs; endorsed candidates; NEC

National Executive Committee
12 union representatives, 7 from constituencies, 5 women, 1 from Socialist Societies, Treasurer, Leader and Deputy Leader – all elected by Conference; plus LPYS representative

Labour Members of the European Parliament

Parliamentary Labour Party
Labour MPs and Labour members of the House of Lords; headed by the Party Leader and Deputy Leader

Regional Council of the Labour Party
There are 11 regional areas. Each holds an annual conference, with representatives from constituency parties. The conference elects a regional executive committee

County Labour Party Management Committee
(Regional Party Management Committee in Scotland.) Representatives from constituency parties and other organisations in the counties

Local Government Committee
In Greater London only: representatives from the General Committees of every CLP in the borough

District Labour Party Management Committee
Representatives of CLPs, unions and other affiliated groups – where two or more constituencies are involved

Constituency Labour Party General Committee
Elected representatives from branches, women's organisations. Labour Party Young Socialists branches, workplace branches and affiliated organisations in the constituency

Constituency Labour Party Executive Committee
The General Committee elects officers and an Executive Committee to look after the detailed organisation of the constituency party

Labour Party Branches
Every Labour Party member belongs first to his or her branch, which is based on boundaries as decided by the General Committee

Other Labour Party Groups and Affiliated Organisations

Labour Party women's organisations, Young Socialists, workplace branches, trade unions and socialist societies which affiliate locally members of the Shadow Cabinet to become members of the Cabinet automatically when the party moves into government, although not necessarily in the ministerial posts which they have been shadowing.

From 1922 to 1980 the Leader of the party was elected exclusively by the PLP. However, after the 1979 General Election, the Hard Left of the party was successful in its long-running campaign to take this power out of the exclusive hands of Labour MPs. Following the agreement at Bishops Stortford in 1981, this power was entrusted to an electoral college in which the three main sections of the Labour movement are represented. Under these arrangements the affiliated trade unions have 40 per cent of the franchise, the PLP has 30 per cent and the constituency parties have 30 per cent. Candidates for the leadership must be MPs and their nominations must be supported by at least 5 per cent of their parliamentary colleagues. Michael Foot was the last Leader of the party to be elected under the old arrangements in 1980 and Neil Kinnock the first to be elected under the new arrangements in 1983.

Main Party Contrasts

The organisation of each of the main parties reflects the contrast between the traditionally hierarchic principles of the Conservative party and the traditionally democratic aspirations of the Labour party. In the former case, this means that party decisions are normally taken expeditiously and implemented without undue debate or difficulty. In the latter case, it means that the origins of party decisions have often been blurred and the implementation occasionally challenged by some of those involved. In short, the Conservative party has tended to be more amenable to firm leadership from the top, whereas the Labour party has often seemed temperamentally and organisationally averse to it.

The problem for Labour has been that it has been difficult adequately to control a party which has served a movement which has aspired to be both ideological and democratic, although the ideology of democratic Socialism holds that there is no conflict between these two characteristics. The problems of the Conservatives have been more subtle, but just as real on occasions. In spite of their autocratic style and tradition, the management of the party has not been trouble-free. For example, exposure to a hostile party Conference can be an unpleasant and tricky ordeal for even the most senior and experienced politicians, especially when the representatives have bayed for blood on one of the more atavistic issues such as decolonisation in the 1950s or law and order in the 1980s.

In the Conservative party effective power is wielded mainly by the Leader, and to a lesser extent by the other senior parliamentary figures, in government or opposition. The senior figures in the hierarchy of the National Union are soothed with knighthoods rather than seriously consulted on matters of policy and on the whole the voluntary side of the party knows its place in the scheme of things. Yet even a powerful Conservative leader cannot afford to ignore party opinion, since the activists can put pressure upon back-benchers who then feel obliged to lobby Ministers or shadow spokesmen as the case may be. It has also been noticeable over the years that Conservative leaders seem to have been more vulnerable than their Labour counterparts to political 'assassination' when they fail to win General Elections or are directly involved in other events politically calamitous for their party.

In the Labour party power has always been more diffuse, since at least since the adoption of the party constitution in 1918 it has been shared between the PLP on the one hand and the affiliated trade unions and constituency parties on the other. This uneasy alliance has been balanced sometimes in favour of the extra-parliamentary elements and sometimes in favour of the PLP. In the 1970s and early 1980s great efforts were made by the constituency parties to seize a larger share of power, heavily encouraged by Tony Benn who sought to make them his own power-base within the Labour movement and to strengthen the NEC against the PLP. Power has tended to reside with the Parliamentary leadership more when the party has been in government and less when it has been in opposition. A great deal has depended upon the inclinations and ambitions of the leading figures in the movement at different times. Yet, as can be seen in the case of Mr Kinnock, if a Labour leader is determined to assert his authority, he can certainly do so, provided he takes care to ensure that he has the backing of the most powerful figures in the party.

The Centre Parties

The organisation of the Liberal Democratic party is essentially federal in that there are separate component parts for England, Wales, Scotland and Northern Ireland. The Liberal Democratic Assembly is composed of representatives from the constituencies, the parliamentary party and the national organisation. It elects the Council which is a smaller body charged with handling the issues which arise between annual Assemblies. A standing committee of the Council provides liaison between the parliamentary party and the constituencies. The party has a National Executive Committee on which are represented all the various sections of the party. This has certain powers of co-ordination, but not much more than that.

The process of party policy making remains ultimately in the hands of the Leader of the party and his principal colleagues and advisers. However the party activists do generate a considerable number of policy proposals and produce a wide range of discussion papers which have to be taken into account by the leadership. National fund-raising, which has often been a problem for the party (and for the Liberal party before it), is the responsibility of a special Finance and Administration Board. Since 1976 the party Leader has been elected by a special Convention of constituency representatives and others, with the former obliged to vote in accordance with the previously balloted views of the rank and file.

The organisation of the Owenite Social Democratic party (SDP) was effectively shattered by the split with the Liberal Democrats following the 1987 General Election. The leader of this rump party, David Owen, now leads no more than a small band of two other MPs and a handful of peers, backed up by a dwindling party membership (about 11 000 in May 1989). The majority of former SDP MPs and the bulk of the party membership chose to join the Liberal Democrats in a ballot of all members held soon after the 1987 General Election. The finance needed to keep the SDP rump going came very largely from David Sainsbury and a few other benefactors, a situation which put its longer-term future in doubt. To most observers the party now appears like a fish with little body and tail. In these circumstances it is probably only a matter of time before it ceases to exist altogether.

5.4 **Constituency Activities**

It is when we consider the constituency activities of the parties that we notice more similarities than contrasts, in spite of the wide variety of people who are involved. For example, both main parties have tried to maintain political activity in all the constituencies, except in Northern Ireland.[14] The centre parties have not been so ambitious and have tended to concentrate their efforts in those constituencies where they already have strong local support or where their electoral prospects look quite good. Constituency organisations vary in size from a few hundred members in areas where parties are weak to more than 10 000 in the strongest areas of the large parties. In all cases they exist to serve the campaigning and fund-raising purposes of.the parties and to enable them to contest both local and parliamentary elections.

Financial Support

Unlike local party organisations in the United States, constituency parties in Britain try to remain solvent and operational throughout the time between General Elections. They are assisted in doing this by the need to contest local elections at regular intervals and occasionally parliamentary by-elections as well. Yet they rely for their continued existence upon individual and corporate subscriptions and donations, made possible by the voluntary efforts and fund-raising activities of the party workers.

In the Labour party, the constituency organisations receive considerable financial support from local trade union branches and in some cases individual MPs are sponsored and financially supported by particular trade unions. In the Conservative party, a considerable portion of the income at constituency level comes from local business and commercial interests, although the bulk of the money is raised from individual subscriptions and voluntary fund-raising activities of all kinds. The centre parties have sought to maintain similar activities at constituency level in order to perform similar political functions, but they often have had to struggle to maintain viable levels of income and support. This has been even more so for the Owenite Social Democratic party as it lost both members and money. Indeed, were it not for the generosity of the party's few remaining national benefactors, the party would not have been able to function at all.

Local Membership

The active members of the various constituency parties come from many different walks of life. In all parties they tend to hold political views which are more zealous and uncompromising than those of the electorate in general. Indeed, if this were not the case, it is unlikely that many of them would be sufficiently motivated to join in the first place or to remain as paid-up members of their political party.

It is difficult to generalise about the membership of constituency parties, since a wide variety of people become involved in politics at the local level at one time or another. Suffice it to say that the active members of Conservative constituency Associations often include middle-aged and elderly women, retired people, farmers and their wives, small businessmen and local traders. The active members of constituency Labour parties often include men rather than women, people in public-sector trade unions, those involved in cause groups and a number of more traditional supporters for whom involvement in Labour politics almost runs in the family. The active members of all the smaller parties tend to be drawn from a wider cross-section of the population. They include many people who are not usually so closely identified with obvious class interests and some who have not been active in party politics at all before.

In the final analysis no generalisations about party membership are really satisfactory. All that can be said with any certainty is that the trends over the years have been characterised by a steady erosion of active support for each of the two main parties and by significantly changing social composition in each case. No one knows exactly how many paid-up members there are in either of the large parties. It has been estimated that the Conservative figure may be about 1.5 million and the Labour figure about 300 000 (not including the block membership of those in affiliated trade unions, which would raise the figure to a nominal 7 million or more). To get some idea of the decline in party membership, those figures can be compared with the figures for 1953 when the national membership of the Conservative party was estimated to be about 2.8 million and that of the Labour party about 1 million on the same basis. It is also noticeable that over the last two decades or so the Conservative party has become less dominated at constituency level by traditional middle-class people, while the Labour party in the constituencies has become more middle-class than it was before. Such social changes at constituency level have had an important effect upon the character of each of the parties in Parliament. The Conservative party under both Edward Heath and Margaret Thatcher moved noticeably 'down market' in its composition and attitudes, while the Labour party over the same period became less closely associated with the interests and outlook of the traditional working class.

Political Power

In so far as members of constituency parties exercise effective political power, they do so mainly through their right to select and, occasionally, de-select parliamentary and local government candidates. Labour activists have greater power than this, since they also have a 30 per cent share in the electoral college which chooses the party Leader. In all the political parties, save the Conservative party, it is accepted that ordinary party members should have some real influence upon the process of policy making.

In the Conservative party the key constituency bodies are the Executive Councils of perhaps 30 to 80 members, composed partly of Association Officers (Chairman, Vice-Chairman, Treasurer and so on), but mostly of representatives of the various wards or branches in the constituency. In the Labour party the key constituency bodies are the General Management Committees, which are composed in the same sort of way, but which are often somewhat smaller. In such gatherings local party activists can have direct and significant influence upon the political process, especially in the Labour party with its procedures for sending resolutions to the annual party Conference where they can become agreed party policy if they secure the necessary two-thirds majority. In view of the fact that roughly two-thirds of all the seats in the Commons have been considered 'safe' for one or other of the two main parties, the power to select the candidate has often amounted to the ability to determine the choice of the MP in many parts of the country. This has been the real foundation of political power at constituency level and it has had to be taken very seriously by MPs and candidates alike.

Candidate Selection

In each of the main parties the candidates for Parliament chosen by the 'selectorates' have tended to be rather different, both from the groups which select them and from the electorate as a whole. There has been a tendency over the years for social convergence between the parliamentary candidates of the two main parties. This has often meant the selection of middle-aged, middle-class men with families in preference to women, blue-collar workers or people from the ethnic minorities.

However in recent times it has become increasingly necessary to qualify this overall description. In the Conservative party there is nowadays a wider variety of candidates for Parliament. Although the privileged origins of some Conservative aspirants remain very noticeable, there has also been a growing number of self-made men and a few women who have managed to fight their way into Parliament. In the Labour party the changes have been even more dramatic in recent years. Nowadays many more Labour candidates are being selected from the ranks of the 'talking classes' in white-collar and public-sector occupations, to the exclusion of many of the more traditional types from the old-fashioned working class. This has coincided with a marked shift towards more radical attitudes in constituency Labour parties which now put a greater emphasis upon the selection of candidates who are eager (or prepared) to carry out the wishes of the party activists. Indeed a preference for radical minority activists (whether blacks, gays or feminists) has been increasingly evident in the London Labour party and in some other areas where such people have got themselves entrenched in local parties.

The position has been rather different in the smaller centre parties. The Liberal party (now the Liberal Democrats) has traditionally attracted men and women of broadly liberal outlook who wished to see the liberal point of view translated into public policy. It has not, however, laid great insistence upon strict adherence to party orthodoxy, although in recent years some of its activists seem to have become conspicuously more zealous, for example on the issue of nuclear disarmament. The Social Democratic party began in 1981 by attracting into its ranks many who had little or no direct experience of party politics, although its few remaining activists must since have learned some hard lessons from their experience of internal strife and fragmentation at the time of the controversial merger with the Liberals in 1987.

While the nature and strength of a candidate's commitment to his party's ideology seems to have become more important in determining his progress in nearly all parties, it is no longer usually the case that the wealth or family connections of an aspiring candidate have much bearing upon the chances of success at constituency level (although it must be said that there have been a few husband and wife or father and son combinations in the House of Commons, and such family connections have not necessarily been a barrier to success). Since the late 1940s all parties have set low limits on the personal donations which candidates or MPs may make to their constituency parties, so it is no longer possible to purchase a nomination, as it used to be, at any rate in the Conservative party, before the Second World War. Yet some candidates still have a better chance of success than others, especially at by-elections, when the parties wish to take no unnecessary chances, and in the competition for the safest seats.

In the Labour party, candidates seeking selection have to be nominated by at least one branch of the constituency party, a process which can often be strongly influenced by the affiliated trade union with the largest representation in the locality. At the national level there are two lists of parliamentary candidates which are kept at party headquarters in London following endorsement of the names by the NEC. List A is made up of trade union-sponsored candidates and List B of the rest. On the whole those on List A have more success in securing candidatures, although they may not do quite so well in the competition for safe Labour seats. Moreover some candidates who emerge as 'favourite sons' of their constituency parties do not appear on either of the national lists, but nevertheless are usually endorsed by the NEC if they are selected. In exceptional cases the modern Labour party has actually limited the range of local choice or even imposed a candidate upon the local party in order to avoid the local selection of a candidate believed to be detrimental to the party's chances at a by-election.[15]

In the Conservative party there is also a list of approved parliamentary candidates which is kept centrally at party headquarters in London. In order to get on this list aspirants have to go through a complicated process of written submissions and personal interviews, as well as a subsequent assessment process. In some cases these stages can prove more difficult than the later appearances before constituency selection committees. Furthermore each constituency Association has the unfettered right to select anyone it likes, even if the person concerned is not on the centrally approved list of parliamentary candidates at the time. Once again the situation is often slightly different at by-elections, in that the Area Agent of the party usually takes great care to guide the constituency selection committee towards a wise choice of someone who is expected to be able to cope with all the extra media publicity that is now associated with modern by-elections.

Initially the Liberals and Social Democrats faced special problems in their candidate selections, since they had to agree upon who should be the standard-bearers for the Alliance in each of at least 600 constituencies at the 1983 General Election. At by-elections during the 1979–83 Parliament they had tended to proceed on a basis of strict alternation between the two parties. However, after the 1987 General Election, the rivalry and disputes between the merged Liberal Democratic party on the one hand and the Owenite Social Democratic party on the other became more acute and effectively self-defeating for both parties. Indeed, the practice of running candidates against each other in some parliamentary by-elections and local elections proved highly damaging to both parties.

5.5 Conclusion

While the two main parties differ quite considerably in their history, ideology and constituency membership, they are more similar in many other respects than some accounts have suggested. When in opposition, each party has tended to use distinctive political language and to develop a distinctive political style in order to differentiate itself from the party in government and often from its own record or behaviour in previous times. When in government, each party has traditionally behaved in a broadly responsible and moderate way and until the early 1970s each pursued policies which belonged within the framework of the postwar consensus.

Since the early 1970s a number of significant developments in each of the main parties led them both to depart quite markedly from their previous adherence to the post-war consensus. The Labour party began to change significantly when in opposition from 1970 to 1974, as Tony Benn and others on the Left of the party began to denigrate the 1964–70 Labour Government for its failure to be sufficiently Socialist. The Conservative party began to change when in opposition from 1974 to 1979 as Sir Keith (now Lord) Joseph and Margaret Thatcher began to redefine the purposes and priorities of modern Conservatism in contradistinction to the policies pursued during the second half of the 1970–4 Conservative Government. As a consequence of these movements of opinion, the ideological gap between the two parties became wider during most of the 1970s and 1980s.

The position began to change yet again in the late 1980s. One result of winning three General Elections in a row was to make the Conservative party increasingly radical and self-confident in its Thatcherite beliefs. On the other hand, another consequence of this chain of Conservative victories was to force the Labour party under Neil Kinnock's leadership to reconsider and revise many of its previously radical policies in a determined and conscious attempt to make its appeal more credible to the mass electorate at the next General Election. The situation has changed once again with the downfall of Margaret Thatcher in November 1990 and the election of John Major to the leadership of the Conservative party in her place.

Only the passage of time and the verdict of the voters will show which of the two main parties has been more successful. Much will depend upon whether the so-called 'new realism' has changed some of the basic values and assumptions of the British people. Much will also depend upon whether the arrival of Mr Major at 10 Downing Street revives the Conservative party's electoral fortunes. And much will depend upon events and influences outside the control of politicians, for example demographic change and technological developments. Indeed a durable or definitive conclusion is not possible, since in party politics, as in life, it is the journey and not the arrival which matters.

Suggested Questions

1. For what principles does each of the main British political parties stand in current circumstances?
2. What are the principal functions of the political parties in the British political system?
3. Where does real power lie in either the Conservative or the Labour party?

Notes

1. S. Beer, *Modern British Politics* (London: Faber, 1969), p. 247.
2. See A. Gamble, *The Free Economy and the Strong State* (London: Macmillan Education, 1988).
3. Since John Major became Leader of the Conservative party and Prime Minister in November 1990, there has been a more emollient style of leadership and a less exclusive approach to politics than under the more crusading Margaret Thatcher. However, there has also been considerable continuity of policy, especially in respect of the party's commitment to sound money.

4. S. Beer, *Modern British Politics*, p. 135.
5. See, for example, the *Statement of Principles* published jointly by the Liberal and Social Democratic parties which was reproduced in *The Times*, 17 June 1981.
6. The elections to the Northern Ireland Assembly took place on 21 October 1982, but the Assembly never functioned properly because the political parties in Northern Ireland refused to co-operate.
7. See R. T. McKenzie, *British Political Parties*, 2nd edn (London: Heinemann, 1963), p. 645.
8. See the Report of the Committee on Financial Aid to Political Parties, Cmnd 6601, (London: HMSO, 1976).
9. *The Spectator*, 8 October 1988.
10. In 1989 it was relatively unusual when the Conservative back-bencher, Sir Anthony Meyer, challenged Margaret Thatcher for the leadership of the party and he attracted only a derisory number of votes. In 1990 when Michael Heseltine challenged Mrs Thatcher for the leadership of the party, things were altogether more serious as the challenger had the tacit backing of about 150 of his parliamentary colleagues. The rest is history. The general point, however, is that these events were dramatic exceptions to the conventional rule in the Conservative party that the leader is not normally challenged as long as he maintains the confidence of the parliamentary party.
11. For further discussion of this subject see L. Minkin, *The Labour Party Conference* (Manchester University Press, 1980).
12. This is because in the Labour Party the NEC shares the policy-making role with the parliamentary leadership, while in the Conservative party policy-making is dominated by the leader and a few senior parliamentary colleagues.
13. See T. Benn, 'The case for a constitutional Premiership', in *Parliamentary Affairs,* Winter 1980.
14. Since the late 1980s there has been pressure from grass-roots Conservatives in Northern Ireland to recreate Conservative Associations in the Province which could again be affiliated to the National Union. This idea was approved in principle at the 1989 Conservative party conference.
15. One of the best examples was when Robert Kilroy-Silk resigned as Member of Parliament for Knowsley North in 1986 having made allegations about Militant infiltration into his constituency party. He was succeeded by George Howarth who was imposed upon the local party by the national hierarchy of the party at Walworth Road in London.

Further Reading

Benn, A., *Arguments for Socialism* (Harmondsworth: Penguin, 1980).
Cole, J., *The Thatcher Years* (London: BBC Books, 1987).
Gamble, A., *The Free Economy and the Strong State* (London: Macmillan Education, 1988).
Kavanagh, D., *Thatcherism and British Politics* (Oxford University Press, 1987).
Kelly, R. N., *Conservative Party Conferences* (Manchester University Press, 1989).
Minkin, L., *The Labour Party Conference* (Manchester University Press, 1980).
Patten, C., *The Tory Case* (London: Longman, 1983).
Riddell, P., *The Thatcher Government,* revised edition (Oxford: Basil Blackwell, 1985).
Seldon, A. (ed.), *UK Political Parties since 1945* (Hemel Hempstead: Philip Allan, 1990).
Young, H., *One of Us*, revised edition (London: Pan Books, 1990).

⑥ Pressure groups

In the British context pressure groups have been defined in a number of different ways. W. J. M. Mackenzie defined them as 'organised groups possessing both formal structure and real common interests in so far as they influence the decisions of public bodies'.[1] Moodie and Studdert-Kennedy defined them as 'any organised group which attempts to influence government decisions without seeking itself to exercise the formal powers of Government'.[2] Samuel Finer defined them as 'organisations . . . trying to influence the policy of public bodies in their own chosen direction, though never themselves prepared to undertake the direct government of the country'.[3]

The expression 'pressure group' is a comprehensive term which subsumes both sectional interest groups and more widely-based cause groups. The former are usually well-established groups defending a vested interest through close and continuous contacts with Whitehall and Westminster and, when threatened, through much more vociferous media campaigns. The latter can be ephemeral organisations which decline or disappear when their goals have been achieved, although in modern times they have played an increasingly influential and continuous role in the political process. However the term presupposes that all pressure groups are promotional in the sense that they seek to promote their various objectives in the most effective possible ways. It also implies that they are irresponsible in the strict sense that they are not democratically accountable to the general public. It is the political parties which have to accept that form of responsibility and which are vulnerable to the verdict of the electorate at every General Election, and at other elections to a lesser extent as well.

6.1 Main Functions

In looking at the main functions of pressure groups, it is necessary to distinguish clearly between interest and cause groups. The former are often defensive in their functions and closely involved with the institutions of central government. The latter often begin as institutional outsiders, but in recent times some of them have attained a degree of prominence which virtually requires their views to be taken into account. In practice, of course, there is considerable overlap between the two types of group and some find a place in both categories.

Interest Groups

In the contemporary British context interest groups have a number of main functions. Firstly, they act as intermediaries between Government and the public. This is a role which has become more important as the scope and complexity of politics have increased and as it has become more difficult for the political parties on their own to perform all the representative functions. This means that they act as spokesmen and negotiators on behalf of clearly defined sectional interests – for example, the National Farmers' Union on behalf of farmers or the British Medical Association on behalf of doctors. It also means that they help all governments to develop and implement their policies by entering into detailed consultations on proposals for administrative action or legislation and subsequently by delivering a measure of public consent to the output of the policy and decision making process. For example, Shelter has had considerable influence upon housing legislation over the years, the Child Poverty Action Group has consistently pressed for improvements to help the poor and especially families with children, and the Magistrates' Association is regularly consulted about the development of the criminal law.

Secondly, they act as opponents and critics of government, especially when the interests of those whom they claim to represent are threatened by government policy. For example, the British Medical Association has been in the forefront of the campaign to resist the present Government's reforms of the National Health Service, while the Bar Council and the Law Society have lobbied heavily against the present Government's proposals for legal reform. Some people might argue that, in behaving like this, they are duplicating or even usurping the rightful role of the political parties. Yet that would really be too stuffy a view in our modern, pluralist democracy. As Robert McKenzie pointed out long ago, 'the voters undertake to do far more than select their elected representatives; they also insist on their right to advise, cajole and warn them regarding the policies which they should adopt and they do this for the most part through the pressure group system'.[4]

Thirdly, they have acted as extensions or agents of government. This is a role which has grown in importance whenever the tendency towards corporatism has grown in our society.[5] For example, the British Medical Association had a number of expert and advisory functions under the auspices of the 1946 National Health Service Act. The National Farmers' Union had a number of analogous functions under the auspices of the 1947 and 1957 Agriculture Acts. The Law Society is responsible for administering the system of state-financed legal aid. Perhaps the most familiar example of corporatism, especially under Labour governments, has been the prominent role played by the Confederation of British Industry (CBI) and the Trades Union Congress (TUC) both as economic interest groups and as virtually obligatory partners with Government in nearly all matters to do with the management of the economy and often much else as well. Examples would include the special employment and training measures which were administered by the Manpower Services Commission set up in 1973, or the regulations made by the Health and Safety Executive under the auspices of the 1974 Health and Safety at Work Act.

Fourthly, they have acted occasionally as substitutes for or outright opponents of Government itself. This is a very rare occurrence in British politics and it is not a role which even the most powerful groups are keen to play, since it can so easily engender a serious and lasting public backlash. If it happens, it is usually the result of either a breakdown of government authority in certain areas of policy or the deliberate implementation of some form of syndicalism.[6] To some extent the former conditions applied in certain circumstances during the serious trade union disruption of essential public services which took place during the 'winter of discontent' in 1979. The latter conditions applied on a local scale during the time of the Meriden Co-operative in the late 1970s, when the workers themselves took over and ran their own motor cycle factory for a while until market forces and Japanese competition got the better of them.

Cause Groups

The main function of any cause group is to publicise its cause in the best available ways in order to promote its particular point of view or defend its particular standpoint. For example, the Campaign for Nuclear Disarmament (CND) has been very active in its efforts to secure favourable media coverage and publicity for its cause of unilateral nuclear disarmament in Britain as an example to the rest of the world. It has sought to do this by organising public meetings, mass demonstrations and other carefully planned media events, as well as by producing a wide range of campaign material and propaganda. Equally, some environmental groups, such as Friends of the Earth or Greenpeace, have used similar techniques in their successful campaigns for environmental improvement, for example the use of returnable bottles or the preservation of rare animal species.

In nearly all cases the most familiar and successful technique of cause groups involves the staging of media events to attract publicity and then further steps to capitalise upon the public attention thus gained by advancing persuasive arguments in suitable supporting material. The publicity techniques may involve an unlikely combination of endorsement by show business personalities and follow-up with detailed and well-researched arguments. Sometimes those concerned even go so far as to undertake difficult or dangerous stunts in order to capture media attention: for example, the Greenpeace campaigns to save whales and seals by sailing small boats into the hunting areas in order to disrupt the activities to which they objected. The media coverage achieved for campaigns of this kind is not an end in itself, but rather a means of getting such issues onto the political agenda and of putting pressure on politicians to take appropriate action. Some other cause groups are essentially defensive; these have included the Wing Airport Resistance Association, which helped to prevent the siting of a third London airport at Cublington in Buckinghamshire, or the M23 Action Group which helped to persuade the Government to drop its plans to extend a motorway through residential Wallington in south London.

6.2 **Organisation and Power**

Pressure groups in Britain are organised in almost as many ways as there are different groups. The pattern of organisation which evolves and the degree of power which can be exerted depend upon a number of different factors. It is therefore worth considering the various aspects in turn.

Nature and Scope of Membership

When the interests of the membership are material and immediate, a group will usually reflect them and concentrate most of its resources upon defending them by whatever means are available. For example, for many years the National Union of Mineworkers (NUM) proved its ability to exploit both the strength of its organisation and the concentration of its interest as a way of gaining substantial material rewards for its members. The result was that the miners managed to stay consistently at or near the top of the industrial earnings league and all governments treated them with wary respect. On the other hand, when the interests of the membership are diffuse and varied, a group will usually find it difficult to secure real advantages for its members. For example, the Consumers'

Association, which has had a paid-up membership equivalent to a mere 3 per cent of all the families in the country, has not proved very effective as a defensive or promotional organisation, although this may now be changing with the growing interest shown by all parties in consumer interests and consumer rights.

The power of a group depends to a considerable extent upon both the coverage and the cohesion of its membership. If a group has a clear identity and purpose and if it manages to attract into its membership a high proportion of those eligible to join, it can be said to have good coverage and is likely to be effective in defence of its members' interests. This has been borne out by the British Medical Association (BMA) which over the years has had over 80 per cent of all practising doctors in membership and which has shown its political muscle during recent public debate about the present Government's reforms of the National Health Service (NHS). On the other hand, if a group seeks to represent a wide range of interests, it is likely to have little natural cohesion and to be rather ineffective in defence of its members' interests. For example, neither the Trade Union Congress (TUC), which seeks to represent more than 100 affiliated trade unions and nearly 10 million individual trade unionists, nor the Confederation of British Industry (CBI), which seeks to do the same for more than 5000 subscribing companies and about 300 employers' associations, has been really effective on behalf of its members, since the need to be inclusive has weakened the cohesion and hence the effectiveness of each organisation. The TUC has had the added problem that the membership of trade unions declined by more than 2 million during the 1980s, while the CBI has had the obvious difficulty of trying to represent employers both large and small in both the private and public sectors. For these reasons, among others, neither organisation has been particularly powerful or effective in recent times.

Loyalty of the Rank and File

The degree of loyalty shown by the rank and file towards their leaders and spokesmen is another aspect of the relative power or weakness of any group. Certainly such loyalty cannot be taken for granted in an age of greatly diminished deference. However, in most circumstances, the leaders of a pressure group have more scope for initiative if they are in the job for life and not subject to periodic recall or re-election, an advantage long enjoyed by several prominent trade union leaders. It is also the case that the leadership enjoys more latitude if the material interests of the rank and file are not directly threatened by any policy initiatives proposed. For example, leadership advocacy of an embargo on the sale of equipment to South Africa has been tolerated and even supported as long as the members of the group concerned had no material interest which was threatened by such a stance.

On the other hand, when the activities of pressure group leaders seem likely to prejudice the interests of the ordinary members, the rank and file are quite likely to reject the lead which is given. For example, Clive Jenkins, who was General Secretary of the Association of Scientific, Technical and Managerial Staffs (now known as MSF), was allowed to indulge in left-wing posturing on virtually any policy issue except the idea of nationalising the banks and insurance companies, since that would have posed a direct threat to the jobs of many of his union's members. Equally, Arthur Scargill, who is still President of the NUM, was opposed by a majority of his own members when he was precipitate in seeking their endorsement for a political campaign of industrial action against the 1979–83 Conservative Government and succeeded only in splitting his union in 1984–5 when he persuaded his Executive to launch an all-out strike against threatened pit closures without first securing the support of his members in a union ballot.

Political Leverage

The power of pressure groups also depends upon the degree of political leverage which they can exert. If a group is in a position to exert significant leverage, it can be truly formidable. Such leverage often takes the form of an ability to deny to the rest of society the provision of goods or services which the community cannot easily do without and which others are not able to supply. For example, power station workers or air traffic controllers can be in such a position, as can computer operators in the civil service or safety workers in the water industry. Currency speculators and company treasurers can also wield comparable financial power in the money markets which amounts to a form of highly effective political leverage. The brewing industry has also shown its ability to sway the present Conservative Government, partly through its ability to exploit a clever and hard-hitting advertising campaign and partly because many Conservative back-benchers realise the significant part which it plays in providing financial support for the party.

   Political leverage on its own may not necessarily be sufficient for the attainment of a pressure group's objectives without the support of other attributes of group power, such as civil service contacts, the ability to use the media effectively and financial or political clout. Yet it can achieve a great deal in our complex, modern society in which such groups can sometimes be in a position to hold the rest of the community to ransom. Only very rarely does it consist in the ability to create completely new balances of power in society which allow one particular group or interest to coerce the rest. On such occasions the government of the day may have to use the full powers of the modern state – for instance, a massive police presence or even military units – in order to counter one brand of ruthlessness with another. No system of democratic government can afford to tolerate, still less allow itself to be defeated by, groups using the sort of leverage through violence or coercion which has become all too familiar in parts of the world today.

Civil Service Contacts

The strength and frequency of contacts with the civil service is another aspect of the power and influence of groups. As J. J. Richardson and A. G. Jordan have pointed out, 'it is the relationships involved in committees, the policy community of Departments and groups, the practices of co-option and the consensual state which account better for policy outcomes than examinations of party stances, manifestos or Parliamentary influence'.[7] On the whole established groups prefer to have a continuous, quiet influence upon the process of government rather than an intermittent and noisy impact based upon the use of media publicity and the staging of public demonstrations. Widely publicised campaigns are something of a last resort for groups which normally succeed in keeping in close touch with the civil service and the rest of the policy-making community. They use their reliable and frequent contacts with Whitehall and the expertise of their own professional staff to influence ministerial decisions and the detailed content of legislation.

In many cases they secure official representation on advisory committees established within the orbits of particular Departments and in this way are able to support and monitor the detailed aspects of policy implementation. This gives them extra status and recognition in Whitehall, rights of access to Ministers when the need arises and opportunities for consultation and influence not available to others outside the charmed circle of customary consultative arrangements in central government. For example, the National Farmers' Union (NFU) was deeply involved in the development and application of British agricultural policy from the 1947 Agriculture Act to Britain's entry into the European Community in 1973. Since then it has had to concentrate more on trying to influence the development of the Common Agricultural Policy, principally in representations to the European Commission and European Parliament through the European farmers' organisation, COPA. Equally, in the 1960s and 1970s, the CBI and the TUC both managed to establish the convention that they should be widely and frequently consulted by central government on all matters of direct interest and concern to them. However, since 1979, neither body has been made so welcome by the Conservative Government, which came to power determined to reduce their status and influence over policy.

Obviously the nature and extent of such consultation has varied from time to time and from government to government, depending upon the priorities and objectives of the Ministers concerned. At least since the establishment of the National Economic Development Council ('Neddy' in popular parlance) in 1962, it was generally accepted practice that what were called 'the two sides of industry' should be consulted by Government on a frequent and extensive basis. Many of these consultations were formalised within the Neddy framework and took place within a large number of so-called sector working parties. Other contacts took place directly between Whitehall officials and representatives of trade unions and trade associations. Such habitual consultation, which was for many years an important element of the policy and decision making process, has been definitely downgraded by the present Conservative Government.

Publicity Value

The publicity value of the causes espoused by different groups is another factor which influences the success or failure of such organisations. For example, the favourable publicity secured by Age Concern in its campaign in the 1970s to get a better financial deal for pensioners was clearly beneficial to that particular cause, although the political priorities of the 1974–9 Labour Government had a lot to do with the outcome as well. Equally the publicity traditionally secured by the Child Poverty Action Group for poor families with children or by Shelter for the homeless was beneficial to those particular sections of society, at any rate as long as Ministers were sympathetic to their arguments.

On the other hand, the publicity secured by the Campaign for Nuclear Disarmament (CND) in the late 1950s and early 1960s had little effect upon public policy at the time, other than to harden the resolve of the then Conservative Government to oppose such a policy. In general, the publicity gained by a group for its cause depends upon the spirit of the times as much as its technical skill in using the media to its own advantage. Thus the public demonstrations and other media events organised by CND and other 'peace groups' in the early 1980s seem to have had more effect upon public opinion than the Aldermaston marches of the

1950s, although in recent years much of their thunder was stolen by the dramatic initiatives of President Reagan and President Gorbachev. While Margaret Thatcher was Prime Minister, they made relatively less headway in influencing the Conservative Government in Britain.

Financial Power

The mere possession of wealth and financial power cannot buy success in pressure group politics, although it obviously helps to pay the bills and to finance the necessary publicity. An examination of the available evidence suggests that not even the most lavishly funded campaigns achieve their objectives simply because they can out-spend their opponents. This may be a tribute to the probity and impartiality of the British civil service or it may reflect the way in which the British party system shields politicians from the full force of group pressures. Whatever the reasons, it is difficult to point to any occasions when money on its own has bought success for a pressure group.

For example, there is no conclusive evidence that the expensive 'Mr Cube' campaign of Tate & Lyle and other producers against the proposed nationalisation of the sugar refining industry in the late 1940s had a decisive influence upon the subsequent decision of the Labour Government not to proceed with such a policy after the 1950 General Election. Indeed the much stronger explanation is that the collapse of Labour's parliamentary majority, from 146 to 5, made it seem politically imprudent for the Government to proceed further with this particular case of nationalisation. Similarly, there is no conclusive evidence that the 'Keep Britain In' campaign of the European Movement in the early 1970s had a decisive effect upon the way in which the British people voted in the 1975 Referendum on European Economic Community (EEC) membership. Nevertheless it does seem that the coalition of political authority represented by the leading personalities of the pro-European campaign did have a positive impact upon the result, since their public reputations then compared favourably with those of the leading personalities on the anti-European side of the argument.

Voting Power

As for the power of groups to deliver votes at elections, twentieth-century British history has shown that the pull of party consistently triumphs over the pull of groups. Ever since the emergence of recognisably modern political parties during the last quarter of the nineteenth century, the nature of our first-past-the-post electoral system and the influence of strong party discipline has left all groups with a poor chance of striking effective political bargains with individual Members of Parliament or parliamentary candidates. Yet this is not to say that certain influential groups cannot exercise considerable influence upon the parties, especially when the latter are in opposition and unshielded by civil service advice.

Unlike the situation in the United States, individual politicians in Britain do not have to construct precarious platforms of electoral support by seeking to appeal directly to powerful interest or cause groups in their constituencies. If their party has been in office, they tend to concentrate upon presenting the record of their party in the most favourable light. If their party has been in opposition, they tend to demonstrate how bad things have been under the stewardship of their opponents and how they could do much better if given the chance. Yet this is not to say that it is ever sensible for a prudent politician to ignore the pressure of groups which are active or influential in his constituency.

Of course, there remains the special case of trade union influence upon the Labour party.[8] This stems from the fact that the creation of the Labour party at the end of the nineteenth century was largely the work of the trade unions and ever since then trade union influence within the wider Labour movement has always been significant and occasionally decisive. Yet no matter how close and crucial this relationship has been over the years, it is unwise to generalise from it when assessing the role of other pressure groups in the British political system.

6.3 Involvement in Politics

Since the British political system is pluralist, liberal and democratic, it affords many opportunities for the involvement of pressure groups in the policy- and decision-making process.[9] Indeed it is impossible fully to describe political activity in Whitehall and Westminster without giving an account of the part played by pressure groups. They have become seemingly inevitable participants in the process of official consultation and as such they contribute to the maintenance of public consent for the acts of government. Their involvement in the policy- and decision-making process is shown diagrammatically in Figure 6.1.

Figure 6.1 Pressure group involvement in politics

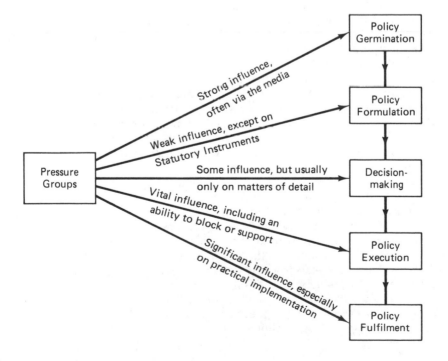

Policy Germination

At the initial stage of policy germination the main role of pressure groups is to identify problems and to get issues onto the political agenda. This is something which they can do rather well and which they are sometimes even encouraged to do by Ministers. This is because the latter often prefer to appear to be responding to external pressures rather than taking unprompted initiatives. For example, the National Society for Clean Air (previously the Smoke Abatement Society) was to a considerable extent instrumental in getting the problems of air pollution onto the political agenda in the 1950s. It then conducted a sustained campaign of publicity and persuasion which helped to bring about the passage of the Clean Air Act in 1956. Equally the Institute of Economic Affairs can claim much of the credit for getting the policy of privatisation onto the political agenda in the 1980s, since it had been campaigning for this for years beforehand.

In playing their part at this early stage of the policy- and decision-making process, pressure groups depend very heavily upon their ability to excite the interest of the media. Without such media assistance many of the campaigns would never get off the ground at all. For example, the creation of the Department of the Environment in 1970 was to a considerable extent a political response to the pressures exerted over many years by the Conservation Society and other environmental groups who had wanted their concerns more clearly represented in Whitehall. It was also a response to the growing public interest in environmental matters which later found international expression at the 1972 Stockholm Conference. Equally, in the 1980s and early 1990s Friends of the Earth, Greenpeace and other environmental pressure groups have had a significant influence upon the pace and direction of recent 'Green' initiatives both at national and at European Community level.

Pressure groups also need to persuade powerful politicians of the good sense and timeliness of their cause. For example, the Road Haulage Association (RHA) worked very closely with leading figures in the Conservative party when the latter were in opposition between 1945 and 1951 and was able to persuade them of the case for the denationalisation of its industry. The result of this pressure was seen in the partial denationalisation of the industry by the Conservative Government soon after its victory at the 1951 General Election. Equally the proponents of employee share ownership, such as Job Ownership Ltd, worked hard and continuously during the 1980s to persuade the Conservative Government that the time had come to give further legislative backing and tax relief to a cause which chimed in well with Conservative thinking on worker participation and wider share ownership.

When pressure groups wish to get issues onto the political agenda, the most effective approach is usually to persuade officials in the relevant Whitehall Department of the importance of their particular problem or interest and then to follow up with expert and detailed advice on how it might be tackled in ways which would be congruent with the principles of the government of the day. A notably successful practitioner of this technique was the National Farmers' Union (NFU) which over the years from the 1947 Agriculture Act until British entry into the European Community in 1973 enjoyed an exclusive and almost symbiotic relationship with the Ministry of Agriculture. This relationship influenced the outcome of every annual farm price review and was also credited with having given rise to the 1957 Agriculture Act, which gave the NFU an even more entrenched consultative role. The other principal way of achieving such an objective is for a group to get on a common wavelength with leading figures in the governing party and then provide them with new ideas which can be presented as a logical development of their existing policies. Once again a good example of the effectiveness of this technique is provided by the way in which so-called political 'think-tanks', like the Institute of Economic Affairs and the Centre for Policy Studies, managed to play the role of intellectual pathfinders for the free market policies of the Conservatives in the 1980s.

Policy Formulation

Pressure groups can also have influence, but not such an important role at the stage of policy formulation. When a political party is in opposition, policy formulation is mainly the work of its leading personalities, who are assisted by officials from the party organisation. When a party is in government, it is mainly the work of civil servants in the Departments concerned. Yet in each case those who formulate policy may well consult pressure groups, provided the latter can be trusted to preserve the necessary confidentiality and are able to supply useful expert advice or information.

The role of groups can be especially significant when policy needs to be formulated as new legislation. For example, the Town and Country Planning Association has made frequent representations over the years and some of its ideas have been incorporated in planning legislation; the Society of Conservative Lawyers had some real influence upon the policy formulated by the Conservative party in opposition during the late 1970s and this made a significant contribution to the subsequent British Nationality Act of 1981. There is therefore a role for pressure groups to play at the stage of policy formulation, although it is not usually as prominent as at other stages of the process.

Decision Making

In a strict sense pressure groups have no direct involvement at the decision-making stage of the political process, since this is essentially a matter for elected politicians. Yet even such an apparently clear-cut statement does not fully reflect the various ways in which political decisions are actually taken in modern Britain. For example, many ministerial decisions are really taken by civil servants acting in the name of Ministers, notably in the detailed and complex area of delegated legislation. Groups with the necessary expertise and access to officials can play an influential part in this aspect of decision making. Examples could be found in the close and frequent contacts between the Law Society and the Lord Chancellor's Department, the Local Authority Associations and the Department of the Environment or the British Medical Association and the Department of Health. However it is interesting that the influence of all these groups has declined under the present Conservative Government, not least because Ministers have been engaged in measures of radical reform affecting each of these vested interests.

Since the introduction of new legislation also involves important decision making of a kind, pressure groups can play an influential part in this stage of the political process as well. For example, the 1982 Criminal Justice Act was influenced at least in important matters of detail by the persistent representations made during the committee stage of the legislative process by groups such as the Magistrates Association or the National Association for the Care and Resettlement of Offenders (NACRO). Similarly the Finance Bills which pass through the House of Commons every year and which contain legislative changes of considerable importance can be influenced in matters of detail by pressure groups with interests to defend or causes to advance. In these various ways groups are involved to some extent at the decision-making stage.

Policy Execution

The real test of effective power for all modern governments is how well they manage to execute their policies. Ministerial decisions or Acts of Parliament are not worth very much if they cannot be implemented in practice, either because of administrative impracticality or because the people who have to execute them decide to withdraw their co-operation.

Formidable delaying power is available to civil servants. If senior civil servants wish to delay the decisions of Ministers, there are many ways in which they can do so. The most gentle technique is simply to go slowly in the administrative implementation of what has already been decided. Another is to suggest further consultations on the detailed implementation of policy with the groups most directly affected. Another is to put up their own Minister to argue with his colleagues that the time is not ripe for a decision in the first place. Most drastic of all is the tactic of deliberate non-co-operation, which was used in many parts of the civil service during the long dispute over pay and conditions in 1981. This did temporary damage to the efficiency of government and led, for example, to long delays in the collection of some public revenues and the payment of some social security benefits.

The role of groups can also be vital, since their active co-operation or passive acquiescence is often a condition of the satisfactory execution of policy. For example, in 1977 the National Union of Teachers refused to co-operate with the Labour Government when it sought answers to a questionnaire on aspects of the school curriculum from all local education authorities in England and Wales. Similarly, the BMA has advised its members not to co-operate with the Health Authorities and others in implementing the present Government's plans for the reform of the National Health Service. In all such cases acquiescence in government policy by the relevant practitioners or workers is an important condition of successful policy execution. Such examples emphasise the key point that one of the main tasks of Ministers is to assess the limits of what is 'politically possible' in a given situation at a given time. In making such assessments, it is clear that the co-operation of the relevant civil servants and pressure groups is a distinct advantage and their non-co-operation a serious liability in the execution of policy.

Policy Fulfilment

A similar point can be made about the final stage of policy fulfilment. Few policies can be brought to fruition without the active co-operation or at least the passive acquiescence of the groups most directly affected. Ministers and civil servants commit serious mistakes if they are ever tempted to equate the political process solely with what happens in Whitehall and Westminster. In modern political conditions there are also many external factors which can influence the success or failure of a given policy. For example, the world-wide commodity price explosion of 1972–3 damaged the counterinflation policies of the 1970–4 Conservative Government, just as the limitations imposed by the 1986 Single European Act restrict the present Government's room for manoeuvre in working towards a single European market by the end of 1992. Such examples inevitably extend the scope of the present discussion beyond the sphere of national politics. Yet it is undeniable that, in our interdependent world, political issues have to be considered in a much wider context if we are to take full account of all the limitations upon the autonomy of national governments.

Politicians may imagine, especially when they have been in office a long time, that they have become the undisputed masters of the political scene. Yet they always do well to remember that in modern political conditions they need the co-operation of interest groups and the support of other external influences if they are to have a reasonable chance of fulfilling their policies.

6.4 **Conclusion**

There are reasons for regarding the activities of pressure groups as broadly beneficial to the British political system and other reasons for regarding them as rather harmful. On the positive side, there are at least four points which can be made. Firstly, they can provide the government of the day with expert information and advice which would not necessarily be available from other sources. Secondly, they can provide frameworks for public participation in the political process between General Elections by all who are unwilling or unable to channel their energies through one of the political parties. Thirdly, they help to define and focus public attention upon issues which may not be ripe for decision but which need nevertheless to be placed on the political agenda. Fourthly, they can provide a form of institutional ratification and public consent for the actions of government which can assist Ministers in the difficult tasks of policy execution and fulfilment.

On the negative side, there are at least four reasons for regarding pressure groups with suspicion if not distaste. Firstly, they tend to give too much weight in the political process to the importance of the concurrent majority – that is, the various sectional groups in our pluralist society – to the detriment of the parliamentary majority – that is, the part of the electorate which voted for the winning party in the House of Commons at the preceding General Election. Secondly, they can become accomplices in a system of government which is based upon exclusive, metropolitan circles of policy and decision making and which may act to the detriment of everyone else. Thirdly, they have reinforced the tendencies towards corporatism in our society and during the 1970s in particular this worked to the detriment of Parliament and the traditions of our parliamentary government. Fourthly, as Douglas Hurd put it in 1986, when reflecting on his experience as Home Secretary, 'the weight of these groups, almost all of them pursuing a legitimate cause, has very substantially increased in recent years and adds greatly not just to the volume of work but also to the difficulty of achieving decisions in the general interest'.[10]

In conclusion, we need to assess the role of pressure groups in parallel with our assessment of the political parties. Both categories of institution play vital roles of mediation and representation which contribute to the working of our political system. Whereas pressure groups are not democratically accountable in the way that political parties have to be, they do share common aspirations to reflect and defend the views and interests of their members. In this way they bring a measure of public consent to the working of the political process and help to endow it with a measure of legitimacy which it might not have otherwise. 'On the other hand, they are increasingly seen by Ministers as 'serpents' which can prevent political decisions being taken in the general interest. Either way, they are among the most significant sources of power, pressure and opinion in the British political system.

Suggested Questions

1. What are the main functions of pressure groups in British politics?
2. Which factors make some pressure groups more powerful than others?
3. At what stages in the political process do pressure groups exert their most effective influence?

Notes

1. Quoted in R. Rose (ed.), *Studies in British Politics*, 3rd edn (London: Macmillan, 1976), p. 343.
2. G. C. Moodie and G. Studdert-Kennedy, *Opinions, Publics and Pressure Groups* (London: Allen & Unwin, 1970), p. 60.
3. S. E. Finer, *Anonymous Empire*, revised edition (London: Pall Mall, 1966), p. 3.
4. Quoted in R. Kimber and J. J. Richardson (eds), *Pressure Groups in Britain* (London: Dent, 1974), p. 280.
5. 'Corporatism' is a term which has often been used pejoratively by those who believe that democratic representation should be territorially based upon constituencies rather than functionally based upon the various sectional interests in society. For our purposes here it is taken to mean the tendency in modern British politics for Government to deal directly with the 'social partners' (that is employers and trade unions) to the detriment perhaps of the elected Members of Parliament. See R. K. Middlemas, *Politics in Industrial Society* (London: Deutsch, 1979) for a fuller discussion of this subject.
6. 'Syndicalism' is a term which was used originally to describe the movement among industrial workers at the end of the nineteenth century (especially in France) of which the primary aim was the transfer of the means of production, distribution and exchange from capitalist owners to groups of workers at factory level. On the British experience of syndicalism see B. Holton, *British Syndicalism, 1900–14* (London: Pluto Press, 1976).
7. J. J. Richardson and A. G. Jordan, *Governing Under Pressure* (Oxford: Martin Robertson, 1979), p. 74.
8. See H. Pelling, *A History of British Trade Unionism* (London: Macmillan, 1963) and H. Pelling, *A Short History of the Labour Party* (London: Macmillan, 1965) for a fuller account of this relationship.
9. See Chapter 15 for a fuller description of the policy- and decision-making process in Britain.
10. Lecture to the Royal Institute of Public Administration, 19 September 1986.

Further Reading

Brennan, T., *Pressure Groups and the Political System* (London: Longman, 1985).
Byrne, P., *The Campaign for Nuclear Disarmament* (London: Croom Helm, 1988).
Crouch, C. and Dore, R. (eds), *Corporatism and Accountability: organised interests in British public life* (Oxford: Clarendon Press, 1990).

Grant, W., *Pressure Groups, Politics and Democracy in Britain* (London: Philip Allan, 1989).

Jordan, A. G. and Richardson, J. J., *Government and Pressure Groups in Britain* (London: OUP, 1987).

Lowe, P. and Goyder, J., *Environmental Groups in Politics* (London: Allen & Unwin, 1983).

Marsh, D. (ed.), *Pressure Politics* (London: Junction Books, 1983).

Miller, C., *Lobbying Government* (Oxford: Basil Blackwell, 1987).

Whiteley, P. and Winyard, S., *Pressure for the Poor: the poverty lobby and policy making* (London: Methuen, 1987).

Wilson, D., *Pressure, the A to Z of Campaigning in Britain* (London: Heinemann, 1984).

7 The media

In considering the media in Britain, we are concerned with more than neutral channels of communication. We are examining some influential participants in the political system, even though they have no formally recognised place in our constitutional arrangements. For better or worse we live in an age which is characterised by the widespread use of the various channels of communication for a broad range of political and other purposes. Politicians need the media and seek every opportunity to get their message across. Equally those who work in the media are not too shy to exert a significant influence over the political process.

7.1 The Current Situation

In the Press

The current situation in the British press is that there are five daily national newspapers of quality, six of the popular variety, four Sunday national newspapers of quality and five of the popular variety. There is only one major evening newspaper in London, *The Standard*, but there are a number of successful regional newspapers in other parts of the country, for example *The Western Morning News, The Yorkshire Post, The Manchester Evening News*, and *The Glasgow Herald*. There are a number of weekly newspapers which give prominence to political issues, for example *The Economist, The Spectator, The New Statesman and Society*. There are also a number of more academic periodicals which deal with political issues, such as *Political Quarterly, Parliamentary Affairs, Government and Opposition* and *Public Administration*. Mention should also be made of the Communist daily newspaper, *The Morning Star*, the revisionist weekly, *Marxism Today*, the satirical and anti-Establishment periodicals, such as *Punch, Private Eye* and *Time Out*, and the publications of the political fringe, such as *Militant, Socialist Worker* and *The Nation*. There is therefore a wide variety of political and other points of view expressed in the British press, although it is worth noting that some of the most widely-read publications are not explicitly political at all: for example, *Woman* or *Woman's Own*.

Until recently one common denominator for nearly all the British press was the difficulty of earning enough money to cover costs and make a profit. Old-fashioned management and chaotic labour relations brought about increasing concentration of ownership as publications were forced to amalgamate with others or close altogether. In Fleet Street in particular virtually every attempt by management to introduce new technology into the production process to make the publications more viable was fiercely resisted by the traditionally-minded print unions. Indeed, the bitter dispute between the print unions and Rupert Murdoch's News International, when the latter moved its production facilities from Fleet Street to Wapping in order to start again with the latest technology and a more realistic and amenable workforce, exemplified both the resistance to change which had characterised the industry and the inevitability of such change once one determined employer managed to break ranks and bust the previous, cosy arrangements between employers and employees in the industry. Prior to that, new titles had proved difficult or impossible to launch and for those which tried and failed, like Eddy Shah's *Today*, there was usually no alternative but to sell to another proprietor with a longer purse. Against this background it is not surprising to find that seven multinational companies or very wealthy families own all the popular national newspapers in Britain and only two individuals – Rupert Murdoch and Robert Maxwell – control huge multi-media empires which between them own about 50 per cent of the British national press. A table of the various national newspapers is set out in Figure 7.1.

In Broadcasting

The situation in British broadcasting at the time of writing is that there are four television channels which provide a national service covering the entire country. There are the two BBC channels with BBC 1 designed to appeal to a mass audience with a mixture of entertainment and information programmes, while BBC 2 puts more emphasis upon its educative role and is prepared to cater for minority audiences as well. There are the two independent channels with ITV (Channel 3) competing for a mass audience directly with BBC 1 and Channel 4 competing with BBC 2 by offering programmes which appeal to a wider range of minority audiences and by acting as a 'publisher' for independent programme makers as well.[1]

The BBC makes and broadcasts most of its own material and is a vertically integrated broadcasting organisation employing thousands of journalists, technicians and programme makers. It is financed from the proceeds of an annual licence fee (currently £77 a year for a colour television) which is levied by law on all who own a television set. Independent television is financed by the proceeds of advertising broadcast during and between its programmes. Its output is produced by 15 different programme companies, each with an exclusive franchise for part of the country for an agreed contractual period (usually 10 years). The BBC is run by a Director-General and his management team who are in their turn responsible to the Board of BBC Governors under a chairman chosen by the Home Secretary of the day. The independent programme companies are answerable to the Independent Television Commission (ITC) which is there to play much the same buffer role as the BBC Board of Governors in relation to the government of the day. The BBC news is gathered and broadcast 'in-house', whereas the news on independent television is provided by Independent Television News (ITN), a separate, non-profit-making organisation established for the purpose and jointly owned by the programme companies.

On radio the BBC has five national channels – Radios 1,2,3,4 and 5 – which each cater for a different segment of the wide range of public interests and tastes. Radios 1 and 2 provide mostly popular music and light entertainment of one kind or another and are beamed very much at the younger audience. Radio 3 caters for minority interests of a more high-brow and cultural variety, as well as providing such traditional services as commentaries of Test Match cricket. Radios 4 and 5 provide most of the solid news, information and analysis of current affairs, and are

Figure 7.1 Main national newspapers

Title & Foundation Date	Publishing Company	Political Leaning	1990 Average Sales
Quality Dailies			
The Times 1788	News International	Pro-Conservative	432 000
The Guardian 1821	Guardian Newspapers	Moderately pro-Left	430 000
Daily Telegraph 1855	Daily Telegraph	Pro-Conservative	1 086 000
Financial Times 1888	Pearson Group	Moderately pro-Right	292 000
The Independent 1986	Newspaper Publishing	Independent	414 000
Popular Dailies			
Daily Mail 1896	Associated Newspapers	Pro-Conservative	1 670 000
Daily Express 1900	United Newspapers	Pro-Conservative	1 562 000
Daily Mirror 1903	Pergamon Press	Pro-Labour	3 130 000
The Sun 1969	News International	Pro-Conservative	3 937 000
Daily Star 1978	United Newspapers	Pro-Conservative	919 000
Today 1986	News International	Pro-Conservative	581 000
Quality Sundays			
The Observer 1791	Lonrho International	Moderately pro-Left	567 000
The Sunday Times 1822	News International	Pro-Conservative	1 187 000
Sunday Telegraph 1961	Sunday Telegraph	Pro-Conservative	587 000
The Independent on Sunday 1990	Newspaper Publishing	Independent	363 000
Popular Sundays			
News of the World 1843	News International	Pro-Conservative	5 036 000
Sunday People 1881	Pergamon Press	Populist	2 588 000
Sunday Express 1918	United Newspapers	Pro-Conservative	1 727 000
Sunday Mirror 1963	Pergamon Press	Pro-Labour	2 911 000
The Mail on Sunday 1982	Associated Newspapers	Pro-Conservative	1 889 000

able to draw upon the work of a wide range of foreign and specialist correspondents.

The BBC also provides local radio services from 30 local radio stations in all parts of the country. These are matched by 50 independent local radio stations throughout the country which are financed, like independent television, from the proceeds of advertising carried on air. Local radio of both kinds puts out a great deal of popular music and other mass appeal programmes in order to ensure an adequate audience, but it also concentrates to a considerable extent on covering local and community issues. To this end there is often considerable emphasis in the programme schedules upon public phone-ins and other forms of audience participation. Many would argue that this has been a healthy development which has boosted the sense of community and democracy in parts of the country where previously it was not all that evident.

7.2 The Problems of the Press

The problems of the press are both internal and external. However, for the purposes of this chapter, we shall be concerned principally with the way in which the activity of the press and some of its methods of working cause disquiet, even hostility among politicians and public alike. Most people in Britain are content that we have such a free press and, if there is a common thread of public criticism, it is invariably along the lines that the press may have become too powerful and especially too invasive of people's privacy.[2] On the other hand, editors and journalists are very often more concerned to defend the rights and independence of the 'Fourth Estate' against what they are sometimes inclined to see as tyrannical Ministers and draconian laws. Obviously, in this age-old struggle between the politicians and the press, there has always been a good deal of hypocrisy and double standards on both sides. This has made it much harder to get at the truth at any time. Nevertheless the following section seeks to touch upon the salient issues and unresolved problems.

Influence and Bias

All the national newspapers have political reporters and commentators who usually take distinctive lines on the political issues of the day. In the popular or tabloid national newspapers, however, the main purposes are to entertain the readers and to maintain or boost the circulation so that the advertisers do not take their custom elsewhere. The result of these two commercial imperatives is that the coverage of political issues is not usually very extensive and certainly not very subtle. Instead the emphasis is put upon ensuring a dramatic and preferably eye-catching presentation of the simplest facts or opinions conveyed in the simplest and most graphic language. Indeed few readers of the tabloid press seem to pay much attention to the political line taken by the paper which they buy, not least because most of them are usually more interested in the sport, scandal or soft pornography which dominate so many pages. The editors also know what sells popular newspapers and usually allocate the column inches accordingly.

As a general rule, the influence of the tabloid press seems to vary inversely with the knowledge or interest of its readers in a given political subject. For example, when *The Sun* (which had previously been a paper supporting Labour) gave strong and unequivocal support to the Conservative party at the time of the 1979

General Election campaign, this appears to have had some influence upon the Conservative voting behaviour of many of its readers, most of whom are unlikely to have voted Conservative before or even to have been particularly interested in political issues. Equally, the *Daily Mirror*, which has consistently supported the Labour party at General Elections since the war, seems to have a significant influence upon the voting behaviour of its readers by persuading many of them, when wavering, to remain loyal to their traditional Labour allegiance. Thus it may be that the relatively 'non-political' nature of such newspapers in normal times and the relative ignorance or lack of interest in politics among most of their readers actually contribute to the political influence which they can have when their editors decide to pull out all the stops.

The quality national newspapers have a more subtle kind of influence, because it is among politicians, civil servants and other political opinion formers that their columns are read most attentively. In this way well-known commentators, such as Samuel Brittan in the *Financial Times*, Peter Jenkins in *The Independent* and Hugo Young in *The Guardian*, can have real influence upon the evolving views of the political elite. Similarly, leading articles, political features and even letters to the editor in such quality newspapers are still taken seriously and carry some weight in Whitehall and Westminster. Such columns may be rather like a house notice board for the political class, but their revelations and their arguments carry disproportionate weight in view of the elitist and metropolitan character of opinion formation in the British political system.

Many on the Left of British politics argue that there is a persistent bias in the national press in favour of the Conservatives and against the views and interests of the Labour party. It is certainly true to say that the *Daily Mirror* is the only national daily newspaper which has consistently supported the Labour party as a matter of editorial policy. Apart from its sister paper, the *Sunday Mirror*, all the other national newspapers can be divided essentially between those which are still broadly in favour of the policies derived from the postwar consensus (for example, *The Guardian, The Observer* and *The Independent*) and those which are invariably pro-Conservative (for example, the *Daily Express*, the *Daily Mail* and *The Times*). Indeed Tony Benn has written with some justification that 'the fundamental criticism of the British newspapers is not that they necessarily support the policies of the Conservative party (although at election time the pro-Conservative allegiance of most of them is not in doubt), but that they support conservative policies whether carried out by a Conservative or a Labour Government'.[3] No doubt some will agree and some disagree with such an observation. Certainly it ought to be modified to take account of the fact that the Conservatives under Margaret Thatcher's leadership became the most radical and least conservative party in British politics and the fact that a paper such as the *Financial Times* has a genuine independence born of its European vocation, while a paper such as the *Daily Telegraph* – which used to be little more than a Conservative house magazine – now adopts a more robust, even critical line towards the present Conservative Government.

Secrecy and Censorship

Another important characteristic of the British press is that it is more inhibited than in most other Western countries by the traditional secrecy of government and the restrictive attitudes in Whitehall towards the unauthorised disclosure of official information. Such secretive habits have been well established for years, at least since the 1911 Official Secrets Act which in Section 2 was meant to deter public servants (including politicians) from communicating and journalists or others from receiving any official information whose disclosure had not been authorised, that is to say by Ministers or by senior civil servants acting on behalf of Ministers. The effect of such draconian legislation was to discredit the whole idea of official secrecy without removing the need for frequent prosecutions over the years. This bred an understandably cynical response from all journalists and many public servants.

Thus there was a wide welcome when the present Government introduced a new Official Secrets Bill in November 1988.[4] This was designed to remove the 'catch-all' provisions of Section 2 of the 1911 Act and replace them with provisions which restrict the application of the criminal law to specific categories of official information, such as defence, security and intelligence, international relations, law and order and the interception of communications (phone-tapping or letter opening). However, since the introduction of the new legislation, it has become perfectly obvious that the effect of the new law upon the press and others is likely to be more restrictive, although less capricious, than the discredited law which it replaced. It is therefore hard to argue that much has been gained in the cause of journalistic freedom.

The same cautious and restrictive attitudes which inhibit freedom of the press are evident in the so-called 'D Notice' system which is designed to prevent the publication in the press of sensitive defence information by the simple expedient of issuing a written warning from an official committee consisting of officials and journalists alike. While this committee has certainly been successful over the years in achieving a degree of self-censorship among those journalists who follow defence and security issues, the 'old boy' nature of the restrictive arrangements and the unpredictability of official intervention has bred further cynicism among those affected.

Similarly restrictive attitudes are reflected in the libel and copyright laws in Britain which also have the effect of inhibiting aggressive and fearless reporting, especially when the subject under journalistic investigation is an individual or a company which has the wealth and self-confidence to use the law to the full. These laws confer extensive powers of prior restraint and hence effective censorship upon those who wish to prevent press publication of anything which they may deem libellous or objectionable by the simple expedient of obtaining a High Court injunction to stop it. They also permit wealthy or determined individuals to go to court to obtain 'justice' in libel cases and, if successful in their suit, to secure from the jury orders for damages which have been known to reach half a million pounds or more.[5] While there is an obvious need for people to be able to protect themselves from libel or defamation, or even intolerable invasion of privacy, at the hands of the media, it is generally considered unsatisfactory that only the rich, the powerful and the well-connected seem to be able to avail themselves of the protection of the law while the rest of the community is neither adequately protected from journalistic excesses nor sufficiently enlightened by journalistic vigilance.

Freedom of Information

Concerted attempts have been made over the years to deal with the problems of secrecy and censorship which affect the British press by introducing proposals designed to promote freedom of information and by pursuing a vigorous pressure group campaign towards this end. In 1978 a report by 'Justice', the British Section of the International Commission of Jurists, recommended the establishment of a Code of Practice on the disclosure of official information by all government Departments and other public authorities to be supervised by the Parliamentary Commissioner for Administration (the Ombudsman).[6] At about the same time a Liberal MP, Clement Freud, introduced a Private Member's Bill designed to legislate for freedom of information along the lines of detailed proposals made a year or so earlier by the Outer Circle Policy Unit.[7] Since that time other back-benchers have tried and usually failed to introduce legislation along similar lines, but their efforts have been usually resisted by the government of the day.

However the Labour and Liberal Democratic parties now favour reforming the law in such a way that a public right of access to official information would be enshrined in statute law and the onus put upon public authorities to satisfy the courts of any justification for non-disclosure. This principle is the reverse of that contained in existing legislation, which holds that all classified information should remain restricted unless its release has been specifically authorised either by a Minister or by a court. The reformers have also wanted to give citizens the right to see their personal files and to establish a reliable register of all official files, except those concerning the security of the state. They have favoured the establishment of some form of appeals procedure against refusals to supply official information and the introduction of a judicial remedy for aggrieved citizens in cases of proven non-compliance with the law. Only certain categories of information, including some defence and security material, information involving commercial confidentiality and that which is safeguarded for reasons of privacy, would be exempt from the provisions of such legislation if it were introduced.

Apart from the inherent unwillingness of most Ministers and civil servants to respond positively to such proposals, the main argument used against them has usually been the extra cost to public funds which would be involved in applying such legislation. Furthermore, in those countries where such legislation has been implemented – for example, Sweden and the United States – the actual experience has been that pressure groups and commercial interests have made greater use of it than ordinary people. At bottom the idea provokes the fundamental antipathy of Ministers, civil servants and most public officials in Britain towards the disclosure of any official information other than that which is unavoidably forced upon them (for example, in answering parliamentary questions) or whose release is believed to be advantageous to the Government's cause. It is not easy to be confident that any Code of Practice or even any new legislation would do much to change such attitudes in a political and bureaucratic elite as congenitally secretive as the one in this country.

The Role of the Lobby

The paradoxical aspect of the position of the press in this country is that, whereas there is so much emphasis upon secrecy and censorship in the formal and legal arrangements, in practice a great deal of information is made available to the press on what are called 'lobby terms'.[8] This practice involves supplying accredited lobby journalists (that is, those entitled to frequent the Members' Lobby and other restricted parts of the Palace of Westminster) with privileged and unattributable information on the strict understanding that there is no disclosure of sources and no attribution of comments. The practice has spread beyond the precincts of the Palace of Westminster to every part of Whitehall, so that every Department (and notably 10 Downing Street) has contacts with trusted journalists who are the privileged recipients of official information and guidance which is deliberately and regularly given to them. Indeed most Ministers and some officials see it as an important part of their job to keep at least a few carefully chosen journalists well informed of what is happening or about to happen in their areas of responsibility. Similarly the journalists concerned find it convenient to take advantage of this form of news management, since it ensures for them a steady flow of news, gossip and opinion on which they can base their stories.

The lobby system has advantages for both the providers and the receivers of such privileged information. For Ministers and officials it can be an effective way of defusing potentially difficult issues through judicious and timely leaks, so that when the information is formally released much of its adverse publicity impact has been removed. A good example of this technique would be the early leaking of rising unemployment figures or an early indication of bad trade figures so that the markets do not respond too badly when the figures are eventually released. The system is also used to fly kites for new policy initiatives in order to get some idea of how they might be received by the media and the public. Occasionally it is used to pursue in the media policy arguments or personality conflicts which are already taking place behind closed doors in Whitehall or Westminster. For example, the Press Office at 10 Downing Street was known to guide friendly journalists towards taking a critical view of a Minister who might have incurred Mrs Thatcher's displeasure – sometimes to the extent that the Minister concerned learnt of his fall from favour more surely from inspired pieces in the press than from any face-to-face contact with the then Prime Minister.[9] It is a moot point whether the use of lobby techniques is desirable and some national newspapers have rather ostentatiously announced that they are not prepared to go along with them. Yet most experienced political journalists still seem prepared to play the game, since it can help them to get a good story and occasionally to increase their circulation.

7.3 The Problems of Broadcasting

The problems of broadcasting are both technological and ideological. They are technological in the sense that there are a number of developments in train which, even if Ministers were to take no action, would significantly affect and change the broadcasting environment now and in the future. For example, the technologies of broadcasting and telecommunications are increasingly converging, so that by one means or another the limitations imposed by spectrum scarcity are likely to be overcome or bypassed. This means that more programme services will be technically feasible both domestically and internationally and these services will be available with improved sound and visual quality. It also means that the range of programme choice could be widened and that the technology of direct payment by subscription could enable that choice to be registered in a cost-effective way. Perhaps most significant, with the spread of satellite television and the growth of global media companies, national media frontiers will begin to blur or disappear, with incalculable implications for public taste, national culture and regulatory control. Indeed eloquent concern has already been expressed in many quarters about the need to safeguard quality, to prevent excessive concentration of ownership, and to work out effective regulatory arrangements, if necessary at international level, in order to match the global reach of the new technologies.

The problems are also ideological in the sense that the Conservative Government seems convinced that 'the growth of (media) choice means that a rigid regulatory structure neither can nor should be perpetuated'.[10] This means that, wherever possible, the Government's approach to broadcasting policy will be made consistent with its overall deregulation policy, although due allowance will have to be made for the 'rules [which] will still be needed to safeguard programme standards on such matters as good taste and decency and to ensure that the unique power of the broadcast media is not abused'.[11] These two statements, which appeared in the same paragraph of the 1988 Broadcasting White Paper, revealed the tensions, not to say contradictions, which have existed in the present Government's policy between the urge to liberalise and the need to regulate, however difficult the latter may prove to be in such a market-led and technology-driven sector. In the Government's view the circle is squared by having both less regulation and better regulation – the latter being defined as 'lighter, more flexible, more efficiently administered'. It remains to be seen whether this synthesis of opposites will be possible in practice and much will depend upon how well the Home Office (the department of regulation in broadcasting) manages to resist pressures from elsewhere in Whitehall for a more ideological approach to the future of broadcasting.

The Power of Television

The power of television has affected many aspects of our society and in the political sphere notably the style and nature of political debate. As Anthony Smith has observed, television has become a well from which society draws many of its common allusions (illusions?) and an important source of social reference points.[12] This means that, in considering the power of television, we need to look not so much at its impact upon voting behaviour (which until recently seems to have been minimal) as at its capacity to influence the way in which the political debate is conducted both between elections and during election campaigns. In essence political issues are often treated as if they were simply another form of public entertainment. This has encouraged the tendency for politicians to perform before the people rather than reason with them. The respectable argument for this practice is that it serves to grab and hold what might otherwise be an uninterested and apathetic viewing public. Yet, while it may produce a greater public awareness of some telegenic issues, it does not necessarily raise the level of public understanding and may even produce a bias against it.[13]

In so far as television has had a discernible effect upon political allegiance in Britain, it seems to have been one of reinforcement rather than conversion, although the early studies on this subject seemed also to suggest that the direct effects upon voting behaviour were rather slight either way. For example, Trenaman and McQuail, in their study of the 1959 General Election (the first televised campaign in Britain), showed that the main effect of television was simply to increase the store of information and opinion available to the electorate.[14] In a follow-up study of the 1964 General Election, Blumler and McQuail showed that the only other discernible effect was to boost slightly the popularity of the Liberal party by giving it an abnormal degree of media exposure.[15] In 1981 television coverage of the newly-formed Social Democratic party seemed to have a similar effect upon its success at parliamentary by-elections at that time. However, with the notable increase in voter volatility in the 1970s and 1980s, it seems plausible that the impact of television upon the outcome of elections became greater than it had been in the late 1950s and early 1960s, when the conventional wisdom on this matter was established. Indeed, during the 1987 General Election campaign, Gallup Polls discovered that 69 per cent of its sample expected there to be too much political coverage on television, while another opinion poll discovered 27 per cent who thought there should be none at all.[16] Certainly the widely-held opinion among the psephological pundits was that Labour had 'won' the media battle against the Conservatives hands down, but this did not seem to make any difference to the level of support for Labour which was the same at the end of the campaign as it had been at the beginning.

Probably the most significant effect of television upon British politics has been manifest in the style and methods of political argument and election campaigning. Since the 1964 General Election campaign the parties have held daily press conferences each morning during the campaign period. This development and the nightly news bulletins on BBC and ITN have had the effect of focusing public attention increasingly upon the party leaders and a few of their senior colleagues. The presence of television cameras and radio microphones on tour with the party leaders has increased the emphasis upon a presidential style of campaigning. This has diminished the role and importance of most ordinary parliamentary candidates, except in very marginal seats or highly-publicised by-elections. One practical consequence of this tendency towards presidentialism has been to diminish still further the value of public meetings as a form of political campaigning, although this is not always the case in sparsely populated rural areas or at important by-elections.

Equally significant in its effect upon British politics has been the tendency for television to personalise, trivialise and sensationalise nearly every political issue. It does this almost unconsciously in that programme producers will always prefer to stage interviews with the party leaders rather than their colleagues or parliamentary spear-carriers (however interesting) and it cannot really afford to be more high-minded or restrained when faced with alternately hysterical and sycophantic competition for the public's attention from the tabloid press. Banner headlines which scream messages like 'Maggie triumphs' or 'Kinnock boobs' have set a hot pace with which television feels obliged to compete. Furthermore, with the antagonistic conventions of the House of Commons having been transposed to the television studios, it is not altogether surprising that the leading television interviewers and personalities tend to regard their clashes with party leaders and other senior political figures as a form of ritual conflict.

Influence and Bias

Just as some on the Left are concerned about anti-Labour bias in the national press, so others in all parties have expressed the view that television is far from being a neutral medium of mass communication. According to this argument, the political effect of television is no longer simply to reinforce existing values and preferences in society, but actually to set the agenda of political discussion. For example, public faith in the impartiality of television news is said to be misplaced, on the grounds that true objectivity can never be achieved by those who produce the programmes. The Glasgow Media Group in particular has argued that the news is not really 'the news', but an arbitrary selection and presentation of certain information and opinion according to the undeclared criteria of those who produce and present the programmes.[17] Interestingly, these left-wing academics are not alone in their suspicion of television decision-makers, but are joined in such feelings by a whole swathe of right-wing political opinion which is convinced that the programme-makers in general and the BBC in particular are out to do them down by innuendo and any other surreptitious method which comes to hand.

If there really is such a media conspiracy against the politicians, it is worth noting that the sense of paranoia is experienced by Left and Right alike. The counter-argument, which has been put by Martin Harrison and Alastair Hetherington, is essentially that political bias on television is in the eye of the viewer and on radio in the ear of the listener.[18] Such sceptics have pointed out that everything really depends upon the broadcast material selected for analysis and that in the case of the Glasgow Media Group the academics were essentially revealing their own prejudices. Equally there are many on the Conservative side of the argument who believe that they have cause to complain about the iconoclastic and even subversive nature of some television programmes. For example, the BBC Panorama programme *Private Lives* which was screened in 1986 purported to equate the life and motivation of an acknowledged IRA terrorist with that of an Ulster loyalist, thus leaving the viewers with the clear impression that the one was morally indistinguishable from the other. Similarly, the TV Eye programme *Death on the Rock* analysed the way in which three suspected IRA terrorists were killed on a street in Gibraltar in broad daylight by members of the Special Air Service (SAS) and conducted its analysis in such a provocative way that there was a major political row and a highly controversial Coroner's Inquest.

In most cases the programme-makers reply to the political charges made against them by arguing that they are either holding up a mirror to some uncomfortable reality or pursuing their vocation as investigative journalists or both. In the final analysis political reporting and editorialising is more a matter of taste and discretion than overt right or wrong doing, unless of course there is any well-founded suspicion that a journalist may have broken the law. In most cases discipline has to be imposed by the professionalism of the journalists themselves and only in the last resort by the courts.

The Power of Radio

Radio is also a powerful medium which has its effect upon both politics and society. The programmes now broadcast by the BBC on its five national channels serve to entertain, inform and educate the public, although Radios 1 and 2 concentrate very heavily on entertainment. Radio 3 caters for a tiny minority audience with a mixture of classical music, drama, poetry readings, academic discussion and brief news bulletins. Radio 4 is the flagship of BBC current affairs and produces a large quantity of high quality news and analysis, together with some lighter music and middle-brow entertainment. Radio 5 is the newest channel offering mainly middlebrow programmes and at the time of writing it is too early to make a definitive assessment. Taken together, the five national channels offer a balanced output which still approximates to the BBC's original Reithian objectives.

The expansion of local radio over the years since the late 1960s has also left its mark upon the quality of life and society at large. The BBC now has 30 local radio stations in England and permission to work towards 38 stations in all, which would cover about 90 per cent of the relevant population. It also has stations in Scotland, Wales and Northern Ireland which fulfil more of a 'national' purpose for those more self-conscious parts of the United Kingdom. The BBC's efforts in local radio are more than matched by the 50 independent local radio stations which now cover about 85 per cent of the entire UK population. Taken together, all these local radio stations in all parts of the country have given an undoubted boost to local consciousness and the more colourful political personalities have thrived in the atmosphere which has been created. Apart from heavy doses of popular music and other forms of light entertainment, the programmes include a considerable number of chat shows and phone-in programmes which provide opportunities for ordinary people to air their views and prejudices and for politicians and other public figures to demonstrate their activity and concern. Thus local radio has undoubtedly contributed to the vitality of British politics at the local level.

In the future, radio has great opportunities for development and expansion, but subject to a lighter regulatory regime in line with the present Government's willingness to see a departure from the traditional Reithian objectives. There will be more wave-lengths available and it is expected that there will be growing demand and potential for additional services, including a new tier of community or special interest radio stations. The likely implications of these developments are that there will be more opportunities for media entrepreneurs to make money out of commercial radio, there will be more competition for the BBC which may be tempted to dilute its public service obligations in order to retain a reasonable share of the audience, and new opportunities may unfold for pressure and cause groups to peddle their ideas in a much more pluralist and deregulated media environment. Many of these changes may affect the nature of politics; all of them will affect the quality of the lives of the British people.

The Impact of New Technologies

It is already clear that new technologies are likely to have a very significant impact upon the media in Britain. The availability of more radio frequencies, as well as the coming of satellite, cable and microwave transmission of television, will make far more services technically possible whether locally, nationally or supranationally. The main constraint on the pace and scale of these developments is likely to be the ability to make all these new services commercially viable within a reasonable period, rather than any serious doubts about the feasibility of the new technologies.

If everything goes well and the new technologies are developed along the benign lines foreseen by their most enthusiastic proponents, then we could see the development of a society which was described by Kenneth Baker, when Minister for Information Technology, as 'better informed . . . more relaxed, less formal, more mobile, less enamoured with structure, more skilled, less ridden with class and social differences and full of scope for more individuality'.[19] Yet if things go differently and the new technologies are developed overwhelmingly for short-term commercial gain and subsequently, perhaps, for manipulative purposes either by powerful media multinationals or by public authorities at the national level (where this can be done) then individual freedom could be eroded, social variety could be stultified and totalitarian tendencies could be spread to an alarming extent.

The likelihood that the traditional distinction between broadcasting and telecommunications will be increasingly blurred or even eliminated by technological developments could mean that there will be a larger range of home-based education, new opportunities for working, buying and selling direct from home, and a range of new consumer services such as electronic mail and telebanking. The present Government seems attracted by the idea of encouraging the progressive introduction of subscription television for the BBC, since it sees this as a way of moving away from the compulsory licence fee in the 1990s and of widening consumer choice by encouraging a broader range of minority and majority interest programmes.

The difficulty with this apparently exhilarating view of the future is that ordinary people may resent having to pay explicitly for mass audience programmes which previously they were able to enjoy 'free' at the time of viewing (the Cup Final, the Grand National, Trooping the Colour and so on) and that those with minority interests (in opera, ballet, vintage cars, for example) may prefer going to the real thing or even watching a video to paying quite large sums for encrypted programmes. In short, it is too soon to tell what will be the impact of the new technologies upon British society and British politics. Taking a favourable view, it is possible to foresee a future in which a more open and competitive broadcasting market can be attained, giving the viewers and listeners greater choice and greater influence, without detriment to the range or quality of the programmes provided. Taking an unfavourable view, these developments could lead to a waste of scarce resources, the erosion of privacy and social diversity, and fatal damage to the present quality and structure of broadcasting.

In April 1983 the Conservative Government announced its decision to encourage the development of cable television in a White Paper produced jointly by the Home Office and the Department of Industry.[20] This policy involved the promotion of a number of pilot projects and the establishment of a new Cable Authority which would award franchises to cable operators and exercise statutory supervision of those services. Since then the technology has languished and the market for cable television and related services has not expanded as fast as the Government expected or wished. In its 1989 Policy Review the Labour party committed itself to the promotion of cable technology on a much more ambitious scale, on the basis of a new fibre-optic network which could only be launched with considerable support from public funds. It remains to be seen whether this will ever happen and the future of cable services in this country now seems linked to the possibility of a future Labour Government.

On the other hand, the growth of Direct Broadcasting by Satellite (DBS) seems rather more assured in that there were originally two systems in operation – Sky Channel, which is owned and managed as part of Rupert Murdoch's media empire, and another consortium, British Satellite Broadcasting (BSB), in which Robert Maxwell has a major interest.[21] In recognition of the high costs of satellite technology (at least at the outset) Parliament decided in the 1984 Cable and Broadcasting Act that DBS companies should normally have a 15-year contract period rather than the eight-year franchise awarded to terrestrial cable contractors. The Government also undertook not to allocate the two additional DBS channels which it had envisaged until BSB had been operational for at least three years. However, in general, the approach of the present Government has been that the market should decide how far and how fast DBS will develop in the United Kingdom and it already seems clear that the relevant market for these purposes will be supranational. Considerable investment is now being made in satellite technology both here and on the continent of Europe and it seems likely that the technology and its regulatory arrangements will have to be developed on an international or supranational basis as well.

As things stand at present, high-powered direct broadcasting by satellite is regulated by the Cable Authority, whereas low- and medium-powered satellite services (if not taken by cable) are not subject to UK regulation at all. In order to close this regulatory gap, the Government proposed three solutions. Firstly, the regulation of programme content by the new Independent Television Commission (ITC) will be extended to cover nearly all satellite services received direct whether from British or foreign satellites. Secondly, foreign satellite services will be monitored here either by the ITC or by the new Broadcasting Standards Council (BSC) whose statutory remit is to guard against obscene or grossly offensive material and then, if need be, notify the British Government so that it can take the appropriate retaliatory action, such as imposing a statutory penalty on those who advertise on such programmes. Thirdly, the British Government will continue to work for agreement on the proposed Council of Europe Convention on Transfrontier Broadcasting which will lay down certain prescribed minimum standards covering both programme content and advertising. Such standards will then be enforced in all the 23 countries through a procedure which will enable the receiving state to take action against any country which allows the transmission of offending services.[22]

It should be clear that the commercial development of such technologies could have very far-reaching implications for traditional ideas of national sovereignty and cultural identity. We have already experienced the invasive consequences of junk food and tabloid television imported from the United States. The problem could be even more serious for other governments, especially in fragile or susceptible societies, if their capacity to influence what their people see, hear and know is greatly reduced. In such a televisual future there is a danger that the bulk of the programmes will become increasingly standardised and monoglot, purveying to the public more and more mid-Atlantic mediocrity designed only to satisfy the global advertisers. The adverse implications for the quality of life in Britain and many other countries could be very disturbing.

7.4 The Media and Politics

There is no doubt that the media have come to play an increasingly important part in the British political system over the last 20 years or so. The journalists, editors, presenters and producers no longer carry conviction if they claim that all they are doing is to reflect what is happening in politics and in society. Indeed the more thoughtful members of the media professions readily acknowledge their ability to influence the agenda of politics and recognise the tensions which media priorities can cause between them and the politicians.

There are really four main points which are made about the role of the media in modern politics. Firstly, it is argued by politicians and others in the public eye that the mass media, and especially television, give a distorted impression of politics and the political world, since bad news is nearly always given precedence over good news, disunity over unity, and gossip and speculation over solid reporting and analysis. Obviously these media tendencies are usually more noticeable in the tabloid press and television, but even the so-called 'quality' media are not above a little distortion or oversimplification when it suits them. The usual explanation is that the imperatives of the market and the need to compete for public attention require the media to behave in this way. Presumably the imperatives will be all the stronger once there has been further liberalisation.

As we have remarked earlier in this chapter, such distortions can take the form of perceived bias in the reporting of the activities and policies of the various political parties. More often, however, the distortion is of a different kind, namely the tendency to personalise and sensationalise complicated political issues for the sake of gaining and retaining the attention of the public. This was all too evident, for example, in the tendency to portray the Thatcher Government in almost presidential terms and to emphasise the gladiatorial nature of the conflict between the two main party leaders. Of course media professionals will reply that this sort of presentation merely reflects political realities, equates with the importance attached to the leadership by the members of each main party and reflects the growing frequency and importance of 'summit' meetings of all kinds. Cynics might add that it also said much about the energy and effectiveness of the press offices of the Prime Minister and Leader of the Opposition respectively. While all these pleas in mitigation might be true, it remains an observable fact that too much of the media coverage of British politics has oscillated between sickening sycophancy and destructive denigration.

Secondly, it is argued by political scientists and others that the media have an unrivalled capacity to set the agenda of politics, often in co-operation, it must be said, with energetic cause or campaigning groups. In one sense this is a more weighty point than the first, since it emphasises what can be one of the most constructive roles played by the media in our political system. Often the positive result is that public attention is brought to new or difficult issues which might not otherwise have received the attention which they deserve from the political parties or established political interests. Two examples of issues which have been raised and dramatised by the media in recent times are the environmental issues of 'Green' politics and the wide range of issues involved in consumer politics in all their forms. Clearly, if the 'Fourth Estate' is doing its proper job in any advanced society where the public is better educated and more aware than its forbears, it will seek to look ahead to warn of impending problems and probe beneath the surface of events to reveal what is really happening and why.

Probably the main reason why some people are made uneasy by this aspect of the media is that they may hold a rather old-fashioned view of political parties as the sole or principal organisations with the right to initiate new political directions. In reality there is bound to be considerable interplay between the politicians and the media in the process of political agenda-setting, as we shall see in more detail in Chapter 15. This is not because politicians are bereft of original ideas, but rather because, for those in opposition or on the back benches at any rate, the process of policy making is often so opaque and secretive that relatively few are able to get in on the act.

Thirdly, whenever the party in power at Westminster has had a comfortable, and sometimes overwhelming, parliamentary majority, there has been a journalistic view that the media themselves have a duty to provide effective criticism and opposition if the official Opposition seems incapable or unwilling to do so. For example, this view was widely held during most of the 1980s, when the

Labour party was more concerned with sorting out its internal affairs than with providing whole-hearted opposition to the Conservative Government. In such unusual circumstances there was a real temptation for those parts of the media which were particularly critical or hostile towards the Conservative party and everything for which it stood to try to fill the gap left by an absent and an ineffective Opposition. Certainly this was how the situation was seen by many Conservative politicians who had long been suspicious, particularly of the BBC. Their resentment towards the BBC spilled over into a growing unwillingness on the Conservative back benches to countenance the continuation of the licence fee arrangements for financing the BBC beyond 1996, when the present Charter expires. It was also reflected in the 1988 Broadcasting White Paper when the Government gave notice of its intention 'to agree licence fee increases of less than the RPI [retail price index] increase in a way which takes account of the BBC's capacity to generate income from subscription'.[23] In other words, it is foreseen that, if subscription television develops as rapidly as Ministers hope and believe, it may be possible to freeze or even reduce the licence fee beyond April 1991.

Clearly all governments are tempted to conclude, especially when they are going through a difficult patch (as the Conservatives did in 1986 at the time of the Westland crisis or again at the time of the 1989 Euro-elections), that the media are largely hostile, or at least unhelpful, to their purposes. This is a normal manifestation of the mutual suspicion which arises between politicians and the media from time to time. For their part, the key people in the media can harbour resentment – as some BBC producers undoubtedly did at the time of the 1982 Falklands conflict – towards what they are inclined to see as ruthless government attempts to manipulate and influence the output of their organisation for party political purposes. While there can never be a final or definitive assessment of the relative rights and wrongs of such grievances, most neutral observers would probably agree that it is not healthy for our democracy when the media feel tempted or entitled to play the role of political opposition to the government of the day and when Ministers for their part feel that they have more to fear from the media than from the official Opposition.

Fourthly, it is argued by many of a traditional disposition that the media in Britain or any other modern society can have a significant, and possibly adverse, impact upon the quality of life by producing a form of cultural pollution. This fear is felt particularly strongly in relation to the possible effects of broadcasting liberalisation as envisaged for the 1990s and it is reinforced by simple observation of the lowering of cultural and ethical standards which is already attributed to the influence of the mass circulation tabloid press.

It is clear from the 1988 Broadcasting White Paper and from subsequent statements made by Ministers to the House of Commons and elsewhere that the Home Office fought a rearguard action against the free market instincts of 10 Downing Street and the Department of Trade and Industry. Yet the outcome in relation to commercial television has clearly been in favour of market forces. As the *Financial Times* put it in a critical editorial, 'British broadcasting faces a future in which bottom line considerations will increasingly dictate the contents of programmes'.[24] Admittedly, Channel 4 is shielded to some extent from the winds of commercial competition and the financial framework for the BBC is safeguarded until at least 1996. Yet in the eyes of many there remains a serious risk (even likelihood) that the quality of broadcasting will deteriorate during the long transition from the present paternalistic duopoly to a highly competitive free market regime mitigated by only the lightest regulation. It is pointed out by the critics of this free market thrust in present broadcasting policy that no other country – not even the United States – auctions television licences to the highest bidder and that what is now proposed for this culturally sensitive area is not yet practised even in more prosaic parts of the economy, such as the allocation of airline routes. Even the Peacock Committee, whose extensive investigation into broadcasting policy provided the intellectual stimulus for the 1988 White Paper, emphasised the importance of achieving a balance between tax finance, advertising and subscription revenue. Yet in the event Ministers decided in favour of a future for British broadcasting which will put the advertisers and the mass media moguls in the driving seat. The worry remains that in such a free market environment the few remaining islands of real broadcasting quality may not survive for very long in a sea of mass media mediocrity.

A fifth concern which has been expressed about the future of the media in this country is that, without adequate rules to prevent it, there could be excessive concentration of ownership which would threaten the Government's commitment to 'Competition, 'Choice and Quality'. As the then Home Secretary made clear in the House of Commons, 'we should regard it as quite unacceptable if British broadcasting were allowed to be dominated by a handful of tycoons or international conglomerates'.[25] He therefore promised effective rules to safeguard diverse broadcasting ownership, editorial diversity, opportunities for new broadcasters and fair competition. Having given those undertakings, the Home Office made it clear that unhealthy concentrations of ownership and excessive cross-media ownership would be prevented. Specifically, the Government did not envisage that a single group would be allowed to own two large television or radio franchises or even two franchises for contiguous areas. Equally, with regard to broadcasting and newspaper cross-holdings, no proprietor of a national newspaper would be allowed to have more than a 20 per cent interest in any satellite, terrestrial television or radio franchise and Ministers also saw a strong case for debarring national newspaper proprietors from having a significant financial interest in more than one such franchise.[26] Such limits would also apply reciprocally to the holders of such franchises who invest in groups which control national newspapers. With regard to the owners of satellite TV channels not using UK broadcasting frequencies but receivable in the United Kingdom, no operator of such a service would be allowed to have more than a 20 per cent interest in any satellite, terrestrial television or radio franchise and cross-interests exceeding 20 per cent would not be permitted. Such limits are laid down in subordinate legislation, now that the Broadcasting Bill is on the Statute Book, and will be capable of variation in future.

While the Government does not intend that the Independent Television Commission and the Radio Authority should have wide discretion in dealing with matters of ownership, it has proposed that these regulatory bodies should be given the enforcement powers necessary to police the rules effectively. These would include the ability to make licence conditions requiring licensees to give advance notice of, and seek prior consent for, changes in their shareholdings. The regulatory authorities would also be able to require changes in a company or a group as a condition of awarding or retaining a licence and to withdraw a licence altogether if a company made false declarations. Taken together, these add up to a formidable range of powers for the regulatory authorities. Yet few observers are convinced that it will be easy to ensure high quality and diversity of ownership once the free play of market forces take full effect. Increasingly, it will be difficult to argue that regulation should be imposed at the national level when so many of the new technologies are likely to require continental or even global regulation. It looks as though the idea of broadcasting in one country will become as obsolete as capitalism in one country and that we shall all have to adjust our traditional assumptions.

In short, in considering the evolving relationship between the media and politics, the approach adopted by the various players is likely to depend upon a mixture of interest, temperament and ideology. Ministers in the present Government have argued that giving more power and choice to the listeners and viewers will engender higher quality and greater diversity in the media within an increasingly competitive commercial environment. Their critics and other sceptics have replied that, although the new technological developments may be inevitable, there is a real danger that genuine choice will be reduced and that quality and diversity will suffer. Only time will tell whether we are about to witness an explosion of media choice and commercial opportunities or whether the Philistines are at the gates.

7.5 Conclusion

We have seen in this chapter how the power of the media in the British political system is in one sense greater, but in another sense not so great as it was in previous times, for example during the heyday of the press barons in the late nineteenth and early twentieth centuries. Today television in particular has a strong influence upon the context and style of British politics, especially during election campaigns. On the other hand, the media do not entirely determine public opinion, nor can they topple governments as, it might be argued, they were able to do in this country on some occasions during the nineteenth century.

Certainly television has had an unsettling and pervasive influence upon the British political system. For most politicians it has acted like a lamp to moths, with the result that they have often seemed fatally attracted to its light. We are already seeing this process at work now that the House of Commons is televised. For the general public television has gained a false aura of impartiality, because most people seem prepared to give extra credence to facts or opinions which are relayed to them in this way rather than in print. However this almost reverential attitude may change as the number of TV channels increases and if the overall quality and integrity of television journalism declines in a much more competitive media environment.

For the opinion-formers television has provided an enormously expanded scope for communication with millions of people who might not otherwise have paid much attention to what they have to say. Yet even that may change in future if the new technologies and new market opportunities bring into being endless varieties of essentially the same media mediocrity. Furthermore the existing dangers of bias, triviality and sensationalism seem unlikely to be dispelled, since they are not even generally acknowledged by those who work in the media. It remains to be seen whether these dangers can be averted and whether television can be developed in ways which will enhance the quality of life and the vitality of democracy.

Against this background it is possible to summarise the overall contribution of the media to our political system as the encouragement of greater awareness of political issues among the general public and the influencing of the political agenda through the choice of issues and personalities which are dramatised in this way. The latter is especially important in pressure group politics in which many different interests and causes compete for the attention of the Government and public opinion alike. It is also true in the broader sense that political priorities are often influenced not so much by the intrinsic importance of particular issues as by the nature and extent of media coverage given to them.

Of course the influence of the media extends beyond the sphere of party politics, since it has a significant effect upon the values, assumptions, attitudes and behaviour of ordinary people. For example, it has contributed to the mindless materialism of modern society by reinforcing the widely-held assumption that individual status and social progress can be measured principally in terms of income received and goods or services purchased. It has also affected public attitudes towards the Government and other public agencies by raising public expectations that problems exposed or discussed by the media will be swiftly solved. On the other hand, it has raised the level of public awareness and prompted more urgent official responses to some of the problems and injustices of the modern world, such as those of environmental degradation or the erosion of human rights in many different countries.

In short, while the media may have made it more difficult for governments to govern by highlighting the flaws and shortcomings in our society and by encouraging a level of public expectations which no government has been able to satisfy, they have also raised the level of public consciousness in ways which have been healthy for our democracy. In forming our own conclusions on their role in the British political system, we should always remember that the media are more likely to be critics than buttresses of those in power and that it is right that this should be so in our pluralist, liberal democracy.

Suggested Questions

1. Describe the structure and organisation of the media in Britain.
2. How influential is the British press?
3. In what ways do radio and television affect the quality of British politics?

Notes

1. Figures published in *The Listener*, 13 December 1990, for the week ending 25 November 1990, for example, showed that the BBC and ITV have a roughly equal share of the most popular programmes. The BBC1 soap opera *Neighbours* attracts over 17 million viewers, while its longer established counterpart on ITV, *Coronation Street*, attracts over 16 million viewers. On BBC2 the most popular programme that week was *Food and Drink* with over 5 million viewers, while on ITV Channel 4 it was another soap opera, *Brookside*, with over 5 million viewers. The flagship news programmes on the BBC are the *Six O'Clock News* and the *Nine O'Clock News* each with over 12 million viewers. Both of these lead ITV *News at Ten* which has 9 million viewers.
2. See the 'Report of the Committee on Privacy and Related Matters' chaired by David Calcutt QC (London: HMSO, 1990) which concluded in para 17.4 that 'the press should be given one final chance to demonstrate that it can put its own house in order'.
3. A. Benn, *Arguments for Democracy* (London: Jonathan Cape, 1981), p. 115.

4. This subsequently became part of the law of the land as the 1989 Official Secrets Act.
5. For example, in July 1987 Jeffrey Archer was awarded £500 000 in damages against *The Star* which had libelled him with allegations about an assignation with a prostitute, and in December 1988 Elton John secured £1 million from *The Sun* in an out-of-court settlement for alleged libel.
6. *Freedom of Information* (London: Justice, 1978).
7. *An Official Information Act* (London: Outer Circle Policy Unit, 1977).
8. For a fuller discussion of the lobby system see J. Margach, *The Anatomy of Power* (London: Star, 1981), pp. 125–55.
9. It is now widely believed that Sir Bernard Ingham, Mrs Thatcher's Press Officer at 10 Downing Street, organised some lobby briefing in Whitehall specifically to discredit Michael Heseltine at the time of the 1986 Westland crisis, and that in the run-up to the 1987 General Election he fell into the habit of describing John Biffen to lobby journalists as 'a semi-detached member of the Cabinet', thus signalling Mrs Thatcher's decision to sack Mr Biffen immediately after the election.
10. See 'Broadcasting in the Nineties: competition, choice and quality', Cm 517, November 1988, para. 2.5.
11. Ibid.
12. A. Smith, *The Politics of Information* (London: Macmillan, 1978), p. 5.
13. This point was well made by John Birt and Peter Jay in *The Times* on 28 February, 30 September and 1 October 1975.
14. See J. Trenaman and D. McQuail, *Television and the Political Image* (London: Methuen, 1961).
15. See J. G. Blumler and D. McQuail, *Television in Politics* (London: Faber, 1968).
16. See M. Harrison's chapter on Broadcasting in D. E. Butler and D. Kavanagh, *The British General Election of 1987* (London: Macmillan, 1988), p. 139.
17. See Glasgow Media Group, *Bad News* (London: Routledge & Kegan Paul, 1981), pp. 12–13.
18. See M. Harrison, *TV News, Whose Bias?* (Hermitage, Berkshire: Policy Journals, 1985) and A. Hetherington, *News, Newspapers and Television* (London: Macmillan, 1985).
19. K. Baker, 'Towards an information economy', speech to the British Association for the Advancement of Science, 7 September 1982.
20. See 'The development of cable services and systems', Cmnd 8866 (London: HMSO, 1983).
21. In November 1990 the launch costs of these two satellite systems proved too onerous and the two companies decided to pool their efforts in one commercial organisation, BSB/Sky. This was clear evidence of the expense and difficulty of creating new broadcasting markets.
22. See 'Broadcasting in the Nineties', Cm 517, November 1988, Chapter XI.
23. Ibid., para. 3.11.
24. *Financial Times*, 14 June 1989.
25. *Hansard*, 8 February 1989, Col. 1011.
26. Ministers seem to have allowed Rupert Murdoch and News International to be an exception to this rule, since Mr Murdoch was allowed to establish Sky Television while retaining ownership of about 30 per cent of the national press in Britain.

Further Reading

Curran, J. and Seaton, J., *Power Without Responsibility* (London: Fontana, 1985).
Curran, J. *et al.*, *Impacts and Influences: essays on media power in the twentieth century* (London: Methuen, 1987).
Glasgow Media Group, *Bad News* (London: Routledge & Kegan Paul, 1981).

Harrison, M., *TV News, Whose Bias?* (Hermitage, Berkshire: Policy Journals, 1985).
Hetherington, A., *News, Newspapers and Television* (London: Macmillan, 1985).
Hetherington, A. *et al.*, *Cameras in the Commons* (London: Hansard Society, 1990).
Margach, J., *The Anatomy of Power* (London: Star, 1981).
Seaton, J. and Pimlott, B., *The Media in British Politics* (Aldershot: Gower, 1987).
Worcester, R. M. and Harrop, M. (eds), *Political Communications* (London: Allen & Unwin, 1982).

8 Public opinion

Public opinion means different things to different people and it has changed its meaning over the years. Whereas Jeremy Bentham defined it as 'a system of law emanating from the body of the people', Robert Peel defined it as 'that great compound of folly, weakness, prejudice, wrong feeling, right feeling, obstinacy and newspaper paragraphs'.[1] A.V. Dicey was more charitable when he defined it as 'the wishes and ideas as to legislation held by . . . the majority of those citizens who have . . . taken an effective part in public life'.[2] On the other hand, V.O. Key was more cynical when he defined it as 'those opinions of private persons which Governments find it prudent to heed'.[3]

Such diversity of definition reflects the different views taken at different times by different people, depending upon the society in which they lived and the political outlook which they had. In Britain in the nineteenth century public opinion was usually considered to be synonymous with the views of the relatively small number of people who were enfranchised and so able to have effective political influence, at least at election time. Nowadays it is generally accepted that public opinion includes the views and prejudices of all adults, no matter how shallow or fitful their involvement in politics. Thus for the purposes of this chapter we may define public opinion as the sum of opinions held on political issues by the entire adult population. The flow of public opinion is shown in diagrammatical form in Figure 8.1.

Figure 8.1 The flow of public opinion

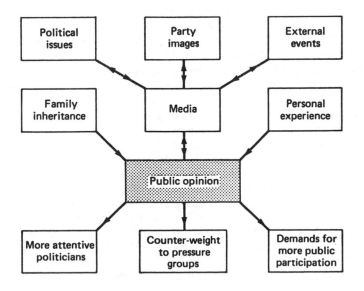

8.1 **The Composition of Opinion**

Consensus and Controversy

There is both consensus and controversy in British public opinion. Indeed there
are many different components of public opinion which vary from issue to issue
and from time to time. As Richard Rose put it, 'there is not a single public with
which the Government seeks to communicate; there is a variety of publics
distinguishable by their degrees of organisation, their policy preferences and their
knowledge or interest in political issues'.[4] The composition of public opinion is
therefore more akin to a mosaic than to a well-defined or predictable diagram.

In Britain for most of the period since the Second World War, at any rate until
the early 1970s, there was a remarkable degree of consensus in public opinion.[5]
This was reflected in the attitudes of the two main parties which both accepted the
wartime commitment to full employment and the postwar commitment to the
Welfare State. In these circumstances the political argument was largely confined
to disputes about the best way to manage the mixed economy and to distribute the
fruits of economic growth. Admittedly, there were some deep divisions of opinion
about some issues, notably in the sphere of foreign policy. For example, the Suez
expedition in 1956, the process of decolonisation in the late 1950s and early 1960s,
and Britain's relationship with the European Community in the late 1960s and
early 1970s all caused serious dissension between and within the main parties. Yet
such arguments took place against a background of basic agreement upon many
other issues of fundamental importance. In such a climate of political consensus it
could be said that the most significant cleavage in public opinion was neither
between Right and Left nor between rich and poor, but between informed and
mass opinion. In other words, the real gulf was between the minority who were in
the know and the rest who were not.

Looking back from the perspective of the early 1990s, we can see that the 1970s
and most of the 1980s were a period of considerable controversy and turbulence in
British politics. Many of the certainties of the postwar consensus broke down
under the pressures of two 'oil shocks' in 1973–4 and 1979–80 which brought in
their wake high and rising inflation and high and rising unemployment. The need
for the Callaghan Labour Government to call in the International Monetary Fund
(IMF) in 1976 and the breakdown of industrial relations during the so-called
'winter of discontent' in 1978–9 represented the low points under Labour. The
inner city riots in 1981 and the year-long coal industry dispute in 1984–5
represented the worst examples of social breakdown during the first two Thatcher
Conservative Governments. Since the 1987 General Election it seems fair to say
that a new political consensus has begun to emerge which looks as though it could
last well into the 1990s. This is based upon the growth of more 'realistic' attitudes
among organised labour (certainly in the private sector) and the deliberate
attempt by Neil Kinnock and the Labour leadership to present the official
Opposition as a party which has learned the lessons of its previous flirtation with
militant Socialism in the 1970s and early 1980s, for example ditching its previous
commitments to massive nationalisation and unilateral nuclear disarmament.
Thus the potential, sub-Thatcherite consensus of the 1990s will probably be based
upon a new commitment to the market economy in both main parties,
counterbalanced in Labour's case by a considerable degree of state intervention
and redistribution of income and wealth, and in the Conservative case by further
moves towards liberalisation within a statutory framework.

Informed Opinion and Mass Opinion

Informed opinion on political issues is opinion held by the minority of people who are 'in the know' and it is usually the result of a recognisably rational process of thought. Typically it is the opinion of politicians at Westminster, civil servants in Whitehall, political journalists, pressure group spokesmen and those prominent in some other walks of life, such as public corporations, local government, the law, the church and the City. In view of the metropolitan character of British political opinion, it often derives disproportionately from interacting London elites, although it can also be influenced by ephemeral intellectual trends which often originate in Oxford or Cambridge. It is therefore essentially the opinion of the Establishment and its licensed critics.[6]

Mass opinion, on the other hand, is often little more than ignorant sentiment, although it is usually based upon significant attitudes, beliefs and ideas which are rooted in popular experience. This means that it has often to be conjured up before it can be said to exist. As V.O. Key observed, 'public opinion does not emerge like a cyclone and push obstacles before it: rather it develops under leadership'.[7] The extent of public ignorance about the basic facts of politics obviously contributes to this situation and has been a matter of record for some time. For example, in 1964 almost a quarter of a representative sample did not know that the coal industry had been nationalised for nearly 20 years. In 1971 another opinion poll showed that only 13 per cent of those questioned could name the six member states of the European Community at a time when the British Government was engaged in widely publicised negotiations for British entry. In 1978 only 46 per cent of those questioned in a national poll could give the name of their MP and a poll in 1979 showed that 77 per cent of those questioned did not know what was meant by the acronym NATO – 30 years after the foundation of the North Atlantic Treaty Organisation.

The high level of public ignorance of the facts of politics persisted during the 1980s. For example, in June 1986 when presented in a MORI Poll with photographs of all the leading Conservative politicians, a representative sample of the public were 100 per cent correct only in their recognition of Margaret Thatcher, 66 per cent correct with Norman Tebbit (then Chairman of the Conservative party) and 51 per cent correct with Sir Keith (now Lord) Joseph. Yet in all other cases less than half of the public correctly identified such senior figures as the Foreign Secretary, the Chancellor and the Home Secretary. Recognition of politicians was no better at local level, since a Gallup Poll in April 1988 showed that 44 per cent of a representative sample could give neither the name nor the party affiliation of their local Councillor. As for the major issues of policy, a Gallup Poll in June 1988 showed that only 29 per cent of a representative sample knew what was meant by the much publicised date of 1992, while 15 per cent associated it incorrectly with the 'Poll Tax' and 42 per cent confessed to having no idea at all.

Bearing in mind all the political communication which takes place, it is perhaps a little difficult to understand why such a degree of public ignorance has existed. The explanation could be that those politicians and others who have something to say are not saying it with sufficient clarity or repetition. It could be that the channels of communication in the mass media are defective for this purpose. It could even be that the public audience is perfectly able to hear, but not really prepared to listen. Simple observation would suggest that politicians and other opinion formers try to impart a great deal of fact and opinion to the general public, perhaps even too much for easy assimilation. It would also suggest that the media, and especially television, are more pervasive and influential than before. Yet it is equally clear that these factors do not necessarily produce a well-informed or enlightened public.

It is possible to identify several plausible reasons for this unsatisfactory state of affairs. It may be because the conduct of political argument on aggressive party lines is not the best way of explaining to the public many of the complicated issues raised in contemporary politics. It may also be because the imperatives of modern journalism and the fierce commercial competition in the media have discouraged editors and producers from giving sufficient coverage or adequate explanation of many difficult political issues. After all, the popular national newspapers are more noted for their coverage of sport, scandal and sex than for intelligent or subtle discussion of important political issues. Equally the radio and television programme-makers are more concerned to compete for a mass audience and to win the battle of the ratings than to provide very much serious coverage of political news and views. As for the attitudes of the general public, anecdotal evidence suggests that most people are largely uninterested in politics and feel bored or even annoyed when the politicians or other opinion-formers seek to foist such things upon them. If we take account of this understandable, psychological reaction to the volume of information made available and the intractability of most of the problems highlighted, it would seem to be more a case of a public which is not really very keen to listen than of politicians and other opinion formers who are not trying to communicate.

In short, mass opinion on most political issues consists of a large component of ignorance, a considerable lack of interest, a certain amount of prejudice, an assortment of received ideas, a smattering of popular mythology, a dose of wishful thinking and considerable rationalisation of personal experience. If this appears to be something of a caricature, then it must be said that there is not much evidence from opinion polls or other systematic sources to disprove it. This appears to be the political reality with which we must live until such time as we develop a more knowledgeable and participatory political culture.

8.2 The Formation of Opinion

Inheritance and Experience

Expert studies have shown that public opinion is formed from a myriad of private opinions, whether personal or group opinions. Such private opinions are often formed quite early in life, usually when people first become aware of political issues. They tend to be derived principally from family influence and personal experience, although the pressures from school, work, friends and neighbours all play a part as well.

In the 1960s Butler and Stokes wrote an important book in which they demonstrated the strength of family influence as a factor in voting behaviour.[8] Although the growth of electoral volatility in the 1970s and early 1980s indicated that its significance had declined, young people today still derive many of their attitudes and opinions from their parents and family influence remains one of the more constant factors in the development of every young generation. Of course, there have always been young people who reject the attitudes and opinions of their parents, either as part of a transient adolescent rebellion or as a function of economic and social mobility. Yet on the whole family influence still plays a major part in the formation of public opinion and even the dramatic increase in one-parent families in the 1980s did not seem to invalidate this thesis.

As for the influence of personal experience, it is obvious that this has a major impact upon the formation of individual opinions. Few people form their opinions on political issues on a basis of detached or altruistic ratiocination, since this is a luxury which is usually available only to those whose material circumstances and educational background allow them to adopt such a Platonic stance. For most people individual opinions are formed in the light of the fortune or misfortune which they experience during the course of their lives, whether at home, at work or at leisure. Indeed, it has been argued that it is the formative experience of young adults which has the most lasting influence upon their opinions later in life. This is known as 'the cohort theory' of opinion formation and it certainly seemed to fit those who came of age in 1945 as well as those who did so in the late 1950s. Some would argue that the theory is still valid, notably in the tendency for those now in their twenties and thirties to reject old-style Socialism and accept many of the tenets of Thatcherite Conservatism. Our cautious conclusion must be that formative experience remains important as an influence upon the formation of public opinion, but that the pace and scale of economic and social change in the modern world has generated much greater volatility than in the past.

Issues and Images

Public opinion is also formed by individual responses to political issues and party images. Traditionally the psephological evidence seemed to suggest that people tend to reconcile their political opinions with their party allegiances, rather than the other way around. In the 1950s and the 1960s neither policy nor ideology seemed to mean very much to the average British citizen whose political opinions and voting behaviour appeared to be largely unaffected by such considerations. Yet evidence drawn from the 1970s and 1980s suggested that political issues do have an impact upon the formation of public opinion and hence upon voting behaviour. For example, Ivor Crewe concluded that 'it was issues, not organisation or personalities, that won the [1979] election for the Conservatives'.[9] Indeed even those who voted Labour on that occasion often preferred Conservative policies, although evidently not enough to persuade them to align their votes with their policy preferences. For much of the 1980s the nature and extent of trade union power was one of the major issues in the political debate and on the whole its salience worked in favour of the Conservatives who were seen to adopt a consistently tougher stance in relation to the trade unions. The same might be said of the issue of nuclear weapons and nuclear disarmament on which Neil Kinnock and the Labour leadership had reluctantly to concede points to the Conservative and Social Democratic positions.

Yet, in considering the influence of political issues upon public opinion, we need to distinguish between the bread and butter issues of daily life (such as inflation, jobs, health or pensions) upon which most people have strongly held views which influence their voting behaviour, and the more esoteric issues of policy (for example, the control of money supply, or theories of nuclear deterrence) upon which some people hold opinions, but which tend not to interest the vast majority. In considering the influence of issues in the latter category, it is as well not to exaggerate the authenticity or originality of the views held by the general public.

Among the more ephemeral considerations which influence the formation of public opinion, the images of the parties and especially of their leaders constitute another important factor in modern political conditions. For example, for decades the Conservative party has managed to preserve an image of competence in government which has led many people to support it even when it may not have appeared particularly warm or sympathetic to most of the general public. Several of its leaders – such as Winston Churchill, Harold Macmillan and Margaret Thatcher – were respected and even occasionally revered for their achievements in office, although they did not necessarily engender feelings of warmth or affection in the hearts and minds of many people. In the mid- and late 1980s, the party's reputation for competence in government was tarnished by the 1986 Westland Affair and the unwelcome surge in inflation and interest rates, with the result that it lost ground to Labour in the opinion polls.

On the other hand, the Labour party has traditionally had an image of understanding and concern for ordinary people which has helped it to retain the voting loyalties of a large part of the traditional working class. This achievement was partly a reflection of the positive personal image of several of its leaders – such as Clement Attlee, Hugh Gaitskell and Harold Wilson – but mainly a tribute to the image of the party as the parliamentary vanguard of the entire Labour movement at a time when the latter had authenticity, fraternity and solidarity. After 1979, however, Labour had more trouble with its image, particularly during the brief period of Michael Foot's leadership in the early 1980s, and it required all the media skills of Peter Mandelson and other Labour image-makers to recreate a positive, modern image for the party. Yet whatever wonders the image-makers may be able to perform with Neil Kinnock and his senior colleagues, it is the performance and credibility of the Conservatives in government which is likely to be decisive in the battle for the hearts and minds of the British people.

The Power of the Media

As we saw in Chapter 7, perhaps the most influential factor in the formation of public opinion in Britain today is the power of the media to reflect, explain or distort the most important political issues and personalities at any time. For example, most of the tabloid press has conducted a ruthless and single-minded campaign to portray the Labour party as completely beholden to the trade unions and the trade unions as stereotypically mindless and militant. Such a campaign would not have been remotely credible to the general public if certain trade union leaders – for example, Arthur Scargill of the NUM – had not played into the hands of the newspaper proprietors by behaving in a manner which might have been calculated to lend credence to their caricatures. Yet undeniably the public's image of the 'loony Left', whether identified with some of the trade unions or some of the town halls up and down the country, has been heavily influenced, even determined, by the columns and pictures in *The Sun*, the *News of the World*, *The Mail on Sunday*, the *Daily Express* and other such hard-hitting newspapers. Conversely these same newspapers and others like them consistently indulged in sycophancy towards Margaret Thatcher in a crude and sustained attempt, one must suppose, to keep the Conservatives in office. It is interesting, however, that this form of hagiography was largely confined to Mrs Thatcher herself, while several of her ministerial colleagues, once they fell from favour, were subjected to character assassination at the instigation of Mrs Thatcher's Press Secretary, Sir Bernard Ingham.

As for radio and television, the part which these broadcast media play in the formation of public opinion is generally agreed to be more insidious, even manipulative. It consists essentially of helping to set the political agenda by influencing the relative salience of different political issues as they waft in and out of the public's consciousness. It is not so much that influential programmes, like the *Nine O'Clock News* or *News at Ten*, consciously set out to tell the general public what to think about a given politician or political issue; but rather that they set the framework of values, assumptions and information within which the public has to try to make up its own mind. In a world in which real public interest in politics is desultory and attention spans are alarmingly short, this form of media influence is obviously both ephemeral and unpredictable. Indeed it may well be that the influence of the media is greater via the medium of mass entertainment programmes, such as *Coronation Street* or *The Archers*, than it is via those more serious programmes which are specifically designed to inform and educate the public. At all events we cannot review the various factors which influence the formation of public opinion in Britain today without laying great stress upon the role of the mass media.

8.3 The Effects of Opinion

More Deferential Politicians

Public opinion in Britain has a variety of political effects. It is arguable that one effect has been to make most politicians more deferential to the wishes of the electorate. While this tendency may seem to have reached its zenith in the time of Harold Wilson (1963–76) who as Leader of the Labour party paid assiduous attention to opinion polls and other psephological data (such as by-election and local election results), it has remained significant at all times in postwar politics, especially when General Elections are imminent. Certainly it has been true in the negative sense that leading politicians both in and out of office usually take considerable care not to put forward policies or take positions which seem destined to encounter powerful opposition from public opinion. Even the redoubtable Margaret Thatcher, who more than any other postwar leader sought to do what she believed to be right almost regardless of the political consequences, adjusted Conservative policy on some occasions in order to take account of the public responses which might have been expected if she and her ministerial colleagues had pressed ahead with certain radical policies in an unaltered form.[10]

This draws our attention to the elusive and controversial concept of 'political impossibility' which has played such an important part in so many political calculations by leading politicians over the years. In essence it can be defined as the influence upon political decision-makers of anticipated public reaction. Some have argued that this is a deleterious influence upon politics, since it can prevent the adoption of radical policies which may be justified as an appropriate response to many of our deep-seated national problems. Others have argued that it is a beneficial influence, since it can be seen as a contribution to our national cohesion, especially during difficult periods of disappointment and relative decline when a less sensitive political approach could prove very damaging. The argument is really between those who regard the conservatism of British public opinion as something of a saving grace, since it constitutes a significant obstacle to the ambitions of the zealots in each main party, and those who see it as a tragedy, since it has often constituted a virtually insuperable barrier to radical action. If the overriding priority is to guard against radical change, then the former view ought to be commended. If it is to make radical change, then the latter view ought to prevail. In any event the outcome is likely to depend upon the personal temperament of the leading politicians who have to carry the responsibilities of government.

Under Margaret Thatcher's leadership in the 1980s the Conservative Government tended to press for what it believed to be right almost regardless of the immediate political consequences. Only a few major revolts on the Government back benches – for example, against the proposed reform of the Sunday trading laws – and the rather more far-reaching inhibitions imposed by Britain's membership of the European Community seemed capable of stopping Mrs Thatcher in her tracks.[11]

A Counterweight to Pressure Groups

Another important effect of public opinion has been the way in which it has provided a useful counterweight to the influence of pressure groups in the British political system. As we noted in Chapter 6, there have been times when it has become very difficult for any government to resist the claims of certain powerful interest groups, such as the National Union of Mineworkers in the 1970s or the British Medical Association in the late 1980s, without appealing over the heads of the group concerned to the general public. This is essentially what Edward Heath sought to do when he called a General Election in February 1974 on the issue of 'who governs?' It is also what the 1979–83 Conservative Government sought to do when it introduced legislation to provide for secret ballots in trade union affairs. In each case the intention of Ministers was to appeal over the heads of obstructive interest groups to the wider public in an effort to fulfil their political purposes. Of course the success of this tactic depends upon the power of the opposing interest group and the degree of public sympathy or support which it can generate for its cause. For example, the BMA campaign against the present Government's reform of the NHS has depended upon the credibility of its propaganda and the willingness of its members to remain solidly behind the union line.

Whenever politicians of the Right or Left invoke the views of the wider public in support of their cause, it is usually a sign that they have been obstructed or opposed by a small but powerful group which seeks to set its sectional interest above that of the general community. This has been as true when Labour Ministers have complained about the pernicious influence of the City of London as when Conservative Ministers have criticised the abuse of trade union power. In each case they have sought to defend the principle that general public opinion has more inherent legitimacy than any sectional group. On the whole it is hard to oppose this principle, since general public opinion has a sounder and more altruistic record than sectional groups on most political issues. Yet every political system also needs safeguards against the tyranny of the majority (or even of a minority of the electorate exploiting a parliamentary majority), since in most societies there have been times when majority opinion has been unfair or unenlightened and temporarily defeated minorities have needed some protection against it. Thus a balance has to be struck which allows fair opportunities for both majority and minority opinion, while retaining a democratic presumption in favour of the former.

The Influence of Opinion Polls

Yet another effect of public opinion has been to give political opinion polls an influence out of all proportion to their true value. Such polls have become the most systematic expression of public opinion between General Elections. When sensibly interpreted, they can provide a useful navigational aid for politicians, whether in government or in opposition. The systematic analysis of opinion poll data has enabled the parties to identify key target groups of voters – for instance, the wives of blue collar workers in the case of the Conservative party or the public sector salariat in the case of the Labour party – and then to concentrate and organise their efforts with particular target groups in mind. Opinion polls also guide the Prime Minister of the day in making the decision about when to call a General Election and they can affect the morale of party activists if the findings are either very good or very bad for a particular party or its leader.[12] While opinion polls are not normally used to determine policy or decision making, it is understandable that they should influence both the development and the presentation of policy. On the other hand, there is a widely held view among practising politicians that both local and European elections (but not usually parliamentary by-elections) are a better guide to the public mood, if not necessarily an infallible indicator of voting behaviour at a future General Election.

Special considerations apply to the role of opinion polls during election campaigns. Some experts have argued that the polls produce a bandwagon effect which assists the party that seems to be on a winning streak. Others have argued for the backlash effect which leads doubting voters to rally to the party that appears to be the underdog. One thing seems certain, however, and that is that opinion polls can have a much more powerful effect upon the actual result at by-elections than at General Elections, since on such occasions they signal to the local electorate which is the best vehicle for an effective political protest.

The Use of Referenda

Still another effect of public opinion is visible in the way in which the growing self-confidence and declining deference of the general public has led to periodic demands for national referenda.[13] These demands have arisen on a variety of political issues, notably those which demonstrate that parliamentary opinion is out of tune with public opinion, for example on the emotive issue of capital punishment. Of course, national referenda have certainly not been a defining characteristic of our constitutional arrangements in Britain and most MPs in all parties have been determined to see that this remains the position. Yet there is always a temptation for political demagogues or other publicity seekers to break ranks with their colleagues in Parliament by calling for national referenda on certain issues when they believe that the results of a plebiscite would be in their favour.

The important and much publicised referenda on Britain's membership of the European Community in 1975 and on devolution to Scotland and Wales in 1979 are still generally considered to have been exceptions which prove the rule. The reason for holding referenda in these special cases was that they were conducted on constitutional issues of great importance in which the very future of Parliament itself was involved. They were therefore clear exceptions to the general rule that we have parliamentary rather than plebiscitary democracy in Britain. On the other hand, it would seem that, once such precedents have been set and the public appetite for direct decision making has been whetted, it may prove difficult for MPs in all parties to resist further demands for referenda on a wide range of political issues, especially when public feelings are running high, powerful cause groups are involved or a majority in the House of Commons is seen to be out of tune with the majority opinion of the general public.

The Impact of Direct Action

Finally, we should not neglect the impact of direct action as a powerful form of non-verbal and non-literate political communication. We should note the fact that at various stages in our history public protest, whether spontaneous or induced, has played an important, sometimes critical, part in the expression of public opinion. We need only instance Wat Tyler and the Peasants' Revolt in 1381, the Peterloo Massacre in 1819, the Chartist Movement in the 1840s, the Suffragette demonstrations in the early 1900s, the Jarrow and other unemployment marches in the 1930s or the inner city riots in the summer of 1981. The miners' dispute of 1984–5 and the Greenham Common demonstrations against American cruise missiles in the mid-1980s provided two more examples of the power of direct action.

Nowadays lawful public demonstrations are usually organised for publicity purposes by minorities who feel strongly about an issue, but who also feel excluded from the regular channels of influence and representation in our society. The fact that some people have recourse to such methods may cast doubt upon the validity of their arguments. Yet more often it reflects their assessment of the chances of attaining their objectives by more orthodox institutional means, such as parliamentary pressure or official contacts in Whitehall. For example, those who believed in the merits of unilateral nuclear disarmament chose to squat outside the Greenham Common air base or to march in large processions through London, since they did not believe that the more conventional means of putting their case would have had as much impact upon the decision-makers. Similarly the Muslim demonstrations in London, Bradford and other cities against Salman Rushdie and his 'blasphemous' novel *The Satanic Verses* illustrated the anger and frustration of the minority Muslim community at the apparent inability of Parliament to respond to their deeply-felt demands. Public demonstrations of this kind have always been a recognised way of seeking publicity for a grievance or support for a cause, and most are conducted in a peaceful and law-abiding manner. Yet they do not always succeed in influencing political decisions in their chosen direction, since the impact upon the general public is often adverse and occasionally counterproductive.

8.4 Conclusion

In summary, public opinion in Britain can be regarded as a source of political legitimacy, a counterweight to the influence of pressure groups, a form of political intelligence and increasingly perhaps as a 'Court of Appeal' in matters of strong public concern or great constitutional importance. Yet its true value is limited by the fact that, in complex issues of national policy, it is usually not based upon sufficient knowledge or experience and is often more of a reflection than an inspiration for the positions taken by leading politicians and other opinion-formers. It is undoubtedly a dynamic factor in the working of the British political system, since it involves a constant and continuous process of two-way communication between the politicians and the people. In the modern age this is most likely to be achieved by extensive use of radio and television. It may even be that televising the House of Commons is making a positive contribution towards closing the communications gap between the politicians and the people.

It is clear, therefore, that political leadership has a major part to play in the formation of public opinion. Yet, if such leadership is to be really effective, it will have to make itself felt beyond the limited confines of Whitehall and Westminster. Metropolitan elites will need to leave the corridors of power and make more frequent contact with the general public in all parts of the country. In any event all opinion-formers will need to have a clearer idea of what they want to say and how best to say it. The key people in the media will need to offer more political news and views and to present such material in balanced and responsible ways. Schools and other institutions of learning will need to put more emphasis upon political literacy in all its forms. Yet, even assuming a reasonable degree of success with all these endeavours, the politicians will still have to keep their fingers crossed and hope that the British people really want to play an active part in our pluralist political arrangements.

Suggested Questions

1. What are the main components of public opinion in Britain?
2. How is public opinion formed and influenced in Britain today?
3. What are the effects of public opinion upon modern British politics?

Notes

1. Both quoted in A. H. Birch, *Representative and Responsible Government* (London: Allen & Unwin, 1964), p. 172.
2. A. V. Dicey, *Law and Opinion in England in the Nineteenth Century* (London: Macmillan, 1905), p. 10.
3. V. O. Key, *Public Opinion and American Democracy* (New York: Knopf, 1961), p.14.
4. R. Rose in R. Rose (ed.), *Studies in British Politics*, 3rd edn (London: Macmillan, 1976), p. 254.
5. See D. Kavanagh and P. Morris, *Consensus Politics from Attlee to Thatcher* (Oxford: Basil Blackwell, 1989).
6. See A. Sampson, *The Changing Anatomy of Britain* (London: Hodder & Stoughton, 1982) for a vivid description of the Establishment in Britain.
7. V. O. Key, *Public Opinion and American Democracy*, p. 285.
8. See D. E. Butler and D. Stokes, *Political Change in Britain*, 2nd edn (London: Macmillan, 1974), pp. 19–151.
9. In H. R. Penniman (ed.), *Britain at the Polls, 1979* (Washington, D. C.: American Enterprise Institute, 1981), p. 282.
10. For example, Mrs Thatcher and her ministerial colleagues deliberately postponed an all-out confrontation with Arthur Scargill and the National Union of Mineworkers until 1984 when all the relevant preparations for a long industrial dispute had been made by the Government and the electricity utilities.
11. Significantly, it was a revolt led by members of the Cabinet which finally precipitated Mrs Thatcher's resignation between the first and second ballots in the November 1990 Conservative leadership contest.

12. It was the fact that the Conservatives trailed a long way behind Labour in the opinion polls during the final 16 months of Mrs Thatcher's leadership which, more than anything else, was responsible for the Cabinet-led back-bench revolt which brought about her downfall in November 1990.

13. See D. E. Butler and A. Ranney (eds), *Referendums: a comparative study of practice and theory* (Washington, D. C.: American Enterprise Institute, 1978) for a fuller discussion.

Further Reading

Clemens, J., *Polls, Politics and Populism* (London: Gower, 1983).

Johnson, N., *In Search of the Constitution* (London: Methuen, 1980).

Jowell, R. *et al.*, *British Social Attitudes* (London: Gower, 1990).

Ranney, A. (ed.), *The Referendum Device* (Washington, D. C.: American Enterprise Institute, 1981).

Teer, F. and Spence, J. D., *Political Opinion Polls* (London: Hutchinson, 1973).

Worcester, R. M. and Harrop, M. (eds), *Political Communications* (London: Allen & Unwin, 1982).

Wybrow, R. J., *Britain Speaks Out, 1937–87* (London: Macmillan, 1989).

Part III
Parliament

9 The Monarchy

In formal terms the Monarchy is one of the institutions of Parliament. With a Queen on the throne every government is 'Her Majesty's Government' and the Monarch still has an important, if largely formal, part to play in our constitutional arrangements. It is the Queen who opens every session of Parliament, who reads the speech from the throne on such occasions and who later in the year gives her royal assent to Bills, without which they could not become Acts of Parliament. Admittedly, the Monarch has long been regarded as one of the 'dignified' as distinct from the 'efficient' parts of the constitution (in Walter Bagehot's nineteenth-century terminology). Yet for all that it is still appropriate that we should consider the Monarchy in this part of the book.

9.1 Powers and Functions

The powers which the Monarchy now possesses are more theoretical than real, since they are based upon no more than conventions and residual royal prerogatives. This means that they can only be used within the confines of well-established custom and practice. If such conventions were ever broken by the Monarch, it would discredit and possibly do fatal damage to the institution of the Monarchy itself.

The Choice of Prime Minister

Whereas George III chose and dismissed Prime Ministers almost at will, Elizabeth II is normally free to choose as Prime Minister only the elected leader of the largest single party in the Commons. It would only be in the exceptional circumstances of a 'hung Parliament' – that is, when no single party has an overall majority in the Commons – that the Queen might be free to choose someone else, if there were to be another leading political figure with a better chance of forming a government which could command the support of a majority in the Commons.

In modern times, however, this has not always been the position. In January 1957, when Anthony Eden became too ill to continue as Prime Minister after the debacle of the Suez expedition, the Queen took advice from Sir Winston Churchill and the Marquess of Salisbury and invited Harold Macmillan to form a new government. In October 1963, when Harold Macmillan became seriously ill and a successor had to be found for the position of Prime Minister, the Queen again took advice – this time from Harold Macmillan himself in hospital – before inviting Lord Home to form a new government. In both cases a new leader of the Conservative party was said to have 'emerged' from the process of informal soundings which characterised the decision making of the party in those days. On the latter occasion, the behaviour of the so-called 'magic circle' was strongly criticised by Iain Macleod and Enoch Powell who subsequently both refused to serve in the Administration of Sir Alec Douglas-Home (the style to which he had reverted after renouncing his peerage in order to sit in the Commons as Prime Minister).

Since 1965 in the case of the Conservative party and 1922 in the case of the Labour party, there have been systematic arrangements to ensure that a new leader is rapidly elected to succeed one who retires or dies. The result is that the role of the Queen is now confined to choosing as Prime Minister whoever has already been elected as leader of the largest single party in the Commons. Of course, when there is a clear change of government following a decisive result in a General Election, the Queen sends for the leader of the victorious party and invites him or her to form a new government.

There has always been the possibility of a more significant role for the Monarch at a time of national crisis or when a General Election has produced a 'hung Parliament'. An example of the first eventuality occurred in 1931 when George V was instrumental in encouraging the formation of the National Government under Ramsay Macdonald in order to get through the Commons the deflationary economic measures which had not been acceptable to a significant part of the Parliamentary Labour party when it had been in power on its own. Another example occurred in 1940, when George VI had some influence upon the choice of Winston Churchill to succeed Neville Chamberlain as Prime Minister after the latter had been discredited by the significant number of abstentions within the Conservative parliamentary party at the end of a crucial debate of confidence on the conduct of the war.

An example of the second eventuality occurred in February 1974 when it seemed possible for a while that the Queen could have been drawn into party political controversy by Edward Heath's attempt to retain power for the Conservatives by offering a pact (and seats in his Cabinet) to the Liberals after his party had been defeated at the General Election. As things turned out, it proved impossible for the Liberal leader, Jeremy Thorpe, to persuade his party to do such a deal with the Conservatives. Thus a few days later Harold Wilson was duly invited by the Queen to form a minority Labour Government.

Dissolution of Parliament

It is now a well-established convention that the Monarch can only dissolve Parliament at the request of the Prime Minister in office within the five-year maximum life-span of a Parliament. It is necessary to go back to the reign of Queen Anne to find the last example of a Monarch exercising this royal prerogative in an independent way. Even in 1913, when it was argued by some that George V might have been within his constitutional rights to have dissolved Parliament in order to give the electorate a chance to pronounce upon the Liberal Government's Bill for Irish Home Rule, A. V. Dicey, the eminent constitutional expert, was not prepared to recommend such a step to the King for fear that it would compromise his neutral position as a constitutional Monarch.

Since that time various views have been advanced about the power of dissolution. One view, which was advocated by some after the very close General Election result in 1950, holds that, if the Prime Minister in office is not prepared to recommend a dissolution in circumstances where it might be considered in the national interest to have one, then the Monarch is entitled to seek other leading figures in the Commons who might be prepared to recommend such a course. In the event such a view did not prevail in 1950 and it has not prevailed since. The

Monarch is therefore bound by the conventional view, which is that she is obliged to accept only the advice of the Prime Minister in office.

There may be a valid distinction, however, between the Monarch's constitutional right to refuse a dissolution on the grounds that it would lead to a premature and unnecessary General Election and the now unsustainable claim by any Monarch to the right to impose a dissolution contrary to the wishes of the Prime Minister in office. In practice, of course, either form of royal initiative would run the serious risk of fatally discrediting the whole idea of constitutional Monarchy in this country. It would involve the Monarchy in apparently taking sides in the party battle and that would destroy its vital asset of political impartiality.

Notwithstanding the conventional wisdom on this matter, there are some conceivable circumstances in which the Queen might be justified in exercising the royal prerogative of dissolution in defiance of the wishes of the Prime Minister in office. For example, if it became clear in the course of a 'hung Parliament' that a minority government had outlived its usefulness and was simply standing in the way of a timely General Election which might produce a clearer parliamentary result, those who advise the palace on constitutional issues might be prepared to emphasise the arguments for such a dissolution. Such a course of action might also have to be considered if a government broke the most basic of electoral rules, namely the five-year maximum life-span of a Parliament, without the necessary all-party support for doing so, as existed, for example, during both World Wars.[1] It must be stressed, however, that these are all hypothetical circumstances which would be most unlikely to arise in modern political conditions.

If the Monarch did proceed along these lines, it is likely that she would win no more than a Pyrrhic victory, since such steps would almost certainly lead to a 'Monarch versus people' clash at the ensuing General Election which would probably be won by the aggrieved political party claiming to represent the will of the people. Even if that were not the outcome, the Monarch would incur the lasting hostility of the aggrieved political party, which could put in jeopardy the very continuation of our constitutional Monarchy. The practical conclusion, therefore, is that any Monarch in this country today has no sensible alternative to accepting the advice of the Prime Minister in office, whatever might appear to be the arguments for doing otherwise.

Assent to Legislation

Royal assent to legislation is another aspect of the Monarch's prerogative which has become purely formal over the years. In the seventeenth century Charles II managed to postpone or quash Bills of which he disapproved by the simple expedient of mislaying them. Queen Anne was the last British Monarch to veto legislation outright. George III and George IV both managed to delay legislation on Catholic emancipation by letting it be known that they were not happy with the idea. Yet today the royal assent is a mere formality and any attempt to make it otherwise would precipitate a constitutional crisis.

Creation of Peers

The Monarch has the power to create new peers and in certain cases it is believed that the palace still has some influence over the final selection from the various names proposed. Certainly there was a time when the use of this particular royal prerogative was formidable indeed. For example, in 1711 Queen Anne created 12 new peers precisely to ensure parliamentary ratification of the Treaty of Utrecht. In 1831 even William IV's threat (at the instigation of his Whig Prime Minister, Lord Grey) to create new peers helped to ensure the passage of the first Reform Bill, against fierce Tory opposition. In 1911 the willingness of George V to create as many as 400 new Liberal peers (discreetly made known by the Prime Minister, Herbert Asquith) caused the hereditary majority of Conservatives in the upper House to give way to the Liberal majority in the House of Commons over what was to become the 1911 Parliament Act.[2]

In contemporary circumstances the creation of new peers by the Monarch has become little more than a constitutional formality. Appointments to the peerage are normally made twice a year when the names of the newly-created peers appear in the Honours Lists. The appointments are made on the basis of advice given and co-ordinated by the Prime Minister in office, although anyone can make suggestions which are then discreetly sifted and assessed by a small unit of civil servants attached to 10 Downing Street before the Prime Minister of the day makes the formal recommendations.

Since 1964 life peerages have been the usual order of the day, mainly because successive Prime Ministers since that time have not felt generally inclined to recommend the creation of any more hereditary peerages. Yet this is no more than a convention of fairly recent times and as such it has always been capable of modification or abolition. For example, immediately after the 1983 General Election William Whitelaw and George Thomas were made hereditary peers on the recommendation of Margaret Thatcher. The former peerage was in recognition of Mr Whitelaw's long and distinguished service to the Conservative party and the nation, culminating in his period as deputy leader of the party since 1975. The latter was in recognition of Mr Thomas's distinguished period as Speaker of the House of Commons from 1975 to 1983. In each case the Queen complied with the Prime Minister's wishes, as is now customary in such matters, although the element of controversy in restoring the principle of hereditary peerages was reduced by the fact that William Whitelaw had only daughters and George Thomas was a bachelor. Even more recent departures from the modern norm in favour of life peerages were the granting of an hereditary earldom to Harold Macmillan in 1984 and the award of an hereditary Baronetcy to Denis Thatcher in 1990 in recognition of his important role in support of his wife when she was Prime Minister.[3]

Granting of Honours

The Monarch is also formally involved in the granting of honours, both civilian and military, to those whom it is customary for the nation to recognise and reward in this way. As with the creation of peerages, this usually happens twice a year when the Honours Lists are published. However there can be special investitures to recognise special events: for example, the honours awarded to those whose acts of conspicuous gallantry had been recognised during the 1982 Falklands campaign. On every occasion the system is a popular and effective way of recording public recognition for those who have made notable contributions to the well-being of British society and who have shone in various walks of life. It also adds lustre to the institution of Monarchy and provides regular opportunities for rewarding service to the community in a way which does not involve bribery or corruption.[4]

Nearly all such honours are awarded by the Monarch on the formal recommendation of the Prime Minister who, in turn, is advised by a small civil service unit attached to 10 Downing Street. Once again this unit sifts and assesses a wide range of recommendations made by MPs and others. Even so, a few honours have remained in the personal gift of the Monarch – for example, the Order of the Garter, the Order of the Thistle, the Order of Merit and the Royal Victorian Order. Usually these awards have no political significance, but are simply a way of signifying the Monarch's personal recognition of an outstanding person, such as Mother Theresa, the Catholic nun working for the hungry and the destitute in Calcutta, who was awarded the Order of Merit by the Queen on her visit to India for the 1983 Commonwealth Conference. Very occasionally such awards do have political significance, as was the case when the Queen awarded Margaret Thatcher the Order of Merit following her resignation as Prime Minister in 1990.

Public Appointments

The Queen plays a formal role in a vast range of public appointments, since all important posts in the civil service, the police, the judiciary, the BBC and the Church of England are filled in the name of the Monarch, not to mention, of course, the ministerial appointments in every government. Once again such appointments are usually made on the basis of advice given or co-ordinated by the Prime Minister, often with the help of the small civil service unit attached to 10 Downing Street which processes the recommendations from all quarters. Senior appointments in the diplomatic service are made on the advice of the Foreign Secretary, in the armed services on the advice of the Defence Secretary, in the police on the advice of the Home Secretary and in the judiciary on the advice of the Lord Chancellor. However, many other senior Ministers effectively have considerable power of public patronage which they exercise in the name of the Monarch and every Prime Minister takes a close personal interest in all the main appointments.

In these circumstances it is not surprising perhaps that some concern has been expressed from time to time about the nature and scope of such political patronage, which is royal in name but ministerial in fact.[5] A number of politicians – notably Tony Benn – and some journalists have been concerned about the lack of prior public scrutiny or subsequent democratic accountability of such public appointments, not to mention the implications for public expenditure in the wide range of public bodies to which such people are appointed. Yet this kind of political patronage has not led the critics to attack the Monarchy, since it is well understood that the Monarch is merely acting as a dignified rubber stamp for appointments which are not really within her control.

Mercy and Pardon

The prerogatives of mercy and pardon are still vested in the Monarch, who is entitled to exercise them on the advice of the Home Secretary of the day. Yet, since the House of Commons voted in 1965 to abolish the death penalty on a provisional basis and since that decision has subsequently been confirmed in successive free votes over the years, it now seems that this particular aspect of the royal prerogative has fallen into disuse. Pardons are granted only after conviction and sentence in rare cases when there is some special reason why a sentence should not be carried out or a conviction should be expunged – for example, a discovery that the evidence on which a conviction was based is actually false. Thus the exercise of this aspect of the royal prerogative has been both formal and rare.

Other Formal Functions

Several important, formal functions are exercised in the name of the Monarch, but actually by Ministers. These include important matters, such as the conclusion of international treaties, declarations of war, the introduction or amendment of colonial constitutions and the establishment of public corporations. In each case the Monarch is acting as a splendid and dignified veil for decisions which are actually taken by Ministers in the government of the day.

In the conduct of foreign policy the royal prerogative to conclude treaties enables Ministers to reach legally binding agreements with other governments or international organisations without having to secure the prior approval of Parliament. For example, the 1972 Treaty of Accession which took Britain into the European Community was signed by Edward Heath as Prime Minister in Brussels without the Government having had to secure the prior approval of Parliament at Westminster. Unlike the position in the United States, where treaties negotiated by the Administration have to secure the 'advice and consent' of the Senate before they can become American law, the position in Britain is that only if treaties have legislative consequences in the United Kingdom does the Government have to involve Parliament. Even then, this need only be done after a treaty has been signed by a Minister on behalf of the Crown.

A declaration of war is made officially in the name of the Monarch, although in the nuclear age such formalities would be of little real interest if time were very short. In the event of a war which directly affected this country, it would be for the Prime Minister and a few senior colleagues and military advisers to take all the key decisions. Such decisions would merely be made known to and ratified by the Monarch as and when appropriate. In the case of the 1982 Falklands conflict, Britain did not declare war upon Argentina, since there were compelling technical and legal reasons for not doing so in the light of our diplomatic efforts at the United Nations and elsewhere. Although the Queen was not therefore required to sign a declaration of war, she was kept informed by the Prime Minister at every stage of the conflict.

Colonial constitutions are promulgated or changed in the name of the Monarch. For example, the constitution of Zimbabwe, which British Ministers under Lord Carrington had negotiated with the representatives of all the parties at Lancaster House in 1979–80, was eventually promulgated in the name of the Queen and later given statutory authority in the Zimbabwe Independence Act of 1980.

The creation of public corporations is also done in the name of the Monarch through the granting of Royal Charters to the bodies concerned. For example, the BBC became a public corporation by Royal Charter in 1926. The various New Towns, such as Milton Keynes or Telford, which were built over the years since the Second World War, were established in a similar way, as were the new universities, for example in Sussex or Essex, which were built in the 1960s and 1970s.

Symbolic Functions

The Queen and other members of the royal family play an important symbolic role in many different ways. For example, the Queen and Prince Philip have made innumerable State visits to countries in all parts of the world ruled by all kinds of regime. She has also played an important role at successive Commonwealth Conferences and in entertaining foreign heads of state or government when they visit this country. In all such activities she and other members of the royal family are serving the national interest, as defined by the government of the day. More generally, the Monarch plays an important symbolic role as Head of the Commonwealth, a title to which she evidently attaches considerable personal significance. This has involved her and other members of the royal family in travelling thousands of miles to different parts of the world to see and be seen by millions of people in the 49 member nations of the Commonwealth. It has also led her to attach considerable personal importance to her annual Christmas broadcasts to the people of this country and the rest of the Commonwealth.

At home the Queen and other members of the royal family are involved by custom and tradition, and sometimes at the instigation of the Government, in the promotion of good causes and in various forms of public ceremonial designed to raise the morale or reinforce the unity of the British people. For example, the Queen usually leads the nation in paying respect to the dead of two World Wars, and other conflicts in which the British armed services have been involved, at the Cenotaph in Whitehall on Remembrance Sunday every year. She and other members of the royal family also pay conspicuous visits to all parts of the United Kingdom, including notably those where the people have suffered from natural disasters (as when hundreds of school children were killed by a coal-tip landslide at Aberfan in 1966) or been involved in serious social unrest (as in the inner city areas of London, Bristol and Liverpool after the 1981 riots). In these and many other ways the Monarchy makes a valuable contribution to the underlying cohesion and morale of the British people.

Unpublicised Functions

The Monarch also performs some unpublicised functions, the most notable of which are her regular and confidential conversations with every Prime Minister in office. On such occasions the Monarch still enjoys what Walter Bagehot once described as 'the right to be consulted, the right to encourage and the right to warn'.[6] In modern circumstances these rights are exercised during her private meetings with the Prime Minister every week when she is at Buckingham Palace and once a year for several days in the late summer when she is on holiday at Balmoral.

The Queen's experience of the affairs of state is now unrivalled in modern times, since in nearly 40 years on the throne she has had nine different Prime Ministers and 13 different governments. She has the undisputed right to see all state papers and in consequence she is almost certainly better informed about key political developments than virtually anyone else in the land. Her private advice to all Prime Ministers must be invaluable in view of the length and variety of her experience of matters of state. Indeed one former Prime Minister apparently accepted the analogy of paying a weekly visit to a psychiatrist and admitted that he could say things to the Queen that he could not say even to his closest political colleagues.[7] The functions of the Monarchy are summarised overleaf in Figure 9.1.

Figure 9.1 Functions of the Monarchy

● *In Parliament*

State opening of Parliament
Royal Assent to Bills
Dissolution of Parliament

● *Other formal functions*

Conclusion of treaties
Declaration of war
Introduction or amendment
  of colonial constitutions
Establishment of public
  corporations

● *Symbolic functions*

Head of the Commonwealth
State visits abroad
Entertaining foreign
  Heads of State in UK
Patronage of good causes
Visits to all parts of UK
Military ceremonial
Religious ceremonial

● *Political functions*

Choice of Prime Minister
Creation of peers
Granting of honours
Public appointments

● *Quasi-judicial functions*

Prerogative of mercy
Prerogative of pardon

● *Unpublicised functions*

Personal contacts with
  the Prime Minister
Confidential advice to
  the Government

9.2 Relations with the Public

Public Attitudes Towards the Monarchy

Although the Monarchy is probably the most revered of our national institutions, it would be a mistake to exaggerate the degree of deference shown towards it by ordinary British people. It tends to appeal more to women than to men and to those of a deferential disposition more than to those who value social equality. An opinion poll in 1969 demonstrated considerable public support for the Monarchy in that only 13 per cent thought it should be ended, 30 per cent thought it should continue as it was, and 50 per cent thought it should continue but change with the times (7 per cent had no opinion).[8] A more recent opinion poll in 1980 showed that the continuing popular appeal of the Monarchy is derived to a significant extent from the fact that it is usually projected to the people as the 'Royal Family', which 80 per cent of those questioned thought to be 'a marvellous example to everyone of good family life'.[9] The same poll also showed that 90 per cent of those questioned preferred the British Monarchy to a republic of the French or American type.

The criticism that the Monarchy is unduly privileged and fundamentally undemocratic cuts very little ice with anyone in Britain except a few dedicated republicans. Nearly all the British people realise and accept that the Monarchy is bound to be financially privileged and well off in other ways. Only 30 per cent of those questioned in the 1980 poll thought that the Monarchy cost the country more than it was worth. Another poll the following year revealed that 76 per cent of those questioned thought that the benefits of the Monarchy outweighed the costs.[10] Thus it seems clear that public attitudes are well disposed towards the Queen and her family. This degree of public support is unlikely to evaporate as long as the Monarch and her advisers recognise the conventions which limit her constitutional position and determine her room for manoeuvre.

Since in the modern television age there is always a risk that familiarity will diminish the respect traditionally shown to the Monarch, the Queen and her advisers have been careful to preserve the vital elements of glamour and mystery which have long enhanced the position of the Monarchy in the eyes of ordinary people. We need only reflect upon the brilliant way in which the 1977 Silver Jubilee celebrations or the 1981 Royal Wedding of Prince Charles and Princess Diana were organised to see that the royal family and its advisers have lost none of their flair for publicity and spectacular ceremonial. Such glittering events, as well as the more homely Christmas broadcasts by the Queen to the nation and the Commonwealth, have done much over the years to tighten the bonds of sentiment and loyalty between the royal family and the British public. On such a basis of affection and respect there seems little doubt that the British people will retain their positive attitudes towards the Monarchy for many years to come.

There is, however, a Marxist critique of the Monarchy which emphasises the part which it plays in holding the country together for the benefit of the ruling class with the clever use of national symbols and popular mystification. It is a thesis which in recent times has been expressed most vividly by Tom Nairn, who has written that 'the Monarchy is little more than the popular visage and social cement of Great Britain's unique version of capitalist development: the prolonged and baroquely gilded hegemony of early or commercial capital over all subsequent phases'.[11] The argument is that the conflicting class interests in British society are to some extent reduced by the widespread respect, even awe, which is felt by people in all walks of life towards the institution of Monarchy and especially the Monarch herself. This 'royal effect' is then intensified for millions of ordinary people by the way in which the mass media present every conceivable aspect of royal activity as a combination of soap opera and fairy tale. Precisely because this media portrayal of the Queen and her family makes them appear at once ordinary and extraordinary, it serves to reinforce a sense of national identity for all British people in all parts of the country and even for the British abroad as well. It provides glittering symbols of national unity, tradition and community which seem capable of anaesthetising what might otherwise become ugly social conflicts. To this extent Marxists regard the Monarchy as little more than a useful weapon in the armoury of the ruling class which has been used to good effect ever since Queen Victoria and her advisers managed to restore the popularity of the Monarchy in the mid-nineteenth century.

Financial Position of the Monarchy

The Queen now receives an annual sum of about £7.9 million of public funds averaged over the period 1991–2000 and allowances totalling about £1.9 million net are paid to the Duke of Edinburgh, the Duke of York, the Queen Mother, Princess Margaret, the Princess Royal and other active members of the royal family. A quarter of the revenue from the Duchy of Cornwall goes to the Prince and Princess of Wales (the other three-quarters goes to the Exchequer), while the royal residences (except for Balmoral and Sandringham), aircraft and yacht are all maintained from public funds. The royal family also has a very large private fortune which has been passed on from generation to generation free of death duties, as well as valuable collections of jewellery, stamps and pictures, some of which are put on show to the public.[12]

This privileged financial position is scarcely challenged, since the vast majority of people in this country believe that the Queen and her family perform their official duties with exemplary charm and efficiency. The few notorious critics of the Monarchy, such as Willie Hamilton, the former Labour MP, have tended to concentrate their criticism upon the cost of supporting the royal household and the somewhat anachronistic character of the Court and its courtiers. In general, however, such critical views are not widely shared. Successive governments have not been criticised for seeing that the Monarchy is adequately supported to enable it to carry out its constitutional duties without financial embarrassment. Indeed any well-founded attempt at a comprehensive cost–benefit analysis of the royal family would almost certainly show that it generates far more income in terms of revenue from foreign tourists and business orders consequential upon royal visits to other countries than it costs the British taxpayers.

Possible Future Problems

It would appear that the position of the Monarchy in Britain is secure both in constitutional terms and in the hearts and minds of the British people. Yet this might not always be the case in future if the Monarchy were to be faced with awkward constitutional problems which required new or unconventional solutions. As Hugo Young has suggested, there are at least three possible scenarios which could put the Monarchy in a difficult position.[13]

One possibility is that an unpopular Prime Minister might carry out a threat to call a General Election in mid-Parliament rather than agree under pressure from senior Cabinet colleagues either to change policy or even to resign the premiership. In such circumstances established political conventions would support the position of the Prime Minister, even if there appeared to be sufficient support in the governing party for a change of policy or even a new Premier or both. Whatever might be the private views of the Queen and her advisers, it seems clear that she would be obliged to grant the wish of the Prime Minister in office, however unpopular that might be with most of the governing party. It would therefore be for the governing party to sort out its own problems of policy and personality rather than for the Monarch to intervene in the dispute.

Another possibility is that a future Labour Government might be committed to the effective abolition of the House of Lords. Indeed, Labour's 1989 policy review suggested that the party will be committed at the next General Election to replacing the present House of Lords with a new Upper House elected by and from the members of newly established regional assemblies. In such circumstances much would depend upon whether the Monarch considered that the new Government had a clear mandate for such a far-reaching constitutional change. If so, she would probably conclude that she had no alternative but to go along with the idea. This would probably involve the creation of perhaps as many as 1000 new Labour peers, whose sole task upon having taken their seats in the House of Lords would be to vote for the Government's Bill designed to bring about their abolition. Yet it is not absolutely certain that the Queen would acquiesce in this procedure, since she might be convinced that the demise of the present House of Lords foreshadowed the demise of the Monarchy itself. In such a constitutional impasse the only way out might be to hold a national referendum on the issue, although even that would require the approval of a majority in the House of Commons, which might not be forthcoming in a Labour-dominated Lower House.

Yet another possibility, which is inherently more plausible, is that the outcome of a future General Election might well be a 'hung Parliament' in which no single party had an overall majority.[14] In such circumstances the Queen would be expected to send initially for the leader of the largest single party in the Commons who would then have to see whether he could form a minority government or arrive at some sort of understanding with one or more of the other parties. Either course would be quite plausible and it would only be in the unlikely event of complete parliamentary deadlock that the Queen might be advised to send for another party leader to form a viable government, rather than agree to an early dissolution very soon after the previous General Election.

The point is that, in any of these circumstances, the Monarch would be involved in some very awkward decisions which could have very far-reaching political consequences. Provided a decent interval had elapsed (about six months minimum), she would probably accede to a request for another General Election in order to allow the electorate to decide. Alternatively, she might charge a party leader with a conditional commission to form a government, which would depend upon his ability to demonstrate that he had the necessary parliamentary support for his Administration. Whatever happened, the Queen might be obliged to play a significant, even decisive, role in the process of government formation. This is not something which she or her advisers would relish, since it might well cast doubt upon the traditional impartiality of the Monarchy in party political matters. This, in turn, could damage the satisfactory relationship which has existed since Victorian times between the Monarchy and virtually all shades of parliamentary and public opinion.

9.3 Conclusion

The Monarchy still holds the supreme position at the apex of British society, yet it does so at the expense of its previous claims (before 1832) to wield real political power. Today it is the quintessence of all that is most dignified and dazzling in our constitutional arrangements. It serves as a powerful symbol of continuity and community which is particularly valuable to ,the nation in difficult or troubled times. In short, it has what Philip Ziegler has described as 'the twin appeals of stability and romance'.[15]

The Monarchy also provides an excellent example of the many paradoxes which abound in the British political system. It is an inherently conservative institution which can facilitate change. Whatever else may be altered, the Monarchy appeals to most people as an unchanging icon, a reassuring symbol. Such seemingly permanent and unchanging institutions can make it easier for people to accept even radical change in other areas of their lives. The Monarchy therefore plays an important part in preserving the cohesion of British society and it contributes significantly to the sense of underlying national unity which helps to hold the British people together. If it did not exist, it would probably have to be invented.

Suggested Questions

1. What are the functions of the British Monarchy?
2. Does the Monarch have any real power in Britain today?
3. Analyse the relationship between the Monarchy and the public.

Notes

1. The Parliaments elected in 1910 and in 1935 were each extended by all-party agreement, in the former case until the so-called 'khaki election' in 1919 and in the latter case until the 1945 election which took place soon after the agreed ending of the 1940 Coalition Government.
2. Some historians have argued that in 1831 the threat of the mob and in 1911 the threat of rebellion in Ireland also played a part in persuading the Conservative peers to give way to the Government of the day in the Commons.
3. Both of these hereditary peerages will continue, since in the former case Harold Macmillan's grandson became the new Earl of Stockton and in the latter case Mark Thatcher will succeed to the Baronetcy on the death of his father.
4. Although there have been occasions in the past when the honours system was abused for political purposes – for example, by Lloyd George as Prime Minister when Maundy Gregory was active on his behalf in offering peerages in return for financial support.
5. Among those who have expressed concern about this are Tony Benn in *Arguments for Democracy* (London: Jonathan Cape, 1981); and P. Holland and M. Fallon in *Public Bodies and Ministerial Patronage* (London: CPC, 1978).
6. W. Bagehot, *The English Constitution* (London: Fontana, 1978), p. 11.
7. A point made by Dr David Butler in correspondence with the author.
8. *The Sunday Times*, 23 March 1969.
9. In *Now*, 8 February 1980 (a weekly news magazine which later ceased publication).
10. *The Guardian*, 22 July 1981.
11. T. Nairn, *The Enchanted Glass* (London: Radius, 1988), p. 241.
12. In 1991 the annuities payable to the Monarch and other members of the royal family amount to about £9.8 million. Various estimates have also been made of the private wealth of the Queen ranging from £10 million to several billion pounds.
13. *The Sunday Times*, 8 November 1981.
14. See D. E. Butler, *Governing Without a Majority* (London: Collins, 1983), pp. 72–134, for a fuller discussion of the issues which could arise in a future 'hung Parliament'.
15. P. Ziegler, *Crown and People* (London: Collins, 1978), p. 199.

Further Reading

Bagehot, W., *The English Constitution* (London: Fontana, 1978).
Butler, D. E., *Governing Without a Majority* (London: Collins, 1983).
Hamilton, W., *My Queen and I* (London: Quartet, 1975).
Hitchens, C., *The Monarchy* (London: Chatto & Windus, 1990).
Martin, K., *The Queen and the Establishment* (Harmondsworth: Penguin, 1963).
Nairn, T., *The Enchanted Glass* (London: Radius, 1988).
Ziegler, P., *Crown and People* (London: Collins, 1978).

⬡10 The House of Lords

The House of Lords, which Walter Bagehot described in 1867 as one of the 'dignified' as opposed to the 'efficient' parts of the constitution, has had a long and varied history during which it has displayed considerable institutional resilience. However, since the 1832 Reform Act, its existence has been characterised by steadily declining political power, offset to some extent by its continuing political influence, especially in the Conservative party.

The 1911 Parliament Act laid the statutory basis for the present limitations upon the power of the Lords. This statute was really a constitutional package which affected both the Lords and the Commons. Its three main components were that Money Bills should become law within one month of being sent to the Lords, no other Bills could be delayed by the Lords for more than two years, and the maximum span of a Parliament should be reduced from seven to five years. Although the 1911 Act restricted the powers of the Lords, it did nothing to alter the composition or functions of the Upper House. Subsequently the 1949 Parliament Act further reduced the delaying power of the Lords to one year, but failed once again to deal with either its composition or functions.

Since then there have been three minor reforms affecting the House of Lords and one further attempt at major reform which failed in the face of fierce Commons opposition. In 1957 daily allowances were introduced for travel to and from and attendance at the House of Lords. In 1958 the Life Peerages Act made possible the creation of life peers (that is, peerages which cannot be inherited), including peerages for women in their own right. In 1963 the Peerage Act allowed hereditary peers to renounce their titles (while retaining the right to claim them at a future date or the right for their heir to inherit the titles), in order to make themselves eligible for election or re-election to the House of Commons.[1]

The one further attempt at major reform which failed was the ill-fated Parliament Number 2 Bill which was introduced by the Labour Government in 1968. This involved both a reduction in the total number of peers and an attack upon the hereditary principle. The essential proposals were that there should be a reformed second Chamber composed of 250 peers with voting rights who would be appointed by the government of the day, together with a larger number of peers who would have the right to speak but not to vote. The existing hereditary peers, who were not among those appointed to the voting category, would be allowed to remain in the non-voting category, although their heirs would not have had even that limited right. The appointed membership would have been reviewed from time to time and altered when necessary in order to ensure that the government of the day always had a voting majority over the principal opposition party, but not necessarily over all the other parties combined. The reformed body would have had a delaying power of six months and a number of other revising and burden sharing functions in dealing with legislation. In the event the proposals were abandoned by the Labour Government in 1969, in the wake of a sustained and effective filibuster by back-benchers on both sides of the Commons led by Enoch Powell and Michael Foot who opposed any reform of the Lords which might have strengthened it in relation to the Lower House.

10.1 Composition

In July 1989, 1185 peers were eligible to attend the House of Lords, although the average daily attendance in 1988–9 was only 317. Under a Standing Order adopted by the House in 1958 peers may apply for leave of absence for the whole or part of a session at any time during a Parliament and in July 1989 there were 152 peers in this category. Equally any peer who wishes to attend the House can do so, even if he has previously been granted leave of absence, provided only that he has received a writ of summons and has given one month's notice of his intention to do so.

Of the total of 1185 peers in the House of Lords in July 1989, 784 were hereditary peers and 354 were life peers. There were also 26 Bishops (including the Archbishops of Canterbury and York) and 21 Law Lords (including the Lord Chancellor and former Lords of Appeal). Twelve peers, who had inherited peerages, had disclaimed their titles for life under the provisions of the 1963 Peerage Act. The House is still, therefore, disproportionately hereditary in composition, even though the life peers tend to play a fuller and more regular part in the proceedings.

Hereditary Peers

The vast majority of hereditary peerages were created during this century and a significant number of them during the time when Lloyd George was Prime Minister (1916–22). Some peerages were created much longer ago – for example, the Dukedom of Norfolk in 1483, the Earldom of Shrewsbury in 1442 and the Barony of Mowbray in 1283 – and are still extant. Very few hereditary peerages have been created since 1964, because successive Prime Ministers since that time have been reluctant to recommend such honours to the Queen. Labour Prime Ministers have been ideologically opposed to the expansion of the hereditary peerage, while most Conservative Prime Ministers have not wanted to appear provocative on the issue. Yet there were notable departures from this custom and practice when, in June 1983, William Whitelaw and George Thomas were created hereditary peers on the recommendation of Margaret Thatcher and in February 1984, when Harold Macmillan finally accepted the hereditary Earldom which he had previously declined on ceasing to be Prime Minister in October 1963.

It should not be assumed that all hereditary peers are mere 'backwoodsmen', since some of them have played a distinguished part in government. For example, Lord Home was Foreign Secretary in the Governments led by Harold Macmillan and Edward Heath, Lord Shackleton was a senior member of Harold Wilson's Administration, and Lord Carrington was Defence Secretary in Edward Heath's Administration and Foreign Secretary in Margaret Thatcher's first Administration. The hereditary peerage has also produced some able and enthusiastic younger peers who have been useful and effective Ministers in successive governments.

Life Peers

All life peers have been created since 1958 and the vast majority of them have been distinguished men and women from many walks of life who have been honoured in recognition of their political or public services. They may be former civil servants or diplomats who retired at the top of their profession, distinguished soldiers, sailors or airmen who rose to the highest military ranks, successful industrialists or prominent trade union leaders, distinguished scientists or other academics, renowned actors or other figures from the world of the arts and the media. In April 1988 there were 47 women life peers, an increase compared with earlier years but still rather a small number.

By far the largest single category of life peers is composed of former politicians from the House of Commons or local government. In the former case, they tend to have been either retired Ministers or previously eminent back-benchers whom the Prime Minister of the day has wished to reward with a seat in the Lords and whose parliamentary skills can be kept in play in the Upper House. In the latter case, they tend to have been distinguished figures from the world of elected local government whose experience in that sphere is seen as an attribute for membership of the Lords. In both cases we can agree with Ian Gilmour, who observed that 'the House of Lords does something to reduce the hazards of a political career and embalms without burying a number of useful politicians'.[2]

Party Divisions

In May 1989 more than one-third of the total of 1185 peers took the Conservative whip and a further 246 were registered as Independents. This means that more than half of those who are eligible to attend are broadly in the Conservative camp, while many of the others are often sympathetic to the Conservative cause. By comparison, the numbers of Labour and Liberal peers are small, even insignificant. In May 1989 there were 116 Labour peers, 60 Liberal Democrats and 23 SDP peers. However the cross-benchers, who do not sit on either side of the House but at the end of the Chamber facing the woolsack, are an increasingly significant and influential group, representing as they do not only the interests of the law and the church, but also independent-minded laymen.

In any case party divisions in the Lords are not usually as sharp or bitter as they can be in the Commons and this is apparent in the relaxed and polite style of debate in the Upper House. Most of the speech-making and legislative work is done by perhaps 60 to 80 particularly active peers, although a larger number usually takes part in divisions. There have been occasions over the years when the natural Conservative majority has sought to amend or delay Labour Government legislation of which it disapproved and a surprising number of occasions on which similar treatment has been meted out to Conservative legislation. Yet, as we shall see, the Conservative peers have usually been rather careful (at any rate since the Second World War) not to use even the limited constitutional power which has been left to them in ways which would provoke a Labour Government or seriously embarrass a Conservative Government. This is essentially because they have recognised that such action could lead to major constitutional conflict and even perhaps to the eventual abolition of the Upper House.

10.2 **Powers and Functions**

Powers

The powers of the House of Lords have been steadily reduced over the centuries. Today they consist essentially of the power of legislative delay (that is, the ability to delay for about one year the passage of a Bill approved by the Commons), the power of legislative revision (that is, the ability to amend and improve a Bill inadequately drafted or considered by the Commons) and the power of well-informed deliberation (that is, the ability to debate the issues of the day in a better-informed and less partisan way than is often the case in the Commons).

The procedures of the 1911 and 1949 Parliament Acts, which confirmed the supremacy of the Commons over the Lords, have been used rather rarely. For example, the 1947 Parliament Bill became the 1949 Parliament Act under the procedures and powers which had been laid down in the 1911 Parliament Act. In 1974–6 the then Labour Government encountered temporary deadlock with the Conservative majority in the Lords over both the Trade Union and Labour Relations Amendment Bill and the Aircraft and Shipbuilding Industries Bill. In the latter case there had been complicated procedural arguments in the Commons about the 'hybridity' of the Bill which had cast doubts upon its constitutional validity and which had encouraged the Conservative peers to insist upon certain amendments which the Labour Government could not accept.[3] Although both Bills were reintroduced under the provisions of the 1949 Parliament Act, they subsequently became law in a form to which the Lords agreed after the Labour Government in the Commons had decided to make further amendments which went some way to meet the objections of the Conservative majority in the Upper House.

In 1980s, when a determined and sometimes highly ideological Conservative Government had a commanding position in the House of Commons, the House of Lords often asserted its constitutional independence. This is because peers taking the Conservative whip, who in any case are not in a numerical majority, often seemed out of sympathy with Margaret Thatcher's brand of ideological Conservatism and preferred the more pragmatic and paternalist approach of traditional postwar Conservatism. When such Conservative 'rebels' aligned themselves with Labour, centre party and cross-bench peers, they were able to defeat the Government on specific issues. For example, in March 1980 the Education (No. 2) Bill, which was later to become the 1981 Education Act, ran into trouble with their lordships on a clause which sought to allow Local Education Authorities to impose transport charges for children in rural areas. The proposal offended both rural and religious interests in the Upper House and in any case had been strongly attacked in the Commons when 13 Conservative MPs had voted against it and 16 more had abstained. The campaign was led in the Lords by the Duke of Norfolk, supported by two former Conservative Secretaries of State for Education, and in the end the Government was heavily defeated by 216 votes to 122, with no fewer than 40 Conservative peers voting against the Government and a further 28 abstaining. No further attempt was made to resurrect the clause and the Treasury was obliged to forego an estimated public expenditure saving of £20–30 million. In all, 10 significant defeats were inflicted upon the Conservative Government by the Lords in the 1979–83 Parliament. Most were on specific points of particular concern to their lordships – for example, the treatment of pensioners and the disabled, rural issues, respect for existing minority rights, and matters of constitutional etiquette.

During the 1983–7 Parliament further government defeats in the Lords ensued. For example, in June 1984 the Local Government (Interim Provisions) Bill, which provided the transitional arrangements for the abolition of the Greater London Council and the other Metropolitan Counties, gave rise to a decisive government defeat (by 191 votes to 143) on a Labour amendment to prevent the proposed cancellation of the 1985 council elections until the main abolition legislation had received royal assent. Since this would have involved too tight a timetable, the Government offered a compromise which allowed the existing Councils to continue for an extra year, but which still cancelled the elections due in 1985. The peers accepted this compromise by 248 votes to 155 in July 1984, so honour was satisfied in what was seen on both sides as a constitutional issue. Such examples clearly indicate that the Lords have been able to administer salutary and timely rebuffs to Labour and Conservative Governments alike. However, in the 1980s there seemed to be a greater likelihood that defeats in the Lords would be allowed to stand, at any rate on certain relatively minor issues which did not call into question any of the main elements of the Government's legislative programme.

Notwithstanding these small successes for the Upper House, the evidence suggests that the powers of the Lords in relation to the Commons are no longer of decisive significance. On the whole the effect of the 1911 and 1949 Parliament Acts has been to inhibit the Lords in the exercise of even the limited degree of power which the law and the conventions still allow. Essentially, as Andrew Adonis has pointed out, 'the peers are only concerned that proper procedures should be followed, that constitutional etiquette should be respected and existing rights be maintained where they are not incompatible with the Government's programme'.[4] In spite of the new-found self-confidence of the Lords in the 1980s, there is no good reason to question this judgement.

Functions

It is a paradox that, as the constitutional powers of the Lords have been steadily reduced over the years since 1911, their functions appear to have grown. The clearest exposition of the functions of the Lords was provided by the Bryce Commission in 1918.[5] It identified four main functions for the Upper House: legislative delay, legislative revision, the initiation of non-controversial legislation, and well-informed deliberation upon the issues of the day. To these four functions we must add the judicial function and the scrutiny functions. The former is performed by the Law Lords in not more than two relatively small Appellate Committees in nearly all cases. The latter are performed by peers from all parties who are appointed to committees specially established for the careful consideration of Private Bills, the scrutiny of delegated legislation flowing from Whitehall Departments, and the scrutiny of draft European legislation flowing from the European Commission in Brussels. The functions of the Lords are summarised in Figure 10.1.

Legislative Delay

In theory, the function of legislative delay is performed by the Lords when they refuse to approve legislation already passed by the Commons. In practice, since 1911 this function has been performed only sparingly, because the Conservative majority in the Upper House has been well aware of the danger that excessive use of this power could hasten the day when a future Labour Government might

Figure 10.1 Functions of the House of Lords

● **Legislative functions**

Legislative delay
Legislative revision
Initiation of non-
  controversial legislation

● **Judicial functions**

Hearing of appeals in
  the Appellate Committee
Hearing of appeals in
  the Judicial Committee
  of the Privy Council

● **Deliberative function**

Well-informed debate on
  the issues of the day

● **Scrutiny functions**

Private Bill Committees
Joint Committee on
  Statutory Instruments
Select Committee on
  the European Communities

decide to abolish the Lords altogether. For example, when the Conservative majority in the Lords opposed the 1947 Parliament Bill which was intended to reduce their delaying power from two years to one year, their opposition was little more than a political gesture and they did not really persist. Accordingly, the Bill duly became law two years later under the provisions of the 1911 Parliament Act.

In 1969, when the Conservative majority in the Lords insisted upon amendments to the House of Commons (Redistribution of Seats) No. 2 Bill, which was designed to free the Labour Home Secretary, James Callaghan, from the legal obligation to lay before Parliament the reports of the Parliamentary Boundary Commissions, the Bill was lost. This was an action which the Conservative peers felt perfectly justified in taking, since they considered that the Labour Government was involved in a cynical attempt to ensure that it fought the following General Election on outdated constituency boundaries which would improve Labour's election chances. In the event the Bill was not reintroduced by the Labour Government in the following session and the recommendations of the Boundary Commissions were eventually implemented by the new Conservative Government after the 1970 General Election.

In the 1974–9 Parliament the Conservative majority in the Lords sought only rarely to use its constitutional delaying power, notably when seeking to exclude ship repairs from the nationalisation provisions of the 1975 Aircraft and Shipbuilding Industries Bill. The legislation was reintroduced in the following session and subsequently became law in 1976 after the Labour Government had agreed to omit the ship-repairing clauses as the price of getting its Bill with the consent of the Lords in good time. As we have already seen, even Conservative Governments in the 1980s felt obliged to compromise with the Lords on certain issues when there were cross-party majorities in the Upper House against some of their measures, for example, rural education or local government reform. Although the majority in the Commons can always get its way in the end if it really wants to do so, on some issues at least modern governments have felt obliged to take account of opposition in the Lords and to respect the limited delaying power still available to the Upper House.

Legislative Revision

The function of legislative revision performed by the House of Lords has long been necessary, especially when dealing with complex or controversial government Bills. This is mainly because MPs very often make inefficient use of the time in Standing Committees when they are supposed to scrutinise and debate Bills clause by clause and line by line. The result is that there is often a need for legislative revision which falls upon the House of Lords, where many of the necessary amendments and new clauses are introduced by Ministers when the Government has had second thoughts about aspects of its own legislation. Sometimes this is a response to continuing pressure from interest groups which have lobbied for or against aspects of the legislation. Sometimes it is simply a matter of doing in the Lords what should have been done in the Commons, if there had been enough time to do so and if all parties when in opposition did not spend so much of the time in Committee simply filibustering on the early clauses of government Bills. This is therefore a function performed by the Lords which is essential to maintaining the quality of legislation and which ensures that the courts do not have to spend too much time subsequently clarifying via case law the original intentions of Parliament. If the Upper House did not perform this function, the Commons would be disinclined to do so, since it would probably oblige them to change their procedures in ways which would result in the emergence of a wholly professional and full-time Lower House.

Initiation of Non-controversial Legislation

The initiation of legislation which is largely non-controversial in party political terms is another useful function performed by the House of Lords. This has the effect of relieving the Commons of at least some of the legislative burden at the beginning of every session of Parliament. Indeed it has been estimated that since 1945 about one-quarter of all government Bills have been introduced in this way. This procedure is particularly appropriate with legislation which is both complex and technical, but which is not a source of fierce party political controversy, such as Bills on data protection or energy conservation. It is also popular with many of their lordships who like to get away from London to their estates or grouse moors well before 12 August every year, an aspiration which can be thwarted if the Upper House has to deal with too much legislation coming from the Commons during the second half of each session.

Deliberative Function

The deliberative function of well-informed debate upon the great issues of the day is another worthwhile aspect of the activities of the House of Lords. This is because the standard of debate and argument in the Upper House is often very high and because the issues are usually approached in a serious and relatively dispassionate way. Indeed the Lords can often find time to debate important and topical issues which might never get an airing in the more partisan and busy conditions of the Commons. In such debates the Lords can also draw upon the wealth of knowledge and experience which is available among their number, especially the life peers who include Fellows of the Royal Society and others of great intellectual and professional distinction. This is therefore one of the activities of the Lords which can have considerable influence in Whitehall and Westminster and upon the climate of informed opinion in the country as well.

Judicial Function

Formerly there was no restriction upon the participation of lay peers in the judicial proceedings of the House of Lords. However, after the O'Connell case in 1844, in which their intervention would have had the effect of overturning the decision of the Law Lords (that is, the Lord Chancellor, the Lords of Appeal and such peers as held or had held high judicial office in a superior court), it became an established convention that they should not take part in the judicial work of the House. Because of the ensuing shortage of peers who had held high judicial office, the 1876 Appellate Jurisdiction Act provided for the appointment of two Lords of Appeal and declared that appeals to the Lords should not be heard unless at least three Law Lords were present. In 1948 the Lords authorised (on a temporary basis at first) the hearing of appeals by an Appellate Committee drawn from the 11 appointed Law Lords and the other senior legal figures already mentioned. After a time this innovation became permanent, so that nearly all appeals to the House of Lords are now heard by the Law Lords sitting as either one or two Appellate Committees, depending upon the number of cases to be heard.[6]

Judgements on appeal to the Lords are still delivered by members of the Appellate Committee meeting in the Chamber, but since 1963 this has taken the form of written opinions from each individual judge. Usually appeals are heard by a committee of five judges and decisions are reached by majority. The judgements of the Law Lords have great authority and have influenced the development of English law over the years. For a long time the Law Lords regarded themselves as bound by legal precedents established in their earlier decisions, but since 1966 they have been prepared occasionally to modify that doctrine by departing from their previous decisions when it has appeared right to do so. This is, therefore, another vital function of the House of Lords, albeit one which is exercised by only a small committee on behalf of the House as a whole.

Scrutiny Functions

Finally there are the very important scrutiny functions of the House of Lords. These are exercised by special committees established for the careful consideration of Private Bills, the scrutiny of delegated legislation flowing from Whitehall Departments, and the scrutiny of draft European legislation flowing from the European Commission in Brussels.

Private Bills (which are Bills to alter the law relating to a particular locality or to confer rights or relieve liabilities from a particular person or class of persons) may be assigned to a committee of five peers for detailed consideration once the legislation has been through the earlier stages of public notification and Second Reading. Such committees have some of the attributes of quasi-judicial proceedings in that the promoters and opponents of Private Bills are usually represented by legal counsel and may call evidence in support of their arguments. Once this committee stage is successfully concluded, the Bill is reported to the House where its subsequent stages are similar to those of a Public Bill.

In the case of Whitehall-delegated legislation, the original Act may confine to the Commons the responsibility for the parliamentary control of the Statutory Instrument concerned, as it does in all fiscal measures. In most other instances the Lords have the same power of control as the Commons. Nevertheless it is rare for the Lords to exercise a legal veto over such subordinate legislation and on those occasions when they have attempted to do so there have often been adverse consequences for the Upper House. For example, in 1968, when the Lords unwisely rejected an Order under the 1965 Southern Rhodesia Act which contained provision for economic sanctions against the illegal regime in that territory, it caused the Labour Government to propose that the power of the Lords to veto Statutory Instruments should be abolished.

In most cases when Statutory Instruments are laid before the House, they come under scrutiny by the Joint Committee (of Lords and Commons) on Statutory Instruments, which consists of seven peers and seven MPs. The duty of the Committee is to consider whether the attention of Parliament should be drawn to a particular Statutory Instrument on any of a number of different grounds – for example, that it would impose a charge upon public funds, that it would be retrospective in effect, that it has been unjustifiably delayed, or that there was doubt as to whether it would be *intra* or *ultra vires*. In short, the Committee may report on a Statutory Instrument on any technical ground which does not impinge upon its merits or the policy behind it. Very few Statutory Instruments are referred to Parliament in this way for further debate, although all those subject to the negative procedure and those subject to the positive procedure which are reported upon unfavourably can be 'prayed against', that is, made the subject of a critical motion put down by MPs or peers for debate on the floor of either House. The main effect of this procedure, in which peers play a full part, is to keep Whitehall officials up to the mark by discouraging them from drafting sloppy or unjust delegated legislation.

As for parliamentary scrutiny of European secondary legislation, committees of each of the two Houses have been in existence since 1974 with scrutiny functions similar to those of the committees which deal with national Statutory Instruments. The House of Lords Select Committee on the European Communities more than matches the House of Commons Select Committee on European Secondary Legislation and is indeed unrivalled in its expertise and depth of scrutiny of European Community affairs. Both of these committees are constantly involved in the scrutiny of European Commission proposals at the draft stage and both may report to their respective Houses with recommendations that particular proposals be debated on the floor of the House. Thus the Lords play a leading part in this increasingly important area of parliamentary control.

The Impact of Television

Whatever the range of powers and functions with which the Lords may be entrusted, Janet Morgan was surely right to point out that 'it is only by monitoring their own behaviour and remaining sensitive to their image in the world outside that they can avoid infringing a web of sanctions explicitly formulated or implicitly understood'.[7] The decision of the Lords in June 1986 to allow the televising of their proceedings on a permanent basis has enhanced the peers' self-confidence about their future and probably their image in the eyes of the public as well. With a regular late-night audience on Channel 4 of 300 000 and a further 200 000 watching a repeat the following afternoon, it is generally believed – at least by their lordships – that this degree of public interest in their proceedings will reduce the pressure for reform or abolition of the Upper House. Only time will tell, and in any case we shall explore the various proposals for the future of the Lords in the following section.

10.3 Proposals for Change

There is a lively and continuing debate about the future of the House of Lords which has taken place within and between all political parties. The Conservatives who are interested in this matter have tended to press for reform of the Upper House in order to strengthen and entrench its position in relation to the Commons. The Labour party has wavered over the years between a wish to reform it and a wish to abolish it. At present it seems to be committed to the idea of transforming it into an assembly composed of representatives elected by or drawn from the various regional assemblies which it proposes to establish if it is returned to power. The minor parties have come forward with a variety of fairly similar reform proposals, most of which would be designed to form part of a wider constitutional settlement. Yet, for as long as the Conservatives remain in office, the likelihood is that the Lords will remain largely unaltered.

Conservative Proposals

Traditionally the Conservative party has been quite interested in reforming the House of Lords, since it has seen such ideas as a way of putting the Upper House on a more secure constitutional basis. Winston Churchill and L. S. Amery were among those who flirted in the 1920s with the idea of turning the Lords into a more functional body capable of directly representing both sides of industry as well as the hereditary peerage.[8] In the late 1940s and early 1950s the Marquess of Salisbury, as the Conservative leader in the Lords, concentrated upon encouraging his noble colleagues to exercise political self-restraint, especially when they faced the radical postwar Labour Government. For example, agreement was reached not long after the 1945 General Election that the Upper House, with its overwhelming Conservative majority, would not divide on the Second Reading of any Government Bill which had been foreshadowed in the 1945 Labour Manifesto.

It was not until the 1970s that serious reform proposals were forthcoming once again from the Conservative side. In 1977 Lord Carrington, then Conservative leader in the Lords, proposed the creation of a reformed second Chamber whose members would have been elected by proportional representation from large regional constituencies. His argument was that such a Chamber would reflect public opinion rather differently from the Commons, since the type of constituencies, the method of election and the timing of the elections would all have been different from those of the Lower House. His main objective was to produce a reformed second Chamber with sufficient democratic legitimacy to survive and prosper as a constitutional check or counterweight to the House of Commons. In 1978 a Conservative committee chaired by Lord Home produced another set of reform proposals which recommended that the membership of the Lords should be reduced to about 400, of which one-third would have been nominated by the political parties and two-thirds elected on a basis of proportional representation from about 250 large territorial constituencies. Neither of these proposals or anything resembling them was implemented then or since. This is mainly because the Conservatives in the Commons have never given a high priority to Lords reform and because the vast majority of the Conservative party in the Commons is opposed to the introduction of proportional representation.

Labour Proposals

Traditionally the Labour party has been less interested in reform than in abolition of the House of Lords. Indeed it has been nominally committed to the abolition of the Lords in their present form since 1934. However, under the influence of R. H. S. Crossman when Leader of the House in the 1960s, the then Labour Government did propose a far-reaching and complicated reform of the Upper House which was embodied in the 1968 Parliament No. 2 Bill to which reference has already been made in this chapter.[9] Since that time the Labour party in the Commons has shown little interest in reforming the House of Lords and it has only been fairly recently that the Labour leadership has begun to show interest in the idea of transforming the present Upper House into an elected Chamber representing principally the interests of the various regions of the United Kingdom, somewhat along the lines of the *Bundesrat* in the Federal Republic of Germany.[10]

Centre Party Proposals

As might be expected from smaller parties which do not do particularly well out of the British political system at present, both the centre parties have favoured the principle of reforming the House of Lords as part of a wider package of electoral and constitutional reform. The Liberal Democrats believe that the present Upper House should be replaced with a new democratically elected second Chamber which would include representatives of the various 'nations' within the United Kingdom (that is, Scotland and Wales) and the various 'regions' of England, as well as some members of the European Parliament.[11] The even smaller Owenite Social Democratic party seems to favour replacing the present House of Lords with a new second Chamber consisting of some members indirectly elected for fixed terms by new regional assemblies and other members appointed for life by the government of the day.[12] In such cases there is a strong temptation to regard these ideas as of academic interest only.

10.4 Conclusion

The debate between those who would like to reform the House of Lords and those who would like to abolish it seems certain to continue. Yet if the Conservative party remains in office, it seems unlikely that any changes will be made. If the Labour party were to win power at the next General Election, much would depend, as before, on the priority which the incoming government gave to this type of institutional reform. It is only if the outcome of the next election were to be a 'hung Parliament', in which the Liberal Democrats were in a position to strike a hard bargain with one of the main parties, that reform of the House of Lords might come about as part of a wider attempt to reach a new constitutional settlement.

The essential choices facing those who consider the future of the House of Lords are either to reform and strengthen it or to leave it alone or to abolish it altogether and go for a unicameral Parliament. If the Conservative party were seriously to contemplate the possibility of losing power at a future General Election, it ought to recognise its interest in reforming the Lords by putting it on a more democratic basis in order to strengthen the constitutional position against possible attack from a future Labour Government. The smaller parties also have a clear interest in the reform of the Lords, but only as part and parcel of the wider constitutional settlement which they favour. Even the Labour party, which used to have an interest in the preservation of the Lords exactly as it is, since this would have strengthened the case for total abolition, now seems more likely either to leave it alone (because of more pressing political priorities) or to reform its composition, powers and functions along the lines already indicated.

Many years ago Peter Bromhead wrote that 'so long as the House of Lords continues by the exercise of voluntary restraint to perform a restricted function in the exercise of political power, there is . . . little reason for altering either its powers or its composition'.[13] Such a complacent view might still make sense today, provided everyone were content that the House of Lords be left alone as a dignified and relatively unimportant anachronism. Yet plainly the Upper House cannot now be so easily ignored, especially on the basis of its performance in the 1970s and 1980s. It may no longer be anything like co-equal with the House of Commons, but it has proved itself capable of providing what Andrew Adonis has described as 'a forum and focus for expert opinion and a dedicated revising Assembly'.[14] In this limited capacity it plays a notable part in the British political system. If it did not exist, it would almost certainly need to be replaced with an institution of comparable purpose and utility.

Suggested Questions

1. Analyse the composition of the House of Lords in Britain today.
2. How well does the House of Lords perform its various functions?
3. Assess the relative merits of reforming or abolishing the House of Lords.

Notes

1. The 1963 Peerage Act was the direct result of the efforts of Tony Benn, then Viscount Stansgate, who was determined to get the law changed so that he and other peers would no longer be disqualified from standing for election to the House of Commons.
2. I. Gilmour, *The Body Politic* (London: Hutchinson, 1969), p. 302.
3. A 'hybrid Bill' is defined in Erskine May (p. 862) as 'a public Bill which affects a particular private interest in a manner different from the private interests of other persons or bodies of the same category or class'.
4. A. Adonis, 'The House of Lords in the 1980s' in *Parliamentary Affairs*, vol. 41, no. 3, July 1988, p. 397.
5. See Report of the Bryce Commission, Cd 9038 (London: HMSO, 1918).
6. The only appeals heard by the House of Lords as a whole are those which happen to be ready between the beginning of the Michaelmas legal term and the autumn parliamentary 'overspill' session – that is, between the beginning of October and the brief period from the end of that month onwards when the Upper House often has to sit to complete its consideration of Bills sent from the Commons.
7. J. P. Morgan, *The House of Lords and the Labour Government, 1964–79* (Oxford: Clarendon Press, 1975), p. 8.

8. See L. P. Carpenter, 'Corporatism in Britain, 1930–45' in the *Journal of Contemporary History*, no. 11 (1976) pp. 9–14; and references to 'Industry and the State' published in 1927 by Harold Macmillan and others.
9. See the introductory paragraphs of this chapter for a description of the Bill.
10. The 1989 Labour Policy Review included a proposal to establish perhaps five regional assemblies in England to match new national assemblies in Scotland and Wales which (together with suitable arrangements for Northern Ireland) would provide the representatives in a reformed Upper House at Westminster.
11. See the Liberal Programme 1982, p. 6.
12. See the Social Democratic Green Paper No. 3 published in 1982.
13. P. A. Bromhead, *The House of Lords and Contemporary Politics* (London: Routledge & Kegan Paul, 1958), p. 16.
14. A. Adonis: *Parliament Today* (Manchester University Press, 1990), p. 168.

Further Reading

Adonis, A., *Parliament Today* (Manchester University Press, 1990), pp. 127–68.
Bagehot, W., *The English Constitution* (London: Fontana, 1978).
Bromhead, P. A., *The House of Lords and Contemporary Politics* (London: Routledge & Kegan Paul, 1958).
Longford, Lord, *A History of the House of Lords* (London: Collins, 1988).
Morgan, J. P., *The House of Lords and the Labour Government, 1964–70* (Oxford: Clarendon Press, 1975).
Norton, P. (ed.), *Parliament in the 1980s* (Oxford: Basil Blackwell, 1985).
Shell, D., *The House of Lords* (Oxford: Philip Allan, 1988).

(11) The House of Commons

Unlike the Monarchy or the House of Lords, the House of Commons still has real power in the British political system, provided it is willing and able to use it. Yet the nature of its power is different from what it was in the nineteenth century, when most of the traditional notions about the House of Commons were established. The modern House of Commons is neither the Government of the country nor even the principal place where most of the decisions or legislation are conceived. It is essentially the stage upon which the party battle is fought, the sounding-board for popular representation and redress, the proving ground for Ministers and shadow Ministers, and the principal forum within which legislation and other decisions of government are criticised and assessed between periodic General Elections.

The essential purposes of the House of Commons have not changed significantly since the last quarter of the nineteenth century. W. I. Jennings described them as being 'to question and debate the policy of the Government and in doing so to bring home . . . the unpopularity (or popularity) of a particular line of policy'.[1] L. S. Amery described them as being 'to secure full discussion and ventilation of all matters . . . as the condition of giving its assent to Bills . . . or its support to Ministers'.[2] Such descriptions are still broadly valid today.

11.1 Composition

The present House of Commons is composed of 650 members elected on a uniform franchise from single-member constituencies of about 67 000 electors on average. The Speaker and his three deputies, who are all elected MPs, take no partisan part in the proceedings (unless a vote is tied, in which case they are expected to vote for the *status quo*), since they are responsible in the chair for seeing that the rules of order are maintained. Of the remaining 646 MPs in July 1989, 372 were Conservative, 228 Labour, 19 Liberal Democrats, 13 Ulster Unionists of various kinds, 4 Scottish Nationalists, 3 Social Democratic and Labour (Parliamentary Irish Republicans), 3 Plaid Cymru (Welsh Nationalists), 3 Owenite Social Democrats, and 1 Provisional Sinn Fein (Revolutionary Irish Republican).

MPs as Representatives

MPs can be seen as more or less representative in two quite different senses. In one sense, we can consider the educational and occupational characteristics of individual MPs. This shows that all sorts and conditions of men and a few women can be found among their number. We can illustrate the point using figures derived from the 1987 General Election results. For example, 99 per cent of Conservative and 70 per cent of Labour MPs came from middle-class or professional backgrounds (when elected), while only 1 per cent of Conservative and 30 per cent of Labour MPs came from working-class backgrounds on the same basis. Of all MPs, 80 per cent had experienced higher or further education and 34 per cent had been to university at Oxford or Cambridge (this latter figure marked a small decline compared with five years before). Of Conservative MPs, 23 per cent have been educated at Clarendon schools (the original nine public schools), as had 3 per cent of Labour MPs, although a significant proportion from each main party had had the advantage of a grammar school education, which has traditionally provided one of the main ladders of opportunity for children from humble backgrounds who are determined to get on and break into middle-class occupations. Thus MPs as a whole are still something of an elite in educational and occupational terms, although increasingly less so when compared with the position in earlier years. As the middle class as a whole has become larger, so the middle-class contingent of MPs has become larger. At the same time the influence of the top public schools and Oxbridge has continued to decline, even in the Conservative party, to a point where we can see a clear social convergence between the parliamentary representatives of both main parties. This has served greatly to diminish the presence of MPs from either end of the social spectrum.

In another sense, we can consider the extent to which the composition of the Commons reflects the composition of the electorate as a whole and especially those sections of the population which traditionally have been under-represented in nearly all our representative institutions.[3] The most obvious example of a disproportion between representation at Westminster and the population as a whole is provided by that of women, who account for 52 per cent of the electorate but only a miserable 6 per cent of all MPs. In the past this has been largely due to the prejudices of Conservative women on constituency selection committees who seem opposed to choosing one of their own sex as a candidate for a winnable seat, and the male chauvinism of traditional Labour activists when choosing candidates for winnable Labour seats. However there are now some signs of a greater willingness – at least on the part of the Labour leadership – to urge the choice of women candidates for Parliament (especially at by-elections), and it may be that the example of Margaret Thatcher's leadership of the Conservative party will have led Conservative constituency women into dropping their hostility to women candidates for Parliament. Equally (as we have already noted in Chapter 3) those who vote for national third parties, such as the smaller centre parties which used to make up the Alliance, are almost as seriously penalised, in this instance by the 'unfair' working of the British electoral system which meant that, at the 1987 General Election, 23 per cent of the votes cast produced only 3 per cent of the seats in the Commons. Furthermore some groups in the electorate are not directly represented at all in the House of Commons – for example, those under 24 and over 80 years old. On the other hand, certain groups seem to be over-represented, notably lawyers, consultants and company directors in the Conservative party; and lecturers, journalists and public-sector workers in the Labour party. Of course, many MPs develop a wide range of interests during their time in the House and this can turn them into very adequate 'virtual representatives' of otherwise under-represented categories in the electorate.[4]

Front-benchers

Paid office-holders in the present Conservative Government (who are entitled to sit on the front bench) make up about 90 out of more than 370 Conservative MPs.

This figure includes 14 Government Whips who draw lower ministerial salaries, but do not speak in the House or act as Ministers in government Departments. The so-called payroll vote (that is, those who are expected to support the Government on all occasions) is supplemented by about 40 Parliamentary Private Secretaries (PPSs), who do not sit on the front bench but who are connected with the Government in that they perform various unpaid tasks for the individual Ministers whom they serve. The Conservative Cabinet in July 1989 had 22 members, of whom 20 were drawn from the Commons, since only the Lord Chancellor and the Leader of the Lords sat in the Upper House.

On the opposition side, the Labour Shadow Cabinet is made up of 20 senior members of the parliamentary party. It is composed of the Leader, the Deputy Leader, the Opposition Chief Whip, the Chairman of the Parliamentary Labour party, the Leader of the Opposition in the Lords and 15 others drawn from the party in the Commons who are elected each year by their colleagues in the parliamentary party. When the Conservative party is in opposition, the members of the Shadow Cabinet are all appointed by the Leader. Junior to the Shadow Cabinet there are about 40 to 50 other opposition spokesmen who are appointed by the Leader to share the front-bench duties of shadowing the various government Departments. In addition, there are about 10 Opposition Whips, including the Opposition Chief Whip and his assistants, who, together with the Leader of the Opposition, are the only members of the Opposition to receive additional salaries from public funds for their parliamentary responsibilities.

Back-benchers

The other 430 or so MPs are all back-benchers who have no direct involvement in government or in the tasks of front-bench opposition.[5] Some are senior, have been in the House a long time and wield a good deal of influence within their parties. A few carry weight in the House as a whole. However most back-benchers are relatively junior, have been in the House for less than 10 years and try to make their way in politics as well as they can. Usually this means that they seek to attract the attention and approval of the party Whips by playing an active part in proceedings both in the Chamber and in Committee 'upstairs'.

The principal duty of back-benchers when their party is in government is to support it with their votes and, to a lesser extent, with their voices in question time and debate. When their party is in opposition their principal task is to attack the Government on every suitable occasion, both in the Chamber and in Committee 'upstairs'. Occasionally some back-benchers choose a more notorious and difficult path by becoming rebels within their own party. Others come to be seen as mavericks or eccentrics. Such deviant behaviour is not normally recommended for those who wish to attain ministerial office, unless they are particularly lucky or clever in staking out ground on which to defy their party's orthodoxy.

The life of a back-bencher in the modern House of Commons is usually more fun in opposition than in government. This is because, in the former case, there are many more opportunities to play a prominent part in the party battle and to catch the attention of the party leadership. It is also because nothing said or done by opposition back-benchers matters very much and such politicians can therefore enjoy the luxury of considerable irresponsibility. When their party is in government, back-benchers have to tread the narrow path between sycophancy and rebellion and they can be forgiven for thinking that all the Whips really want is their presence in the division lobbies in support of the Government at the appointed times. Certainly junior back-benchers in both main parties have cause to complain about the privileges given to Privy Councillors (that is, very senior back-benchers, nearly all of whom have held ministerial posts at an earlier stage in their careers) and to the spokesmen of minor parties, since both categories are more likely to be called in debates and to catch the Speaker's eye at Question Time. This is mainly a reflection of the seniority principle which influences the pecking order at Westminster and indeed in most other Parliaments around the world. It is also a reflection of the well-established Westminster convention that the Speaker should try to ensure a hearing for minority points of view and indeed for dissidents within the main parties as well. For example, a back-bencher who intends to abstain or vote against his party will normally be given a chance to explain his intentions during the course of the debate.

Pay and Conditions

All MPs receive a parliamentary salary from public funds (£28 970 in 1991), together with a range of parliamentary allowances for secretarial help and research (just over £27 000 a year in 1991). Ministers receive various salaries according to their level in the Government (ranging in 1991 from just over £50 000 for the Prime Minister to just over £20 000 for a Parliamentary Secretary), as well as a proportion of their parliamentary salaries (about £22 000 in 1991) in recognition of the fact that they have the same duties towards their constituents as their back-bench colleagues.

Apart from the Speaker and his three deputies, the only MPs not in the Government who have additional salaries paid from public funds are the Leader of the Opposition (about £35 000 in 1991), the Opposition Chief Whip (about £27 000 in 1991) and the Assistant Opposition Whip (about £17 000 in 1991). These financial arrangements symbolise the long-standing commitment to the concept of constitutional opposition and give financial expression to the traditional idea of 'Her Majesty's Loyal Opposition'. Indeed Britain was the first parliamentary democracy to make such arrangements for leading members of the Opposition in recognition of their constitutional duty to oppose the government of the day.

The conditions of work for MPs have improved over the last decade or so, although many of the arrangements reflect the lingering amateurism which still characterises so many of the traditional habits and assumptions of politicians at Westminster. For example, when the Chamber was rebuilt after the Second World War, it was decided to leave the size and shape as it had been before the German bomber attack, namely rows of opposed benches and a total seating capacity for no more than about three-quarters of those entitled to take a seat. This was done in order to reflect both the combative nature of the proceedings and the conversational, occasionally intimate atmosphere of many debates.

Equally there is still a shortage of suitably equipped office premises for individual MPs and many have to make do with a desk, telephone and filing cabinet in a room shared with several of their colleagues. This will change when the new parliamentary building in Bridge Street is complete in the early 1990s, now that MPs seem to have overcome their previous fears about the likely public reaction to their voting large sums of public money to improve their own facilities.[6] The traditional approach to these matters has reflected the fact that every British government prefers to deal with a traditional House of Commons composed of amateur and part-time MPs, rather than professional and full-time politicians able to monitor the Executive on more equal terms. Furthermore many MPs now have such a burden of constituency work and committee responsibilities that they spend little time in the Chamber, except when present for questions or for particular debates in which they hope to intervene. This has changed somewhat with the televising of the Commons which has lured many more MPs into the Chamber in order to be seen in action by their constituents and the general public. Nevertheless it remains true that MPs have had to perform an increasingly varied and arduous range of political tasks in physical conditions which have been largely unchanged since the late nineteenth century.

11.2 Principal Powers

The powers of the House of Commons are diffuse, variable and rather difficult to define. They are not set out in any single document or defined in any court rulings. In cases of dispute the most reliable guide is Erskine May, the reference book which covers the whole of parliamentary procedure according to the precedents established over the centuries by successive Speakers and codified by successive Clerks of the Commons.[7]

Theory and Practice

In theory, the House of Commons has very great power in our British constitution. This could be said to include the power to make and unmake governments, to topple Prime Ministers, to safeguard the liberties of British citizens, to bring to light and remedy injustices, and even to legislate itself out of existence and the country into a dictatorship.

In practice, the power of the Commons is usually subsumed in the power of the government of the day, which rules through Parliament as long as it retains the voting support of its party majority in the Commons. It is therefore misleading to refer to the powers of the Commons in any way which implies that such powers are separate or distinct from those of modern single-party government. In normal parliamentary conditions, when one of the main parties has an overall majority in the Commons, the power of the House as a representative institution is wielded mainly by the official Opposition in its constant efforts to draw attention to the shortcomings of government policy and to criticise, delay and occasionally obstruct the course of government legislation. There is, however, an important, if delicate role for government back-benchers, as representatives of those in the electorate who voted for the party in office and as occasional critics of government policy when they believe that it is falling short of party commitments or public expectations.

Only on very rare occasions since 1945 has the power of the House of Commons really made itself felt. One famous earlier example was in May 1940, when the result of a vital confidence debate led Neville Chamberlain to resign as Prime Minister and so make way for Winston Churchill to succeed him as this country's wartime leader. A more recent example was in March 1979, when at the end of another confidence debate the opposition parties united to defeat the then

Labour Government and so precipitated the May 1979 General Election which brought the Conservatives to power. On the whole, however, such examples of parliamentary power have been rare in modern times and most governments have got their way in Parliament most of the time, at any rate on the issues which really mattered.[8]

The Power of Influence

In most normal circumstances the House of Commons has to rely upon the power of influence – that is, influence upon the politicians in government, influence upon the policies of Government and influence upon political opinion in the country. Effective influence in the Commons is frequently exerted in a discreet manner before the event, whether in party committees or in private conversation. On the other hand, the exercise of overt parliamentary power is usually confined to the rare occasions when the authority of a Minister or the Government as a whole is in jeopardy. For example, when it became clear at the beginning of April 1982 that Ministers in the Foreign Office and the Ministry of Defence had lost the confidence at any rate of the vast majority of the Conservative party in the immediate aftermath of the Argentinian invasion of the Falklands, Lord Carrington and most of his ministerial team at the Foreign Office resigned and John Nott at the Ministry of Defence offered his resignation, which was only refused at the time by Margaret Thatcher because the nation was by then effectively at war. In crude and capricious parliamentary conditions this was a graphic example of the power of the Commons. More recently, Nicholas Ridley, as Secretary of State for the Environment from 1987 to 1989, became increasingly unpopular with Conservative voters – and hence with Conservative back-benchers – because of his apparent disdain for many of the shibboleths of 'green' politics. This message was conveyed with increasing intensity by Conservative back-benchers via the Whips to Mrs Thatcher during the summer of 1989, with the result that she was left with no alternative but to move Mr Ridley from the Department of the Environment in her July 1989 Cabinet reshuffle.

The defeat of the Callaghan Government in March 1979 exemplified something rather different. In that case the Labour Government had really sown the seeds of its own destruction when it had brought forward its proposals for legislation on devolution which proved unacceptable both to a significant minority of its own back-benchers and to the minor parties. This was bound to be disastrous at a time when the Labour Government had lost its overall majority in the Commons and could only continue in office as long as it proceeded on a basis which was broadly acceptable to all these disparate elements.

Over the period since 1945 such examples of real parliamentary power have been rare. At most General Elections the electorate has voted and the electoral system has worked in such a way as to ensure that one of the main parties has had an overall majority in the Commons large enough to withstand most back-bench rebellions and the erosion which takes place through death and retirement during the normal span of a Parliament. In such circumstances the power of the Commons has not normally been manifested in successful attempts to censure Ministers, still less to defeat governments. Instead it has been exercised through constant back-bench influence upon Ministers, and through the constant interplay between governments striving to get their legislation through Parliament and oppositions striving to criticise and delay them in doing so.

Parliamentary culture

The House of Commons has often been described as 'the best club in London'. If this is so – and there would be many members of Whites or the Garrick to challenge it – it says a good deal about the atmosphere within which its business is conducted. It is an atmosphere in which the cut and thrust of the party battle is balanced by a political camaraderie which often makes it easier to form friendships across the floor of the House than with other members on the same side. It is an institution which relies upon the pretence that all its members are 'honourable' and that all are equal in terms of their democratic legitimacy. Yet, in an institution in which there are supposed to be no second-class members, it is remarkable how some are more equal than others, and how front-benchers and Privy Councillors seem to be able to play all the best parts. The main explanation, of course, is that the traditional procedure, much of which dates from the 1880s, assumes that debate and discussion will be conducted largely by the parliamentary giants of the day and that the rest will be content with minor roles as spear-carriers or cheer-leaders. This established tendency is reinforced by the simple fact that the Chamber itself is rather small (deliberately so) and that no more than about three-quarters of those entitled can possibly find a seat on the green benches when the House is full – for example, on Budget Day or for the opening speeches by the Prime Minister and the Leader of the Opposition on the first day of the debate on the Queen's Speech. In short, there are only a limited number of opportunities for MPs to shine during prime parliamentary time at Westminster, and most of these are taken by senior Ministers or their 'shadows' on the opposition front bench.

Another interesting aspect of parliamentary culture in the House of Commons is the extent to which the institutionalised party conflict is organised, even ritualised, by the party Whips working through what are known as 'the usual channels'. This phrase is a euphemism for the sometimes heated and vigorous discussions which take place every day that the House is sitting behind the scenes and off the record between the Leader of the House and the Chief Whip for the Government and the Leader of the Opposition and the Opposition Chief Whip for the official Opposition. Without the benefit of these discussions, which often include Ministers, Whips and their opposite numbers on the opposition front bench, the whole place would probably grind to a halt. As it is, the essential deal between the two sides is based upon two assumptions: that the Government must get its business done (that is, get through its legislation more or less intact) and that the Opposition must have its full opportunities to oppose and, within limits, to decide what is urgent or newsworthy and what is uncontentious or acceptable and hence a suitable subject for full co-operation. In support of this generally pragmatic approach to the conduct of parliamentary business is the basic British idea that it is the duty of Her Majesty's Loyal Opposition to oppose the government of the day, and the understanding that there are few problems which cannot be solved by the Whips on each side acting in tacit co-operation.

Indeed the co-operative principle is reflected in the attitudes and behaviour of individual MPs who all strive very hard, as soon as they get to Westminster, to secure 'a pair' – that is, a member on the other side who will agree on specific occasions to stay away from the division lobbies when the votes are called, so that the overall result of the vote is not affected. Such 'pairing' is an invaluable practice for those with long parliamentary careers and can serve to mitigate what is otherwise the tedium and exhaustion of staying up half the night to vote on matters about which most members know little and care less. However such personal arrangements are only allowed to operate on what are called two-line Whips – that is, those votes on which each side agrees in advance that the matter to be voted upon is not of the utmost party-political significance.

A final aspect of parliamentary culture which is worth mentioning is the fondness of MPs in all parties, but especially on the Conservative side, for dining clubs and informal political gatherings of all kinds. It is sometimes said that the afternoon hours at Westminster resemble nothing more than a coffee-shop or a smoke-filled bazaar, while the evening hours are often whiled away quite agreeably in the Smoking Room, on the terrace in summer or around various dining tables among self-consciously exclusive groups of like-minded MPs. In the Labour party, the various factions usually like to meet, talk and perhaps plot in the Tea Room. In the Conservative party they prefer the Members' Dining Room or private rooms on the terrace level or even their own London homes. The common denominator on all these occasions is the indulgent exchange of political gossip and ideas, something which is the very stuff of politics in all parliamentary assemblies around the world. The views of such groups, as and when they are clarified, are then propounded and taken forward by the MPs concerned, who lose little time in passing on the essence of their discussions either to the party Whips or sometimes, in suitably veiled form, to lobby journalists. It is in these ways and at these *symposia* (in the Greek sense of the word) that much political opinion at Westminster is moulded and developed. If a full and accurate account is to be given of life in the House of Commons, attention should be paid to these organisations, whether the Manifesto Group (now disbanded), the Tribune Group or the Campaign Group in the Labour party – all of which have organised their own slates of candidates for the annual elections to the Shadow Cabinet; or gatherings such as the 92 Group, the Lollards, One Nation or the No Turning Back Group in the Conservative party, which compete for influence over policy and offer ladders of promotion to ministerial office for ambitious back-benchers.

11.3 Main Functions

In 1867, Walter Bagehot suggested that the House of Commons needed to do the following: 'elect a Ministry, legislate, teach the nation, express the nation's will and bring matters to the nation's attention'.[9] If we were to translate these functions into modern terms, we would say that the House of Commons has to provide most of the Ministers in any government, to scrutinise and pass legislation, to give a lead to public opinion on the great issues of the day, and to seek redress for the grievances and concerns of ordinary people. There are, of course, other vital functions performed by the modern House of Commons, notably parliamentary control of the Executive and party political conflict on the parliamentary stage. Yet the essential functions of the House have not changed very much since the time when Walter Bagehot made his authoritative pronouncement. The functions of the Commons are summarised in tabular form in Figure 11.1.

Figure 11.1 Functions of the House of Commons

Representation and redress

On behalf of constituents
On behalf of causes
On behalf of interests

The legislative process

First Reading
Second Reading
Standing Committee
Report Stage
Third Reading

The party battle

In the Chamber
In Committee 'upstairs'
In the media

Parliamentary control

Oral questions
Written questions
Select Committee investigations
Delegations to see Ministers
Letters to Ministers

Representation and Redress

The oldest function of Members of Parliament is to represent the interests of their constituents and to seek redress of their grievances by the government of the day. This function, which has been performed ever since the establishment of Parliament in the thirteenth century, is still a vital task for MPs in modern conditions. There are a number of different ways in which it is carried out. These range from having a quiet word with the Minister in the Division Lobby to signing an Early Day Motion with other MPs in order to signal the breadth and depth of support for a particular cause or complaint. They include such techniques as writing a letter to a Minister enclosing documentary evidence of a constituent's complaint, leading a delegation to lobby a Minister in his Whitehall office, putting down a Parliamentary Question for written answer in order to get a Minister's response on the record in *Hansard*, putting down a Parliamentary Question for oral answer in order to be able to make a point on the record in the Chamber, and applying to the Speaker for an Adjournment Debate at the end of the day's parliamentary business or an Emergency Debate immediately after Oral Questions and any Ministerial Statements. As must be evident from this brief description, there are many channels of representation available to MPs when pursuing this aspect of their duties. It is also quite normal for them to begin with one of the lower-key methods and resort to the more dramatic ones only if the former do not have the desired effect. This wide range of possible techniques for publicising the concerns or grievances of constituents gives back-bench MPs a degree of power in their dealings with Ministers and civil servants which the latter take very seriously indeed.

If MPs did not speak and intervene on behalf of their constituents when the latter feel frustrated by the bureaucracy of central or local government or cheated of their democratic rights as citizens, many people might conclude that our form of democracy was a sham and withdraw their loyalty and respect. As it is, the public has a pretty cynical attitude about the role and usefulness of MPs, at any rate until such time as they may encounter some modest success in dealing with the bureaucracy of government with the help of their MP. On the other hand, when a conscientious MP is able to provide effective help for a troubled constituent it can make the beneficiary of such political intervention more likely to appreciate the value of our particular form of parliamentary democracy. To the extent that MPs are able to fulfil this important function, we have discovered at least one significant reason why our political system has survived so long, notwithstanding many grander disappointments and disasters over the years.

The Party Battle

Another function of Members of Parliament is to act as party-political publicists, whether in defence of their party when it is in office or in criticism of the Government when their party is in opposition. The party battle, which became notably more polarised in the 1970s and early 1980s, has been criticised from several quarters, especially by the smaller centre parties whose interests are not well catered for in the procedural arrangements at Westminster and whose political stance has long been critical of confrontational politics. However there are points to be made in favour of the party battle. It encourages the voters to take an interest in national politics between General Elections, to consider at least two sides to every political argument and to pay some attention to policy issues. Without the political drama of the party battle at Westminster and in the studios of the media, it is likely that the political process would lose much of its vitality and that the non-political influence of the bureaucracy would increase. Of course there are those who would welcome such an alternative, but even they would have to concede that it would produce a form of government which was less accountable and less democratic.

While it must be acknowledged that many people pay little or no attention to politics, without the stimulus of the party battle there might be even less public interest and even more public apathy. Certainly the evidence shows that the relative success or failure of the opposition parties in criticising the government of the day and putting forward their own alternative proposals does have a cumulative effect upon public opinion and hence upon the voting behaviour of at least the more attentive voters. Opposition parties may not always get all the publicity which they would like, but they can often be successful in sowing the seeds of doubt and resentment about the performance of the party in office. To this extent the party-political battle makes its contribution to the working of our political system.

The Legislative Process

Another well-recognised, but not always well-understood function of Members of Parliament is the scrutiny and approval of legislation. It is the function which most members of the public mention when asked about the activities of Parliament. Over recent years it has absorbed an increasing amount of parliamentary time as the scope and complexity of legislation has increased and as the public – and especially pressure groups – have come to make greater and greater demands upon government. Only in the 1980s were there some signs that public expectations might be moderating, but this may not be a reliable indicator of future trends.

The legislative process in the Commons begins with First Reading. This is the name of the formal stage at which printed copies of a Bill are laid on the table of the House and made available in the Vote Office for all MPs and other interested parties to read and consider. After an appropriate interval, this is followed by

Second Reading (usually about a fortnight later) when a debate takes place for about six hours during which the broad purposes of the Bill are discussed and at the end of which a vote is usually taken to show whether or not the House approves of the Bill. This is the stage when the senior Minister in charge of the Bill sets out the broad arguments for it, the chief opposition spokesman sets out the broad arguments against it (unless the Bill is wholly uncontentious, in which case detailed criticism and constructive suggestions are more likely to be forthcoming), interested back-benchers on both sides of the House make national or constituency points, and junior Ministers and opposition spokesmen wind up the debate during the final hour by attempting to take up or answer the various points made by others during the course of the debate. At the end of such debates on all Government Bills the votes are 'whipped', which means that MPs are expected to vote as their party has decided, unless they have powerful reasons for doing otherwise – for example, conscientious objections to the Bill or overriding constituency reasons for opposing it.

Assuming that a Bill is approved by the House at Second Reading, it is then usually referred to a Standing Committee 'upstairs' where it is debated in detail and at length by a committee of between 16 and 50 MPs chosen to reflect the party balance in the House as a whole. This means that a typical Standing Committee may be made up of one or two Ministers in charge of the Bill, a Government Whip and perhaps a dozen or more back-benchers on the government side, ranged against a variety of opposition MPs whose composition depends upon the nature and extent of political interest in the Bill, but who will invariably include one or more Opposition spokesmen and an Opposition Whip who between them carry much of the burden of proceedings at the committee stage. The task of a Standing Committee is to debate a Bill clause by clause and line by line. This usually involves the opposition members putting down a large number of detailed amendments, some of them probing and some seeking to alter the Bill in significant ways. This requires the Ministers in charge of the Bill to answer each separate debate and, if necessary, to persuade their own back-benchers to vote against any amendments unacceptable to the Government if the Opposition is not prepared to withdraw them. Once all the debates on amendments and on each clause 'stand part' have been concluded, new clauses can be proposed and debated, provided they fall within the scope of the long title of the Bill. In the case of a complex and controversial Bill, the later stages in committee often have to be timetabled, that is, if the Government can get the necessary 'guillotine' vote at the end of a brief debate on the floor of the House. This procedure does at least ensure that all parts of the Bill are discussed, however briefly, during the committee stage and that the passage of the Bill through committee is not unduly delayed by opposition filibustering. Yet even with the benefit of this time-tabling procedure, some Bills may involve a committee stage of 100 hours or more and large parts of Bills may not be adequately discussed in the Commons.

After an appropriate interval (usually several weeks), the Bill is then returned to the floor of the House where it goes through the stages of Report and Third Reading. These are usually taken together and may last for six hours or more – in other words, often more than one day of debate. The Report stage is the time when the House as a whole (that is, including those who did not serve on the Standing Committee) can debate and vote upon not only the amendments which may have been passed during the committee stage but also any new amendments or new clauses which may have been accepted by the chair for debate on the floor of the House. It is out of order for opponents of the Bill to go over ground already traversed during earlier stages of the legislative process. Third Reading, which follows immediately, is usually no more than a brief and fairly repetitive debate on the general merits or demerits of the Bill as it stands. It is concluded by yet another vote on the main principle of the Bill, in which MPs vote according to the guidance of their party Whips.

By this stage the House of Commons has usually concluded its scrutiny of a Bill, unless subsequently the House of Lords insists upon any substantial amendments. If this happens, the Commons has later to consider them. If all the Lords amendments are approved by the Commons, the Lower House simply sends a message to the Upper House notifying its agreement. If, however, the Lords amendments are not acceptable to the Commons, the Lower House sends a message containing its reasons for disagreement and possibly some counter-amendments. It is then for the Lords to decide whether to persist with its opposition or to give way gracefully in the light of the fact that the Commons can always eventually get its way under the terms of the 1911 and 1949 Parliament Acts. On nearly all occasions since 1945 their lordships have considered discretion to be the better part of valour.

Since the vast majority of Lords amendments are inspired by the need for technical or drafting improvements to Bills, nearly all of which are made at the instigation of Ministers in the light of criticisms voiced during earlier stages of the legislative process in the Commons, such amendments usually cause no difficulties in the Lower House. They merely underline the usefulness of having a bicameral legislature. Once a Bill is out of the Lords, it is virtually in its final form and awaits only the formality of Royal Assent. The whole process from First Reading to Royal Assent normally takes between six months and one year, although it can be speeded up dramatically in cases of emergency legislation – for instance, Bills to deal with terrorism or civil disorder have been put through all stages of the legislative process within 24 hours when necessary.

Parliamentary Control

Yet another vital function of Members of Parliament is to control or monitor the activities of the Executive. This is probably the most necessary, but also the most difficult function which has to be carried out by the House in modern conditions. Traditionally it was assumed that ministerial accountability to the Commons at Question Time and in debate was broadly adequate to ensure parliamentary control of the Executive. Yet, with the steady extension of government activity over the last 50 years or so, it has become clear that such a traditional approach is not sufficient and needs to be supplemented by other institutional devices if central government and its agencies are to be properly monitored, let alone controlled by the elected representatives of the people.

Thus the system of Parliamentary Select Committees, which can be traced back to its origins in the Public Accounts Committee established in the 1850s retrospectively to oversee departmental public expenditure, has had to be reformed and extended in successive attempts by the House of Commons over the years to achieve some effective parliamentary control over the Executive. Following the latest and probably most comprehensive stage of reform in 1979, there is now one of these all-party and supposedly non-partisan committees for each area of central government activity, as well as a number of non-departmental committees which have survived from previous Parliaments.[10] These Select Committees, each of which is usually composed of between nine and 11 MPs reflecting the party political balance in the House, meet regularly (perhaps two days a week) to oversee and investigate their particular areas of government activity. In the course of their investigations they can call for persons and papers, and their findings are normally written up in substantial reports produced for the benefit of the House as a whole. In normal circumstances they have no legislative role, although on a few occasions they have been used as parliamentary mechanisms for the exploration of policy ideas at the pre-legislative stage.[11] While they do not match in any way the scope and power of Congressional Committees in the United States, they do represent the first systematic attempt in Britain to improve parliamentary control of the Executive, at any rate since it has been widely recognised that the traditional forms of ministerial accountability to the Commons as a whole do not guarantee the achievement of this vital parliamentary objective.

It remains a matter of considerable controversy whether or not the Westminster parliamentary system, which is now so dominated by the forces of party discipline and the habits of voting on party lines, can ever exercise truly effective parliamentary control of the Executive. This controversy was thrown into sharp relief by the experience of the so-called Westland Crisis in 1986.[12] In January 1986 there was a serious disagreement in the Cabinet over the future of the British helicopter industry and especially the firm of Westland. The Secretary of State for Trade and Industry, Leon Brittan, favoured a link-up for the firm with the Americans; the Secretary of State for Defence, Michael Heseltine, favoured the construction of a European helicopter consortium. The internal arguments became very sharp, with a good deal of leaking and counter-leaking of privileged information and the crisis was brought to a head by Michael Heseltine's dramatic resignation from the Cabinet in protest not only against his failure to win the policy argument but also against the Prime Minister's role in the whole affair. The Prime Minister made an oral statement to the Commons and was extensively questioned on the floor of the House. A few days later there was an emergency debate on the floor of the House when Mrs Thatcher was obliged to defend her position, but when equally she and the Government had the full support of the Conservative Parliamentary party on a three line Whip. Three different Select Committees of the House felt impelled to investigate the matter – the Defence Committee on the defence aspects, the Trade and Industry Committee on the industrial aspects and the Treasury and Civil Service Committee on the aspect of ministerial relations with civil servants. In the event it was the Defence Select Committee, under the chairmanship of a senior Conservative, Sir Humphrey Atkins, who had been in his time both Lord Privy Seal and Chief Whip, which really tried to take the lead in the investigation on behalf of the House as a whole.

The two senior departmental Ministers involved in the affair, Leon Brittan and Michael Heseltine, were prepared to testify to the Select Committee, although the former (who had belatedly and reluctantly resigned) steadfastly refused to go beyond what Margaret Thatcher had said on the floor of the House. The Government would not allow key civil service witnesses (including Sir Bernard Ingham, then Press Secretary at 10 Downing Street) to be cross-examined by the Committee, on the grounds that they had already been questioned by Sir Robert Armstrong, the Cabinet Secretary and Head of the Civil Service, who had been appointed by the Prime Minister to conduct an internal Whitehall inquiry; and that it was for Ministers, and not their private secretaries and personal staff, to give evidence to Select Committees. Accordingly the Committee had to make do with two cross-examinations of Sir Robert Armstrong, who had in effect to speak for the Prime Minister and the Private Office civil servants most closely involved in the whole affair. When the Committee published its two reports on the affair – one on the defence implications of the Westland crisis and the other on the Government's decision making – it was the latter which caused the most stir and the greatest difficulty for the Government when it came to formulate its written reply.

In its reply, which was eventually published in October 1986, the Government roundly condemned the Committee's attempts to investigate the conduct of individual civil servants on the grounds that this would have blurred or cut across the traditional lines of accountability from civil servants to Ministers and from Ministers to Parliament. Furthermore the Government steadfastly stood by the so-called Osmotherly Rules (the 1980 Whitehall Memorandum of guidance for officials appearing before Select Committees), which had advised that the principle of democratic accountability was secondary to the principles of commercial confidentiality, national security and 'good government'. Gavin Drewry has written 'the Westland affair raised fundamental questions about the relationships between Ministers and civil servants, and indeed about the nature of Cabinet government itself'.[13]

What these and other similar events seem to show is that ultimately even the new structure of Select Committees with all its pretensions and growing *esprit de corps* was effectively rather powerless when faced with a strong and determined government which, for its own reasons, did not want to bow down before the instruments of parliamentary power and which was confident of its ability to use its own power on the floor of the House (via whipped party votes) to trump that of any Select Committee. In the British political system governments can get away with such high-handed behaviour and Parliament invariably has to acquiesce in it, because Select Committees have no independent existence or guaranteed constitutional rights of their own (as US Congressional Committees do) other than those which are conferred upon them – and which, by the same token, can be taken away from them – by the House as a whole, which today means the government using its whipped majority if necessary. The only way in which this double-Nelson could be broken would be if a future government were committed to, or had imposed upon it in a 'hung Parliament', the goal of a new constitutional settlement complete with a Bill of Rights, an independent Supreme Court, proportional representation and freedom of information. Such developments seem unlikely to be brought about.

As Bernard Crick warned more than 20 years ago, we should not read too much into the idea of parliamentary control in Britain, since in this country it means 'influence not direct power, advice not command, criticism not obstruction, scrutiny not initiative, and publicity not secrecy'.[14] Yet even these attenuated forms of parliamentary control should not be underrated in a political system which has never been characterised by clear-cut and unambiguous power relationships. Furthermore a degree of parliamentary control to match that exercised by Congress in the United States would only be possible in this country if we moved to an explicit separation of powers set out in a codified constitution and guaranteed by an independent Supreme Court. Such a revolutionary change is unlikely to be brought about in a political system where it is the Government of the day and the official Opposition (the putative alternative government) which effectively control the House of Commons.

11.4 **The Prospects for Reform**

The prospects for reform of the House of Commons are limited by the fact that the power of Parliament is usually a euphemism for the power of government ruling through Parliament, and by the fact that there is an inherent tension between the interests of the Executive and those of the legislature which is supposed to control it, in other words between actual and potential Ministers on the one hand and all back-benchers on the other. In most normal circumstances when the governing party has an overall majority in the Commons, any reform (that is to say, any strengthening) of the power of the Commons is likely to mean a relative weakening of the power of government. The only developments which could alter this state of affairs would be the implementation of electoral reform on the basis of some kind of proportional representation, probably within the context of wider constitutional reform involving a newly codified constitution. Since those who benefit most from the present arrangements seem unlikely to agree to such far-reaching changes, it is easy to see why the cause of parliamentary reform has made such little headway over the years.

Select Committee Developments

In the 1960s and 1970s the main focus of parliamentary reform was upon the extension and strengthening of Select Committees. Between 1965 and 1969 there was considerable impetus in this direction under the aegis of R. H. S. Crossman, Leader of the House for some of that time. However these positive developments in the scope and power of Select Committees were nipped in the bud between 1969 and 1971 when some of the committees (for example, Education and Science, Agriculture and Scottish Affairs) were terminated, largely because their activities had become somewhat embarrassing to the Government of the day.

Notwithstanding these set-backs, the later 1970s saw a steady growth in the number and scope of Select Committees and arguably in their impact upon the political process as well. It may have been no coincidence that this took place at a time when the then Labour Government had either a very small majority or (from 1977 to 1979) no overall majority at all. In other words, Select Committees tend to flourish when the government of the day does not have a sufficiently commanding position on the floor of the House to keep them down. At any rate there were some celebrated instances during the period 1974–9 when Select Committee reports had considerable influence upon the general political debate at Westminster. For example, the General Sub-Committee of the Expenditure Committee produced a series of reports which contained powerful criticism of Treasury policy. Similarly the Trade and Industry Sub-Committee produced some controversial reports on the Labour Government's financial support for British Leyland and Chrysler UK. Such committee work made its mark upon the general party battle, because it dealt with topical and highly political aspects of policy and offered weighty criticism of the Executive on a bipartisan basis which proved embarrassing to the Government Whips and the 'rebel' MPs alike. Such consequences emphasised the inherent tension between effective parliamentary control and traditional party government in Britain.

After the 1979 General Election, the Conservative Government agreed to the establishment of a reformed structure of Select Committees which consisted of 14 Departmental Committees and five (now seven) non-Departmental Committees which were allowed to survive from the previous Parliament.[15] It is as yet unclear whether this structure of Select Committees has done more for effective parliamentary control than the arrangements which applied before. The evidence from what happened in the aftermath of the 1986 Westland crisis would suggest that it has not. However it might be best to suspend final judgement, since so much obviously depends upon the general party arithmetic in a particular Parliament. Essentially, Select Committees are involved in a continuous process of explanatory dialogue with the government of the day rather than any more combative form of real parliamentary control. The activity of the Commons is still dominated by the two front benches working through their respective party Whips and through what are described as 'the usual channels' – that is, direct and informal contacts between senior members of the Government and the official Opposition.

Other Procedural Reforms

On the whole the prospects for parliamentary reform do not look very good, unless it is supposed that there will be other measures of wider electoral and constitutional reform as well. As S. A. Walkland has pointed out, 'Parliamentary reform cannot be effective in a vacuum or . . . within the confines of the present political structure of the House.'[16] The underlying political conditions do not seem to have changed since that observation was made in the early 1980s, so it remains doubtful whether parliamentary reformers can be justifiably optimistic about the prospects of progress.

Some of the minor procedural reforms made in the 1980s have not amounted to very much. For example, the idea of making it conventional in Second Reading and other major debates that back-bench speeches between 6 p.m. and 8 p.m. should be limited to 10 minutes was tried in 1979–80 and again from 1984 for a further experimental period. Equally a new mixed procedure was introduced for some public Bills which are of a technical and largely non-controversial nature. Here the first three sessions of the Standing Committee stage are conducted on an investigative basis (similar to a Select Committee) before reverting to the normal committee procedure for the rest of that stage of the legislative process. At the time of writing this mixed procedure has been used on very few occasions.[17]

There are, of course, some far-reaching parliamentary reforms which might be made one day. These include the idea of imposing an obligation on the House to debate all major Select Committee reports, the setting aside of one day a week when the House sits exclusively for committee work or consideration of draft European legislation, and the timetabling from the beginning of all Government Bills in order to ensure that they are properly considered in their entirety.[18] However all these ideas have proved too radical for the controlling forces in the present House of Commons and for their more traditionally minded supporters on the back benches. Consequently the Procedure Committee proposal for a new Legislative Business Committee to lay down timetables in advance for the committee stages of those Government Bills likely to require more than 25 hours in Standing Committee was rejected by the Commons as a whole at the end of a wide-ranging procedural debate on 27 February 1986. On the other hand, some proposals have been broadly accepted by the present Government, including the idea that departmental estimates should be examined each session by the appropriate Select Committees and that opposition debating time (now known as Opposition Days) should be reduced in order to allow more time in the Chamber for debates on public expenditure, defence, the European Community and Scottish affairs.[19]

Perhaps the most significant proposals put forward in the 1980s were those made in 1980 by the Armstrong Committee on Budgetary Reform.[20] These included the idea that the Commons should consider the revenue and expenditure sides of the annual budget together on the basis of a provisional Treasury document published several months in advance of the actual budget, so that fuller account could be taken of parliamentary views and other relevant developments. The 1979–83 Thatcher Administration went some way towards accepting this idea, which was also endorsed (unsurprisingly) by the Treasury Select Committee. In its reply to that Committee the Government agreed to a substantial increase in the information available to the Commons by including estimates of revenue, expenditure and borrowing for the following financial year in the annual economic forecast published by the Treasury every November. It also agreed to provide more information about public expenditure plans for the following year, as well as guidance on the implications of any future changes in the structure of taxation and National Insurance contributions which might be implemented in the following Budget. This procedure was duly brought into effect for the first time in 1982 and the annual Autumn Statement published by the Treasury each November is now an enlarged and more informative document as a result.

The Impact of Radio and Television

Finally, since November 1989, the proceedings in the Chamber of the House of Commons have been broadcast live on radio and television, as happens in many other countries. This idea had been under discussion in Britain at least since the early 1960s. For a long time there was nothing more adventurous than a limited experiment which began in the late 1970s with live radio transmission of a few particularly newsworthy exchanges or debates in the Commons. It tended to concentrate upon Prime Minister's Question Time every Tuesday and Thursday afternoon and a few major debates or occasions of particular media interest, such as the annual Budget statement by the Chancellor of the Exchequer, the May 1978 debate on nuclear fuel reprocessing at Windscale, the April 1982 debate on a Saturday morning at the outset of the Falklands conflict, and the January 1986 debate on the Westland crisis.

The present position (in 1990) is that the producers of BBC radio programmes normally use edited extracts from the tape recordings of the proceedings in the Chamber as the raw material for programmes which are transmitted after the event, such as *Today in Parliament* or *The Week in Westminster*. However, since the opening of the new session in November 1989 it has been possible for the general public to watch the proceedings live both in the Chamber and 'upstairs' in certain newsworthy Select Committees. Originally, this was only an 'experiment' in televising the House, but in July 1990 the House voted to make the arrangements permanent.

No one can be quite sure what will be the eventual impact upon the House of Commons of televising the proceedings in the Chamber. Certainly, it would be unwise to argue either way on the basis of recent experience in televising the House of Lords, because the style and content of debate in the Upper House is so different and because the media were on their very best behaviour in a determined attempt to demonstrate to the doubters and opponents that there was really nothing to fear from such developments. The proponents of televising have argued that it brings the proceedings of the Commons closer to the public – indeed, into the very sitting-rooms of people throughout the country – and that in the process it can enhance public understanding and support for the working of our parliamentary democracy. They have also argued that, were the House to have continued to resist the televising of its proceedings, it would have been condemning itself to a situation of increasing quaintness and irrelevance in the eyes of ordinary people who have become used to being able to watch all the leading political personalities perform in front of the cameras either on BBC *Question Time* or in specially arranged television interviews and discussions on all the main television channels.

The opponents of televising, on the other hand, have argued that it can have the effect of trivialising and possibly sensationalising the proceedings in the Commons, partly because the media are always more interested in the trivial and the sensational than in the dull but worthy aspects of what happens, and partly because certain Members of Parliament are not able to resist the temptation of playing up to the viewers. The opponents are also convinced that, whatever special arrangements may be made at the insistence of the House to limit the ambitions of the media and their publicity-conscious allies among MPs, in the longer term the imperatives of television are likely to predominate over the more traditional parliamentary practices. They therefore fear that the decision to allow televised proceedings will be the beginning of a slippery slope at the bottom of which the House will find that it has been changed out of all recognition and almost certainly for the worse.

11.5 Conclusion

In summary, the House of Commons has a range of powers and functions which can be formidable or merely nominal, depending upon the party balance and the personal inclinations of the 650 MPs. In most normal circumstances, when the governing party has an effective overall majority, the government of the day is able to dominate the House, provided only that it retains the confidence and voting support of its own back-benchers. In the rarer circumstances when the parliamentary results of a General Election have been very close or inconclusive (for example, after both elections in 1974) the government of the day is vulnerable not only to dissatisfaction on its own back benches, but also to defeat at the hands of the combined opposition parties. It was parliamentary conditions of this kind which forced James Callaghan, the Labour Prime Minister, to embark upon the so-called Lib–Lab Pact with the Liberals in March 1977 and which later led to the parliamentary defeat of the Labour Government by the combined opposition parties in March 1979.

There are many paradoxical aspects of the House of Commons which ought to discourage sweeping generalisations. All that can really be said is that the House carries out its various tasks with varying degrees of efficiency and success. It is reasonably effective as a forum for popular representation and public redress. It is best known as a dramatic stage for party political conflict, although in this its position has increasingly been usurped by stage-managed confrontations in radio and television studios. It is quite good at the detailed scrutiny of legislation (except when the Opposition decides merely to filibuster), but rather bad at modifying legislation against the wishes of the Government because of the power of party discipline imposed by the Government Whips. It is gradually becoming more effective as a mechanism for the supervision and control of the Executive, although in this respect recent evidence is not very encouraging and it is never likely to emulate the power and independence of the United States Congress because in Britain we have no formal separation of powers.

In short, while the House of Commons is theoretically supreme in the constitutional arrangements of this country, in practice it is usually controlled by the government of the day in most normal parliamentary circumstances. This position is unlikely to change unless and until there are far-reaching reforms of our procedural, electoral and constitutional arrangements. Furthermore such changes are unlikely to be made unless a future General Election produces another 'hung Parliament', in which the government of the day is forced to do a deal on all these matters with the opposition parties. Even then it might well be possible for the governing party to thwart such changes by following a policy of divide and rule in its dealings with the opposition parties. Thus it is unwise to be dogmatic when considering the House of Commons, which is still inherently powerful but usually subordinate to the will of the government of the day and, of course, the will of the electorate at periodic General Elections.

Suggested Questions

1. To what extent do members of the House of Commons reflect the views and interests of the British electorate?
2. How well does the House of Commons perform its main functions?
3. What changes need to be made to improve parliamentary control of the Executive?

Notes

1. W. I. Jennings, *Parliament*, 2nd edn (Cambridge University Press, 1969), pp. 7–8.
2. L. S. Amery, *Thoughts on the Constitution* (Oxford University Press, 1947), p. 12.
3. See J. Blondel, *Voters, Parties and Leaders* (Harmondsworth: Penguin, 1974), pp. 130–57; and A. Mitchell, *Westminster Man* (London: Thames Methuen, 1982), pp. 141–55.
4. 'Virtual representation' was best defined by Edmund Burke in 1797 when he wrote in a letter to Sir Hector Langrishe that it was representation 'in which there is a communion of interests and a sympathy in feelings and desires between those who act in the name of any description of people (i.e. MPs) and the people in whose name they act (i.e. particular sections of the general public), though the trustees (the MPs in the days before mass suffrage) are not chosen by them'.
5. Indeed, it is significant that less than one-third (31 per cent) of the House of Commons in July 1989 had direct experience of government at any time as a Minister or a Whip.
6. In December 1983 the House of Commons voted to approve a plan for the refurbishment of buildings on Bridge Street, Westminster, which are intended to provide about 280 new units of office accommodation for MPs.
7. The latest (21st) edition of Erskine May appeared in 1990 and was edited by the present Clerk of the Commons, Sir Clifford Boulton. It is particularly useful as a work of reference on current parliamentary practice.

8. The power of party in Parliament is, however, something which is ever present in modern conditions, as became painfully evident to Mrs Thatcher in November 1990 when she was challenged by Michael Heseltine for the leadership of the Conservative party and eventually withdrew after the first round of the contest to be succeeded as party leader and Prime Minister by John Major who came first in the second ballot.

9. W. Bagehot, *The English Constitution* (London: Fontana, 1978), p. 170.

10. Since 1979 there have been the following Select Committees: Agriculture; Defence; Education; Employment; Energy; Environment; Foreign Affairs; Home Affairs; Scottish Affairs; Social Services; Trade and Industry; Transport; Treasury; and Welsh Affairs. There have also been seven non-departmental Select Committees which in many cases were longer established: Parliamentary Commissioner for Administration; Public Accounts; Statutory Instruments; European Legislation; Consolidation Bills; Procedure (Supply); and Televising the House. The arrangements for all Select Committees are co-ordinated by a small Liaison Committee composed of Chairmen of the committees.

11. For example, in the 1970s Select Committees were occasionally asked by Government to look into possible ideas for future fiscal legislation – for example, Corporation Tax in 1970–1, Tax Credit in 1972–3 and Wealth Tax in 1974–5.

12. The different but overlapping aspects of the Westland affair were examined by no fewer than three House of Commons Select Committees – Defence; Trade and Industry; and Treasury and Civil Service. See especially the Defence Select Committee Report: 'Westland plc, the Government's decision making', H.C. 519, 1985–6, for further details.

13. G. Drewry (ed.), *The New Select Committees*, 2nd edn (Oxford: Clarendon Press, 1989), p. 417.

14. B. Crick, *The Reform of Parliament*, revised edition (London: Weidenfeld & Nicolson, 1968), p. 80.

15. See note 10 above.

16. In S. A. Walkland and M. Ryle (eds), *The Commons Today* (London: Fontana, 1981), p. 294.

17. Notably, for Bills on Deep Sea Mining, Special Education, Criminal Attempts, and Mental Health.

18. For an elaboration of these ideas see the First Report from the Select Committee on Procedure, 1977–78, H.C. 588–I, (London: HMSO, 1978); and the Second Report from the Select Committee on Procedure, 1984–85, H.C. 49–I, (London: HMSO, 1985).

19. See the First Report from the Select Committee on Procedure, 1980–81, H.C. 118–I, (London: HMSO, 1981).

20. See W. Armstrong *et al.*, *Budgetary Reform in the UK* (Oxford University Press, 1980) for a fuller exposition of these ideas.

Further Reading

Adonis, A., *Parliament Today* (Manchester University Press, 1990).

Drewry, G., *The New Select Committees*, 2nd edn (Oxford: Clarendon Press, 1989).

Griffith, J. A. G. and Ryle, M., *Parliament* (London: Sweet & Maxwell, 1989).

Hetherington, A. *et al.*, *Cameras in the Commons* (London: Hansard Society, 1990).

Judge, D. (ed.), *The Politics of Parliamentary Reform* (London: Heinemann, 1983).

Norton, P. (ed.), *Parliament in the 1980s* (Oxford: Basil Blackwell, 1985).

Radice, L., *Member of Parliament* (London: Macmillan, 1987).

Rush, M., *Parliament and the Public*, 2nd edn (London: Longman, 1986).

Ryle, M. and Richards, P. G. (eds), *The Commons Under Scrutiny* (London: Routledge & Kegan Paul, 1988).

Taylor, E., *The House of Commons at Work*, 9th edn (London: Macmillan, 1979).

Walkland, S. A. (ed.), *The House of Commons in the Twentieth Century* (Oxford: Clarendon Press, 1979).

Part IV
Central Government

⑫ Prime Minister and Cabinet

The term 'Prime Minister' was no more than a tenuous convention from the time of Robert Walpole (1721–42) to the time when Lord North insisted that his Administration resign *en bloc* in 1782 when he lost favour with King George III. Indeed, on a number of occasions during the eighteenth century, the most powerful politician of the day, Lord Chatham, was actually the leading Secretary of State in administrations led by others, such as Lord Pelham or Lord Newcastle. Until the beginning of William Pitt's Administration in 1784, all Prime Ministers were chosen because of their good relationships with the Monarch and they survived in office because of their ability to manage the House of Commons.

The term 'Cabinet' is older in origin and was first used during the reign of Charles II. At that time the King used to summon a few favoured members of his Privy Council for consultations in his private apartments and such people became known as members of his 'Cabinet' after the French word for private quarters. For a time they were also known as the 'Cabal', which happened to be an acronym for the names of those involved – Clifford, Arlington, Buckingham, Ashley and Lauderdale.

The office of Prime Minister and the institution of the Cabinet evolved together throughout the nineteenth century. Until the 1832 Reform Act the Prime Minister and Cabinet were answerable to the Monarch almost as much as they were to Parliament. The extension of the franchise in 1832 meant that the Prime Minister and Cabinet became more answerable to and dependent upon shifting majorities in the House of Commons. Further changes occurred after the 1867 Reform Act as the growing power of nationally organised political parties began to limit the independence of individual MPs. One of the consequences was the increased political stature of the main party leaders, such as William Gladstone and Benjamin Disraeli, who alternated as Prime Minister for nearly 20 years. In 1878 the title of 'Prime Minister' was recorded officially in a public document for the first time when Benjamin Disraeli signed the Treaty of Berlin on behalf of the British Government. Another equally important development during this period was the growth of the power of the Cabinet in relation to the House of Commons. By the time of Lord Salisbury's second Administration (1886–92) Britain had moved essentially from parliamentary government of the classic type to Cabinet government of the modern type – that is, government through Parliament rather than government by Parliament.

Statutory recognition of the office of Prime Minister was not formally complete until 1937 when the Ministers of the Crown Act provided the Prime Minister of the day with a salary and a pension from public funds, yet to this day the powers and responsibilities of the Prime Minister are not defined by statute. Like the institution of the Cabinet, the office of Prime Minister provides a classic example of the importance of conventions in British constitutional arrangements.

In theory, the Cabinet now constitutes the supreme decision-making body in the British political system. Yet in practice, as we shall see, the Prime Minister has become more than first among equals in any modern government. In political terms, the most effective sanctions against Cabinet decisions of which people may disapprove are a decisive back-bench revolt in the governing party or the verdict of the electorate at the subsequent General Election. The Prime Minister and Cabinet are also influenced in an imprecise but real way by the views of their own back-benchers in the House of Commons, the need to take account of the Opposition's demands which can affect the progress of government business in Parliament, their relations with party activists, pressure groups and the media, and their assessment of public opinion at any given time on any given issue. All these factors qualify and refine the power and authority of the Prime Minister and Cabinet.

12.1 Cabinet Machinery

Composition and Functions

The Cabinet in modern Britain has been composed of between 19 and 24 senior Ministers (including the Prime Minister) who meet every Thursday morning around the large table in the Cabinet room at 10 Downing Street. It subsumes a large network of committees, both ministerial and official, and it depends for its efficient operation upon the work of the Cabinet Secretary and about 200 civil servants in the Cabinet Office. The latter is the administrative nerve-centre of central government and responsible for recording all Cabinet and Cabinet committee decisions and then communicating them to those who need to know in the various Departments in Whitehall.

Certain very senior Ministers have a place in every Cabinet – for example, the Chancellor of the Exchequer, the Home Secretary and the Foreign Secretary. Some other Ministers have a place by dint of the geographical area which their Department represents in government – for example, the Secretaries of State for Scotland, Wales and Northern Ireland. Occasionally, some important Ministers, such as the Secretary of State for Transport, are included in the Cabinet at one time and excluded from it at another, depending upon the competing claims of other Ministries and the personal preferences of the Prime Minister of the day. In a few rare cases a senior Minister may belong to the Cabinet, but draw no public salary for it in view of the upper limit on the permitted number of such paid positions (currently 23). The Government Chief Whip is not a member of the Cabinet, but invariably attends all Cabinet meetings.

The Cabinet meets formally once a week for about two and a half hours at a time, although extra meetings are arranged as and when the need arises. Owing to its size there is no question of all its members taking an active part in all discussions. Some may remain silent because their Department is not involved in the issue under discussion. Some may not get a chance to speak about an issue because they have to be away on the day in question, in which case another Minister from their Department will deputise if need be or the senior Minister concerned may submit something in writing to the Prime Minister. Indeed it is just as well that the Cabinet proceeds in this way, since, if every Cabinet Minister spoke on every item of Cabinet business, the agenda would never be covered in the time available. At the invitation of the Prime Minister other non-Cabinet Ministers (for example, the Law Officers) may attend Cabinet meetings when necessary, but they remain in the room only for the period when the item or items affecting them are under discussion.

''Cabinet committees are an essential and integral part of Cabinet government. They are usually composed of the relevant Ministers according to the subject under discussion and chaired by the Prime Minister or another senior Cabinet Minister. They are normally empowered to take decisions on behalf of the entire Cabinet. Only in cases of serious disagreement are matters referred back to the full Cabinet for final resolution. Few substantial issues are taken by full Cabinet which have not already been dealt with in some way in bilateral meetings between the Prime Minister and the relevant Departmental Minister or by the relevant Cabinet committee. Thus one of the main purposes of such meetings is to reach decisions which can then be put to full Cabinet simply for formal ratification.' When Cabinet committees cannot reach agreement or when the issues under consideration are too important to be settled at a smaller meeting, the whole Cabinet has to argue things out in order to reach agreed conclusions which bind the entire Government.*

Cabinet committees can conveniently be divided between standing committees – such as the Economic Committee, the Home and Social Affairs Committee, the Overseas and Defence Committee, and the Legislation Committee – and *ad hoc* committees which are usually classified under a 'miscellaneous' heading and which remain in being only as long as necessary to resolve a particular issue of policy. Many of the standing committees and the sub-committees spawned by them are chaired by the Prime Minister, since they deal with the most important issues of policy. Decisions reached in such committees do not necessarily require subsequent ratification by the Cabinet as a whole. 'Miscellaneous' committees are normally chaired either by the Prime Minister or by a senior Cabinet Minister and meet for as many discussions as necessary in order to resolve the matters at issue. For example, in recent years such committees have dealt with the replacement of the Polaris force with Trident, the abolition of the Greater London Council (GLC) and the other Metropolitan Councils, the imposition of spending cuts upon departmental Ministers, the de-indexing of social security benefits, the annual rate support grant for local authorities and the reform of the National Health Service. It is normal for the decisions of such committees to require subsequent ratification by the full Cabinet or at least one of its standing committees. Yet in all cases the key to successful working of such committees is that they are empowered to take decisions on behalf of the whole Cabinet and they can do so without any political or constitutional difficulty in most cases.

Senior civil servants and the military Chiefs of Staff are not members of the Cabinet, at any rate in peacetime. Yet they have occasionally participated in some Cabinet committee discussions – for example, in the special circumstances of the 1982 Falklands conflict, when the Chief of the Defence Staff and a few very senior civil servants played a significant part in support of what the press called the 'War Cabinet'. In the broader framework of Cabinet government, junior Ministers play a frequent and useful part in Cabinet committees where they can relieve senior Ministers of many of the burdens of collective decision making. Indeed junior Ministers are the workhorses of the Cabinet committee system and they can make or mar their reputations when performing this aspect of their ministerial duties.

Support in Whitehall

Meetings of the Cabinet and its committees would not proceed as smoothly as they usually do were it not for the fact that ministerial meetings are prepared and

Figure 12.1 The Cabinet Machine

Committee initials	Chairman	Functions
Economic, Industrial and Scientific		
EA	Margaret Thatcher (Prime Minister)	Economic affairs and strategy, energy policy, changes in labour law, the most important EEC matters
E(EX)	Margaret Thatcher	Export policy
E(NI)	Margaret Thatcher	Public-sector strategy and oversight of the nationalised industries
E(NF)	Nigel Lawson (Chancellor of the Exchequer)	Nationalised-industry finance
E(LA)	Margaret Thatcher	Local-government affairs
NIP	Nick Monck	Official committee on nationalised-industry policy
E(PSP)	Nigel Lawson	Public-sector and public-service pay policy
E(DL)	Nigel Lawson	Disposal and privatisation of state assets
E(PU)	Leon Brittan (Trade and Industry Secretary)	'Buy British' policy for public purchasing
E(CS)	John MacGregor (Chief Secretary, Treasury)	Civil Service pay and contingency plans for Civil Service strikes
E(OCS)	Anne Mueller (Cabinet Office official)	Official committee for preparing contingency plans
PESC	John Anson (Treasury official)	Committee of finance officers handling the annual public expenditure survey
OCS	Sir Robin Nicolson (Chief Scientist, Cabinet Office)	Official Committee of Chief Scientists
OCS(I)	Sir Robin Nicholson	Official Committee of Chief Scientists on International Policy
IT(O)	Sir Robin Nicholson	Official Committee on Information Technology
Oversea and Defence		
OD	Margaret Thatcher	Foreign affairs, defence and Northern Ireland
OD(O)	Sir Robert Armstrong (Cabinet Secretary)	Permanent secretaries' group shadowing OD
OD(E)	Sir Geoffrey Howe (Foreign Secretary)	EEC policy
EQ(S)	David Williamson (Cabinet Office official)	Committee of deputy secretaries servicing OD(E)
EQ(O)	M. R. H. Jenkins (Foreign Office official)	Official committee on routine EEC business
OD(SA)	Margaret Thatcher	Committee on the South Atlantic, the so-called 'War Cabinet' of 1982
OD(FAF)	Margaret Thatcher	Committee on future arrangements for the Falklands
OD(HK)	Margaret Thatcher	Future of Hong Kong

Committee initials	Chairman	Functions

Home, Legislation and Information

Committee initials	Chairman	Functions
L	John Biffen (Leader of the Commons)	Legislation
QL	John Biffen	Preparation of the Queen's Speech
H	Lord Whitelaw (Lord President)	Home affairs and social policy, including education and housing
CCU	Douglas Hurd (Home Secretary)	The Civil Contingencies Unit of the Cabinet Office, which prepares plans for the maintenance of essential supplies and services during industrial disputes
H(HL)	Lord Whitlaw	Reform of the House of Lords (abandoned after a few meetings in 1982–3)
HD	Douglas Hurd	Home (i.e. civil) defence
HD(O)	Christopher Mallaby (Cabinet Office official)	Official committee shadowing HD
HD(O)L	Not known	Updating wartime emergency legislation
HD(P)	David Heaton (Home Office official)	Updating of central- and local-government civil-defence plans
TWC	Sir Robert Armstrong	Transition to War Committee, which updates the 'War Book' for the mobilisation of Whitehall and the Armed Forces in a period of international tension
EOM	Anne Mueller	Monthly meeting of Whitehall establishment officers on personnel policy
MIO	Bernard Ingham (Press Secretary, No. 10)	Weekly meeting of chief information officers
MIO	Bernard Ingham	Special group for handling economic information. Meets infrequently owing to persistent leaking

Intelligence and Security

Committee initials	Chairman	Functions
MIS	Margaret Thatcher	Ministerial steering-committee on intelligence which supervises MI5, MI6, the Defence Intelligence Staff and GCHQ and fixes budget priorities
PSIS	Sir Robert Armstrong	Permanent secretaries' steering-group on intelligence; prepares briefs for ministerial group
JIC	Sir Colin Figures	Joint Intelligence Committee, which prepares assessments for ministers, collating intelligence from all sources and circulating them weekly in the 'Red Book'
JIC(EA)	Sir Colin Figures	Economic-intelligence assessment
SPM	Sir Robert Armstrong	Security and policy methods in the Civil Service
Official Committee on security	Sir Robert Armstrong	Permanent secretaries' group on internal Whitehall security
Personal Security Committee	Sir Robert Armstrong	Official group supervising the working of positive vetting, polygraphs, etc.

Committee initials	Chairman	Functions
Ad hoc		
MISC 3	John Dempster (Lord Chancellor's Department official)	Public-records policy
MISC 7	Margaret Thatcher	Replacement of the Polaris force with Trident
MISC 14	Nigel Lawson	Policy innovation
MISC 15	Formerly head of CPRS; post now defunct	Official group for briefing MISC 14
MISC 21	Lord Whitelaw	Ministerial committee which meets each autumn to fix the level of rate- and transport-support grant for local authorities
MISC 32	Robert Wade-Gery[a] (Cabinet Office official)	Deployment of the Armed Forces outside the NATO area
MISC 42	Robert Wade-Gery[a]	Military assistance (for example, training of personnel) for the armed services of friendly powers
MISC 51	Robert Wade-Gery[a]	Commodities needed for strategic purposes (for example, oil)
MISC 54	Lord Soames[c]	Future of Civil Service Pay Research
MISC 57	Robert Wade-Gery[a]	Contingency planning for a miners' strike
MISC 58	John Dempster	Liberalising the declassification of official documents
MISC 62	Lord Whitelaw	The 'Star Chamber' for forcing spending-cuts on departmental ministers
MISC 79	Lord Whitelaw	Alternatives to domestic rates; rate-capping
MISC 83	David Goodall[b]	Internal constitutional arrangements for the Falkland Islands
MISC 87	Nigel Lawson	De-indexing of benefits
MISC 91	Margaret Thatcher	Choice of ALARM anti-radar missile
MISC 94	Peter Gregson (Cabinet Office official)	Detailed preparation for a miners' strike
MISC 95	Mrs Thatcher	Abolition of the GLC and the metropolitan counties
MISC 97	Nicholas Barrington (Foreign Office official)	Preparation for 1984 London Economic Summit
MISC 101	Mrs Thatcher	Day-to-day handling of the 1984–5 miners' strike
MISC 103	Unknown	Public-sector housing policy
MISC 107	Lord Young (Employment Secretary)	Training of 14–18 year olds
MISC 108	Lord Young	Freeing small businesses from red tape
MISC 111	Mrs Thatcher	Future of the Welfare State
MISC 115	Lord Young	Tourism and Leisure
MISC 117	Lord Whitelaw	Acid rain
MISC 119	Lord Young	Deregulation
MISC 121	Mrs Thatcher	Inner cities
MISC 122	Mrs Thatcher	Handling of the teachers' dispute, 1985–6

[a] Sir Robert has since left the Cabinet Office.
[b] David Goodall has since left the Cabinet Office.
[c] Lord Soames resigned from the Government in September 1981.

Source: The bulk of this table and the explanation provided for it have to be cited as private information. From Peter Hennessy, *Cabinet* (Oxford: Basil Blackwell, 1986).

supported by official meetings of senior civil servants from the various Departments concerned. It is this parallel structure of official committees which keeps government business moving along and makes it possible for the Cabinet and its committees to dispatch a great deal of government business in a rather expeditious way. Cabinet Office officials usually chair these official committees which are intended to maximise the areas of potential inter-departmental agreement and to define, if not minimise, the areas of potential disagreement. Since each Department tends to respect the interests and responsibilities of every other Department and since there is an established Whitehall hierarchy, with 10 Downing Street and the Treasury at the top and the smaller or newer Departments – for example, the Department of Transport or the Department of Energy – at the bottom, the outcome of inter-departmental discussions at official level often reflects the balance of bureaucratic power in Whitehall. This may facilitate the collective decision-making process, but it can also make for minimalist, inter-departmental compromises which may lower the quality or reduce the effectiveness of the decisions eventually taken. In other words, a significant price can be paid for the collegiate conventions of Whitehall.

The outcome of Cabinet discussions and of inter-departmental discussions at official level is also affected by the relative standing and authority of the various Ministers whose Departments are involved with an issue at a given time. Thus, if the Chancellor of the Exchequer and the Chief Secretary have won battles with their Cabinet colleagues over the control of public spending, the Treasury will be even more formidable than usual in its dealings with other Departments. Equally, if Foreign Office Ministers have been proved wrong, or even had to resign, over sensitive issues – such as the Argentinian attack on the Falklands in April 1982 – then that Department will find its authority in Whitehall somewhat diminished, at any rate for a while. The only sure rule in British central government is that it is usually wise to enlist the support of 10 Downing Street in any important inter-departmental battle.

In the process of central government the Cabinet Office has a vital role to play in ensuring fast and efficient communication of inter-departmental decisions to all who need to know of them throughout Whitehall. This 'central' Department, which consists mainly of civil service 'high flyers' seconded from other Departments, communicates government decisions in the form of extracts from Cabinet or Cabinet committee minutes to those parts of the government machine which have to act upon them. This means that in the first instance such decisions are communicated to the Private Offices of the Ministers concerned, from where they are further relayed within the respective Departments.

The minutes of the Cabinet and Cabinet committees are drawn up by officials of the Cabinet Office under the overall direction of the Cabinet Secretary. It is open to the Prime Minister and, indeed, any other Minister to see the minutes in draft, to point out errors and ask for suitable amendments. Yet, if this is to be done, it has to be done within 48 hours, so such requests are not very frequently made and even less frequently granted. In short, Cabinet Office officials keep a tight grip upon this aspect of Cabinet government.

From 1971 to 1983 the Cabinet was assisted in its deliberations by the Central Policy Review Staff (CPRS).[1] This was set up by Edward Heath as a small advisory body within the Cabinet Office designed to give intelligent and dispassionate advice to the Cabinet on matters of policy affecting the entire Government. Under the initial direction of Lord Rothschild it seemed to achieve this objective and proved itself to be a useful source of independent and sometimes heretic advice to Ministers. Yet subsequently it seemed to lose its way and suffer diminished effectiveness. This was partly because it encountered formidable opposition from senior officials in the Treasury and the Cabinet Office who disapproved of some of its work – especially that on public expenditure and political priorities in the early 1970s – and partly because the Labour Government in the late 1970s drew it away from its original purpose into short-term, inter-departmental trouble-shooting which pu. it too much in the political limelight for its own good.

The final straw which probably brought about the demise of the CPRS was the fact that some people in Whitehall were not prepared to preserve the confidentiality of its sensitive reports to Ministers during the 1979–83 Conservative Government. One notorious example in the autumn of 1982 involved the unauthorised disclosure of a report which questioned the future ability of the Government adequately to finance much of the Welfare State and notably the National Health Service. This caused considerable embarrassment to Margaret Thatcher and her ministerial colleagues at a difficult time for the Government. It was not altogether surprising, therefore, that Mrs Thatcher abolished it soon after the Conservative victory at the 1983 General Election.

10 Downing Street

In addition to the formal structure of Cabinet government, successive Prime Ministers have had other sources of advice available to them at 10 Downing Street. Lloyd George began this practice with his so-called 'Kitchen Cabinet' during the First World War and it has continued in one form or another ever since. Winston Churchill during the Second World War had the help of Lord Cherwell; Clement Attlee after the war had Francis Williams; Harold Macmillan had John Wyndham; Harold Wilson had Marcia Williams; and Margaret Thatcher had her own personal advisers, including Sir Anthony Parsons, Sir Alan Walters, Sir Charles Powell and Sir Bernard Ingham.

Since 1964 there has also been a Policy Unit in 10 Downing Street consisting normally of fewer than a dozen advisers brought in to serve the Prime Minister of the day and to assist in any way thought appropriate. The personnel of such a Unit have varied from government to government, depending upon the outlook and inclinations of the Prime Minister of the day. For example, James Callaghan depended quite heavily upon Dr Bernard Donoghue, an academic from the London School of Economics, for advice on issues of domestic policy; whereas Magaret Thatcher had advice and support from Sir John Hoskyns, a businessman, Ferdinand Mount, a journalist, John Redwood, a banker and politician, and Professor Brian Griffiths, an academic economist. Whether such advisers are installed in a Policy Unit or work more informally for the Prime Minister of the day, their contributions to the really big issues of Cabinet government are probably no more than marginal in most cases. Yet, whenever there are moves towards a more presidential style of government and the occupant of 10 Downing Street plays an increasingly significant role as the final arbiter of all government decision making, such close advisers can wield increasingly disproportionate influence.

12.2 **Prime Ministerial Power**

The Prime Minister of the day could be described as the most powerful person in Britain. Certainly the reality of Prime Ministerial power has been recognised for some time by practising politicians and academic observers alike. Yet the nature and extent of such power is a matter of continuing controversy and there remain some significant constraints upon its exercise, no matter who occupies the premises at 10 Downing Street.

Conflicting Interpretations

There have been at least two strongly conflicting interpretations of Prime Ministerial power in Britain. On the one hand, Harold Wilson, one of the longest serving peacetime Prime Ministers, has concluded that 'the predominantly academic verdict of overriding Prime Ministerial power is wrong'.[2] In making this forthright comment, Lord Wilson was probably reflecting upon his own experience of having to preside over a number of Labour Cabinets which contained powerful and determined personalities who did not take kindly to excessive Prime Ministerial leadership. On the other hand, Lord Morley in his biography of Sir Robert Walpole (the longest-serving Prime Minister of all time) – but with his friend and colleague William Gladstone very much in mind – wrote as long ago as 1889 that 'the flexibility of the Cabinet system allows the Prime Minister to take upon himself a power not inferior to that of a dictator, provided always that the House of Commons will stand by him'.[3] This view has had its strong adherents ever since, including Sir Anthony Eden (later Lord Avon) who wrote in his memoirs that 'a Prime Minister is still nominally *primus inter pares* [first among equals], but in fact his authority is stronger than that'.[4]

The best way of assessing these conflicting interpretations is to examine the various aspects of Prime Ministerial power in order to see which of the two schools of thought is best supported by the evidence of history. Yet even at this early stage in the argument it is tempting to agree with the commonsense view expressed by Herbert Asquith more than 60 years ago, when he wrote that 'the office of Prime Minister is what its holder chooses and is able to make of it'.[5] In the light of the entire history of the office, it is difficult to dissent from this concise view expressed by one of its most distinguished occupants.

The Power of Patronage

The Prime Minister has the power of political patronage. This is manifested principally in the power of appointment to and dismissal from ministerial posts in government. Once a party leader has accepted the royal commission to form a new government, he can fill the 100 or so ministerial posts as he sees fit. However, in terms of practical politics, there are always a number of senior figures in any party who virtually select themselves for ministerial office and some others whom it would be imprudent for any new Prime Minister to exclude. Other considerations which come into play in the course of government formation are regional balance, ideological leaning and simple age, as well as political debt and personal allegiance. Thus, although the Prime Minister can do virtually as he likes when making government appointments (and increasingly so as time goes by), his

Power of Patronage.
theoretically fill any of 100 posts at will.
However

freedom of manoeuvre is always limited in practice by common prudence and political calculation.

Equally, the Prime Minister can always ask for the resignation of any member of the Government on the grounds that the Minister concerned is not up to the job or is too old or that the office is needed for someone else. Nevertheless the most usual motives for Prime Ministerial dismissal of a Minister of Cabinet rank are either to remind the governing party and the public of the reality of Prime Ministerial power by having a 'reshuffle' or to put a more personal and distinct stamp upon the Government by getting rid of Cabinet Ministers who are widely known to have crossed or disappointed the Prime Minister and then replacing them with others more in tune with the occupant of 10 Downing Street. For example, in September 1981, Margaret Thatcher sacked three Cabinet Ministers (Lord Soames, Sir Ian Gilmour and Mark Carlisle) at least two of whom had displeased her in this way, and appointed three new ones (Norman Tebbit, Nigel Lawson and Lady Young) at least two of whom were then close to her own brand of Conservatism. Such power of dismissal can sometimes be used more capriciously than the power of appointment, but in each case Prime Ministers are well advised not to abuse their power, as this can rebound seriously against them. For example, when Mrs Thatcher moved Sir Geoffrey Howe from the Foreign Office in her Cabinet reshuffle of July 1989, he and his friends reacted to what they took to be a gratuitous insult by letting it be known that she had been willing at one time to offer him the post of Home Secretary instead, without the knowledge of the incumbent of that office, Douglas Hurd. Thus at one fell swoop she succeeded in offending two of her most senior ministerial colleagues and damaged her own political reputation in the process.

The Prime Minister of the day also has a wider and more general power of political patronage which stems from his right to advise the Monarch on many of the public appointments made in the name of the Crown. This means that a considerable number of important positions in the higher reaches of the British Establishment are effectively in the gift of the Prime Minister of the day when they fall due for appointment or reappointment. For example, Permanent Secretaries in Whitehall Departments, Bishoprics in the Church of England, the Governorship of the Bank of England, the chairmen of nationalised industries and key appointments to a host of other public bodies all depend to a considerable extent upon finding favour with the Prime Minister of the day, although other Ministers also make such recommendations within their own Departmental spheres. In view of the highly influential nature of many of these positions, such appointments can have considerable wider significance. For example, the appointment of a former clearing bank chairman to be Governor of the Bank of England or the appointment of an expatriate Scottish businessman to be successively chairman of British Steel and then British Coal fell into this category. Such Prime Ministerial patronage, whether exercised positively to favour some or negatively to block others, is a formidable aspect of Prime Ministerial power.

Power within the Government

It goes without saying that the Prime Minister of the day normally has considerable power within the Government. Indeed many would argue that a strong Prime Minister has the ability to dominate the Government by setting its strategic purposes and political priorities. This is done in a number of different ways, all of which are facets of Prime Ministerial power. It is achieved through the

Hire/hire. Power of P.M. Patronage in — length of
100 positions. government. time in office.

Hailsham. (1977) Democratic dictatorship.

Prime Minister's control of the Cabinet agenda, his right to establish and pick the members of Cabinet committees, his practice of chairing the most important committees and discussions, his right to summarise the sense of Cabinet meetings, his preferential access to the best available advice both in the civil service and outside, his freedom to take an overall and non-departmental view of political issues, his pre-eminent position in the eyes of the media, his power of appointment and dismissal and, above all, his leadership of the governing party in the House of Commons.

During the 1980s when Margaret Thatcher was at 10 Downing Street, the power of the Prime Minister within the Government increased and was refined still further very largely at the expense of the Cabinet as a whole. This happened for a number of reasons. It was partly an obvious consequence of Mrs Thatcher having led her party to three consecutive General Election victories. More insidiously, however, it was a consequence of her ability to transform the membership of the Cabinet over a period of years from one in which she was effectively a prisoner of her own first Cabinet, which had been largely inherited from Edward Heath's leadership in the early 1970s, to one which she was much more able to dominate because all but one of its members (Sir Geoffrey Howe) owed their position in Cabinet to her. It was also a consequence of her marked preference for bilateral meetings with key Ministers as an effective and disciplined way of resolving policy problems, rather than have recourse to the more traditional, and less controllable, methods of Cabinet committees or full Cabinet. No one should really have been surprised by these developments, since Mrs Thatcher gave due warning of her intentions and her preferred method of working in government when she told Kenneth Harris in a now famous newspaper interview given before the Conservatives came in power in 1979 that 'it [her Administration] must be a conviction Government – as Prime Minister, I could not waste time having any internal arguments'.[6]

As must be clear by now, the extent of Prime Ministerial power within government is a subject of continuing controversy, since the situation is constantly changing in response to changing political circumstances. Furthermore the available evidence often comes from witnesses or participants who were strongly committed for or against a particular Prime Minister, while most outside observations are inevitably speculative in view of the blanket of official secrecy in which the process of Cabinet government is shrouded. The honest investigator is left with not much more than a series of impressions of one Prime Minister as compared with another or of the same Prime Minister at different times. The real dilemma is that those who might be reliable and objective witnesses of the political drama do not normally gain access to the theatre, whereas those who were privileged to be on stage are not normally the most reliable witnesses when they eventually go on record, often many years after the events in question. Although no definitive conclusions can sensibly be drawn about this aspect of Prime Ministerial power, there is strong circumstantial evidence that in peacetime modern Prime Ministers have wielded greater power within the Government than their predecessors usually did.

Power in Parliament

The Prime Minister of the day usually has formidable power in Parliament. This is partly because the power of appointment and dismissal can do so much to determine the political fortunes of the MPs in his own party and partly a reflection of the Prime Minister's leading role in the gladiatorial battle between the two sides of the House at Question Time. Clearly the extent and nature of such power has varied from time to time, depending upon the personal position of the Prime Minister and the political habits of his party. For example, much depends upon the extent to which the Prime Minister can rely upon the loyalty and support of his parliamentary colleagues; much depends upon the efficiency and subtlety of the Government Whips; and much depends upon the personal standing of the Prime Minister in the eyes of the media and the general public at a given time.

On the whole Conservative Prime Ministers seem to have been more powerful in relation to their parliamentary followers than Labour Prime Ministers in relation to theirs. This is mainly a reflection of the contrasting origins, organisation and habits of each of the major parties. Whereas the Conservative party has been traditionally both hierarchically organised and deferential towards its leader, the Labour party has tended to be more democratic in its aspirations and more egalitarian in its outlook. On the whole this has made it somewhat easier for Conservative Prime Ministers to preserve their authority than for Labour Prime Ministers to preserve theirs, although the contrast should not be exaggerated, since there have been relatively strong and decisive Labour Prime Ministers – for example, Clement Attlee – and relatively weak and indecisive Conservative Prime Ministers – for example, Sir Anthony Eden or Sir Alec Douglas-Home.

In general, all peacetime Prime Ministers during this century have usually exercised effectively dominant power within their own parliamentary parties as long as they have continued to hold their high office and have been able to count upon the loyal support of the great majority of their own back-benchers.[7] Once they have left 10 Downing Street and have been defeated at the polls, they have become even more vulnerable to challenges from their rivals, especially in the Conservative party, which traditionally has been unsentimental in its attitude towards election losers.

Party-political Power

The Prime Minister of the day can have great power over the fortunes and destiny of the party which he leads. In the Conservative party this stems from the usually dominant position of the party leader which is enhanced when combined with the office of Prime Minister. In the Labour party the situation is usually not so clear-cut, since Prime Ministerial power has to be shared to a greater extent with the parliamentary party, the affiliated trade unions and the constituency parties, all of whom have a guaranteed place in the Labour party constitution. Labour Prime Ministers have therefore had their problems with the National Executive Committee of the party, since nearly all the other members of the committee have their own power-bases within the Labour movement which enable them to take an independent line if they so choose. Furthermore, whereas the authority of a Conservative Prime Minister is generally recognised, if occasionally resented, at all levels of the party which he leads, the paramount position of a Labour Prime Minister is not always recognised and often challenged by his party colleagues in private and sometimes in public as well.

In no case is the party-political power of the Prime Minister more significant than in the exclusive right to recommend to the Monarch the time of dissolution within the five-year maximum span of a Parliament. The exercise of this aspect of

Prime Ministerial power can have lasting effects for good or ill upon the political fortunes of his party and the destiny of the country. A few examples will illustrate the point. Clement Attlee decided to call a General Election in 1951, even though the Labour Government which he led had an overall majority of five in the Commons and more than three years of its parliamentary term still to run.[8] The result was a narrow victory for the Conservatives and the beginning of 13 years of Conservative rule. Edward Heath decided to appeal to the country by holding a General Election in February 1974, even though the Conservative Government which he led had a comfortable majority in the Commons and nearly 18 months of its parliamentary term still to run. The result was a narrow victory for the Labour party and the beginning of more than five years of Labour rule. James Callaghan appeared to err in the other direction when he decided not to call a General Election in October 1978 against the advice and instincts of nearly all his senior colleagues and contrary to the confident expectations of many of his most powerful trade union supporters. The main political consequence was that the Labour party missed what was probably its best opportunity to win another term of office at a time when there was relative industrial peace and some evidence of economic revival. When the General Election eventually took place, in May 1979, it was against a background of the so-called 'winter of discontent' among the trade unions and the defeat of the Labour Government in the Commons in the vote of confidence of March 1979. The result was the election of a Conservative Government on the basis of the largest swing since 1945. In this and many other cases, it can be argued that this particular aspect of Prime Ministerial power has had very significant political consequences.

National Power

In contemporary political conditions the Prime Minister of the day has considerable national power in the sense that he has considerable status and prestige, even allowing for demystified public attitudes and widespread public cynicism. Of course the symbols of Prime Ministerial power should not be confused with the substance, but they are nevertheless important as part of the aura of power which surrounds all heads of government in modern political conditions. Certainly this particular aspect of power is strongly reinforced by the sycophantic attention which many in the media devote to nearly every facet of Prime Ministerial activity. It is also dramatised by the modern tendency for British Prime Ministers to attend frequent summit meetings with their opposite numbers from other countries. As such it is a notable aspect of the current tendency towards presidentialism, from which the British political system is by no means immune.

The national power of the Prime Minister is enhanced every time there is a real crisis or a requirement for particularly swift and decisive national leadership. This is especially true in time of war, but it is also true in relation to matters of national security in time of peace. For example, it is usually the Prime Minister who has to act decisively in the event of a spy scandal affecting the Government or a major industrial crisis which threatens essential services. Equally in foreign affairs it is the Prime Minister who has to give a clear lead when British national interests are seriously threatened, as Sir Anthony Eden did at the time of Suez in 1956 or Margaret Thatcher did at the time of the Falklands conflict in 1982. Similar considerations would also apply in the awful event of full-scale war involving the possibility of a nuclear exchange between this country and another. Although this aspect of Prime Ministerial power is minor in comparison with that of the American or Soviet Presidents, it will remain the most awesome facet of Prime Ministerial responsibility as long as Britain retains an independent nuclear weapons capability.

12.3 The Role of the Cabinet

It is difficult to consider the role of the Cabinet in Britain in a way which separates it from consideration of the office of Prime Minister. Yet there are some important points which can be made about the ideas of Cabinet government and collective responsibility which also serve to illustrate some of the real limitations upon the exercise of Prime Ministerial power. John Mackintosh provided a useful framework for analysis when he wrote that the major tasks of Cabinet are 'to take or review the major decisions (of Government), to consider (though not necessarily at the formative stage) any proposals which might affect the future of the Government, and to ensure that no departmental interests are overlooked, thus giving the work of the Government a measure of unity (and coherence)'.[9] It is therefore worthwhile to consider each of these aspects in turn.

Important Decision Making

In theory, the Cabinet is the most important decision-making body in British central government. It is supposed to play this vital role because there is no other institution so well-placed or well-qualified to meet the need for decisive arbitration at the apex of central government. After all there is formally no chief executive in British central government and all executive power is vested by Act of Parliament in the various Secretaries of State and other ministerial heads of Whitehall Departments. Thus, whatever the reality of Prime Ministerial power, the Cabinet is supposed to be the most important decision-making body if only to give institutional expression to the important idea of collective responsibility.

Some have argued that in modern times it has invariably been the Prime Minister of the day who has taken all the really important decisions, albeit usually after appropriate discussion with a small number of senior ministerial colleagues. There is evidence to support this view in the 1947 decision to develop a British nuclear weapons capability, the 1956 decision to invade the Suez Canal Zone and the 1982 decision to send a Task Force to recapture the Falklands. Yet even such apparently Prime Ministerial decisions had to be cleared with a few very senior Ministers and subsequently endorsed by the entire Cabinet.

There are several reasons why the Prime Minister of the day usually comes out on top in the decision-making process. The main reason is that in every modern Cabinet the Prime Minister has been more than simply first among equals. This happens partly for the reasons already given in the section on Prime Ministerial power, but also because the civil service habitually deals with Ministers in an hierarchical way. Indeed it can be convenient to have a Prime Minister who is head and shoulders above all his Cabinet colleagues, since this offers opportunities for individual Ministers to outflank their colleagues by enlisting the support of 10 Downing Street at the decisive stage in any inter-departmental argument.

As it happens, nearly every Cabinet in modern times has divided quite conveniently into two layers: a 'first eleven' of very senior Ministers who carry real weight and authority in the Government and a 'second eleven' who, although in charge of Departments or holding Cabinet rank, count for much less. Indeed, Winston Churchill sought at one time in the early 1950s to formalise this division by nominating a few 'Overlords' from among his most senior Cabinet colleagues to supervise and co-ordinate the work of clusters of other Cabinet Ministers. In the late 1960s Harold Wilson also experimented with the idea of creating an 'inner Cabinet' composed of fewer than half a dozen of the real political heavyweights in the Cabinet. None of these formal arrangements has worked very well when it has been tried, but informal divisions along such lines seem to evolve in every Cabinet.

It seems that in every Cabinet it is the Prime Minister who usually holds most of the high cards in dealings with his Cabinet colleagues. He can manipulate the membership of Cabinet committees in order to exclude those who are most likely to challenge his preferred course of action or to include those who can be relied upon to support it. He can also exploit the possibilities of bilateral meetings between 10 Downing Street and individual Departments in order to divide and rule any potential opposition to his policies in Cabinet. Indeed, if he preserves a political axis with the Chancellor of the Exchequer, there are few, if any, occasions on which the two of them can be defeated by their Cabinet colleagues.

In any case the doctrine of collective responsibility means that the invidious choice facing any member of the Cabinet who is really unhappy about an important government decision is either to threaten resignation, with the risk that the Prime Minister may choose to accept it, or to bite his lip and risk losing political credibility in the eyes of his Department and his political colleagues. Clearly this is not an attractive choice, yet most Cabinet Ministers faced with this dilemma have chosen the latter course on most occasions. In modern British politics resignation from the Cabinet on policy or personal grounds is usually a one-way ticket to eventual obscurity.

In the Conservative party it is necessary to go back to Anthony Eden in 1938 or Peter Thorneycroft in 1958 to find examples of senior Cabinet Ministers who chose to resign over significant policy differences with the Prime Minister of the day.[10] Michael Heseltine's dramatic resignation in January 1986 was partly because he lost the policy argument over the future of Westland helicopters, but mainly because he was completely fed up with the way in which the then Prime Minister had handled the dispute between him and Leon Brittan at the Department of Trade and Industry. In the Labour party it is normal to refer to Aneurin Bevan in 1951 or George Brown in 1968, yet in both of these rare and celebrated cases clashes of personality with the Prime Minister of the day played a major part as well. Occasionally there has been a tendency in both Conservative and Labour Governments for disaffected members of the Cabinet to convey their disapproval of certain aspects of government policy either via unauthorised private conversations with lobby journalists or in carefully coded public speeches designed to be just within the bounds of collective responsibility, while marking out important differences which distance them from the prevailing government orthodoxy. Such techniques can be regarded as a tribute to the durability and flexibility of collective responsibility and they were used quite often with impunity by Peter Walker during his surprisingly long ministerial career in Margaret

Thatcher's Cabinet. Yet it is also worth noting that in two other cases in the 1980s this technique led to the dismissal of the Cabinet dissidents concerned.[11]

Thus the Cabinet is still the forum within which all the most important decisions of government are ratified, if not actually taken. It is therefore the body in whose name the Government takes its most important decisions, even when the actual decision making is done by the Prime Minister alone or by smaller ministerial groups. It can be a formidable brake upon Prime Ministerial power and individual ministerial initiative, yet it seems to have had a rather limited role in modern times, at any rate in all but emergencies and other exceptional circumstances.[12]

Review of Key Problems

Another vital role of the Cabinet is the review of key problems which can affect the future of the Government. To the outside observer this would appear to be an activity upon which any Cabinet worthy of the name ought to concentrate. After all, where else but around the Cabinet table should there be serious and timely discussion of such vital subjects as the concept of sustainable development, the apparently intractable task of defeating inflation, or the difficulties of meeting public expectations in the modern Welfare State? Yet sadly the truth seems to be that this aspect of the work of the Cabinet has often been neglected in favour of dealing with more urgent political issues.

In recent years every regular Cabinet agenda has included an item on the following week's parliamentary business (when Parliament is sitting), an item which permits the Prime Minister or Foreign Secretary to give a brief report on current international developments or recent international conferences with implications for Britain, and often an item which allows the Chancellor of the Exchequer to report upon the state of the economy as indicated by the latest official statistics. Of course any member of the Cabinet may apply to the Cabinet Secretary to have a particular item included on the agenda of a future meeting, but it is not uncommon for such requests to be turned down or for the matter to be referred to an appropriate Cabinet committee at the behest of the Prime Minister, who is in effective control of the Cabinet agenda. On most occasions when the Prime Minister does this, he is merely acting as a good chairman by seeking to get decisions taken at as low a level as possible consistent with the importance of an issue. However, in the case of a real emergency or if a Cabinet Minister is not prepared to accept the decision of a Cabinet committee, the Prime Minister should ensure that the matter is put immediately on the agenda of the full Cabinet. Any other response would lead to a deterioration in the general atmosphere of mutual trust in the Cabinet and this would not be in the interest of any Prime Minister, however powerful. In general, therefore, the preparation and timing of Cabinet decisions is very much in the hands of the Prime Minister of the day, which gives the holder of that office a real advantage in any Cabinet battle.

The fact that successive Prime Ministers and senior officials in the Cabinet Office have not always encouraged the Cabinet as a whole to discharge its responsibility for strategic policy review of this kind can be attributed to a number of different reasons. Firstly, it is doubtful whether regular Cabinet meetings are the appropriate occasions on which to attempt this task, since senior Ministers are always very busy and short of time – they have departmental business to manage, parliamentary demands to respond to and a variety of public engagements both here and abroad to fulfil. Secondly, the Cabinet exists mainly to settle or endorse the big decisions which have already been carefully prepared in Whitehall and which may even have been taken (in effect at any rate) by the Prime Minister and a few senior ministerial colleagues in advance of regular Cabinet meetings. In these circumstances it is not surprising that the Cabinet has a poor record in this respect.

Just occasionally, of course, the Cabinet does engage in intensive and extensive discussions of this kind. This happened with the discussions in the Churchill Cabinet about British withdrawal from Egypt in 1954, the discussions in the Macmillan Cabinet about European policy in the late 1950s, the discussions in the Heath Cabinet about policy towards Northern Ireland in 1972–3, and the discussions in the Callaghan Cabinet in 1976 when it was necessary to agree upon a package of public expenditure cuts to satisfy the conditions of the IMF loan to Britain. Reflective discussions also take place from time to time in the more informal setting of Chequers, the Prime Minister's official country residence, but these are usually focused on a single theme and do not necessarily involve the entire Cabinet. In general, therefore, most regular Cabinet discussions are largely pre-ordained and even somewhat ritualistic. The Cabinet retains the supreme decision-making power in our political system, but it has usually been a disappointment to those who have looked to it for deep or intense discussions on the key political issues of the day. The awkward truth may be that such discussions are simply never easy when as many as 22 leading politicians meet around a table for two and a half hours (and often less) once a week and mainly when the House is sitting.

Inter-departmental Co-ordination

The third important role of the Cabinet is to ensure inter-departmental co-ordination in the development of government policy. In the opinion of many well-informed observers this has been the most notable role of the Cabinet in recent years. It is obviously a vital aspect of Cabinet activity, since it helps to impart a degree of coherence and unity to government policy and so reinforces the doctrine of collective responsibility. Indeed it could not really be otherwise, since senior Ministers cannot be expected to be bound by Cabinet decisions affecting their spheres of responsibility if their departmental interests and political points of view have not been adequately taken into account. Such inter-departmental co-ordination helps to guard against the taking of political decisions by one Department which may have unintended or even adverse consequences for other Departments. It is also intended to contribute to the administrative efficiency of any government, in that it can help to avoid both unnecessary duplication in Whitehall and the creation of awkward and unintended gaps in the scope of official action.

More generally, it is clear that single-party government in Britain needs to be united government if the political system is to work satisfactorily. The Cabinet is the main institutional expression of this unity and it is therefore vital that its decision-making procedures should contribute to rather than detract from the essentially collegiate nature of central government in Britain. Whenever a Cabinet is seriously split on policy – as the Callaghan Cabinet was in 1976 over the IMF demand for public expenditure cuts or the Thatcher Cabinet was in 1979–81 over the general thrust of macroeconomic policy – the morale and effectiveness of the whole Government suffers. It is therefore not surprising that all Prime

Ministers strive mightily to avoid such splits and deal promptly with them when they occur.

12.4 Conclusion

Considerable controversy continues to surround the issues raised by the respective roles of Prime Minister and Cabinet in modern British politics. There is no consensus of opinion among academic observers or practising politicians, although, as time goes by, more and more people have been persuaded that we live in an increasingly presidential political system.

Many still agree with John Mackintosh, who wrote that 'the weight of evidence does suggest that British Prime Ministers are in a position of very great strength as against their colleagues and within the whole framework of British government'.[13] Others may agree with George Jones, who wrote that 'the Prime Minister is the leading figure in the Cabinet whose voice carries most weight, but he is not the all-powerful individual which many have recently claimed him to be'.[14] However Robert Blake probably came to the most balanced conclusion when he wrote that 'the powers of the Prime Minister have varied with the personality of the Prime Minister or with the particular political circumstances of his tenure'.[15] On the whole this last interpretation seems to accord most closely with the historical evidence. It allows for the fact that there have been times when Prime Ministers have carried all before them – as in the immediate aftermath of General Election victories or other political triumphs – and times when powerful Ministers or the Cabinet collectively have asserted their authority over weak, lazy, sick or discredited Prime Ministers. Such are the vagaries and realities of politics.

Although we have been looking in this chapter at two distinct components of the British political system, the fortunes of Prime Minister and Cabinet are nearly always inextricably linked. Whatever their respective roles and capabilities, neither can function satisfactorily without the consent and co-operation of the other. In so far as each is limited in the exercise of political power, the constraints are essentially political rather than constitutional, practical rather than theoretical. It is the other actors in the political process – the political parties, pressure groups, the civil service, the media and public opinion – which keep both Prime Minister and Cabinet in check. Indeed in the modern world it is the passage of events, often in other countries, and the verdict of the British electorate which usually determine their fate.

Suggested Questions

1. Describe the structure and organisation of Cabinet government in Britain.
2. How powerful is the Prime Minister in modern Britain?
3. Can Cabinet government counteract the tendency towards presidentialism in British central government?

Notes

1. See T. Blackstone and W. Plowden, *Inside the Think Tank* (London: Heinemann, 1988) for a fuller account of the Central Policy Review Staff.
2. H. Wilson, *The Governance of Britain* (London: Weidenfeld & Nicolson, 1976), p. 8.
3. Quoted in R. Blake, *The Office of Prime Minister* (London: OUP, 1975), p. 50.
4. A. Eden, *Full Circle* (London: Cassell, 1960), p. 269.

5. H. H. Asquith, *Fifty Years of Parliament, Vol. II* (London: Cassell, 1926), p. 185.
6. *The Observer*, 25 February 1979.
7. This last condition of Prime Ministerial power is critical, as was made clear by the circumstances which led up to Michael Heseltine's challenge to Margaret Thatcher for the leadership of the Conservative party in November 1990, and hence the office of Prime Minister. This challenge to a very powerful Prime Minister and her subsequent downfall was the culminating consequence of consistently low opinion poll ratings for Mrs Thatcher since July 1989 and a growing conviction in the Cabinet and the Conservative parliamentary party that it would not be possible to win the next election under her leadership.
8. On the other hand, it can be argued that Clement Attlee did not really have any choice, since his senior Cabinet colleagues had either died (e.g. Ernest Bevin and Stafford Cripps) or were exhausted after 11 years continuously in government (e.g. Herbert Morrison and Hugh Dalton), and since he was under pressure from some of his senior colleagues to go to the country at that time in any case.
9. J. P. Mackintosh, *The British Cabinet*, 3rd edn (London: Stevens, 1977), p. 414.
10. In April 1982 Lord Carrington and his ministerial colleagues at the Foreign Office resigned because of their failure to foresee or prevent the Argentinian invasion of the Falklands, not because of any fundamental policy difference with the rest of the Government.
11. In December 1980 Mrs Thatcher dismissed Norman St John Stevas for flippancy and loose talk to the press, and in September 1981 she dismissed Sir Ian Gilmour for his political heresy on the main issues of economic policy.
12. It was, indeed, exceptional political circumstances in the Conservative party which led so many members of Mrs Thatcher's Cabinet to tell her after the first round of the party leadership contest with Michael Heseltine in November 1990 that she could not win on the second ballot and ought, therefore, to withdraw to make way for someone else in her Cabinet who could defeat the challenger.
13. In A. King (ed.), *The British Prime Minister* (London: Macmillan, 1969), p. 198.
14. In A. King (ed.), *The British Prime Minister*, 2nd edn (London: Macmillan, 1985), p. 216.
15. R. Blake, *The Office of Prime Minister*, p. 51.

Further Reading

Benn, A., *Diaries*, Vols. I, II, III and IV (London: Hutchinson, 1987–90).
Blake, R., *The Office of Prime Minister* (Oxford University Press, 1975).
Callaghan, L. J., *Time and Chance* (London: Collins, 1987).
Castle, B., *Diaries*, Vols. I and II (London: Weidenfeld & Nicolson, 1980 and 1984).
Hennessy, P., *Cabinet* (Oxford: Basil Blackwell, 1986).
Kavanagh, D., *Thatcherism and British Politics* (Oxford University Press, 1987).
King, A. (ed.), *The British Prime Minister*, 2nd edn (London: Macmillan, 1985).
Rose, R. and Suleiman, E. (eds), *Presidents and Prime Ministers* (Washington, D.C.: American Enterprise Institute, 1980).
Wilson, H., *The Governance of Britain* (London: Weidenfeld & Nicolson, 1976).
Young, H., *One of Us*, revised edition (London: Pan Books, 1990).

13 Ministers and Departments

Britain is a country with a long tradition of centralised government. Some of the public offices of central government have been in existence for centuries. For example, the first Lord Chancellor was appointed by Edward the Confessor, the Exchequer developed in the twelfth century and the office of Lord President of the Council dates from 1497. Some of the Departments of central government are now over 200 years old. For example, two of the most prestigious Departments were established in 1782 when George III created a Department for Foreign Affairs and a Department for Home and Colonial Affairs (now the Home Office).

Since the mid-nineteenth century Departments of central government have been created, reorganised and dissolved. For example, the Board (Department) of Education was established in 1870 with a Minister directly responsible to Parliament for the whole area of public education. The Board (Department) of Agriculture and Fisheries was converted into a Ministry in 1919 after the struggle to feed the nation during the First World War. The Air Ministry was created in 1937 to organise the national response to the growing threat from German air power. More recent examples include the Department of the Environment, which was established in 1970 as one of the super-Departments designed to secure better co-ordination in Whitehall and the Department of Energy, which was established in 1974 as a response to the energy crisis at that time.

Yet few departmental arrangements last for ever. For example, the 1974–9 Labour Government split the super-Departments into several smaller Departments – for example, the Department of Transport was re-established as a separate Department outside the Department of the Environment and the Department of Trade and Industry was split into a Department of Industry, a Department of Trade and a new Department of Prices and Consumer Affairs. Equally, the 1979–83 Conservative Government abolished the Civil Service Department and redistributed its functions between the Treasury and the Cabinet Office, the 1983–7 Conservative Government recreated the Department of Trade and Industry but transferred some of its functions to an enlarged Department of Transport, while the present Conservative Government has split the Department of Health and Social Security into separate Departments of Health and Social Security respectively. Thus there has been both change and continuity in the organisation of British central government.

13.1 The Work of Departments

Throughout the entire period of departmental government in Britain there has been only one serious examination of the overall structure of central government. This was carried out by a committee chaired by Lord Haldane which reported to Lloyd George's Government in 1918.[1] The two main recommendations of the report were that departmental boundaries should be based upon functional criteria (such as health, agriculture or defence), and that the Cabinet should be kept as a compact policy-making body at the apex of central government. Neither recommendation has been implemented fully or deliberately over subsequent years. Thus it has been quite common for Departments based on function to coexist with some based on tradition (such as the Home Office) and others based on geography (such as the Scottish Office or the Northern Ireland Office). Furthermore Cabinets have had as few as five members (Winston Churchill's War Cabinet in 1940) or as many as 24 members (Harold Wilson's Cabinet in 1975).

A limited attempt at departmental reorganisation was made by the Heath Government in 1970. This stemmed from careful preparation in opposition and was set out in a White Paper published soon after the Conservative election victory.[2] It marked the culmination of a trend in the 1960s towards the creation of super-Departments, the adoption of a managerial style of government, and deliberate attempts to strengthen the central co-ordinating Departments in relation to the rest of Whitehall. Yet only the emphasis upon the strengthening of the central Departments (such as the Treasury and the Cabinet Office) really substantiated the rhetoric about a new managerial style of government.

Departmental Structure

The departmental structure in Whitehall today consists of 19 main Departments, including the three legal Departments. In political terms the most important are the Treasury, the Foreign Office and the Home Office. Yet, in terms of the public spending for which they are responsible, the Department of Social Security, the Ministry of Health, the Ministry of Defence and the Department of Education are the most significant. In formal terms there is no Prime Minister's Department, although the staff at 10 Downing Street and in the Cabinet Office provide effective civil service support for the Prime Minister of the day.

Apart from the Prime Minister, there are a few other non-departmental Ministers, such as the Lord President of the Council (now also the Leader of the House of Commons), the Leader of the House of Lords, and the Chancellor of the Duchy of Lancaster (often the post given to the party chairman when the Conservatives are in office). Such senior non-departmental Ministers are often assigned important tasks of policy co-ordination, such as the chairmanship of Cabinet committees or the oversight of government information policy. Such offices can also be a convenient way for the Prime Minister of the day to include close political colleagues in the Cabinet – for example, the chairman of the party in the case of the Conservatives – without burdening them with departmental responsibilities. The structure of Departments is shown in diagrammatic form in Figure 13.1 over the page.

Within each major Department the normal pattern is for there to be a Secretary of State or Minister of Cabinet rank as Department head, supported by at least one Minister of State at the second level and perhaps two or more Under-Secretaries at the third level. Obviously, there are variations in this pattern which flow mainly from the nature and scope of each Department's responsibilities. For example, the Department of the Environment has one Cabinet Minister, two Ministers of State and four Under-Secretaries, whereas the Welsh Office has only a Cabinet Minister, one Minister of State and one Under-Secretary. The Treasury is distinctive in many ways, not least in having two Cabinet Ministers – the Chancellor of the Exchequer and the Chief Secretary – and normally the backing of the Prime Minister as well (who is known formally as the First Lord of the Treasury).

Figure 13.1 The structure of Departments

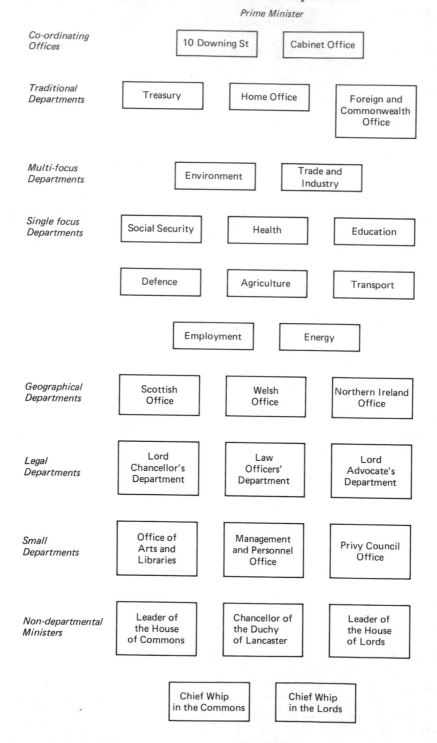

Just as the number and importance of Ministers varies from one Department to another, so the number of civil servants working in each Department also varies considerably. For example, the Ministry of Defence, the Department of Social Security and the Department of the Environment each employ more than 80 000 non-industrial civil servants, whereas the Treasury only employs about 3800 and the Department of Education and Science about 2400. The explanation for this wide discrepancy is that in the former category we find two of the remaining super-Departments, whereas in the latter category we find small, but important, Departments whose functions are essentially supervisory.

Government Functions

It is difficult to generalise about the way in which central government works in Britain. So much depends upon the personality and outlook of the senior Ministers concerned and a good deal depends upon the various departmental habits and traditions. According to the traditional view propounded by Sir Ivor Jennings, the essential features of British central government are 'the clear division between politicians and public servants and the close relationship between policy and administration'.[3] This emphasises one of the key paradoxes of British central government. On the one hand, there is a clear theoretical distinction between the role of Ministers, who are supposed to determine the policy and take all the decisions, and that of civil servants, who are supposed to advise Ministers and see that the business of government is conducted in conformity with the policy laid down by Ministers. On the other hand, there is the practical impossibility in modern British government of sustaining such a clear distinction. Hence we find yet another example of the inherent contradictions which are to be found in the British political system.

Most Ministers have to work very hard, often for between 12 and 18 hours a day. There are official papers to be read and approved, ministerial correspondence to be read and signed, frequent meetings both within their own Departments and bilaterally with other Departments or 10 Downing Street, meetings of the Cabinet or Cabinet committees to attend, meetings to be held with outside bodies and the representatives of various pressure or interest groups, parliamentary committees to attend, parliamentary questions to be answered, parliamentary debates in which to take part, official visits to be made to various parts of the country and abroad, foreign visitors to be welcomed and entertained, journalists and others in the media to be briefed, interviews to be given, meetings of the European Community and other international organisations to attend, and constituents and party activists to be kept content. Such an inventory provides no more than a superficial and incomplete sketch of the range of ministerial activities, since it is impossible to give a definitive description of a working life which is inherently so varied and unpredictable.

Civil servants for their part, and notably those in the senior administrative grades who are based in Whitehall, do their best to ensure that Ministers are adequately briefed on all matters with which they have to deal. Yet at the same time they try to see that Ministers are not over-burdened with unnecessary paper work or matters which can be handled by officials. This means that one of the key roles of senior civil servants, and especially those who work in ministerial Private Offices, is that of 'gate-keeper' in the information-gathering and decision-making process of central government. Every day such civil servants have to decide whether to refer matters to Ministers for political decision or whether to deal with issues themselves within the confines of established government policy. Although there is a natural tendency for civil servants to err on the side of caution by referring all politically sensitive matters to Ministers, their 'gate-keeper' role gives them considerable influence within central government and the veil of official secrecy behind which they work makes it hard for the outside observer to evaluate just how satisfactorily they perform their tasks.

Perhaps the most characteristic aspect of activity in Whitehall is the work which is done in the extensive network of inter-departmental committees both at political level in Cabinet committees and bilateral ministerial meetings and at official level in the inter-departmental committees made up of officials from the Departments concerned. Since many of the issues with which central government has to deal are too broad and complex to be handled within the sphere of a single Department, the process of inter-departmental co-ordination by officials is vital to much of the policy- and decision-making process. It is of great assistance to Ministers, most of whom are usually too busy with their other duties to devote as much time as they would wish to the preparation of policy decisions. It also puts a considerable burden upon the Prime Minister and officials at 10 Downing Street and in the Cabinet Office, who have to see that the various strands of policy are pulled together. The process of government would not work so smoothly without such inter-departmental co-ordination by officials, but the quality of decision making may not be improved by doing things this way.

Another important aspect of the work of British central government is the frequent and extensive consultation which takes place between officials and various client or pressure groups. Nowadays nearly every Department finds it useful to consult widely with such groups, not so much about which policy to adopt as about the detailed effects and implications of policy already determined by Ministers. For example, the Ministry of Agriculture has worked very closely (some would say too closely) with the National Farmers' Union in accordance with the statutory duties of consultation laid down in the 1947 and 1957 Agriculture Acts. Equally the Department of Trade and Industry keeps in contact with the Confederation of British Industry and the wide range of Chambers of Commerce and Trade Associations (although less so these days in view of the non-interventionist instincts of the Conservative Government). In short, nearly all Departments make it their business to keep in touch with the various interest and cause groups which have an interest in their spheres of departmental responsibility, although the extent and intensity of these contacts, at any rate at ministerial level, has clearly diminished under the present Government. Certainly any government which totally spurned or neglected such contacts would lay itself open to serious criticism in the media and in Parliament, so political prudence dictates that Ministers and officials at least go through the motions, if nothing more.

13.2 The Role of Ministers

The role of Ministers in British central government can be simply defined as the taking of decisions on matters of policy and the defence of that policy in Whitehall, Westminster and the country at large. Within their Departments Ministers act essentially as political jurymen who take decisions on the basis of advice supplied to them by their civil servants. Of course Ministers are always free to ignore or discard such advice, but this does not happen very often. Civil servants do not usually recommend courses of action or inaction which they know would be unacceptable to Ministers at the time. Ministers for their part often do not have the time or the inclination to question or reject most of the policy advice which is put to them. Only very strong and self-confident Ministers or those who are engaged upon implementing clearly established party policy usually manage to dominate their Departments.

Every Government since the war has contained a few senior Ministers who have been able, more often than not, to get their way with officials, with their ministerial colleagues and with Parliament. Of course this has applied particularly to strong and determined Prime Ministers, such as Clement Attlee and Margaret Thatcher, yet it has also applied very clearly to some other leading figures who have not been Prime Minister. One obvious example of such a ministerial heavyweight was Ernest Bevin, who was Minister of Labour in the wartime Coalition Government and Foreign Secretary in the postwar Labour Government. Another example was Duncan Sandys, who was successively Commonwealth Secretary and Defence Secretary in Conservative Governments in the 1950s. Another was Denis Healey, who was Labour Defence Secretary, 1964–70, and Labour Chancellor of the Exchequer, 1974–9. Another was Viscount Whitelaw, who was successively Leader of the House of Commons and Northern Ireland Secretary in the 1970–4 Heath Government, and Home Secretary and Leader of the House of Lords in Margaret Thatcher's first two Administrations. Another was Nigel Lawson, who was Chancellor of the Exchequer in Mrs Thatcher's Government from 1983 to 1989 and Energy Secretary for two years before that. It is not easy to define what qualities such Ministers have had which have earned them the accolade of 'political heavyweights'. Yet experienced observers know one when they see one. Force of character and political experience undoubtedly play an important part, but so does ministerial competence in their various posts and Prime Ministerial backing.

Ministerial Responsibility

Ministerial responsibility is the key concept in British central government. It has endured since the nineteenth century because it still has advantages for Ministers and civil servants alike. Ministers benefit from the fact that it puts them in a privileged position in which they are the main beneficiaries of official information and advice. Civil servants benefit from the fact that it gives them considerable influence over government policy and decision making without the formal need to accept public responsibility for the outcome.[4]

Within a Department the senior Minister is theoretically responsible for everything which happens and can be held to account by Parliament for acts of commission as well as omission. For example, the resignation of Lord Carrington and most of his ministerial colleagues in the Foreign Office in April 1982 was a recognition of his Department's failure to foresee and prevent the Argentinian invasion of the Falklands. On the other hand, John Davies did not resign as Secretary of State for Trade and Industry in 1971 in the wake of the Court Line collapse or in 1972 after the failure of Vehicle and General, even though in both these celebrated cases it could have been said that ministerial responsibility was involved. Thus there are no hard and fast rules which determine the nature or extent of ministerial responsibility in all cases and the outcome depends upon an unpredictable mixture of precedent and political circumstance.

The chain of responsibility in a Department is hierarchical, which means that civil servants and junior Ministers alike report to the senior Minister at the head of the Department and it is he who has to take the ultimate responsibility for their action or inaction. Of course there have been times when junior Ministers have been so out of sympathy with the policy of their Department or the Government as a whole that they have felt bound to resign. Yet on the whole junior Ministers stay at their posts and only tender their resignations if they are obliged to do so in the course of a ministerial 'reshuffle' organised by the Prime Minister of the day.

Indeed it seems that individual ministerial responsibility has been blurred and eroded in modern times by the size and complexity of modern government. This means that it has been effectively impossible for any senior Minister to be aware of, let alone control, everything which happens in his Department. For example, thousands of planning appeals have to be decided every year by the Secretary of State for the Environment, many of them important and nearly all of them complicated and contentious. Yet no Minister in that position can possibly hope to consider all of them personally, so junior Ministers and civil servants effectively take the decisions in the senior Minister's name in all but a few outstanding cases. Thus in most cases individual ministerial responsibility has become little more than a constitutional shibboleth, a convenient fiction for parliamentary and civil service purposes, but a doctrine which is put strictly into practice on very few occasions.

On the other hand, collective ministerial responsibility is more of a reality in modern political conditions because it reflects the collegiate and usually cohesive nature of single party government in Britain. It is really a way of expressing the fact that all Ministers, Whips and, indeed, Parliamentary Private Secretaries are bound by government policy and are expected to stand by it and to speak and vote for it, at any rate in public. While no politician can really be expected to believe totally in everything which he has to support in public for reasons of party loyalty, those whose activities are covered by collective ministerial responsibility are expected nevertheless to support the Government on all occasions. If they feel unable or unwilling to do so, they are supposed to resign. It should come as no surprise that this convention has not always been fully observed, especially on those occasions when governments have been so split that it has been effectively impossible to enforce and it has therefore been suspended altogether.[5] It is unwise, however, for those covered by collective responsibility to test the boundaries of the permissible too obviously or too often, since in doing so they are quite likely to invite dismissal by the Prime Minister of the day. On the whole, therefore, collective ministerial responsibility has become more of a convenient shield for Ministers and the rest of the so-called 'payroll vote' than an effective mechanism of parliamentary accountability.

Parliamentary Accountability

In theory, the proper constitutional check upon the power of the Executive in Britain is to be found in ministerial accountability to Parliament. This is supposed to be achieved in three ways. None of these is adequate on its own, but taken together there are some safeguards for the public interest.

Firstly, there are the opportunities for MPs to hold Ministers to account during proceedings in the Chamber of the House of Commons – that is, at Question Time, following ministerial statements and during debates. Yet the scope for real parliamentary control in such proceedings is limited by the ability of most competent Ministers to answer points in the House without revealing any new or substantial information if they do not want to do so. Experience also shows that such proceedings are often rather an empty ritual, since any attempt at genuine parliamentary control usually gives way to mere party-political point-scoring and invariably the media have discovered (or been briefed about) the points at issue long before Parliament gets its chance.

Secondly, there are the opportunities for MPs to probe ministerial thinking and government policy during Select Committee investigations and during the committee stage of Government Bills. These have proved to be somewhat more effective mechanisms of parliamentary control. Yet, in the former case, the usefulness of such investigations is limited by the general unwillingness of all governments to act upon the findings of Select Committees and occasionally even to allow key ministerial or official witnesses to appear before the committees at all.[6] In the latter case, legislative scrutiny by the Opposition in Standing Committees has to be set against the voting power of the Government majority, both in the committees themselves and subsequently on the floor of the House at Report and Third Reading. Such proceedings provide a form of parliamentary accountability, but not genuine parliamentary control.

Thirdly, there are the various opportunities for MPs to use their power of publicity to dramatise the errors of Ministers or the shortcomings of government policy. The principal effect of this form of parliamentary accountability has been to encourage habitual caution on the part of civil servants and to reinforce the tendency for Whitehall Departments to play safe in the conduct of government business. Indeed it is the capricious and unpredictable quality of such parliamentary accountability which has led both Ministers and officials to treat it with wary respect. This has had a marked influence upon attitudes and working practices in Whitehall and has sometimes discouraged bold or imaginative decision making by Ministers. It may also have lowered the quality of decision making in British central government.

Thus, if we examine the various forms of parliamentary accountability, we discover that none of them has proved to be a guarantee of effective or responsible government. The lack of proper accountability has been most marked in the detailed areas of policy covered by Statutory Instruments, the secondary legislation which is drafted by civil servants in the name of Ministers and lawfully implemented under the authority of existing statutes. In effect, legislation of this type is no longer within the realm of effective parliamentary control. Although there is a Joint Committee of the Lords and Commons which has the task of overseeing the spate of secondary legislation which pours out of Whitehall, the problem has really become unmanageable now that there are more than 2000 Statutory Instruments issued each year. The volume of such secondary legislation and the shortcomings of existing parliamentary procedures for dealing with it are such that genuine parliamentary accountability is really unattainable.

The other notable area in which parliamentary accountability is clearly defective is that of European legislation. Under the 1972 European Communities Act the British Government is obliged to implement automatically the regulations issued by the EEC Commission, notably in the spheres of agriculture, trade and competition policies, and to find appropriate national means of carrying out the directives which flow from decisions taken by the Council of Ministers. In 1974 the House of Commons established a special Select Committee to sift draft European legislation and to make recommendations as to whether or not the various items were sufficiently important to merit a debate on the floor of the House. As things have turned out, such debates are normally brief and late at night, if and when the 'usual channels' find time for them at all. In some cases it has not even proved possible to find time to debate a particular draft European proposal before it is considered by the Council of Ministers or before it is promulgated by the Commission as directly applicable European legislation. This means that it may well become law in this country before there has been any consideration of its merits or otherwise by MPs on the floor of the House.

One answer to the problem of insufficient parliamentary accountability in this area of executive action is for the tasks of scrutiny and control to be performed by the directly elected European Parliament which does now have some enlarged rights of 'co-decision' with the other Community institutions in specific areas of European Community activity. Yet this does not seem to be a complete answer as yet, and in any case many of the national Parliaments in the Community remain jealous of their historic rights to legislate and to hold Ministers to account. The result is that there is now what has been called a 'democratic deficit' in the Community which can only be closed either by a great leap forward towards fuller political integration in Europe, with much greater powers for the European Parliament, or by a dramatic reassertion of democratic control by national Parliaments, which seems both unlikely and unattainable.[7]

In reflecting generally upon the history of parliamentary accountability in Britain since the Second World War, we must conclude that it has been notable more for the tendency of Ministers to escape the shackles of real accountability than for the ability of Parliament to impose its will and control upon Ministers.[8] While there were the celebrated cases of the Crichel Down affair in 1954 and the Argentinian invasion of the Falklands in 1982, each of which led to the resignation of the Cabinet Minister considered most culpable, in modern times such cases have proved to be exceptions to the general rule that Ministers and civil servants can make grievous mistakes without ever really being subjected to full and effective parliamentary control. They may get sacked later on when the heat has died down and the public attention has turned elsewhere. Yet at the relevant time when they ought to be under parliamentary control, Ministers are only accountable in the sense that they have to answer to Parliament, not in the sense that they are really controlled by it.

13.3 The Problems of Government

The problems of government vary from Department to Department and from time to time. The key question which has to be faced by all governments is whether or not Ministers are really in full control of their Departments and therefore able to give the necessary political impetus to the Government as a whole. In this section we shall examine some of the problems which make it hard to give a convincing, affirmative answer to this basic question.

Ministerial Workload

One major problem of British central government is the heavy workload which Ministers have to bear, especially Cabinet Ministers in charge of large Departments, such as Environment, Defence or Trade and Industry. The very size, scope and complexity of such Departments works against the idea that the senior Minister should be able to dominate or control every aspect of his Department's activities. Yet this is what he is expected to do, notwithstanding the extra demands upon his time which are imposed by the nature of modern British politics. Indeed, in view of the collegiate nature of Cabinet government in Britain, it is a problem with which all senior Ministers have to cope to a greater or lesser extent.

One way of lightening the burden upon Ministers is to reduce the size of the public sector. This has happened over the last decade as a result of the present Government's policy of privatisation, but Ministers are still left with a public sector which accounted in 1989 for about 40 per cent of Gross National Product. Thus the area of activity for which Ministers are held directly or indirectly responsible has diminished, even if the extent to which the general public seems to blame Ministers for things which go wrong has increased inexorably over the years presumably as a reflection of the politicisation of all aspects of modern life.

Another possibility would be to reduce the range of tasks which Ministers are expected to perform – for example, by relieving them of their constituency duties, as in France, or their responsibilities for administrative oversight, as in Sweden. While the former idea is probably unthinkable in Britain, because back-benchers like to ensure that Ministers have to encounter and deal with the same constituency problems as themselves, some progress has been made towards implementation of the latter idea with the establishment of new Departmental Agencies to do some of the run-of-the-mill administrative tasks previously done by Departments.[9]

Of course the problem of ministerial workload is exacerbated by some of the conventions of central government in Britain, notably the assumption that Ministers will consult widely and systematically before taking major decisions or introducing important new legislation. Admittedly, many of these consultations with interest groups and relevant experts are conducted by civil servants on behalf of Ministers. Yet Ministers still have to lay down the political guidelines for such discussions and in the most important cases often have to take a leading part as well. A balanced solution to the problem would take account of all these factors. Yet, no matter which solutions are adopted, Ministers will always require great personal energy and strong political will to perform all their tasks successfully.

Departmental Policy

Another major problem of central government is the continuously powerful influence of established departmental policy. This may not make itself felt very much during the first year or two of a government's term of office, but it can assume considerable importance as time goes by if the political momentum of the party in office begins to falter. This phenomenon was particularly noticeable during the period of the postwar consensus from 1945 to 1973 and especially in the well-established Departments with long traditions and considerable self-confidence, such as the Foreign Office or the Home Office. Yet the outcome of such quiet struggles between Ministers and civil servants has never been a foregone conclusion. Much depends upon whether Ministers individually – and notably the Prime Minister – are determined to carry out their policies and to impose their authority upon the Government. If they are so determined, both the realities of political power and the conventions of Whitehall enable them to get their own way whatever the personal preferences or reservations of their senior civil servants. If they are not so determined, then the inertia of departmental policy may triumph in the end.

The strength of departmental policy is enhanced by the habits of ministerial and civil service life. This is because it has been customary for Prime Ministers to shift Ministers and move them from post to post quite frequently, sometimes simply to assert Prime Ministerial authority, but usually to broaden the experience of their most promising ministerial colleagues. This has produced an average tenure in a single ministerial office of about two years in postwar British governments, with the result that most Ministers are precluded from making anything more than a temporary or marginal impact upon the political issues with which their Departments have to deal. It is also because it has been customary to move civil servants in the higher administrative grades even more frequently from one job to another both within a single Department and sometimes between Departments. In many instances this means that key administrative staff may stay in a post for only a year or two, with the result that they do not have time to develop real expertise in their own policy area. This happens mainly for reasons of career development and is largely for the benefit of those who have been identified as 'high flyers' early in their civil service careers. The inevitable consequence is that even the best civil servants rely heavily upon what their departmental 'experts' tell them and especially upon what is already in the departmental filing cabinets, in other words the accumulated wisdom of established departmental policy. Such tendencies can only be overcome by sustained political will on the part of Ministers and significant changes in civil service career development policy.

The Quality of Advice

Another problem of central government is the quality of official information and advice available to Ministers. While such material is a source of strength for Ministers in relation to the Opposition and all back-benchers, it does not necessarily strengthen their position within their own Departments. This is because many of the politicians who become Ministers are likely to be posted to a Department about which they know little or nothing in advance and which deals with areas of policy of which they have had little or no previous experience. Even when a Minister appoints an expert personal adviser from outside the civil service, such an outsider is likely to be 'domesticated' by the Department and is unlikely, on his own, to be able to provide his boss with sufficiently persuasive, countervailing advice to match or defeat the established departmental view. The result is that, unless Ministers are engaged in the implementation of clear Manifesto commitments or are pushing through other forms of unambiguous party policy, they are seldom provided with a sufficiently compelling view of the available alternatives to existing policy and are therefore often obliged to rely upon the conventional advice from their departmental civil servants.

This is an unfortunate state of affairs, for two reasons. Firstly, the best answers to many of the most difficult problems of central government are not necessarily found either in the liturgy of party Manifestos or in the drawers of departmental filing cabinets. Secondly, the policy- and decision-making process is deprived of a good deal of high-quality information and advice from 'outsiders' who are both expert in their field and independent of Government. Some of this may be changing slightly for the better with the growing tendency for every Prime Minister to hold all-day seminars and other 'brainstorming' sessions at Chequers or 10 Downing Street, but it is noticeable that the initiative for such lateral thinking usually has to come from the very top if it is to happen at all. Undoubtedly there is room for the quality and breadth of advice available to Ministers to be improved and this may be one way of doing it.

13.4 Conclusion

Well-qualified observers of British politics and some distinguished practitioners have argued for years about whether Ministers are really in control of their Departments. As long ago as the 1850s Lord Palmerston wrote to Queen Victoria that 'Your Majesty will see how greatly such a system [of government] must place in the hands of the subordinate members of public Departments [civil servants] the power of directing the policy and the measures of the Government, because the value, tendency and consequences of a measure frequently depend as much upon the manner in which it was worked out [that is, administered] as the intention and spirit with which it was planned'.[10] This was one of the earliest and most perceptive statements of the now familiar argument that in the process of government the power to administer can be as important as the power to decide. In other words, civil servants can have nearly as much effective power as Ministers, even though the constitutional conventions do not admit it.

On the other hand, Herbert Morrison wrote in the 1950s that 'if the Minister in charge [of a Department] knows what he wants and is intelligent in going about it, he can command the understanding, co-operation and support of his civil servants'.[11] This statement from a senior Labour Minister with departmental experience dating back to before the Second World War could be interpreted as an affirmation of ministerial dominance in Whitehall. Yet it could also be interpreted as a back-handed compliment to the power of the civil service and a warning that Whitehall officials tend to fill any power vacuum which may be left by Ministers. Clearly it is necessary to refine the conventional statement that Ministers decide the policy and civil servants simply carry it out. The contemporary realities are more subtle, and the traditional model takes insufficient account of the complexities of modern government.

In modern political conditions it is, of course, possible for Ministers to exercise clear leadership, but this has usually become less likely as each General Election has receded further into the past. In this respect Margaret Thatcher and her senior ministerial colleagues were distinctly unusual and might be regarded as one of the exceptions which prove the rule. All senior Ministers may believe that they are in complete charge of their Departments. Yet civil service control of official advice to Ministers, the long time-scale and great complexity of decision making in government, and the limited scope for truly effective political intervention in the problems of modern society – especially if attempted purely at a national level – all tend to reduce the impact and effect of ministerial leadership. The broad conclusion must be that Ministers may be in charge of their Departments, but only within the limits set by established administrative procedures and uncompromising political realities.

Suggested Questions

1. Describe the work of British central government.
2. What is the role of Ministers in British central government?
3. Are the problems of British central government capable of solution within the existing institutions and conventions?

Notes

1. See *Report of the Committee on the Machinery of Government*, Cd 9230 (London: HMSO, 1918).
2. See *Report on the Reorganisation of Central Government*, Cmnd 4506 (London: HMSO, 1970).
3. W. I. Jennings, *Cabinet Government*, 3rd edn (Cambridge University Press, 1959), p. 133.
4. The conventional wisdom on this matter has been significantly eroded in modern times by the fact that all recent governments have, to some extent, abandoned the pure theory of ministerial responsibility. The point was very well made by the late David Watt at the time of the 1986 Westland crisis when he wrote: 'if Ministers allow blame to rest with individual, identifiable civil servants, they must expect two consequences: critics of Government actions will hold officials publicly responsible; and the civil servant will claim, and deserve, the right to defend himself in public, if necessary by shifting blame back on to Ministers' (*The Times*, 7 February 1986).
5. For example, in 1931 there was an open 'agreement to differ' in the National Government on the issue of tariff reform; and in 1975 during the European Referendum campaign Labour Cabinet Ministers were allowed to argue against each other on public platforms.
6. For example, when a Select Committee sought to cross-examine Labour Ministers on public financial support for Chrysler UK in the 1970s, the then Prime Minister, James Callaghan, prevented any of his Cabinet colleagues from appearing before the Committee. Equally, as we noted in Chapter 11, not all the key official witnesses were permitted by Margaret Thatcher, when Prime Minister, to testify before Select Committees in the wake of the 1986 Westland crisis.
7. In 1989 the House of Commons began belatedly to address this problem when the Select Committee of Procedure considered the matter and issued a cautious report. See 'Scrutiny of European legislation', H.C. 622, 1988–89, Vols. I and II. See also the Government's response: 'Scrutiny of European legislation', Cm 1081 (London: HMSO, 1990).
8. See A. H. Birch, *Representative and Responsible Government* (London: Allen & Unwin, 1964), pp. 141–8; and J. Bruce-Gardyne and N. Lawson, *The Power Game* (London: Macmillan, 1976), pp. 10–37.
9. Among the first wave of Departmental Agencies to be established by the end of 1989 were: the Vehicle Inspectorate, Companies House, the Stationery Office, Warren Spring Laboratory and the Civil Service College.
10. Quoted in H. Parris, *Constitutional Bureaucracy* (London: Allen & Unwin, 1969), p. 114.
11. H. Morrison, *Government and Parliament* (Oxford University Press, 1959), p. 311.

Further Reading

Birch, A. H., *Representative and Responsible Government* (London: Allen & Unwin, 1964).

Brown, R. G. S. and Steel, D. R., *The Administrative Process in Britain*, 2nd edn (London: Methuen, 1979).

Bruce-Gardyne, J. and Lawson, N., *The Power Game* (London: Macmillan, 1976).

Henderson, N., *The Private Office* (London: Weidenfeld & Nicolson, 1984).

Kaufman, G., *How to be a Minister* (London: Sidgwick & Jackson, 1980).

Marshall, G., *Constitutional Conventions* (Oxford: Clarendon Press, 1986).

Parris, H., *Constitutional Bureaucracy* (London: Allen & Unwin, 1969).

Pollitt, C., *Manipulating the Machine* (London: Allen & Unwin, 1984).

Theakston, K., *Junior Ministers in British Government* (Oxford: Basil Blackwell, 1987).

14 The civil service

In Britain the standard definition of a civil servant is still the one which was formulated by the Tomlin Commission in 1931, namely 'a servant of the Crown employed in a civil capacity who is paid wholly and directly from money voted by Parliament'.[1] In April 1990 this definition covered about 562 000 people in all. Of this total about 69 000 were industrial civil servants employed principally by the Ministry of Defence and other government agencies. The remaining 493 000 were non-industrial civil servants, about one-quarter of whom worked in central London while the other three-quarters worked in the other offices of central government in all parts of the country.

In this chapter we are concerned only with the civil servants who work directly for Ministers (popularly known as 'Whitehall') and specifically with those in the higher administrative grades. We are dealing, therefore, with the administrative elite at the heart of British central government.

14.1 Composition and Functions

The 19 main Departments vary greatly in size and character, from the Department of Energy with about 1000 civil servants to the Ministry of Defence with about 89 000. Indeed the three largest Departments – Defence, Social Security and the Inland Revenue – account for just under half the total of non-industrial civil servants. In a typical Whitehall Department about two-thirds of the civil servants are involved in the administrative tasks of government, while the remaining one-third perform a wide range of tasks of a technical, scientific and support nature. In Whitehall as a whole about 4000 civil servants are involved in the policy- and decision-making process, although of these only about 2000 at the senior levels have close and frequent contact with Ministers. It is this small administrative elite which sets the conventions of Whitehall and determines the character of the civil service in Britain.

The Personnel

In the higher administrative grades the traditional dominance of experienced generalists still holds sway and influences both the character and the quality of the civil service at every level. There are three main reasons for this.

Firstly, the civil service has not escaped from the influence of the 1854 Northcote–Trevelyan Report which defined the role of civil servants as being 'to advise, assist and to some extent influence those who are set over them from time to time'. This still means that in the higher administrative grades no particular value is placed upon the possession of specialist skills, except perhaps the skill of administration which is thought to be best acquired by experience on the job.

Secondly, there is a traditional disdain for professional expertise which was expressed by Lord Bridges (once Secretary to the Cabinet) when he defined a good civil servant as one 'who knows how and where to find reliable knowledge, can assess the expertise of others at its true worth, can spot the strong and weak points in any situation at short notice, and can advise on how to handle a complex situation'.[2] This still means that in the higher administrative grades no great value is placed upon the possession of relevant expertise, with the exception perhaps of the expertise of administration. As the saying goes, the experts are supposed to be on tap but not on top.

Thirdly, there is the traditional tendency for the young recruits into the administrative elite to come disproportionately from those with a middle-class background and an arts degree from Oxford or Cambridge. Certainly this was true when the composition of the civil service was examined for the Fulton Committee in 1967.[3] It appeared still to be true in the mid-1970s when the matter was investigated by the Labour party.[4] Figures provided by the Civil Service Commission in 1978 showed that 63 per cent of the direct entrants into the administrative grades came from Oxford or Cambridge universities.[5] Figures for similar entrants in 1988 showed a clear bias in favour of people with arts or social science degrees, since 59 were arts graduates, 16 social science graduates and only 11 were graduates in science or technology. The figures also showed that of the 89 administration trainees and top grade Higher Executive Officers who took up their appointments in 1988, 36 had graduated from Oxford or Cambridge, while the remaining 53 were graduates of other universities or polytechnics. The 1988 cohort produced the highest ever proportion of non-Oxbridge entrants, but the proportion of female entrants was still only 33 per cent.[6]

Thus the sort of people who qualify for the career path which leads to the most influential positions at the senior levels of the civil service are still very much the product of the values and outlook of their predecessors who select them. The main consideration is to find promising young men and women with what is described as 'a good, all-round intellect'. Good judgement and reliability are qualities which are highly valued, as well as clarity of expression and an ability to work effectively with others. On this basis the administrative grades of the civil service still attract some of the best qualified and most able young people in every generation. Yet, as long as such young people continue to form an elite which is broadly a reflection of the older elite which selected them, the character of the top civil service is likely to change only slowly, if at all.

Main Functions

The main functions of the higher administrative grades in the civil service can be summarised as follows: informing and advising Ministers, helping them to formulate policy or make decisions, carrying out the subsequent administrative tasks, representing Ministers in meetings with other Departments, pressure groups and members of the public, and managing the bureaucracy of central government. It will be convenient to look at each of these aspects in turn.

Civil servants are the main source of information and advice for Ministers. When a Minister needs to know something or has to prepare for a meeting, to make a speech, to answer questions in Parliament or to appear on the media, it is the civil servants in his own Department (and sometimes in other Departments as well) who provide the necessary information and advice. Usually this is provided in writing in the form of background papers and other internal memoranda. It is often supplemented (or even replaced) by oral information and advice given at

Figure 14.1 Civil service staff in post, 1 April 1990

Departments (Grouped by Ministerial responsibilities)	Total Staff* Full-time equivalents	Non-Industrials					
		Full-time			Part-time		
		Male	Female	Total	Male	Female	Total
Total all departments	562,388	257,517	219,397	476,914	1,810	34,829	36,639
Agriculture, Fisheries & Food	9,881	5,299	3,851	9,150	35	585	620
Intervention Board for Agric Produce	860	402	376	778	7	156	163
Cabinet Office (incl OMCS)	1,484	667	740	1,407	12	121	133
CHANCELLOR OF EXCHEQUER							
Treasury (incl CISCO)	3,135	1,449	1,007	2,456	10	134	144
Customs and Excise	26,864	16,903	9,454	26,357	42	973	1,015
Inland Revenue	66,063	28,098	34,334	62,432	298	6,950	7,248
National Savings, Department for	7,027	2,323	4,348	6,671	20	692	712
Central Statistical Office	999	500	460	960	1	76	77
Government Actuary	62	47	13	60	2	1	3
Information, Central Office of	739	416	303	719	3	11	14
National Investment and Loans Office	41	20	21	41	–	–	–
Registry of Friendly Societies	130	82	47	129	1	1	2
Royal Mint	973	243	127	370	–	14	14
HM Stationery Office	3,201	1,180	824	2,004	6	91	97
DEFENCE							
Defence, Ministry of	141,373	57,910	30,356	88,266	240	2,960	3,200
EDUCATION AND SCIENCE							
Education and Science, Department of	2,560	1,180	1,303	2,483	4	151	155
EMPLOYMENT							
Employment, Department of	37,268	11,982	22,619	34,601	134	5,183	5,317
Training Agency	10,870	5,648	4,515	10,163	36	697	733
Advisory Conciliation & Arbitration Serv	613	374	213	587	1	51	52
Health and Safety Commission/Executive	3,640	2,067	1,352	3,419	44	284	328

ENERGY							
Energy, Department of	1,024	680	315	995	4	46	50
Office of Gas Supply	23	17	6	23	–	–	–
Office of Electricity Regulation	143	79	64	143	–	–	–
ENVIRONMENT							
DOE (excluding PSA)	6,074	3,046	2,418	5,464	27	140	167
PSA (excluding the Crown Suppliers)	19,584	9,122	3,498	12,620	50	412	462
The Crown Suppliers	967	403	374	777	–	10	10
Ordnance Survey	2,530	1,932	470	2,402	2	78	80
Office of Water Supply	64	37	22	59	8	2	10
FOREIGN AND COMMONWEALTH							
FCO	7,979	5,387	2,441	7,828	9	94	103
Overseas Development Administration	1,512	844	625	1,469	1	49	50
HOME							
Home Office	42,721	30,750	8,155	38,905	171	1,238	1,409
LORD CHANCELLOR							
Lord Chancellor's Department	10,454	4,159	5,679	9,838	180	1,051	1,231
Land Registry	10,771	4,028	6,226	10,254	52	974	1,026
Public Record Office	421	226	170	396	7	43	50
NORTHERN IRELAND OFFICE	194	97	85	182	–	3	3
PAYMASTER GENERAL'S OFFICE	831	249	457	706	12	237	249
SCOTLAND							
Scottish Office	10,274	6,890	2,639	9,529	26	223	249
Scottish Courts Administration	917	471	416	887	3	58	61
General Register Office, Scotland	303	148	141	289	–	28	28
Registers of Scotland	997	512	475	987	–	20	20
Scottish Record Office	114	68	30	98	–	11	11
Health, Department of	5,422	2,738	2,553	5,291	16	178	194

continued overleaf

Figure 14.1 (cont'd)

Departments (Grouped by Ministerial responsibilities)	Total	Non-Industrials					
	Staff*	Full-time			Part-time		
	Full-time equivalents	Male	Female	Total	Male	Female	Total
Total all departments	562,388	257,517	219,397	476,914	1,810	34,829	36,639
SOCIAL SERVICES							
Social Security, Dept of	80,890	28,100	48,490	76,590	212	8,239	8,451
Office of Population Census and Survey	2,126	754	1,276	2,030	14	172	186
TRADE AND INDUSTRY							
Trade and Industry, Department of	11,793	6,601	4,556	11,157	46	672	718
Export Credits Guarantee Department	1,349	701	623	1,324	–	51	51
Office of Fair Trading	350	169	179	348	1	3	4
Office of Telecommunications	121	77	44	121	–	–	–
Transport, Department of	15,513	8,389	5,969	14,358	40	1,222	1,262
Welsh Office	2,284	1,102	983	2,085	6	164	170
OTHER CIVIL DEPARTMENTS							
Charity Commission	416	216	192	408	2	14	16
Crown Estate Office	38	25	13	38	–	–	–
Crown Office (Scot) & Proc Fiscal Service	1,066	357	672	1,029	11	63	74
Crown Prosecution Service	4,710	1,980	2,631	4,611	9	188	197
Law Officers Department	20	10	10	20	–	–	–
Lord Advocate's Department	19	13	5	18	–	2	2
Office of Arts and Libraries	60	33	26	59	2	–	2
Privy Council Office	34	16	18	34	–	–	–
Serious Fraud Office	84	54	28	82	1	2	3
Treasury Solicitor	413	247	160	407	2	11	13

* Part-timers working more than 10 hours counted as half units.
Source: *Staff in post in the Civil Service* (HM Treasury: HMSO, 1991)

internal departmental meetings, since this can be quicker in an emergency and some Ministers prefer to be briefed in this way. On the whole civil servants do not produce original work for these purposes, since they do not have the time or the aptitude for the necessary research on which it would have to be based. They act essentially as filters and interpreters of existing information which they derive either from departmental sources or from outside experts to whom they have access.

Civil servants help Ministers to formulate policy and to make decisions by presenting them with option papers which encompass a range of possibilities and policy recommendations. They also provide the information and advice against which Ministers can test the soundness or otherwise of their own ideas and their party political commitments. The complex role of civil servants in the policy- and decision-making process will be described more fully in Chapter 15.

Civil servants carry out the administrative tasks of central government in accordance with the political guidelines laid down in previous ministerial decisions. If this is not possible in certain cases because new situations have arisen, reference is usually made to the appropriate Minister or Ministers for further policy guidance. Even though the administration of policy can be as important as the actual policy decisions, civil servants are trained to avoid behaving in such a way as to preempt or nullify the decisions of their political masters. On the whole they seek faithfully to carry out the policies which they have helped Ministers to formulate and the decisions which they have helped Ministers to take.

Civil servants have an important role as representatives of Ministers at meetings in Whitehall and elsewhere. These may be meetings with Ministers or officials from other Departments, with the spokesmen of pressure groups or with members of the general public. On occasions civil servants may speak on behalf of Ministers within the carefully defined limits of existing policy – for example, when giving evidence to a Select Committee or taking part in the discussions of an inter-departmental committee. On other occasions within Whitehall civil servants may state their Department's position slightly differently from their Ministers, since they may be involved in an exercise of departmental 'kite-flying' or devil's advocacy in order to test or probe some aspect of the conventional wisdom in Whitehall. There is normally a clear distinction between the degree of latitude which is allowed to them in the privacy of internal Whitehall meetings and the orthodox way in which they are expected faithfully to reflect government policy in meetings with outsiders. Of course, some meetings between civil servants and outsiders are held on a confidential basis and on such occasions the officials concerned may be reasonably frank and expansive with a few knowledgeable outsiders whom they know from experience they can trust. Yet it takes a long time for outsiders (that is, anyone not covered by the Official Secrets Act) to build up such trust in the eyes of officials and on the whole information is exchanged or imparted only to those who have a clear 'need to know'.

Finally, there is the very important function for civil servants in the highest grades, namely that of seeing that the bureaucracy of central government is managed in such a way as to ensure the greatest practicable efficiency and effectiveness in the civil service. This is an aspect of their duties which has been accorded much greater importance by Ministers in the present Government who have been determined both to reduce civil service numbers and to increase the efficiency of those who remain.

Ever since the implementation of the Northcote–Trevelyan reforms in the second half of the nineteenth century, the Permanent Secretary of each Department has had to take personal responsibility (as the senior official) for the management of his Department and to act as its Accounting Officer when answering to the Comptroller and Auditor-General and the Public Accounts Committee. In practice, however, most of the day-to-day management tasks within Whitehall Departments have been delegated to other senior civil servants at slightly lower levels in the various departmental hierarchies, while the important matters of civil service pay and conditions are handled centrally in Whitehall by the Treasury and the Management and Personnel Office (now within the Cabinet Office). Indeed the efficient management of Whitehall Departments is regarded by the present Conservative Government as being of such importance that all senior Ministers have been urged (often without much conspicuous success) to play a direct part in the management of their Departments. Perhaps it is an indication of the hopelessness of that appeal that the Government has turned to the idea of Departmental Agencies as a potentially more fruitful way of ensuring that large chunks of administrative activity are more efficiently managed in semi-autonomous units. This is an interesting development which we shall discuss below.[7]

14.2 Key Aspects

There are several key aspects of the civil service in Britain. In this chapter we shall concentrate on those which have had a significant effect upon the British political system. Accordingly we shall begin by considering some of the most influential Whitehall conventions and then go on to discuss the strengths and weaknesses of the civil service, including the issues raised by the nature and limits of civil servants' loyalty to Ministers.

Whitehall Conventions

Perhaps the strongest convention in Whitehall is that the main duty of senior civil servants is to advise Ministers on matters of policy and to assist them in their dealings with Parliament and the public. This means that they look up to Ministers rather than down to the administration of their Departments, as one senior civil servant has put it.[8] The tasks of bureaucratic management and control have tended to be seen as rather tedious and unattractive chores by most of the talented officials who have reached the top of the civil service over the years. Notwithstanding the attempts made following the 1968 Fulton Report and again by the present Conservative Government to instil more managerial attitudes into senior civil servants, the results have appeared to be rather patchy and may prove ephemeral. This is because policy advice to Ministers really has to come first when it is needed and because the whole Whitehall machinery has been designed mainly to serve Ministers in their dealings with Parliament and the public.

Another related convention is that civil servants invariably take their instructions only from their superiors in their own Departments or directly from Ministers and not from anyone else. This means that the lines of authority and accountability are strictly vertical and that, to get anything done in a Whitehall Department, it is necessary for Ministers (or civil servants acting on their behalf) to give the initial instructions. This tends to put a considerable burden upon

Ministers and the civil servants working directly for them in their Private Offices. It also means that a clear and decisive lead from Ministers is usually essential if Departments are to respond to events quickly and with good effect.

Another familiar Whitehall convention is that the administration of policy should be carried out according to the highest standards of probity and equity, preferably avoiding all forms of political embarrassment for Ministers. In the civil service this has often put a premium upon a defensive and cautious approach to policy and decision making and has meant that undue emphasis has been laid upon trying to see that neither Parliament nor the media nor the general public get more than minimal opportunities to identify shortcomings or failures in government policy. This is often an heroic and futile exercise, since events have a way of destroying the best laid plans of mice and men. Yet on a day-to-day basis it can mean that the correct conduct of government entails the minimum of administrative flexibility and too few opportunities for local management initiatives. With any luck this may now be changing following the present Government's acceptance of a report from its own Efficiency Unit outlining three main ways in which the management of central government could be improved.[9]

Another well-established convention in Whitehall is that the government of the day should have at all times a coherent and defensible position on every policy issue with which it has to deal. This is seen as a minimum requirement for satisfactory Cabinet government based, as it is, upon the principle of collective responsibility. Yet it does mean that a great deal of civil service time and effort is spent upon producing agreed solutions with which all Departments can concur, even if such solutions may not be the most appropriate or desirable in the circumstances. Thus the coherence and defensibility of policy has often come before opportunities to adopt simple or radical solutions to the problems with which central government is faced.

Essentially, all these civil service conventions flow from traditional adherence to the principles of ministerial responsibility and parliamentary accountability. The former dictates that civil servants should regard the support of Ministers as their principal and overriding task. The latter ensures that civil servants are habitually cautious, even unimaginative, in the way that they perform their tasks. In both cases the dominant conventions really derive from assumptions long held at Westminster and the political imperatives of parliamentary government.

Strengths and Weaknesses

As we have already seen, the British civil service has both strengths and weaknesses which stem mainly from the nature of British parliamentary government and the people involved in it. In many cases the weaknesses are merely the counterparts of the strengths which have been widely recognised for many years. The position can be regarded from at least two contrasting angles, so it is unwise to be dogmatic when making an assessment. In any case, the situation changed quite fast and probably with significant long-term consequences under the Thatcher Government, so our judgements now need to be tentative and provisional.

One obvious strength is the intellectual and administrative ability of those in the higher administrative grades. This reflects the high entry standards for this group and the continuing attractions of a career in the administrative grades for many of the ablest students from our best universities. It also reflects the fact that an elite group of administration trainees is selected each year, so that these 'fliers' can then be put into a special fast stream for accelerated promotion to positions of great responsibility. Such people are given early chances to enhance their reputations and to leaven their intellectual abilities with the yeast of hard experience in various parts of the administration. Increasingly they are now able to benefit from short secondments to the private sector as well, although this can also lead some of them to decide not to return. In general, however, the result of this successful elitism is the formation and constant renewal of a small cadre of highly-trained and very able practitioners of public administration whose main strength is the ability to see that the decisions of Ministers are efficiently implemented within the realm of government.

On the other hand, it can be argued that the particular kind of ability demonstrated by this elite group of civil servants is too generalist and arcane to be truly beneficial to Ministers grappling with all the problems of modern government. Unfavourable contrasts have often been drawn with the rather different qualities of comparable officials in the higher grades of the French civil service where the cadres have the dual advantage of intellectual distinction and a more specialised, technical training from the *Ecole Nationale d'Administration* or one of the other *Grandes Ecoles*.[10] Similarly some of those on the Left of British politics have criticised the narrow and socially unrepresentative composition of the civil service elite and have argued that the situation will not be satisfactory until such cadres are recruited from a much wider economic and social background.[11] The assumption in this case is that bourgeois civil servants will tend to dilute and sometimes negate the political purposes of a Labour Government.

Another strength of the British civil service has been its traditional impartiality and apparent ability to work satisfactorily for Ministers of contrasting political persuasions. Of course individual civil servants retain their own private political views, but professionally they have to be prepared to carry out the policies of the government of the day without complaint or obstruction and this is clearly what they do. Resignations from the civil service on policy or political grounds are very rare, although a growing minority do leave the public service for higher financial rewards in the private sector – as with, for example, Inland Revenue inspectors who join private accountancy firms.

On the other hand, there have been critics of the civil service who have interpreted this vaunted political impartiality as tantamount to patient and practised obstruction of the more radical political purposes of democratically elected governments. Complaints of this kind have been expressed on both the Left and the Right of British politics. On the Left, Tony Benn and others have made the point in speeches and articles reflecting upon the experience of the 1974–9 Labour Government.[12] On the Right, Sir John Hoskyns (the first head of Margaret Thatcher's Policy Unit at 10 Downing Street) criticised civil servants for withholding the last 5 per cent of commitment to the policies of any government simply in order to preserve their credentials for serving a future government of a different political persuasion.[13] It would seem from such matching complaints that the civil service is at least even-handed in its instinct for political impartiality and caution. Yet we cannot be sure that such criticism, whether from the Left or from the Right, is not really an attempt to make the civil service the whipping-boy for the political failures of all governments.

As for the almost complete absence of corruption in the civil service, this must obviously be regarded as a virtue of British central government. With very few exceptions British civil servants are people of the highest personal integrity who do not succumb to the temptations of bribery and corruption which damage the reputation of governments in many other countries.[14] Such venality is more evident in local government in Britain, presumably because there are more opportunities at that level for both councillors and officials to do favours – for example, in relation to planning permission – in return for personal financial gain.

Obviously no one would claim that the almost total absence of corruption in the British civil service is anything but a strength for the system. Yet it might be argued that the price which we have had to pay for this probity and rectitude is an attitude of stuffy and unadventurous caution which has been criticised by those who look to the civil service for more spark and imagination. Such criticism is almost certainly misplaced, partly because even a little corruption in order to get things done in any political system is invariably very corrosive of personal and institutional standards, and partly because in our political system it is for politicians and Ministers to take initiatives and for civil servants then to carry them out on behalf of the government of the day.

The Loyalty Issue

The British civil service has long been admired for its sense of dedication and commitment to public duty. This is based upon the traditional civil service ethos which holds that civil servants must be scrupulously fair in their dealings with Parliament and the public. It reflects what has sometimes been described as 'the mandarin culture' of Whitehall; that is to say, the belief held by Permanent Secretaries and other senior civil servants that there is something which can be called 'the public interest' which is normally defined by Ministers in the government of the day, but which occasionally has to be defended by senior civil servants if and when it seems to come under unreasonable political attack. In this respect, it is slightly analogous to the duty which may be felt by the Monarch from time to time to a concept of the public interest which may be different from that which is recognised by Ministers.

There are at least two views of this aspect of the civil service. The favourable view is held by those who basically do not trust any politicians – a fairly widespread feeling in British society – and who therefore welcome the existence of certain bureaucratic 'stabilisers' in the political system. In the eyes of such people, who include many managers of large companies and other well-meaning technocrats, life would be much simpler if there were always a high degree of continuity in government policy and in the regulatory arrangements which govern their affairs from one year or even one decade to the next. In so far as British politics are thought by many to have suffered from a surfeit of ideology and political polarisation in the 1970s and early 1980s, there are those who look eagerly and appreciatively to the civil service to provide this stabilising and moderating influence upon governments of both Left and Right. It is the argument for what might be called the gyroscopic role of the civil service – its alleged ability to draw most policy and nearly all governments back to the middle of the road before too long.

The critical view, which is shared with almost equal vehemence by 'conviction politicians' of the Right and the Left, is that the British political system is based upon the principle of 'winner takes all' and in that context it is Ministers, whoever

However, another view is that Ministers.

they may be, who have the absolute and exclusive right to define the national or public interest, while the duty of civil servants is simply to carry out their wishes in the most effective way unless and until the ruling party is dismissed by the electorate at a subsequent General Election. For most of the time this controversy does not arise in any acute form, since civil servants smoothly and faithfully carry out the policy decided by Ministers, but there have been instances – some more important than others – when the boot seems to have been on the other foot. On those occasions civil servants in strong and established Departments appear to have been able to convince their Ministers at least of the desirability of certain policies to which the latter may not have been committed initially. For example, in the 1950s senior civil servants in the Home Office apparently were able to persuade at least two successive Home Secretaries of the desirability of retaining capital punishment for murder, notwithstanding the publicly declared abolitionist views of the Ministers concerned. Equally in the 1960s it appeared that civil servants in the Foreign Office were able to convince Foreign Secretaries in successive Conservative and Labour Governments that Britain should apply to join the European Community, even though each incoming government had had strong reservations about doing so.

The idea of a civil servant seeking to set his conception of the public interest above that of Ministers was, however, illustrated best by the case of Clive Ponting, who deliberately passed two classified documents concerning the sinking of the *Belgrano* during the Falklands conflict to Tam Dalyell, the Labour MP who had been relentlessly pursuing this issue ever since 1982.[15] When this was discovered after a rigorous internal investigation in the Ministry of Defence, Mr Ponting was charged with contravening Section 2(1)(a) of the 1911 Official Secrets Act and in 1985 taken to court, where he pleaded not guilty to communicating the documents unlawfully on the grounds that it had been his duty 'in the interests of the state' to inform Parliament (via Mr Dalyell), because Ministers had misled Parliament about the sinking of the *Belgrano* and the Select Committee investigating the affair was in danger of being misled as well. Although the trial judge, Mr Justice McCowan, said in his guidance to the jury that 'the interests of the state' were synonymous with the policies of the government of the day, the jury eventually thought otherwise and found Mr Ponting not guilty. For our purposes here the main issues highlighted by this interesting case were, firstly, whether a civil servant has the legal right to communicate classified information against the wishes of his Minister on the ground that it is his duty to see that Parliament and public are not misled and, secondly, whether a civil servant has a professional or ethical duty to a concept of 'the public interest' which is superior to, and may not be the same as, that which is defined by Ministers. The judge argued against both these propositions, but the jury and a good part of the press and public opinion seemed more inclined to be sympathetic to Mr Ponting's view. The outcome was a technical victory for Mr Ponting and a moral victory for those who believe that the government of the day has no monopoly right to define the public interest. Yet Ministers and the Government's supporters in the country could legitimately argue in reply that, if Mr Ponting really felt unable on grounds of conscience to accept the action of his Minister, then his correct course would have been to resign from the civil service rather than break the conditions of his employment by passing classified documents to someone who was unauthorised to receive them.

filtering /
diluting

Other Familiar Criticisms

Among the other familiar criticisms which are made of the British civil service is the charge that senior civil servants are disinclined to approach the problems of government sufficiently in the long term or in the round. It is said that there is too much concentration upon immediate political issues within the sphere of each Department. In so far as this is true, it stems from a natural bureaucratic instinct to play safe and from working habits in Whitehall which have always attached considerable importance to the orderly division of labour between Departments. Furthermore, in a system of government which is so heavily influenced by the political requirements of Ministers, it is perhaps naive to expect civil servants to set broader or more distant targets than those of the politicians whom they serve. Indeed, in the light of the sensitive issues discussed in the previous section, it would not be well received by most politicians if civil servants attempted to do this.

Perhaps the most recurrent refrain in the criticism from political quarters has been that the civil service seems either unwilling or unable fully to embrace radical policies, or at least radical departures from existing policies. It is argued that civil servants demonstrate this tendency by filtering or diluting nearly all new ideas which do not fit into the current political wisdom. Yet, as long as such initiatives come from the Prime Minister or other senior Ministers, civil servants are much less likely to act as a brake upon political radicalism; indeed they are likely to carry them through with dutiful efficiency. Everything depends upon the source of the new ideas and who gives the instructions. If the new ideas stem from Ministers, they are invariably accepted, albeit sometimes with private misgivings. If they come from anyone else, no matter how expert or enlightened, they are much more likely to be regarded as unwelcome heresy.

The main explanation for this characteristic of civil service behaviour seems to be that, while civil servants are trained faithfully to carry out ministerial wishes, they are naturally reluctant to entertain new ideas which would disrupt or challenge the conventional political wisdom of the time. An important subsidiary explanation may be that some Ministers are too lazy or narrow in their political outlook to welcome such ideas, while others are too ambitious or beholden to their party leadership to take any risks.

This problem would not matter very much if the Prime Minister and other senior members of the Government had more frequent opportunities for fresh thinking and intelligent reflection while in office, or if there were better institutional arrangements in Whitehall to ensure that the conventional wisdom of every government was constantly challenged and tested from within. Yet on the whole this is not the case and it is left to critics in the Opposition or the media to 'think the unthinkable'. Unfortunately such sparring is not usually very helpful, since all governments have a tendency to close ranks against criticism from such sources. Political criticism should not be regarded as heresy and political exorcism is not necessarily the most appropriate response.

14.3 Methods of Control

There are a number of different methods of controlling the civil service. Each of them is used to a greater or lesser extent, but none of them has been sufficient on its own. It has proved necessary to use them all in combination in a continuing effort to achieve real and lasting control on democratic principles.

Ministerial Responsibility

The classic method of controlling the civil service in Britain is based upon the traditional doctrine of ministerial responsibility. This may have been effective during the second half of the nineteenth century when the scope and complexity of government was very much smaller than today. In modern conditions its efficacity is much more dubious, as a number of knowledgeable witnesses have pointed out.[16]

In theory, ministerial responsibility is supposed to mean that Ministers are held to account for everything which happens or fails to happen within the spheres of their departmental responsibility. In practice, modern government has become so large and complex that no Minister, however energetic or hard-working, can possibly achieve such an ideal. Indeed, as Michael Heseltine pointed out soon after becoming Secretary of State for the Environment for the first time, 'I had general advice on every policy issue, but no analysis of how each part of the [departmental] machine operated, why it operated in that way and how much it cost'.[17] Without such basic management information, let alone the necessary inclination and expertise to make use of it, most senior Ministers in modern times have been unable (or uninterested) to control their Departments in anything like the full meaning of the term.

Admittedly the Thatcher Government sought to introduce a new Management Information System for Ministers (MINIS) throughout Whitehall which was supposed to enable them to set out the objectives, priorities, costs and results of every aspect of their Departments' activities, so that waste and duplication were eliminated and efficiency and effectiveness were enhanced.[18] Yet this systematic approach has not appealed to all senior Ministers, some of whom remain convinced that such managerial activity does not constitute the best use of their time and energy and who doubt whether they personally have the aptitude for it. As long as ministerial responsibility continues to be interpreted by some senior Ministers in the traditional way, there is unlikely to be full and effective control of all aspects of modern central government based upon the concept of ministerial responsibility.

Bureaucratic Hierarchy

Another traditional method of controlling the civil service is based upon the concept of bureaucratic hierarchy. This also dates from the second half of the nineteenth century and the civil service reforms which flowed from the Northcote–Trevelyan Report of 1854. It has always presupposed that Ministers are responsible for the elaboration of policy, while civil servants are responsible for the public administration which carries it out.

In theory, such a division of labour in Whitehall appears quite logical and ought to work well. After all, as mentioned earlier, every Permanent Secretary at the head of a Department is also the Accounting Officer for his Department and directly answerable to the Comptroller and Auditor-General and the Public Accounts Committee for every item of public spending in his departmental budget. In practice, the senior civil servants at the top of the various departmental hierarchies are normally preoccupied with their role as the leading policy advisers to Ministers and so disinclined to spend much of their time on the tedious but necessary tasks of managing their area of public administration. Yet it must be admitted that this established convention of Whitehall behaviour was modified under the Thatcher Government. The result was that most senior civil servants responded positively to the wish of Ministers that more of their time should be devoted to the exercise of tighter bureaucratic control over the administrative machinery of central government.

Administrative Efficiency

A more modern method of controlling the Whitehall bureaucracy is based upon the principle of administrative efficiency. This assumes that it ought to be possible to apply in the civil service some of the business techniques used in the private sector. It was one of the main thrusts of the Fulton Report in 1968, which advocated the introduction of 'accountable management' into the civil service, and it has been promoted intermittently by governments ever since. It attaches special importance to the use of business techniques, such as the achievement of a given level of output with less financial input, the comparison of different methods to achieve a given objective, and the use of cost–benefit analysis in the process of decision making.

Such techniques imported from the private sector have not always proved transferable to the public sector where the goals, constraints and criteria of success or failure are rather different. In the private sector, the principal goal is usually profit, the constraints are largely imposed by the market, and the criteria of success or failure include the assessments made by investors and the rate of return on capital and labour employed. In the civil service, on the other hand, the goals tend to be ill-defined and changeable, the constraints include considerations of equity and public interest, not to mention the problems of parliamentary accountability, and the criteria of success or failure depend very much on the changing priorities and prejudices of transient senior Ministers. In short, it is hard to see how it would be sensible to try to run the Whitehall part of the civil service as if it were Sainsbury or Marks & Spencer, although there are obviously useful lessons which can be applied to the conduct of the more straightforward administrative tasks which are performed increasingly in separate operational units situated outside Whitehall.

In spite of the inherent problems of applying this approach to the management of the civil service, the Thatcher Government demonstrated that it is possible to make progress in this direction. The so-called 'Rayner scrutinies' (named after Lord Rayner, who was a Managing Director of Marks & Spencer before becoming Mrs Thatcher's first adviser on efficiency in government) identified potential financial savings in some of the routine support services in Whitehall – for example, typing pools, messenger services and car transport. The scrutiny of government research and development establishments also revealed potential financial savings of at least 15 per cent, while the review of the non-office activities of government – such as H.M. Coastguards or the Property Services Agency – indicated areas of further financial savings.[19] On the other hand, not all such scrutinies have been a success, especially when the proposals have seemed politically unacceptable to government back-benchers. For example, in 1981 it was suggested in one such scrutiny that certain payments made to pensioners through Sub-Post Offices should be made fortnightly rather than weekly or in some cases no longer made at all. This was anathema to millions of elderly people who raised such a protest with MPs that Ministers soon felt obliged to drop the idea.

Ministers in the present Government have also been keen to expand the role and importance of the Government Accountancy Service within every aspect of government. This has proved quite an uphill struggle, since it is difficult for the public sector to recruit and retain enough good accountants when most of them can earn so much more in the private sector. To date there are now about 820 fully qualified accountants in post in Whitehall. There is obviously a long way further to go in this direction before the influence of professionally trained accountants really makes itself felt in all parts of central government.

Judicial Scrutiny

A final method of controlling the civil service is that of judicial scrutiny by the courts and other quasi-judicial bodies, such as administrative tribunals. The attraction of this method is that it can provide a framework of standards for good administrative practice without being too legalistic in the mechanisms used.[20] Yet it is doubtful whether the system of administrative law in this country is sufficiently developed really to achieve its purpose in this respect. This is because so far the courts have taken only limited steps in this direction, notably on those occasions when the doctrine of *ultra vires* has been applied in certain cases brought against local authorities charged with going beyond the bounds of their proper competence.[21] This form of judicial control has been applied only sparingly to central government, largely because it conflicts with the traditional principle of ministerial accountability to Parliament, but it may become more evident as the European Court gradually gets involved in more and more cases of definitive arbitration in those areas of public policy where Community legal competence is established.[22]

Hitherto, the most notable step in this direction for the benefit of the ordinary British citizen was taken in 1967 when Parliament decided to establish the Parliamentary Commissioner for Administration (the so-called Ombudsman) with the statutory authority to investigate public complaints of maladministration in central government Departments and (later) in the National Health Service as well.[23] Although the Ombudsman has always been limited by the fact that he has no powers of general initiative or legal enforcement, his office has been able over the years to rectify faulty procedures in the civil service and has occasionally led Whitehall Departments to make *ex gratia* payments by way of compensation to citizens with clear and justified grievances. His powers of publicity and persuasion, backed by the House of Commons Select Committee which monitors his work, have proved to be a significant addition to the range of methods available for the control of the civil service in Britain.

14.4 The Next Steps

There are a number of further developments which could change the civil service in a variety of far-reaching ways. Some are logical extensions of what has already happened over the past decade and more. Others would involve major new departures in our constitutional arrangements in this country. All are likely to be difficult to achieve, given the familiar problems of reforming an established bureaucracy.

Ministers as Managers

One development, which is a logical extension of policy already initiated by the Thatcher Government, would be for all Ministers to take on the main responsibility for the management of their Departments. So far this idea has been more evident in rhetoric than in action, and it has evidently appealed more to some Ministers than others. It implies that all Ministers should take a much more direct and continuous interest in the management of their Departments and spend a good deal of their time acting as if they were the chief executives of large public corporations. Such an approach may be practicable for a Minister in charge of one of the smaller Departments, such as Energy or Employment. It is bound to be more difficult in the larger Departments, such as Defence or Social Security, and in the Departments, such as the Treasury or Education and Science, where the actual administration of policy is largely the responsibility of other institutions.

Furthermore, if the idea is to work, it would probably require the appointment of more Ministers in nearly every Department (a move which would be limited at present by the 1937 Ministers of the Crown Act), the creation of several smaller Departments by breaking up the remaining super-Departments, and deliberate steps towards simpler forms of public administration reflecting reduced government activity in general. It would also be easier to implement if Ministers were relieved of many of the burdens of parliamentary accountability (for example, parliamentary Questions once a month) and the responsibilities of constituency representation (as happens in France). Since few of these conditions are likely to be met within the British parliamentary system, the idea is unlikely to be implemented to any significant extent.

Officials as Managers

Another development, also a logical extension of policy already initiated by the Thatcher Government, would be for senior officials to spend more of their time and energy managing their Departments. This idea has been promoted very strongly by Ministers in the present Government as one way of securing greater efficiency and effectiveness in the civil service. As stated in a 1981 White Paper on this subject, 'an integral part of the Government's policy is to tackle the underlying obstacles to efficiency [in the civil service] by creating the right conditions for managers to manage and by bringing on and rewarding those who are successful'.[24] This has involved increasing the responsibilities of line managers, securing better management information, insisting that Departments pay fully for common services, putting greater emphasis upon managerial skills in the training of civil servants, and encouraging officials at all levels to propose ways of increasing the efficiency of the bureaucracy.

For a number of reasons there have been some difficulties in getting this new managerial ethos established and accepted in the civil service. Sir Robert Armstrong, when Secretary to the Cabinet and Head of the Civil Service, pointed out to a Select Committee that 'civil servants have tended to find policy work more glamorous and more interesting than management work'.[25] Another problem is that, whereas it may be possible to measure the typical policy inputs of money and manpower employed, it has always proved more difficult to measure the output of government policy in a useful way. Since these problems are inherent in the process of British central government, the Treasury and Civil Service Select Committee felt able in its report to recommend no more than 'greater devolution of management, and strengthened central review of the effectiveness and efficiency with which management operates'.[26] In responding to the Select Committee, the Thatcher Government made it clear that it wanted to see all Departments follow three basic principles. These were that 'the objectives for policy and administration should be clear, the responsibility for attaining objectives and for the management of resources in so doing should be defined, and the information needed to exercise the responsibility should be provided'.[27] On the face of it, these were reasonable requirements.

Whether or not it proves possible fully to implement such principles, the insistence upon the role of officials as managers is likely to have a number of longer-term consequences. It may mean that Ministers will need to seek more policy advice from their Private Offices, which may have to include more special advisers who serve them with an explicitly political remit. It may mean significant changes in the recruitment and training of civil servants, since at any rate those destined for senior administrative positions will need to develop real managerial skills at an early stage of their careers. It could even mean the evolution of two-tier recruitment and career development within the civil service, with some civil servants destined for an explicitly managerial role and some being recruited (often from outside the civil service) for the enlarged political role of providing policy advice for Ministers. Under the Conservative Government since 1979, we have already seen the growing politicisation of the higher grades of the civil service – with all the current Permanent Secretaries having been appointed by Margaret Thatcher. It seems most unlikely that any future government would not follow suit.

Structural Reform

Another development which has gathered momentum is the idea of reforming the structure of Departments by differentiating between the bulk of civil service work, which tends to be administrative and repetitive in character, and the work of the policy-making elite, which is concerned almost entirely with the requirements of Ministers. Such a reform is aligning the Whitehall structure more closely with the pattern in Sweden or West Germany, where the policy-making Ministries are often quite small and significantly political in their orientation, while the execution of policy is entrusted to larger administrative Agencies which have considerable managerial autonomy.

In Britain this idea was pioneered by the Heath Government in the early 1970s when it experimented with the practice of 'hiving off' sections of Whitehall Departments into quasi-autonomous Agencies, such as the Civil Aviation Authority in 1971 and the Manpower Services Commission in 1973. It was taken a good deal further by the Thatcher Government, following the influential report submitted to the Prime Minister by the so-called Efficiency Unit in 1988. This group, under the leadership of Sir Robin Ibbs, a director seconded from ICI, recommended that to the greatest extent possible the executive functions of central government should be carried out not by traditional Departments but by specially designated Agencies. Each Agency is accountable to a Minister who in turn is accountable to Parliament for its performance. The Agencies have generally been set up within existing Departments and their staff continue to be civil servants.[28]

Margaret Thatcher accepted the main recommendations of the report on behalf of the Government in a statement to the House of Commons on 18 February 1988. In doing so, she indicated that it would 'set the direction for further development of management reform in the civil service'.[29] She added that the Government would develop a continuing programme for establishing such Agencies and would seek to apply the lessons of the experience gained. Among the first such Agencies to be established have been the Stationery Office, the Meteorological Office and the Employment Services part of the Department of Employment. Ministers have also decided upon the radical step of putting the Social Security offices throughout the country onto an agency basis, thus shifting the largest single chunk of Whitehall administrative work. It seems that the idea is well and truly launched and that in due course it may bring about far-reaching changes in the ethos and practices of the public administration in Britain. Indeed the establishment of Agencies outside the sphere of Departments amounts to the privatisation of parts of the civil service.

Certainly the present Government has not been shy about its attempts to transfer various activities, in whole or in part, from central government into the private sector. The main idea behind these various forms of 'contracting out' is that certain tasks can be performed in the private sector both more cheaply and more efficiently then in the public sector. For example, the Ministry of Defence has put many of its cleaning requirements out to private contractors, the Property Services Agency (which has itself been privatised) has had some minor maintenance work on the government estate done by private contractors, and Health Authorities in all parts of the country have been encouraged to have their hospital catering, cleaning and laundry done by private firms under contract. The objective has been either to use competitive tendering to squeeze better value for money from the existing public sector workforce or to secure cheaper contracts for services from firms in the private sector. It must be added, however, that the latter approach has not always been beneficial in the longer term, since private firms have been known to secure their contracts on a loss-leader basis, only to raise their prices later on, and since their standards of quality and reliability have sometimes proved too low for the specialist tasks required. The most striking, and tragic, example illustrating the latter point was the apparent ease with which in 1989 a group of IRA terrorists was able to penetrate the defences provided by a private security firm which had been engaged by the Ministry of Defence to guard the barracks of the Royal Marine school of music in Deal.

It could be argued, however, that the most significant structural reform of the civil service made by the Conservative Government since 1979 has been its deliberate and continuous reduction in the overall size and cost of the civil service. In May 1979 there were 732 000 civil servants and the number was steadily reduced to 562 000 in April 1990. The result is that Britain now has the smallest civil service since the Second World War. This reduction has been achieved by a combination of improved efficiency, cutting functions, privatisation (including contracting out), hiving-off to other public sector bodies and policy changes resulting in a reduced workload in some areas, such as public housing. It remains to be seen whether it will be possible to go much further down this road in the 1990s.

Judicial Control

A final idea for the future, which has been advocated by those who are attracted by continental European or American models of government, is that the civil service in Britain should be subjected to comprehensive judicial control in a formal way. This would require the development of a fully-fledged system of administrative law in this country, including perhaps the use of special administrative courts on the pattern of the *Conseil d'Etat* in France or the *Bundesverfassungsgericht* in West Germany. Such far-reaching legal and constitutional changes could not be made in Britain unless there were prior all-party agreement. Although this may seem unlikely, there is a real possibility that developments in this direction will gradually be imposed upon us by the European Court as it finds itself drawn into more and more definitive arbitration between private interests and the public administration in those areas of policy, and hence civil service activity, covered by European Community law.

14.5 Conclusion

On the basis of the evidence adduced in this chapter it is reasonable to conclude that the higher grades of the civil service wield considerable power and influence within British central government. Yet such senior officials are by no means necessarily the dominant forces in their Departments. Ministers remain in charge and their constitutional authority is not questioned by civil servants. Officials are there to guide, assist and advise their Ministers, not to control them. As Denis Healey (one of the heavyweights in successive Labour Governments) has observed, 'a Minister who complains that his civil servants are too powerful is either a weak Minister or an incompetent one'.[30] In other words, if the relationship between Ministers and civil servants works as it is supposed to do, there is no problem of over-mighty officials.

On the other hand, there is still a problem caused by the ethos and conventions of Whitehall which can frustrate the intentions of Ministers (especially junior ones) and lower the quality of policy and decision making in government. This happens because the top 2000 or so civil servants in the bureaucracy of central government have tended to form a self-conscious network within the 'village' atmosphere of Whitehall.[31] In these circumstances they are apt to share a range of common assumptions, to put a high value on agreed solutions, and to close ranks almost instinctively against heretics or outsiders. For years until 1979 many of them considered themselves to be engaged essentially in the orderly management of national decline. This was often expressed in an elegant, laconic pessimism about Britain's chances of competing successfully with her rivals in the modern world. While it would be claimed by sympathisers with the present Government that this defeatist mood was dispelled by the more exhilarating approach of Ministers in the 1980s, there are still few signs that top civil servants wield much creative power. Rather they seem committed to an honourable, if slightly circumspect, sense of public duty.

In these circumstances we must conclude that the civil service in Britain today is not exactly master or servant in our political system. It is more like a necessary ballast which helps to keep the ship of state on an even keel.

Suggested Questions

1. Is the composition of the British civil service well-suited to the needs of the time?
2. Do civil servants really run the country?
3. What are the most appropriate and effective ways of controlling the civil service in Britain?

Notes

1. Report of the Tomlin Commission, Cmnd 3909 (London: HMSO, 1931).
2. Lord Bridges, *Portrait of a Profession* (London: CUP, 1950), p. 25
3. See the Report of the Fulton Committee, Cmnd 3628 (London: HMSO, 1968).
4. See B. Sedgemore, *The Secret Constitution* (London: Hodder & Stoughton, 1980), pp. 148–53.
5. See P. Kellner and N. Crowther-Hunt, *The Civil Servants* (London: Macdonald, 1980), pp. 121–3.
6. See Civil Service Commission Annual Report, 1989.
7. See section below on 'The Next Steps', pp. 218–22.
8. See D. Howells, 'Marks & Spencer and the Civil Service: a comparison of culture and methods' in *Public Administration*, Autumn 1981.
9. The report, entitled 'Improving management in Governmen, the next steps', suggested that to begin the process of change there should be three main priorities: (1) systems and structures in each Department should enhance the effective delivery of policies and services; (2) the staff in each Department should have the relevant experience and skills; and (3) real pressure should be sustained for continuous improvements in value for money.
10. For example, in a Report on the Civil Service by the House of Commons Select Committee on Expenditure, H.C. 535, 1977.
11. See B. Sedgemore, *The Secret Constitution*, pp. 11–48.
12. See A. Benn, 'Manifestos and Mandarins' in W. Rodgers *et al.*, *Policy and Practice: the experience of Government* (London: RIPA, 1980), pp. 57–78.
13. See J. Hoskyns, 'Whitehall and Westminster, an outsider's view', in *Fiscal Studies*, November 1982.
14. Cases, such as the Poulson Affair which came to a head in July 1972, in which civil servants and Members of Parliament were implicated in corrupt practices, have been very rare in modern times.
15. For a fuller analysis of the 'public interest' defence see R. Thomas, 'The British Official Secrets Acts 1911–39 and the Ponting Case', in R. A. Chapman and M. Hunt (eds), *Open Government* (London: Routledge, 1989), pp. 95–122.
16. For example, see H. Young and A. Sloman, *No Minister* (London: BBC, 1982) pp. 19–31.
17. *Sunday Times*, 16 December 1979.
18. MINIS was described in paras 23–6 of the Third Report of the Treasury and Civil Service Select Committee, H.C. 236–I, 1981–2.
19. The total cumulative savings from the so-called efficiency scrutinies since 1979 came to £1.5 billion by early 1991, see *Hansard*, 7 February 1991, Col. 215.
20. See G. Drewry, *Law, Justice and Politics* (London: Longman, 1975), pp. 75–6.
21. For example, in the 1981 case of *Bromley Council* v. *the Greater London Council* in which the Law Lords ruled that the GLC had gone *ultra vires* by subsidising London Transport fares to an excessive extent via precepts upon the rates of the outer London Boroughs.
22. See section on the legal and constitutional implications of Britain's membership of the European Community in Chapter 19 below, pp. 319–24.

23. See Chapter 18 below, pp. 306–7, for a fuller description of the role of the Ombudsman.
24. 'Efficiency in the Civil Service', Cmnd 8293 (London: HMSO, 1981), para. 16.
25. Quoted in 'Efficiency and effectiveness in the Civil Service', Third Report from the Treasury and Civil Service Select Committee, H.C. 236–I, para. 21, 1981–2.
26. Ibid., para. 73.
27. Government observations upon the Third Report, Cmnd 8616, para. 25.
28. The Government's thinking on these new Departmental Agencies was outlined in a White Paper 'The financing and accountability of Next Steps Agencies', Cm 914 (London: HMSO, 1989). The progress made in this direction was later summarised in 'Improving management in Government, the Next Steps Agencies', Cm 1261 (London: HMSO, 1990).
29. *Hansard*, 18 February 1988, Col. 1149.
30. Quoted in H. Young and A. Sloman, *No Minister*, p. 25.
31. See H. Heclo and A. Wildavsky, *Private Government of Public Money* (London: Macmillan, 1981).

Further Reading

Bruce-Gardyne, J., *Ministers and Mandarins* (London: Sidgwick & Jackson, 1986).
Chapman, R. A., *Ethics in the British Civil Service* (London: Routledge & Kegan Paul, 1988).
Drewry, G. and Butcher, T., *The Civil Service Today* (Oxford: Basil Blackwell, 1988).
Fry, G. K., *The Changing Civil Service* (London: Allen & Unwin, 1985).
Hennessy, P., *Whitehall* (London: Secker & Warburg, 1989).
Kellner, P. and Crowther-Hunt, N., *The Civil Servants* (London: Macdonald, 1980).
Metcalfe, L. and Richards, S., *Improving Public Management* (London: Sage, 1987).
Rodgers, W. *et al.*, *Policy and Practice: the experience of Government* (London: RIPA, 1980).
Williams, W., *Washington, Westminster and Whitehall* (London: CUP, 1988).
Young, H. and Sloman, A., *No Minister* (London: BBC, 1982).

⬡15 Policy and decision making

In this chapter we are concerned with the policy- and decision-making process of British national politics, but only with the two main parties since none of the other parties has held the reins of office since the Second World War. We may define policy as a deliberate course of action or inaction worked out by the leading figures of the two main political parties with the help of others in order to define their political purposes and, to some extent, the methods by which they intend to achieve them. We may define decision making as an act by a Minister or Ministers collectively (and occasionally by civil servants in the name of Ministers) to select a particular course of action or inaction on a matter of public policy. Such definitions may seem rather abstract and general, but, if they are to reflect the varied realities of modern British politics, this is bound to be the case.

At the outset it is worth heeding Richard Neustadt's observation that 'in Britain governing is meant to be a mystery'.[1] This can be attributed to a number of different factors. Firstly, there is the pervasive official secrecy of British government, which can be traced back at least to the 1911 Official Secrets Act and which is still firmly established as one of the ruling conventions of conduct in Whitehall. Secondly, there is the tendency for all Ministers and civil servants to exploit the fact that their privileged access to official information is a form of real power in this and any other political system. Thirdly, there are the limitations imposed upon all investigations in this area by the fact that those who might be able to dispel the mystery are usually inhibited from doing so by the requirements of official secrecy (at least until many years after the event) while those academics and others who would be willing to do so are not usually given sufficient access to the evidence.

For these and other reasons it is not easy to identify all the characteristics of the policy- and decision-making process in Britain, let alone to draw all the right conclusions about what actually happens. Yet an attempt will be made in the following pages, necessarily in a rather schematic way. The process is shown diagrammatically in its sequential stages in Figure 15.1.

15.1 Stages in the Process

In many ways it is somewhat artificial to divide the policy- and decision-making process into a number of discrete stages, since in real life there is always a good deal more overlap and confusion than such a neat presentation would suggest. However it is a useful way of clarifying the way the process works and of identifying the key participants and procedures. In default of a better method, we shall proceed in this way.

Figure 15.1 The policy and decision making process

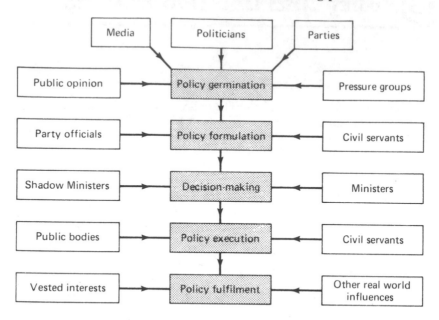

Policy Germination

The process begins with the stage of policy germination. This usually takes place when a party is in opposition, although it has to take place also when a party is in government if one party continues to win a succession of General Elections.

In the Conservative party, what usually happens is that the leadership identifies a problem or set of problems arising from its previous experience in office or its observation of the current economic and political scene, and then decides upon the need for a new policy or the reconsideration of an existing policy in a particular area. It has then to see whether there are the necessary sources of information and advice within the party fold to enable it to embark upon the formulation of policy proposals. If it seems that there are, the leadership will probably press ahead by setting up a policy group to look into it. On the other hand, if it is clear that there are not sufficient sources of information and advice within the party and its orbit, efforts are made to enlist the assistance of sympathetic and expert outsiders who can be trusted to keep a confidence and who have both the time and the inclination to help the party in such policy work.

When Margaret Thatcher was leader of the party, the more ideological thrust of Conservative policy was strongly influenced by self-styled 'think tanks', such as the Institute of Economic Affairs (IEA), the Centre for Policy Studies (actually established by Sir Keith Joseph and Margaret Thatcher in 1975) and the Adam Smith Institute. All of these bodies, and notably the IEA, which was founded in the 1950s, have been unrelenting campaigners for a free market approach, not only in economic policy, but increasingly in other spheres of policy as well. Over the period 1975 to 1990 they had a significant agenda-setting role in Conservative policy making and thrived under the appreciative patronage of Mrs Thatcher.

In the Labour party, policy germinates in a rather different way which reflects the different organisational and ideological tradition of the party. Political power and influence over policy has traditionally been more diffuse within the entire Labour movement. Consequently, ideas and pressure for the germination of policy come from a wider variety of sources, such as constituency activists, internal party pressure groups (such as the Socialist Environmental Association) and affiliated trade unions, as well as many friendly academics, intellectuals and experts in mass communication. The role of the parliamentary leadership has often been to act as something of a brake upon policy germination rather than an accelerator of it, especially at those times in the party's history when the Left has been in the ascendant in the constituencies.

The approach to policy making has been rather different since the 1987 General Election when Neil Kinnock and his closest colleagues and advisers decided upon the need for a thorough policy review in the wake of Labour's third electoral defeat in a row. In organisational terms, the conclusion that was drawn was the absolute necessity to keep the policy-making process firmly within the control of the party leader and his most trusted collaborators in the parliamentary party and on the National Executive Committee. In policy terms, Mr Kinnock evidently came to the conclusion at an early stage that only a revisionist and modernising approach to Labour policy would suffice if the party were to be able to make a convincing appeal to the British electorate in the 1990s. This implied, for example, leading the party towards more explicit acceptance of the mixed economy and away from the old formulations on nationalisation. It has also involved the party leadership in a sustained effort to square the circle on defence policy by committing the party to a position which appears to involve both acceptance of the Trident missile system if and when Labour next comes to power and a determination to switch resources on a massive scale from the defence budget to other domestic and social programmes. The truth is that the Labour leadership has done its homework on British public opinion and has been prepared for the first time since Labour left office in 1979 to make concessions to the realities of the new political consensus.

In the case of each main party the mechanisms just described may be characterised as the pure models of policy germination. In practice this stage of the process is often much more hit-or-miss, since it is bound to be influenced by developments in the political environment which produce a greater or lesser degree of pragmatism, depending upon the correlation of political forces at any particular time. The Labour Policy Review 1987–9 was a good example of the reactive model of policy germination in that the Labour leadership felt obliged to take account of the so-called 'new realism' engendered by more than 10 years of Thatcherism in power. Equally the almost revolutionary change in Conservative policy, for which the seeds were sown by Sir Keith Joseph and Margaret Thatcher during the period 1975–9, also fitted a reactive model of policy germination. The only difference is that in the latter case the party leadership was reacting to the previous failures which it had experienced in office rather than the relative success of the policies of its opponents, as was the case with Labour in the late 1980s.

At this early stage of the process, the key questions are who defines the problems to be solved, who sets the priorities for the policy work to be undertaken, and according to what ideological or institutional criteria are the various policy groups established? When a party is in opposition and seemingly down on its luck, it is invariably the party leadership which tries to take charge of the agonising reappraisal which is normally thought to be necessary when a party has been heavily or decisively defeated at the polls. When a party is in government, somewhat different considerations usually apply, since it is the school of experience in office which often leads to the germination of new policy once the initial burst of ideological enthusiasm has been exhausted.

It now appears that the normal rules which have traditionally governed this stage of the process when a party is in office were largely disregarded when Mrs Thatcher led the Conservative party as Prime Minister. Admittedly, the 1983 Conservative Manifesto was not particularly substantial in terms of content nor particularly radical, largely because the election was called at rather short notice in the after-glow of victory for Britain in the 1982 Falklands conflict. Yet during the following Parliament Mrs Thatcher and her closest colleagues moved decisively to rectify this 'mistake' or missed opportunity by insisting upon a much more radical Manifesto for the 1987 General Election.

Accordingly, the Conservatives fought the 1987 election on the basis of some quite radical and daring political commitments, some of which, such as the Community Charge and water privatisation, proved to be unpopular with their supporters and opponents alike. Once again Thatcherite Conservatism seemed to flout the traditional canons of postwar British politics by renewing and strengthening the party's commitment to radical, 'conviction politics' at precisely the stage when in analogous circumstances previous governments of Right or Left would probably have become consolidators rather than radicals.

Policy Formulation

The next stage in the process is that of policy formulation. By this we mean the translation into coherent policy proposals of the political ideas which have germinated in the ways just described. This is also a stage which takes place more systematically when a party is in opposition than when it is in government, although each situation will need to be examined if we are to get a complete picture.

In the Conservative party, policy formulation is usually the work of party officials and others who draft the papers in which the policy proposals are contained. Of course, such people work under the careful direction and control of the chairmen of the policy groups concerned and indirectly of the party leader and his most senior colleagues. For years this drafting work was done by the officials of the Conservative Research Department, which had been a relatively small but rather competent back-room organisation staffed mainly by bright, young graduates with further political ambitions. Since the Department was absorbed directly into Conservative Central Office in 1980 (ostensibly for reasons of economy) its role has not been so prominent in this aspect of party work and it has become more of a briefing and propaganda unit for the party as a whole.

In the Labour party, the work of policy formulation is done by analogous people employed by the party's Research Department. They work under the direction and control of the leading politicians in charge of the various policy groups, which in turn are located within the formal structure of policy committees and sub-committees under the auspices of the National Executive Committee. Thus, except for the drafting of some of the most important policy documents (such as some of those produced in the 1987-89 Policy Review), this work is done mainly by party officials who will not themselves be directly involved in the execution of the policy if and when the party is returned to office.

In government, of course, the policy formulation stage can be rather different, since Ministers have the benefit of official information and advice from civil servants. Nevertheless, the real work of drafting and redrafting the policy proposals which may or may not find their way into the party Manifestos is still done mainly by party officials and other trusted scribes working within the structure of party policy groups, since it would be constitutionally improper to ask civil servants to do it.

In the Labour party, the structure of such groups tends to be as elaborate when the party is in government as when it is in opposition, since the National Executive Committee still provides the framework for what in the past has sometimes amounted to a rival policy-making process with which the more moderate parliamentary leadership has had to contend. However the situation now seems to be very different in that Neil Kinnock and his closest colleagues have obviously succeeded in imposing their authority upon the comprehensive Policy Review. Even in former times, Labour Ministers and shadow Ministers remained free to decide which of the many policy commitments proposed by policy groups established under the auspices of the National Executive Committee they would accept and which they would reject as far as final inclusion in official party policy was concerned. When in government, Labour Ministers have also retained considerable flexibility and discretion in deciding upon the methods and timing for the implementation of even the most unambiguous policy commitments, as will doubtless be the case next time Labour is in office.

In the Conservative party, the structure of such policy groups tends to be less elaborate when the party is in government than when it is in opposition. This is because there is no equivalent of Labour's National Executive Committee with which the parliamentary leadership has to contend and because the party leader and his closest colleagues retain almost complete control of the policy formulation stage of the process. Policy groups are therefore established by the leader of the party and these are normally chaired by senior members of the Commons or the Lords and supported by party officials or other trusted people within the party orbit. In the first instance, the actual drafting of policy proposals is usually done by the party officials who act as secretaries to the various policy groups, although they tend to work under the close supervision and control of the various policy group chairmen, many of whom will be senior Ministers. The policy proposals are considered by the groups and often redrafted or refined in the light of such discussions. They are then submitted for further consideration by the relevant Minister or Ministers and in all important cases referred to the Prime Minister and Party Chairman for approval before any decision is taken about inclusion in or exclusion from the party Manifesto.

It must be added, however, that there is growing cynicism and even resentment in certain quarters of both main parties at the way in which the germination and formulation stages seem to have been captured in recent years by the leader of each party, assisted only by a few hand-picked colleagues and party officials. In so far as most MPs and others are not given the chance to be directly involved in the various policy groups which are established, there is resentment at being excluded and having to fight an election on a programme which has been drawn up by others. In so far as a few of them are directly involved in the groups, there is a widespread recognition that they have been co-opted into what is often a placebo exercise designed essentially to make them feel involved, even though their participation is of little real consequence and all the big decisions will be taken by the party leader in any case.

Decision Making

The next stage in the process is that of decision making. On all important or politically sensitive issues this is the work of Ministers or shadow Ministers as the case may be, and invariably of the party leaders.

In opposition, the requirements and procedures are quite simple. Usually all that is necessary is that the Shadow Cabinet should meet to accept or reject the policy proposals which have been formulated and refined in the ways already described. Of course there are some issues which require lengthy discussion even at this stage and which cannot be resolved at a single meeting. Yet in most cases, by the time that a policy formulation reaches this stage in the process, the actual decisions can be taken quite quickly, not least because the leader and his closest colleagues will have taken care to prepare the ground before the meeting.

In government, this stage of the process is both more varied and more complex. Some government decisions can be taken quite quickly by individual Ministers acting within their allotted spheres of responsibility. Some are taken by groups of Ministers within a particular Department. Yet nearly all important government decisions affect a variety of departmental interests and therefore have to be taken at least by Cabinet committees and often by the Prime Minister after appropriate consultation with a few very senior colleagues. It is difficult to make any definitive generalisations about decision making at meetings of the Cabinet and its committees. It would appear that in full Cabinet most decisions are taken quite expeditiously and it is only when the Cabinet has to deal with the most difficult and contentious political issues – for example, the IMF-imposed public expenditure cuts under the 1974–9 Labour Government – that it has had to return to the same issues on several occasions. This really underlines the lengths to which Whitehall officials go to prepare the ground for difficult Cabinet decisions, and the considerable efforts which all Prime Ministers make to facilitate smooth Cabinet decision making, whether by holding prior bilateral meetings with key colleagues or by manipulating the substance and timing of the Cabinet agenda.

When a Cabinet committee has to make a decision on a particular subject, the terms of reference are usually supplied to the chairman by the Prime Minister or, occasionally, by the Cabinet as a whole. It is then for the chairman of the committee to hold as many meetings as necessary in order to reach a decision which can be recommended to the Cabinet, often within an agreed period of time. In the later stages of the 1964–70 Labour Government it became conventional that any member of the Cabinet who was not on a particular Cabinet committee would not challenge the decisions of the committee in full Cabinet without the prior approval of the Prime Minister or the chairman of the committee concerned. Indeed the whole rationale of Cabinet committees is that they should be able to take decisions on behalf of the Cabinet without normally having to submit them to a further formal stage of decision making in full Cabinet. Only if they function in this way can they truly be said to save the time and energy of the Cabinet. Yet it also remains true that the conventions of collective responsibility and the traditions of Cabinet government entitle all Cabinet Ministers, if they are sufficiently determined, to pursue a particularly sensitive or important political issue in full Cabinet if they insist (sometimes backed by a threat of resignation) upon having it put on the agenda.

Some Prime Ministers have found it necessary to lay down strict ground rules for Cabinet decision making (such as the example given in the paragraph above), especially if the members of a Cabinet are not sufficiently amenable to Prime Ministerial leadership. Others have not found it necessary to act so formally, because for various reasons they have been able to dominate and control their Cabinet colleagues. In all cases the nature of the decision making is likely to depend upon the balance of power and experience within a Cabinet, and upon the political circumstances of the time.

Policy Execution

Next comes the stage of policy execution. This is the stage at which Whitehall excels, provided the decision has been clearly taken by Ministers and clearly minuted by officials. The real difficulties tend to occur later, in that the law of unintended consequences applies to policy and decision making as much, if not more, than to other spheres of human activity.

Policy execution normally follows immediately after the three stages already described. As far as civil servants are concerned, its roots can be traced back to an earlier stage in the process. Once the broad objectives of a party's policy have been set and a General Election campaign has begun, it is for civil servants in all the various Whitehall Departments to prepare position papers designed to assist incoming Ministers to implement their policies, no matter which party is authorised by the electorate to form the Government. Thus incoming Labour Ministers may have advice on their desks on how best to implement their policy of economic intervention, while new Conservative Ministers may have comparable advice on further stages of privatisation. The advice is neither sanguine nor cautious, but merely intended to suggest the most effective ways of executing the policies of the incoming Government, while emphasising the practical consequences of implementing the various political commitments.

From then on the initiative is with Ministers and their behaviour varies according to their personal drive and ambition, and the extent to which the party commitments in their own Departments are given priority by the Government as a whole. If a Minister is charged with the execution of a policy which is given a high political priority and if the commitment is clearly expressed in the party Manifesto or other formal statements by the party leadership, then it will usually be a straightforward matter of taking the appropriate ministerial decisions for the initiation of administrative action in Whitehall or new legislation at Westminster, whichever is appropriate. On the other hand, if a Minister has to execute a policy which has been given a low political priority by his party, then he will probably have little alternative to preparing the ground with suitable administrative action and speeches or putting in a fresh departmental bid for a future place in the legislative timetable. In anticipation of future progress he can, of course, try to improve his Department's prospects by stimulating interest in Parliament and the media, and by mobilising support in relevant pressure groups and public opinion. If he does all these things successfully, he will increase the chances of making a mark for himself and his Department at a later stage.

Assuming that the appropriate decision has been taken, the stage of policy execution is initially the responsibility of the Cabinet Office if the decision was taken by an inter-departmental Cabinet committee. It does this by communicating the decision to all the Departments and other public bodies which need to know about it. For example, if a decision concerns a nationalised industry, it will be communicated by the Cabinet Office to the relevant Department which supervises the industry in question, which will in its turn be responsible for seeing that the decision is conveyed to the chairman and board concerned. If the decision involves matters of local government responsibility (such as planning, housing or land use), it will be communicated to the Department of the Environment for onward transmission to the local authorities in England, and similarly to the Scottish, Welsh and Northern Ireland Offices for decisions which affect people living in those parts of the United Kingdom. All such civil service communication is carried out between the Cabinet Office and the appropriate ministerial Private Offices which are then responsible for further communication within the respective Departments. It therefore complements and supports the direct communication between Ministers which takes place in the relevant Cabinet committees and on other more informal occasions in Whitehall, the House of Commons and elsewhere.

If a decision requires legislation, it becomes the responsibility of the Minister or Ministers who will have to pilot the legislation through Parliament. The Department or Departments concerned have to work very closely with legal experts from the Office of Parliamentary Counsel who act as legislative draftsmen for the entire Government. Indeed, the role of these parliamentary draftsmen can be of considerable significance, since the precise wording of Bills can sometimes be almost as important as the fundamental principles involved.

If the execution of a government decision requires new primary legislation, the process begins with an important pre-parliamentary stage within the confines of Whitehall. This often involves extensive consultations between civil servants in the Departments concerned and relevant experts and other interested groups both within and outside the web of government. Such detailed consultations may continue for many months on the basis of draft legislative proposals, and it is not unknown for the results of this work to be rejected by the Legislation Committee of the Cabinet if the timetable is too tight or the legislative programme too full or the likely political outcome too dubious. By the time that a proposed Bill is ready for inclusion in the Queen's Speech at the beginning of a parliamentary session in November, it can usually be assumed that its content has been fully discussed in this way and that the eventual outcome will be a piece of acceptable and workable law. On the other hand, there are occasions when ministerial decisions or even draft Bills are introduced at the eleventh hour on the basis of only minimal or perfunctory discussion even within the Government. Recent examples would include the decision to abolish the Greater London Council and the other Metropolitan Councils which was taken by Margaret Thatcher and a few ministerial colleagues just before the 1983 General Election campaign, or the decision to hold a fundamental review of the National Health Service, which seems to have been sprung upon the rest of the Government by Mrs Thatcher during a television interview on *Panorama* in January 1988.

In other instances, the execution of a government decision may only require secondary legislation, in other words a Statutory Instrument issued under the authority of an existing Act of Parliament. Once again there are usually detailed consultations within Whitehall with a wide range of relevant experts and interested groups. Indeed such consultations are particularly important in such cases, since the subsequent procedures for parliamentary scrutiny of Statutory Instruments are widely regarded as cursory and inadequate.

If the decision falls within the sphere of lawful administrative discretion provided for Ministers by legislation which is already on the Statute Book, the Minister concerned normally acts in an executive capacity and then communicates directly with the persons or bodies concerned via departmental circular or by ordinary letter or memorandum. In some cases the decision may entail the delegation of executive responsibility to statutory bodies which already have lawful powers in certain specified areas, such as local authorities or public corporations. Yet in most cases it is a matter of departmental action carried out directly on behalf of the Minister concerned by the civil servants in his Department. As we saw in Chapters 13 and 14, this means that it is usually impossible to maintain a credible distinction between policy and administration, and the execution of policy is often as important as the decision actually taken.

Policy Fulfilment

The final and most problematic stage in the process is policy fulfilment. Recent British history suggests that it is the stage at which the failures of successive governments have been most marked. Among the reasons for this may be that governments have tried to do too much, pursued often mutually contradictory policies, had to share power with formidable interest groups, found themselves constrained by expected or revealed public opinion, and been obliged to work within the limiting framework of established social assumptions and the uncompromising realities of the modern world. Faced with such difficulties, successive governments have sought to ensure the fulfilment of their policies by using one or more of the following political techniques.

Firstly, there is the technique of accommodation. This is a standard political technique whereby governments seek to neutralise any threats to their policies by the simple expedient of accommodating critical points of view and absorbing critical people. It may take the form of co-opting troublesome or obstructive individuals onto official consultative committees or appointing them to positions of responsibility on public bodies or simply holding privileged discussions with powerful groups with a view to incorporating at least some of their ideas or concerns into government policy. It is certainly one of the most effective and well-tried methods, since it can turn critics or adversaries of government policy into compliant or at least semi-pacified partners. Yet it is not usually enough to ensure the fulfilment of policy.

A second technique is that of manipulation. This is really little more than a sinister term for the well-tried art of political persuasion and it subsumes such often-practised techniques as news management – that is, attempting to influence public opinion via careful and deliberate guidance of the media. This technique has been used with varying degrees of success at least since the early 1950s when governments began to adjust the timing of their decisions on economic policy in order to maximise the chances that the peaks in the economic and political cycles would more or less coincide. This technique, which has usually involved deliberately boosting the economy a year or two before the expected date of a General Election, can be seen to have worked in 1959 and 1987. Yet it has also been an uncertain and risky practice which invites swift electoral retribution for those who try it, but get it wrong.

A third technique is that of public opinion mobilisation. This is really a matter of seeking the support of the 'silent majority' in order to redress the political balance against the influence of vociferous and articulate minorities. As an exercise in political leadership, it is no easier than the other techniques already mentioned and can be more difficult in view of the problems involved in trying to hold public opinion constantly to one particular line and then translating it into actual voting behaviour when necessary. Such difficulties are illustrated by the familiar tendency for many people to give strong support in answering publc opinion polls to the general idea of income restraint, but then to act individually or collectively in flagrant disregard of the principle. Nevertheless there are various ways in which this technique can be applied. These may involve the use of powerful rhetoric, constant repetition of simple points, persuasive argument designed to appeal to the man in the street, symbolic gestures designed to evoke a favourable public response and specially commissioned political advertising or opinion polls. None of these methods has proved decisively effective, so sensible politicians usually fall back on the more traditional methods of rational argument and emotional appeal.

Finally, there is the technique of political shock treatment. This involves confronting the public with the full implications of failing to support government policy. In a sense this is a technique which was used by the Thatcher Government in its efforts to change public attitudes radically and permanently in the vital area of economic productivity and industrial performance. It is certainly a technique which has been successful in the past at times of clear and present danger – as in 1940 when Winston Churchill appealed so successfully to the British people as they stood alone against Nazi Germany – and it may also have worked for the Conservative Government during the 1982 Falklands conflict when public opinion rallied strongly behind the British armed forces. Yet there can be no certainty that it will work in normal circumstances during times of peace and relative prosperity, so governments are wise not to try it too often and even then not to count upon it.

15.2 Key Aspects

The Post-war Consensus and its Legacy

It should be clear from the foregoing description of the policy- and decision-making process in Britain that it is essentially a continuous process which proceeds from week to week, month to month, year to year and even government to government. This is mainly because the central problems of government have remained the same over the decades since the Second World War, regardless of which party has been in office. Every government has been faced with the need to maintain and improve the competitiveness of the economy, every government has wrestled with the problems of securing adequate resources for the Welfare State without imposing an intolerable burden upon the wealth creators; every government has had to cope with the diplomatic implications of Britain's relative economic and political decline in the postwar world. It is also because the civil service has a natural preference for orderly and continuous government, something which is to be expected from a permanent and politically impartial bureaucracy. Because of this institutional inertia in the system, once a policy consensus becomes established, it requires a prolonged period of disappointment with its consequences – even when exploited by a radical political leadership fully prepared to embark upon new directions – for the thrust of policy to change and a new consensus to emerge. Looking back at the period since 1945, we can see that this is exactly what has happened in Britain.

For about 25 years after the Second World War the continuity of British government policy stemmed from the high degree of broad policy consensus which had emerged within the Coalition Government during the war. This consensus was extended and carried forward with conviction by the postwar Labour Government, which has been widely recognised as one of the great reforming Administrations in Britain this century – the other two being the Asquith/Lloyd George Liberal Administration of 1906–16 and the Thatcher Administration from 1979 to 1990. It continued to apply under both Conservative and Labour Governments in the 1950s and 1960s – hence the term 'Butskellism' which was used to describe the policy approach followed by R. A. Butler (Conservative) and Hugh Gaitskell (Labour) when they were prominent policy makers within their respective parties. It was not until the early 1970s – about the time of the Yom Kippur War in 1973 and the first oil crisis in 1974 – that the postwar consensus in Britain began to crumble, although there had been some harbingers of this development in the more radical, free market policies attempted by the Heath Government from 1970 to 1972. By 1979, when the Conservatives were returned to office under Margaret Thatcher's leadership, the era of the postwar consensus was effectively over, having been destroyed in the 1970s by the hammer blows of unstable economic performance and disappointed public expectations which, in turn, created the preconditions for the new ideological approaches to politics adopted by each of the two main parties.

Such discontinuities of policy as there have been since 1945 have usually been the result of governments having to respond to great events or other developments over which they had little or no control. For example, the decision taken in 1947 by Clement Attlee and a few of his senior colleagues in the postwar Labour Government to develop an independent nuclear weapons capability for Britain stemmed largely from the unwillingness of the US Congress to allow the Truman Administration to share American nuclear weapons information with even its closest ally abroad. The decision taken in 1956 by Anthony Eden and a small group of senior Ministers to send British forces to invade the Suez Canal Zone was a response to the threatening behaviour of President Nasser of Egypt which, in its turn, had been provoked by the refusal of the American Government to help finance the construction of the Aswan Dam. The decision taken in 1960 by Harold Macmillan and a few close advisers to open negotiations with the Six with a view to full British membership of the European Community derived mainly from the failure of the British Government a year earlier to negotiate a wider European Free Trade Area with the same countries. The decision to devalue the pound taken in 1967 by Harold Wilson and a few senior ministerial colleagues became more or less inevitable once the authorities could no longer contain the serious pressure upon the pound in the foreign exchange markets and could no longer rectify the persistent problems with the balance of payments. The decision taken in 1972 by Edward Heath and a few senior colleagues to impose direct rule from Westminster upon Northern Ireland stemmed mainly from the Government's sense of exasperation with the unwillingness of the Protestant majority to make any real concessions to the Catholic minority in the sensitive sphere of civil rights. The decision taken in 1976 by James Callaghan, Denis Healey and a few senior advisers to apply to the International Monetary Fund for a massive loan to assist the British economy became necessary when international confidence was withdrawn from the policies pursued by the Labour Government during the period 1974–6. The decision taken in 1982 by Margaret Thatcher and a few senior ministerial colleagues to send a Task Force to the South Atlantic to recapture the Falklands after the islands had been invaded by the Argentinian armed forces was equally unexpected, but became unavoidable because of the unacceptable political damage which would have been inflicted upon the Government if any other course of action had been adopted. All of these examples were decisions which entailed notable discontinuities of policy, yet really permitted no other government response. In every case they appear aberrant in the context of the policy consensus prevailing at the time, but, looking back with the wisdom of hindsight, they were really unavoidable.

The New Ideological Politics?

After 1979 the British people experienced a new era of Thatcherite 'conviction politics' which was reflected in the radical decisions taken by the Conservative Government under Mrs Thatcher. Of course the foundations for these mould-breaking policies were laid when the Conservative party was in opposition in the late 1970s, at a time when it succeeded very largely in winning the intellectual argument against the then Labour Government. For its part, the Labour party had also become more ideological in the 1970s, partly as a result of the disappointment of its activists with the minimal, Socialist achievements of the 1964–70 and 1974–9 Labour Governments, and partly as a response to the Thatcherite onslaught of the early 1980s. The result of these parallel developments in the two main parties was political polarisation and the virtual disappearance of the common ground of the postwar consensus. This created a vacuum in the centre of British politics which the Alliance of Liberals and Social Democrats sought to fill following its creation in 1981 and for several years thereafter.

This new era of ideological politics stemmed from the tendency of each main party, when in opposition, to return to ideological first principles in an attempt to formulate radical and often uncompromising policies for implementation upon its return to government. The effect of this kind of policy making was to lead the government of the day to claim that it had a mandate for every single commitment made in its Manifesto at the previous General Election, no matter how damaging or unpopular it might prove to be. It produced sharp discontinuities of policy in the 1970s and was reflected in the largely ideological approach of the Conservative Government in the 1980s. It is now uncertain, however, whether this ideological polarisation between the two main parties will persist into the 1990s, partly because the present Conservative Government has shown signs of a wish to consolidate, but mainly because Mr Kinnock's Labour Opposition wants to win power more than it wants to cling to all the old ideological shibboleths of the Labour Movement. This means that each of the two main parties seems to be gravitating towards the new centre of British politics, although it is plain that the centre ground has been shifted by Thatcherism significantly to the Right as compared with the situation in the 1960s and 1970s.

Those who relished the era of ideological politics in Britain, but who feel disconcerted by the current, centripetal tendencies of the two main parties, are the ideological zealots who usually come into their own when their party is in opposition, but who, in the case of the Conservative party, managed to sustain a remarkable influence upon the Conservative Government during most of the 1980s. Indeed, this was one of the most remarkable features of British politics in the 1980s – the extent to which, against all the odds, the party in power became more rather than less ideological as its period in office continued. This must really be attributed to the singular leadership of Margaret Thatcher, which encouraged such people to blossom in a way which would have been most unlikely under all previous postwar Conservative leaders. It must be added that the ideological approach to policy and decision making brought some real success for the Conservative party and could be justified on certain conditions. Firstly, when a party is in opposition, its leaders must succeed in mobilising sufficient public opinion in support of their ideas. Secondly, during every General Election campaign, they must make their policy intentions crystal clear, so that it is difficult for their opponents to argue afterwards that the electorate was never warned. Thirdly, in government they must constantly explain and justify their actions to the satisfaction of at least the politically attentive public. If they succeed in doing all these things, then their policies will have a good chance of commanding sufficient public acquiescence, if not positive support, to ensure a satisfactory outcome.

It may be that leading politicians in all British political parties are now moving, however reluctantly in some cases, towards a new policy consensus based upon a considerable dose of Thatcherite 'new realism' in the economic sphere, but leavened with an equally significant concern for social responsibility and the quality of life in the non-economic sphere derived largely from the priorities of the opposition parties. Yet it is always worth remembering that policy is developed by all political parties in conditions of considerable uncertainty and flux, not least because developments in the real world and the political responses necessary continue to be as unpredictable and contradictory as ever.

15.3 Strengths and Weaknesses

There are both strengths and weaknesses in the policy- and decision-making process in Britain. It is neither one of the best nor one of the worst of its kind in the liberal democracies. It has some characteristics which are universal and some which are peculiar to this country. In any event it ought to be assessed on its merits.

Strengths

The most obvious strength is the ability of the process to translate party-political commitments into government action or legislation. This derives principally from the way in which the electoral system is capable of turning a minority of the votes cast in the nation as a whole into a majority of the seats won by the victorious party in the House of Commons. Thus it enables a particular interpretation of the popular will to be transformed into executive or legislative action by the government of the day, usually without encountering any insuperable obstacles, at any rate in Whitehall and Westminster. However even the most powerful government can be vulnerable to a back-bench revolt on its own side, as was evident, for example, in the defeat of the Thatcher Government in 1986 on its proposal to liberalise the Sunday trading laws.

Another strength of the process is its efficiency in turning ministerial decisions into administrative action or legislation. This is a tribute largely to the efficiency of civil servants in Whitehall and their special skills in the sphere of public administration. It means that the writ of Ministers usually runs quite effectively throughout Whitehall and its satellite institutions (always assuming that Ministers have a coherent and collegiate view), but much less certainly in the quasi-autonomous spheres of public corporations and local government, and hardly at all in the private sector unless reinforced by the full backing of the law. For example, the Conservative Government since 1979 has had endless difficulties in imposing its policy of public expenditure restraint upon local authorities, and has put at least 23 Bills through Parliament in its repeated attempts to curb local authorities by legislative means.

Yet another strength of the process is its ability to cope with abrupt and radical changes of policy. Any institutions of government which have this ability to accommodate changes of political direction so quickly and completely must be very robust. What is more, such changes are made without any significant change in the administrative personnel involved, which contrasts sharply with what happens in other democracies, such as the United States. However this too has changed somewhat in recent years, with the growing politicisation of the higher grades in the civil service, and the tendency for Conservative and Labour governments alike to employ more 'special advisers' and other party-political auxiliaries whose involvement in the process of policy making can be very influential.[2]

Weaknesses

There are also some notable weaknesses in the process which might be considered to outweigh the strengths just enumerated. For example, it can be argued that the robust flexibility of the process has permitted too many abrupt and often damaging discontinuities of policy. As has already been pointed out, these have stemmed from the determination of politicians in office slavishly to implement their party-political commitments, and from the polarisation of attitudes and policies between the two main parties, notably in the 1970s and early 1980s.

Paradoxically, another weakness in the process is that there has been too much unimaginative continuity of thinking in Whitehall which has often stymied the chances of radical initiatives. It used to be the case that this brought virtually all governments back to the safe middle ground of British politics within two or three years of every General Election. It reflected the gyroscopic influence of the top civil service which Shirley Williams (after her spell in the 1974–9 Labour Government) described as 'a beautifully designed and effective braking mechanism'.[3] However, as the Thatcher Government came to seem more permanently entrenched during the 1980s, it increasingly revealed a tendency for at any rate the highest grades of the civil service in Whitehall to take on the prejudices and assumptions of their political masters.

Another weakness of the process is that it encourages both Ministers and civil servants to pay too much attention to short-term political considerations at the expense of the quest for fundamental long-term solutions to the nation's most serious and intractable problems. While this is partly a function of the relatively short political timescale imposed by the five-year maximum span of a Parliament, it is mainly due to the congenital tendency of nearly all politicians to give priority to what appears to be urgent over what they know to be important, largely because they believe that most voters expect quick results.

Another weakness of the process is that both Ministers and civil servants tend to rely too heavily upon a rather narrow range of official information and advice. This is perhaps inevitable, since civil servants control the flow of people and advice to their Ministers and because this advice so often reflects only what is available in departmental files or supplied by a limited range of expert opinion. In other words, because of the weight of Whitehall tradition and the habit of official secrecy, the policy process in Britain tends to be less eclectic than in many other Western countries where governments tend to be more open and the maintenance of coalitions is more important.

Another weakness of the process has been described as governmental 'overload'.[4] Essentially, this means that Ministers and some senior civil servants often have far too much to do in too little time. This can be attributed to a number of different causes, among which are the increase over the years in the scope and complexity of modern government, the growth of the international dimension of decision making (especially in the European Community) and the impact of modern mass communications which has led Ministers to feel that they have to be informed about (and perhaps comment upon) an amazing variety of developments, allegations and rumours revealed or dramatised by the media. It seems that this is particularly true at the very top levels of British government where the most senior Ministers have to bear disproportionate burdens of paper work and discussion.

A final weakness of the process could be said to be the rather limited scope for parliamentary or public participation. This is mainly because central government in Britain is still regarded as the exclusive and secret preserve of a chosen few. Policy ideas, especially in their formative stages, are not usually shared with anyone who is not thought to have a clear need to know. Perhaps the most notable group among the company of the excluded are back-benchers in all parties who invariably learn of new developments long after the media have got the story. Even though the House of Commons is supposed to be the first to be informed when Parliament is sitting, it seems unlikely that this problem will be solved to the satisfaction of ordinary MPs as long as the Executive makes up its mind behind a veil of official secrecy and Parliament is therefore presented with so many *faits accomplis*.

15.4 Possible Improvements

This is not the place to consider in any detail the wide range of possible changes which have been proposed from time to time in order to improve the policy- and decision-making process in Britain. It is sufficient here to mention only a few of the more familiar suggestions which have been made in order to give a flavour of the reformist discussion which has taken place.

Increased Support for the Opposition

Some people have argued that there should be increased support for the Opposition, so that it can be better informed and briefed on the great issues of the day. To this end they have suggested the creation of a small but capable Department of the Opposition to advise and inform opposition politicians and so enable them to argue against Ministers on a more even footing. The less overt purpose of such an innovation would be to keep the policy making of any opposition party more closely in touch with the realities of the outside world and so reduce the risk that it will be captured by the views and prejudices of unrepresentative minorities. It is also argued that this would raise the quality and sophistication of policy making in opposition and ensure that Parliament as a whole was slightly less dominated by the might of Government.

Another way of achieving the same objective of 'educating' the Opposition would be to give all politicians not in the Government much fuller and more frequent access to official information and advice. This already happens to some extent in the case of Privy Councillors (former Ministers of senior rank) who can see restricted official information on privileged terms. It also happens during the Standing Committee stage of some complicated Government Bills when the MPs concerned are supplied with detailed official briefing on every clause and government amendment. The principle could perhaps be extended more widely in Parliament if Ministers felt sufficiently self-confident to allow it.

Yet another way of achieving a similar objective would be to provide all political parties with substantially greater support from public funds, as happens in many continental countries, perhaps in proportion to the votes which they receive at elections or the money which they are able to raise by their own efforts. This would enable parties in opposition to employ more of their own advisers and so enable their front-bench spokesmen to be better informed and more effective in their various roles. It would not, of course, guarantee a higher standard of opposition, since that depends most upon the motivation and capabilities of the politicians concerned.

Wider Advice for Ministers

Another proposal which has been put forward is that there should be a wider range of advice available to Ministers from a wider range of people.[5] This could be achieved by bringing into Whitehall a larger number of 'special advisers', but it could just as well be achieved by opening up the higher grades to recruitment and staffing from a wider range of backgrounds with more provision for full-time civil servants drawn from the private sector and other organisations on specific short-term contracts. This could have a positive effect on the quality of policy and decision making in central government which can be adversely affected by the rather narrow and cautious attitude of the more traditional senior civil servants.

Some businessmen with experience of central government, such as Sir John Hoskyns who headed Margaret Thatcher's Policy Unit during her early years in 10 Downing Street, would take this idea a good deal further by opening up civil service recruitment to permit the employment in each Department of perhaps 10 to 20 policy officials drawn from the private sector to serve in government on fixed-term contracts for market rates of pay.[6] The idea is that such officials would be likely to offer Ministers support and advice which would be more completely in tune with the political purposes of the Government. This would be fine if the purpose of government were seen simply as a matter of forcing through Whitehall and Westminster a particular political programme, but, bearing in mind that much of government is necessarily reactive as well as proactive, it is not beyond all doubt that people from such external backgrounds would be best qualified to assist Ministers in a crisis or political upheaval. In short, even if such an exhilarating change were made, it is not self-evident that it would produce a higher quality of policy and decision making in central government.

Structural Changes in Whitehall

Another proposal which has been made from time to time is that there should be structural changes in Whitehall in order to make the centre more powerful in relation to the various individual Departments. This has led some people, such as Lord Hunt, a former Cabinet Secretary, to propose the creation of a new central Department, such as a fully-fledged Prime Minister's Department or an enlarged and reinforced Cabinet Office.[7] Such changes have usually been suggested in order to strengthen the hand of the Prime Minister in the policy- and decision-making process and to encourage greater coherence in government policy overall. However, in the light of events leading up to the resignation of Nigel Lawson, the Chancellor of the Exchequer, in October 1989, it is no longer self-evident that the shortcomings of the policy-making process derive from insufficient Prime Ministerial influence. Indeed, in what has become essentially a 'presidential' system of government when one party has a strong leader and an overwhelming parliamentary majority, it now seems that the real need is for more genuine Cabinet government. In so far as there may be a problem of excessive 'Departmentalism' in Whitehall, the most appropriate solution would seem to be a return to the more effective and timely use of the Cabinet and its committee system rather than any further attempt to reinforce what is already seen by many as excessive Prime Ministerial power.

Greater Role for Parliament

Finally, some people have been attracted by the idea that Parliament should be given a greater role in the policy- and decision-making process. This would add a more creative role to the main characteristic of traditional parliamentary activity, which is that of legitimation and the mobilisation of consent for the acts of government. It would almost certainly require the further development of the existing structure of Select Committees in ways which would enable those parliamentary bodies to be more deeply involved in the formative stages of policy making. For example, it might mean enabling Select Committees to consider legislative proposals at the pre-legislative stage or to influence taxation and public spending decisions at a stage in the budgetary cycle before final decisions are taken by Ministers. In general, such an enhanced role for back-benchers would probably require the strengthening of the independent sources of expert advice now available to Parliament by establishing new supporting institutions along the lines of the General Accounting Office or the Office of Technology Assessment which serve the US Congress. Yet, even with the benefit of such institutional strengthening of Parliament, there would still be considerable obstacles to taking such developments very far in a parliamentary system which has long been based upon the principle of Executive initiative and parliamentary response.

15.5 Conclusion

A balanced conclusion to the issues raised in this chapter would seem to be that the policy- and decision-making process works rather well in Britain, but only if its performance is measured in terms of its relatively smooth operation in Whitehall and Westminster. Outside the walls of these twin citadels, the process is not so satisfactory or effective, especially since it is not very good at mobilising the understanding or consent of the general public. Even the interest groups and others who are consulted fairly regularly by Ministers and civil servants cannot feel confident that they have much more than a marginal influence upon either the process or the outcome. While they may occasionally do better in exceptional circumstances, it is normally the very senior politicians and their closest advisers who monopolise both the discussions and the decisions. Party-political criteria dominate the process, which seems to leave little scope for uncommitted outsiders.

In the future, the process will probably change quite significantly as it becomes more complicated in its variables and more bound up with the process of policy and decision making in the European Community. At the same time, as the public gradually becomes more aware and better informed, there could be increased difficulty for the politicians and civil servants to keep up with rising public expectations. In such circumstances all the key players would be wise to explain more fully to the general public the limitations which are inherent in a process based upon strong ideological competition and a tendency towards mutually exclusive positions. Britain may have a robust and mature system of policy and decision making, but we would be foolish to take unnecessary risks with it as long as the problems of government are so hard to solve.

Suggested Questions

1. Describe the policy- and decision-making process in British central government.
2, Where does real power lie in the policy- and decision-making process?
3. How could the policy- and decision-making process be made more accountable to the general public?

Notes

1. Quoted in R. Rose (ed.), *Policy Making in Britain* (London: Macmillan, 1969), p. 292.
2. For example, Sir Alan Walters, Mrs Thatcher's personal adviser on economic policy, was a factor in the resignation of Nigel Lawson as Chancellor in October 1989, since his influence over the then Prime Minister's approach to monetary policy became so great and so visible as to make it politically impossible for Mr Lawson to continue in office.
3. In W. Rodgers *et al.*, *Policy and Practice, the experience of Government* (London: RIPA, 1980), p. 81.
4. Lord Hunt of Tanworth, a former Cabinet Secretary who had served four different Administrations, elaborated this point in a lecture given to the Chartered Institute of Public Finance and Accountancy on 9 June 1983.
5. Perhaps the foremost proponent of wider advice for Ministers from a more open and flexibly recruited civil service is Peter Hennessy in his magisterial book *Whitehall* (London: Secker & Warburg, 1989).
6. See J. Hoskyns, 'Whitehall and Westminster, an outsider's view' in *Fiscal Studies*, November 1982.
7. Lord Hunt outlined four possible options, but expressed no strong preference as between a full-blown Prime Minister's Department, a strengthened Cabinet Office, a recreated and strong Central Policy Review Staff, and an enlarged Prime Minister's Office.

Further Reading

Ashford, D. E., *Policy and Politics in Britain* (Oxford: Basil Blackwell, 1981).

Benn, A., *Diaries*, Vols. I, II, III and IV (London: Hutchinson, 1987–90).

Bruce-Gardyne, J. and Lawson, N., *The Power Game* (London: Macmillan, 1976).

Healcy, D., *The Time of My Life* (London: Michael Joseph, 1989).

Hennessy, P., *Whitehall* (London: Secker & Warburg, 1989).

Richardson, J. J. and Jordan, A. G., *Governing Under Pressure* (Oxford: Martin Robertson, 1979).

Rodgers, W. *et al.*, *Policy and Practice, the experience of Government* (London: RIPA, 1980).

Smith, B., *Policy Making in British Government* (Oxford: Martin Robertson, 1976).

Part V
Other public institutions

⑯ Local government

It is important to distinguish at the outset between local government, which can be defined simply as directly elected local authorities, and local administration, which includes the regional and local offices of public corporations and the local administration of justice. In this chapter we shall concentrate upon directly elected local authorities, in other words primary local government.

16.1 Structure and Personnel

The structure of local government is different in the different parts of the United Kingdom. It is represented diagrammatically in Figure 16.1.

England and Wales

The structure of local government in England and Wales was reformed by the 1972 Local Government Act which came into effect in 1974. It reduced the previous mosaic of about 1400 local authorities to six large Metropolitan authorities (outside Greater London, which had been created as a single authority by the 1963 Greater London Act), 47 County authorities (for example, Devon, Kent, Norfolk, Dyfed), 36 Metropolitan District authorities (of which the largest was Birmingham with a population of more than one million), and 333 County District authorities (representing areas with local populations ranging from 60 000 to 100 000 in most cases). Thus a total of about 420 local authorities replaced the previous 1400 or so, and the interdependence of town and country became the guiding principle of the structure of local government.

At the most local level, the former Parish Councils were retained and their powers were increased, though to a limited extent. About 300 former Urban Districts and small Boroughs became Parish Councils. Parishes of more than 200 inhabitants were required to elect a council, whereas those with fewer inhabitants than this were encouraged to practise the direct democracy of parish meetings.

Figure 16.1 The structure of local government

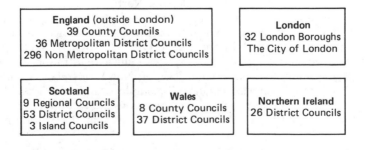

England (outside London)
39 County Councils
36 Metropolitan District Councils
296 Non Metropolitan District Councils

London
32 London Boroughs
The City of London

Scotland
9 Regional Councils
53 District Councils
3 Island Councils

Wales
8 County Councils
37 District Councils

Northern Ireland
26 District Councils

The 1972 Act also established separate local government Boundary Commissions for England and Wales. These bodies have kept the structure of local government under review and are empowered to propose boundary changes from time to time in order to take account of population movements and other social changes.

The Greater London Council and the six other Metropolitan Counties were abolished by Acts of Parliament in 1984 and 1985 which came into effect on 1 April 1986. This meant that the large conurbations, namely Greater Manchester, Merseyside, South Yorkshire, Tyne and Wear, West Midlands and West Yorkshire, no longer had any democratic representation at that level of local government. The functions of the Metropolitan Counties were reallocated to the Borough and District Councils, statutory joint boards and other public bodies. The abolition of these upper-tier authorities was intended to remove a source of bitter conflict with central government, save money after incurring some transitional costs, and provide a simpler and more accountable structure of local government in the large Metropolitan areas.

Scotland

The present structure of local government in Scotland was determined by the 1973 Local Government (Scotland) Act which came into effect in 1975. This involved the creation of nine Regional Authorities (with populations ranging from about 2 500 000 in Strathclyde to fewer than 100 000 in The Borders) and 53 District Authorities within the regions. The division of functions between the two levels of local government is similar to that in England and Wales, except that the three island areas (Orkney, Shetland and Western Isles) are each single, all-purpose local authorities.

Northern Ireland

The present structure of local government in Northern Ireland was largely determined by the 1972 Local Government (Northern Ireland) Act which came into force in 1973. It created a single level of local government by establishing 26 District Councils based upon the main population centres in the Province. The Districts vary considerably in area and resources, with populations ranging from about 13 000 to about 350 000. Under a subsequent reorganisation of local government in 1977, which was precipitated by the way in which the Protestant majority had abused its position of local power, the District Councils were stripped of all but some minimal functions, such as street cleaning and sanitation, markets and abattoirs, and recreational facilities.

All the more important functions of local government in the Province are carried out either by central boards under the Northern Ireland Office (dealing, for example, with housing, police, fire services and electricity supply) or by area boards (dealing, for example, with health, personal social services, education and libraries) or directly by the Northern Ireland Office (town and country planning, water and sewage services, roads and car parks, vehicle registration and licensing, for example). Although the local councillors in Northern Ireland have severely circumscribed direct functions, they have some indirect influence when they sit as nominees on the various area boards and some consultative influence when they hold formal discussions with Ministers and officials in the Northern Ireland Office.

Councillors and Officials

The composition of local authorities in England and Wales can be summarised by saying that each County Council has between 60 and 100 elected councillors and each District Council has between 30 and 80 elected councillors. In each case councillors are elected for fixed four-year terms. At present those elected to the London Borough Councils, the County Councils and the non-Metropolitan District Councils are elected *en bloc* every four years, whereas in the Metropolitan District Councils outside London one-third of the councillors is elected every third year in a *tranche*. For electoral purposes the Counties are divided into single-member constituencies, whereas the Districts and London Boroughs are divided into wards, each represented by between one and three councillors, depending upon geographical area and population.

At every level of local government the chairman of the council is elected annually by his fellow councillors. In those Districts which are predominantly urban, the chairman takes the honorary title of Mayor and presides in that capacity over the council proceedings. However the real power in all councils is wielded by the leader of the majority party and, to a lesser extent, by the political chairmen of the key committees – for example, education, finance, housing and social services. Most councils have a Policy and Resources Committee (or its equivalent) which normally includes the chairmen of all the main committees and acts as a sort of 'Cabinet' for the local authority. Councillors of all political persuasions usually serve on more than one committee and the membership of committees reflects the relative strengths of the political parties in the local authority concerned. Since many local authorities are politically dominated by one particular party, this usually means that the key committees are controlled by the majority party in the locality and are run in conformity with that party's political ideas and interests.

Councillors are not much more representative of the general public than are Members of Parliament. To be eligible for election, however, they must live or work in the local authority area itself. There is not a great deal of statistical evidence about their make-up and socioeconomic characteristics. A survey conducted in 1964 revealed that only 12 per cent of councillors were women, only 19 per cent were blue-collar workers, and the average age was 55 years.[1] In 1977 the Robinson Report confirmed that the general characteristics of councillors had not changed very much, since at that time they were still predominantly male, middle-aged and middle-class, although the proportion of women had risen slightly to 17 per cent.[2]

Research into the characteristics and attitudes of councillors carried out for the Widdicombe Committee in 1985 showed that fewer than one in five councillors were women and that the majority of councillors were still aged 55 or more.[3] However, with the exception of the English shires and the Welsh local authorities, all authorities showed an increase in the number of councillors aged 45 or less, with the most marked increases in London and Scotland. In general, Metropolitan councillors have been getting younger on average, while shire councillors have retained their older age profile. Councillors had higher educational qualifications than the public as a whole and were more likely to have stayed on at school beyond the age of sixteen. Almost a quarter of the councillors who took part in the survey had obtained a degree or higher qualification, compared with only 5 per cent of the general population.

Since the time of the Robinson Report in 1977, there has been an appreciable fall in the proportion of councillors in paid employment – 60 per cent in 1985 compared with 72 per cent in 1976. This was matched not by an increase in the number declaring themselves to be unemployed, but rather by an increase in the number defined as retired. Councillors were drawn from a much narrower range of occupational backgrounds than would be found in the population as a whole, with 41 per cent coming from a professional or managerial background and only 5 per cent from semi-skilled or unskilled manual occupations. Of those councillors in paid employment at the time of the survey, 36 per cent were employed in the public sector (exactly the same as the population as a whole) and of those almost half were employed in local government, notably as teachers, lecturers, social workers or administrators. The practice of people being councillors in one local authority while being employed as officials of another local authority caused some controversy and even hostility, especially among Conservatives in their attitude towards Labour-controlled local government. It was one of the things which the Widdicombe Committee was asked to examine and it led to the inclusion of a measure in the 1989 Local Government and Housing Act which enabled the Government to prohibit council officials on salaries of more than £19 500 a year from standing for election in local government.

Local authority officials are the other vital element in local government. In general, they assist councillors in much the same way as civil servants assist Ministers, but there are some significant contrasts with the civil service, especially the fact that the key officials in local government are normally well-qualified professionals in the particular sphere of local government activity in which they are engaged. Thus Chief Education Officers are often former teachers, Directors of Social Services are often former social workers, and Chief Planning Officers are often qualified planners, surveyors or architects. They can therefore have a considerable influence upon the policy of their local authorities by using their professional knowledge and experience in their work with elected councillors.

The main similarity between local government officials and civil servants in central government is that both are expected to remain politically neutral and faithfully to carry out the policies of their political masters. In local government the principal effect of such political neutrality is that most policy decisions are heavily influenced by the technical and expert advice of the officials concerned. Of course, the decisions are always taken by the councillors, but there can be occasions when they appear to be acting as little more than political spokesmen for the officials. On the other hand, there has also been more recent concern – especially in the Conservative party – that some local government officials appear to be uncomfortably 'political' in their motivation and their actions, notably in Labour-controlled local authorities in inner city areas. Doubtless similar perceptions are held in the other direction by some of those strongly committed to the Labour party when they look at the behaviour of local government officials in the Conservative-controlled rural areas. A balanced conclusion would seem to suggest that these things are largely in the eye of the beholder, although it should be added that both local and central government seem to have gone through a particularly 'political' phase in the 1980s.

16.2 Powers and Functions

The powers and functions of local government in England and Wales are set out in the relevant statutes, notably the 1972 Local Government Act. Such legislation specifies the powers which are to be exercised by the various levels of local government, and there is a clear understanding that all powers which are not statutorily designated for local authorities remain the preserve of central government – assuming that Parliament has provided the necessary statutory powers in the first place. Indeed Parliament is always able to modify or even abolish aspects of local government in this country, as we saw when the Conservative Government put legislation through Parliament in 1984 and 1985 to abolish the GLC and the other Metropolitan County Councils. The distribution of powers and functions between the various different kinds of local authority is shown in tabular form in Figure 16.2.

Statutory Duties

Local authorities are given statutory duties in Acts of Parliament. The Westminster legislation sets out what the statutory duties shall be in each case. This means that local authorities have to perform certain functions which Parliament has assigned to them and they carry out their duties in accordance with the terms of the legislation. For example, the 1944 Education Act stipulated that local authorities should be responsible for providing public education for all

Figure 16.2 The distribution of local authority powers and functions

● *Metropolitan District Councils*

Education
Social services
Libraries
Museums and art galleries
Housing
Most development control
Local planning
Refuse collection
Environmental health
Parks, open spaces
Coastal protection

● **Non-Metropolitan County Councils**

Education
Social services
Libraries, museums and art galleries
Structure planning
Transport planning
Highways and traffic
Refuse disposal
Consumer protection
Fire service
Parks, open spaces
Coastal protection
Police

● **Non-Metropolitan District Councils**

Housing
Planning
Refuse collection
Environmental health
Museums and art galleries
Parks, open spaces
Coastal protection
Municipal bus services

children in their areas who are within the statutory age range for school education. Equally the 1972 Chronically Sick and Disabled Persons Act laid statutory duties upon local authorities to provide care for all such people within their areas in the various ways prescribed in the legislation. Or again the 1977 Homeless Persons Act imposed a statutory duty upon local authorities to house the homeless, provided the latter satisfy certain prescribed conditions and have not made themselves voluntarily homeless. Even when the statutes provide some latitude for local authorities as to how exactly they should carry out their statutory duties, subsequent advice and circulars from central government usually ensure that minimum standards of provision are set and adhered to.

Discretionary Powers

Local authorities are also given discretionary powers in Acts of Parliament. Once again the Westminster legislation sets out in each case the areas and the extent to which such powers may be exercised. This means that local authorities are endowed with discretionary powers to provide certain services, provided they wish to do so and assuming they can raise the necessary finance. For example, the 1969 Children and Young Persons Act gave local authorities the discretionary powers to do all sorts of caring and compassionate things for young people in trouble, but failed to make the necessary extra financial provision without which it has proved very difficult to implement large sections of the Act. More recently, during the period of public expenditure restraint imposed by the Conservative Government since 1979, many local authorities have pressed for discretionary rather than mandatory powers whenever they have been affected by new legislation, so that they can have a better chance of living within the tight financial limits set by central government. Thus the discretionary powers, which used to be seen as a way of extending local provision of national services, are now regarded by many local authorities as a convenient way of saving money, since this allows them to reduce or withdraw such services without incurring legislative or judicial penalties.

Division of Functions

The division of functions between the various levels of local government is fiendishly complicated and has been subject to a number of changes over the years. To simplify the matter, it is best to describe the situation in England as it has been since the 1985 Local Government Act, which abolished the Greater London Council and the Metropolitan County Councils. In England this left a structure of 39 County Councils, 296 non-Metropolitan District Councils, 36 Metropolitan District Councils and 32 London Borough Councils, plus the City of London.

The County Councils have statutory responsibilities for transport, highways, police, fire service, court administration, overspill housing, strategic planning, consumer protection, refuse disposal, education, public libraries and personal social services. The non-Metropolitan District Councils have statutory responsibilities for housing, local planning, environmental health, minor roads, licensing of public houses and places of entertainment, and the registration of births, marriages and deaths. The Metropolitan District Councils have the same statutory responsibilities as the non-Metropolitan District Councils, with the addition of education, public libraries and personal social services. The upper and lower levels of Metropolitan local government used to share statutory responsibility for museums and art galleries, parks and open spaces, municipal swimming baths, regional airports and land acquired for development. However, since the abolition of the Metropolitan Counties in 1986, these tasks have been taken on by the Metropolitan Districts. Only police, fire services and public transport have been transferred to statutory joint boards, while a few residual functions (such as land drainage, flood protection and some arts sponsorship) have been transferred to other public bodies.[4]

16.3 Financial Arrangements

The financing of local government has long been both complicated and controversial in Britain. Ever since the early 1950s local authority spending has grown steadily and usually at a faster rate than the economy as a whole. This was bearable in the 1950s and 1960s when the British economy was growing at about 3 per cent a year and there was general public and political support for a constantly expanding public sector. However, since the 1976 financial crisis, when the then Labour Government had to call in the IMF, successive governments of both main parties have felt it necessary to control all forms of public spending. Local authority spending, which accounts for about one-quarter of the total, has been no exception to this rule. In such circumstances relations between local and central government have been very strained and in the 1980s struggles over local government finance and local government spending were exacerbated by sharp differences of party politics between Conservative-controlled central government and Labour-controlled local government.

The financial problems of local government have not been made any easier by the fact that so much new legislation proposed by central government and passed by Parliament has financial implications for local authorities for which they have not always been sufficiently compensated by the Exchequer. A vast range of new statutory duties has been placed upon local authorities over the years in fields such as housing, education, social services and community care. Yet, under the present Conservative Government in particular, local authorities have not received all the financial support from the centre which they felt they needed, while at the same time they have been prevented by law from raising the extra finance which they needed from local sources – traditionally, domestic and business rates.

The Methods of Local Government Finance

The methods of financing local government have varied over the years in Britain. In general, however, local authorities relied upon revenue from local rates (property taxes) levied according to a complicated formula on domestic, commercial and industrial (but not agricultural) buildings within their designated areas; together with financial support in various forms from central government and some limited income from rents, fees and charges.

Rates, which traditionally raised nearly half of the revenue needed to finance local services, were assessed on the rateable value of the land or buildings concerned. In theory they represented the rent at which the property could be let (if there were a market for such lettings), minus the notional cost of repairs, insurance and other maintenance expenses. They were paid every year (normally in two or more instalments) and the abstruse calculations upon which they were based were reviewed about every 10 years by the Inland Revenue in periodic revaluations which took account of inflation and any improvements to the property over the intervening period. Although rates were an unpopular form of taxation, it was never easy to identify a simpler or more cost-effective way of raising large sums of revenue from local sources.[5]

The rest of the money needed for local government revenue support came traditionally from a system of central government grants to local authorities. These took two main forms. Firstly, there were specific grants in aid of particular local purposes – for example, 50 per cent of local police expenditure or 90 per cent of mandatory student grants, or specific housing subsidies for poorer tenants. Secondly, there were general grants to the rate funds of individual local authorities in order to increase their overall income, notably in those parts of the country with a poor rateable base.

The total amount of Rate Support Grant (RSG) was fixed every year by the Department of the Environment in co-operation with the Treasury and after consultation with the local authority associations and the Consultative Council on Local Government Finance. The RSG was composed of a needs element assessed for each local authority mainly on the basis of demographic factors, a resources element paid to those authorities where the rateable base was below the national average, and a domestic element designed to bring some relief to all domestic ratepayers. The most notable characteristics of the system were a bias in favour of income redistribution from the richer to the poorer parts of the country, and considerable power for central government in its ability to switch or withhold grants from individual local authorities.

In the twentieth century, the 1929 Local Government Act was an important early bench-mark which abolished the previous system of assigned revenues from national taxation and replaced it with a system of specific grants for specific local services, together with a block grant from the Exchequer to each local authority. In 1948 this was supplemented by a system of deficiency payments to those local authorities with rateable values below the average. In 1958 the entire array of complicated financial support for local government was rationalised and the RSG was introduced. This largely replaced the former variety of specific grants with a new general grant to each local authority, which was calculated on a basis of needs, resources and domestic elements. Further legislation in 1963 permitted individual local authorities to raise an additional rate of up to 1p in the pound for specific local purposes, if they chose to do so. This was increased to 2p in the pound by the 1972 Local Government Act.

The whole question of local government finance was examined by the Layfield Committee in the mid-1970s.[6] This concluded that the main shortcoming in the system was the lack of clear accountability for local government spending. Its principal recommendation was that the financing of local government spending should be recast on the basis of a prior political choice about the broad direction in which the relationship between local and central government should be developed. Most of the committee favoured a move towards greater local responsibility by supplementing the rates with local income tax raised by the major spending authorities. However the Labour Government of the day responded to the report by denying that it was necessary to choose between a centralist and localist approach, so an opportunity for thoroughgoing reform was missed.[7]

When the Conservatives returned to power in 1979, they were determined to give a high priority to controlling local government spending, encouraging local authorities to deliver services more efficiently and reducing the number of detailed controls over local government. Under the 1980 Local Government Planning and Land Act the Government sought to introduce a better framework for the distribution and control of public funds for local government. To do this it decided to introduce block grants paid to every local authority. This system was designed to ensure that all local authorities of the same kind (for instance, all Shire Counties or all London Boroughs) could provide a similar standard of local services if they levied a similar rate in the pound. It also sought to escape from reliance upon past expenditure as a measure of local need and to base such measurements upon an objective view of the costs of typical standards of local service. While the new system was supposed to discourage local authorities from overspending, it was also supposed not to reduce the freedom of local authorities to determine their own local priorities within financial limits.

Under the 1982 Local Government Finance Act the first Thatcher Government went one stage further in its policy of tightening the financial controls upon local authorities. The Act prevented local authorities from raising supplementary rates and precepts during the course of the financial year and subjected their activities to further financial scrutiny by the newly established Audit Commission. Under the 1984 Rates Act a further legislative attempt was made to curb excessive rate increases by individual local authorities and to provide a general reserve power for the limitation of rate increases by all local authorities. This policy of 'rate-capping' had some limited success in controlling the overspending by what Ministers saw as spendthrift local authorities and hence shielded ratepayers from some of the worst financial consequences. However it also led some local authorities into the greater complexities of so-called 'creative accounting' and succeeded in reducing the rate of increase in local authority spending from about 3 per cent per year in real terms at the beginning of the 1980s to about 1 per cent per year in real terms by the end of the decade.

In spite of all these efforts by central government, the system of local government finance with all its controls and anomalies became increasingly discredited, with the result that Ministers felt obliged to look for even more radical solutions. As Nicholas Ridley, when Secretary of State for the Environment, made clear at the 1986 Conservative party Conference, the Government had a clear choice: 'either we go on legislating until we have a framework of law within which the abuses can be contained with more central control; or we make local authorities fully accountable to their electors and ensure that those who vote for local extravagance and depravity [sic] pay for it'.[8] It was not long thereafter that the Government clearly chose 'local democratic accountability' and came forward with a new set of proposals which figured prominently in the 1987 Conservative party Manifesto. These proposals involved the abolition of domestic rates, their replacement with a so-called Community Charge (levied on nearly everyone aged 18 or over within each local authority area), the introduction of the so-called Uniform Business Rate in place of non-domestic rates, and a simplified system of block grants to local authorities according to their population numbers and their needs in place of the previously complicated RSG formula.

On being returned to power at the 1987 General Election, the Conservative Government set about implementing its Manifesto pledges to reform the system of local government finance at the earliest possible date. Even though there was considerable opposition and misgiving in Conservative ranks, a Bill was introduced early in the Parliament which later passed onto the Statute Book as the 1988 Local Government Finance Act. Ministers argued that the Community Charge would improve democratic accountability for local authority spending, since about twice as many people would have to pay as had paid domestic rates before (36 million as opposed to 18 million in the former system in England). They also argued that it would be fairer than domestic rates, since the cost of local government services would be spread more evenly over all those who use them. In short, it was seen by the Government as an extension of the charging principle (hence the name Community Charge) and a useful way of promoting financial discipline in local government by creating a larger constituency of support for the restraint of local spending. As for the Uniform Business Rate, Ministers argued that it would prevent profligate local authorities from putting up their business rates to pay for their ambitious political and social spending programmes and that it would protect business ratepayers (once the initial revaluation had been made) from future rate increases above the rate of inflation.

The Government's original idea was to phase in both the Community Charge and the Uniform Business Rate over a period of years, so that the voting public would not face too large a financial adjustment in any one year. However that idea was largely abandoned as far as the Community Charge was concerned following grass-roots pressure at the 1988 Conservative party Conference, mainly from Scottish Tories who had pioneered the shift to the new form of local government financing a year before their fellow citizens in the rest of the United Kingdom. The consequence was a decision to introduce the Community Charge in England and Wales in April 1990 at levels which were mitigated for some local authorities and exacerbated for others by the effects of the so-called 'safety net' arrangements. These were to last for one year only and ensure that local authorities with low spending patterns and those with high rateable values would have to subsidise to some extent others with high spending patterns and low rateable values. A further complexity was introduced at the 1989 Conservative party Conference when David Hunt, then Local Government Minister, announced that additional steps would be taken to see that no individual Community Charge payer would be more than £3 a week worse off as a result of the change in the first year of the new system, provided that the local authority in which he lived did not spend at a level higher than its so-called Standard Spending Assessment. On the other hand, the Uniform Business Rate, which was introduced on the basis of the first rating revaluation in England and Wales since 1973, is being phased in over a five-year period from April 1990 with safety net arrangements to limit the size of both the gains and the losses from the new system in any one year. Thereafter – that is, in 1995 and beyond – there will be regular statutory revaluations of business property every five years.

At the time of writing it is very difficult to predict exactly what will be the effect of these new financial arrangements upon local government, although it is clear that they are unpopular with a large part of the electorate. There are a minority of clear gainers, such as single-person households in low-spending local authority areas, those who live in houses larger than they need (unless they have two or more grown-up children living at home) and businesses in previously high-rated or high-spending local authority areas. Yet, as is so often the case in politics, the gainers say very little in favour of the changes, while the losers say a very great deal against them and may well cast their votes accordingly at the next General Election.

16.4 Central–Local Relations

The relations between local and central government have seldom been easy or unambiguously defined. In the nineteenth century there was a lengthy search for a system of local government which would be both efficient and democratic, although not necessarily for a relationship with central government that was designed to be mutually beneficial. Throughout the twentieth century there have been notable occasions when the usual habits of co-operation between local and central government have broken down and thus given rise to serious misunderstanding and conflict. In general, however, local authorities have faithfully performed their statutory duties and acted within the statutory constraints laid upon them by Parliament.[9]

Constitutional Relations

The constitutional relations between local and central government have varied greatly over the centuries in Britain. Between 1688 and 1835 the effective independence of local government could hardly have been greater, since there was virtually no interference from central government and only minimal control. However, since the 1835 Municipal Corporations Act, the power and influence of central government have grown steadily and there has been an apparently remorseless tendency towards the centralisation of political power. This should not be thought particularly surprising in a unitary state, such as Britain, in which all the legal power and authority of local government has always derived from Acts of Parliament and in which local government has been able to rely only on local elections and local pride to buttress its sense of legitimacy in dealings with central government.

Today the constitutional relationship between local and central government is invariably described by Ministers as a partnership, but by councillors in much less flattering terms and, occasionally, as a central dictatorship. In Whitehall and Westminster not much more than lip-service is paid to the idea of partnership with local government, partly because many local authorities tend to be controlled by local politicians from the opposition parties, but mainly because local government is now dependent upon the decisions of central government for about three-quarters of its income and, ultimately, for its very existence.

There is, therefore, a paradoxical aspect to the relationship between local and central government which is explained partly by the historical fact that until modern times virtually all civil government in Britain was local government (for example, through Justices of the Peace), partly by the important tradition that national services should wherever possible be provided locally, and partly by the tendency for central government to act via the agency of local authorities rather than directly via its own regional and local organisation. It might have been more logical to have clear-cut statements and constitutional rules about the division of powers and responsibilities between local and central government, and then to have entrenched such arrangements in a new constitutional settlement. Yet the principle of parliamentary supremacy has not permitted such an outcome and it seems rather unlikely that it ever will. Consequently the compromise which has been reached is to accord to local government a clearly subordinate constitutional position, while allowing it a more co-ordinate relationship with central government when dealing with the wide variety of practical issues which arise on a day-to-day basis.

Political Relations

Political relations between local and central government have not been easy in modern times, since they are often characterised by inherent conflicts of interest and incompatible political objectives. This was especially true in the 1980s when an ideological Conservative Government in Whitehall had a long-running battle with a number of much more 'political' local authorities led by left-wing Labour politicians of a campaigning disposition. Of course there is bound to be tension or worse in a relationship which depends upon mutual understanding and co-operation between inherently unequal partners. Furthermore the relationship is bound to become rather bitter when central government seeks to impose tighter financial constraints upon local authorities and when many local authorities are run by politically motivated men and women with principles and objectives which are entirely at odds with those of Ministers. Since 1979 the Labour party has been particularly strong in urban local government, especially in the inner city areas and in the great conurbations of the Midlands and the North. This has led some prominent figures in the Labour party, such as Ken Livingstone in Greater London or David Blunkett in Sheffield, to regard Labour-controlled local authorities as bastions of opposition to the Conservative central Government and to abandon most pretence at co-operation between the two levels of democratically elected government. Such suspicion and resentment has been mutual, much to the detriment of the traditional conventions which previously facilitated comparatively civilised relations between the two levels of elected government in this country.

Even in difficult economic circumstances, and with fraught political relations, the partnership between local and central government is supposed to involve some sharing of decision-making powers. Yet most people in local government would probably agree with N.P. Hepworth when he wrote that 'local government does not share in the decision making of central Government; it makes representations, but that is not the same thing'.[10] On the other hand, from the point of view of central government, the partnership can seem quite real, in that many aspects of government policy depend for their success upon the active and willing co-operation of local government. For example, overall public expenditure restraint is dependent upon local government co-operation at a time when local authorities account for one-quarter of total public spending, even if the planning total has now been redefined to exclude those categories of local spending which are financed exclusively by local government. Similarly many of the statutory obligations placed upon local government by Parliament are couched in broad terms of principle which leave the precise methods of implementation very much in the hands of local authorities, not to mention the discretionary powers whose use or non-use depends entirely upon local government decisions. Furthermore the local authorities have learned to combine in order to maximise their influence upon central government. They do this through their representative bodies – the Association of Metropolitan Authorities, the Association of County Councils and the Association of District Councils – and in strictly financial matters through the Consultative Council on Local Government Finance.

While the relationship between local and central government is reasonably clear-cut in constitutional terms, it has often been ambiguous and even hostile in political terms. Neither level of government can really afford to alienate the other and neither can achieve all its objectives without the co-operation of the other. Local government now depends more heavily than before upon central government for financial support, since with the introduction of the Uniform Business Rate in 1990 no less than three-quarters of total local spending is financed either by central government grants or by the new form of business rates whose level in any year is determined by central government. On the other hand, central government depends heavily upon local government for the local administration of national services, although increasingly the present Conservative Government has insisted that responsibility and provision need not always be in the same hands now that the privatisation and contracting-out of local services has begun to spread.

16.5 Methods of Central Control

There are four principal methods by which central government seeks to control local government. Of these financial control is the most important, but we shall consider the others first.

Legislative Control

It is the legislative control in Acts of Parliament which establishes the nature and extent of the subordinate powers conferred upon local government. As J.A.G. Griffith has explained, 'within the terms on which these powers are bestowed, local authorities are autonomous bodies and a Department (of central Government) which proposes to control the way in which or the extent to which local authorities exercise their powers must be able to point to statutory provisions authorising this intervention'.[11] Thus legislative control provides legal safeguards for local government as well as a means of control for central government.

Such legislative control can take various forms. In many cases the original legislation confers upon Ministers the power to make detailed regulations which are binding upon local government. For example, it is customary for Whitehall to issue Statutory Instruments which set out the building regulations to be observed in the construction of buildings and the planning regulations to be observed in carrying out local property or transport developments. In some cases local authorities are given power to make by-laws about public footpaths and other very local matters. Yet it is always made clear in the original Westminster legislation that these by-laws must be confirmed by the relevant Minister. Of course this legislative control involves two-way influence and communication, since the representative bodies of local government are always consulted in the preparation of Westminster legislation which affects local authorities.

Policy Control

Another form of central control is provided by the power and influence of government policy. This can take various forms, depending upon the priorities of the party in office in Whitehall and the legal basis of the relationship between local authorities and the different Departments of central government. For example, the 1948 Children Act and the 1969 Children and Young Persons Act each stipulated that local authorities should exercise statutory functions in this area of policy under the guidance of the relevant Ministers, which has meant in effect the policy pursued by the government of the day. Similarly the Secretary of State for Education and Science has a supervisory and promotional role in relation to the organisation of schools and the supply of teachers in all the local education authorities in England and Wales. This power derives from the 1944 Education Act, as amended by the 1988 Education Reform Act, and it has been exercised by successive governments in accordance with their own particular education policies.

Another example of policy control by Ministers and their civil servants in Whitehall can be found in the sphere of housing policy. Successive Conservative governments have promoted policies of home ownership and home improvement, while successive Labour governments have promoted policies of public sector house building and rent control. In these ways the policy of the government of the day has had a considerable influence upon the behaviour of local authorities. Sometimes it has led to bitter conflict between the two levels of government, with local authorities vainly seeking to resist the policy favoured by central government – for example, resistance to the right-to-buy provisions of the 1980 Housing Act by Labour-controlled Norwich. Yet in the end central government has the whip hand, since, if the existing statutory position is not sufficiently compelling, the party in office in Whitehall can always use its parliamentary majority to put through further Westminster legislation to curb or eliminate what it sees as intolerable resistance by local government.

Administrative Control

Administrative control is another form of central control which derives from central government's responsibility for setting national standards and promoting the efficiency of local government. Ever since the nineteenth century it has been accepted that many functions of government in Britain should be national services locally administered. This has always implied the need for administrative control via national standards drawn up by Whitehall civil servants and enforced in many cases by powerful, independent Inspectorates. For example, in the case of education there is regular supervision of local education authorities by the officials of HM Inspectorate of Education. In the case of the police, the payment of central government grants to police authorities is conditional upon there being satisfactory reports from the officials of HM Inspectorate of Constabulary.

Although the range and power of administrative controls exercised by central government over local authorities has become increasingly formidable over the years, there have been brief periods when there was a countervailing tendency at work. For example, the 1979–83 Conservative Government sought to reduce the number and scope of such controls in the hope of thereby reducing the burden of compliance costs upon the private sector. It also believed that, by freeing local authorities from many forms of detailed supervision and administrative control, it would be possible for them to perform their statutory duties in a more cost-effective way. Some provisions in the 1980 Local Government and Planning Act were designed for precisely that purpose. Since that time the tendency has been rather in the other direction, with central government seeking to interfere and control the activities of local government ever more obsessively.

Financial Control

The most powerful form of central control has always been the financial control exercised by central government. This can be traced back at least to the 1929 Local Government Act in which the earlier system of assigned revenues was abolished and replaced with a system of specific grants, together with a block grant from central government to each local authority. In 1948 this system of financial control was supplemented by a system of deficiency payments to those local authorities with rateable values below the average, and in 1958 the whole system was rationalised to enable a new block grant (the Rate Support Grant) to replace the wide variety of specific grants which had grown up over the years. At every stage from then until the present day financial support from central government has been synonymous with financial control by central government, especially as the proportion of total local government spending financed by central government grants or locally raised taxation entirely under the control of central government has now risen to three-quarters. Little more than lip-service has been paid by central government to the idea of encouraging a degree of financial independence for local authorities, because the Treasury has always been determined not to relax its control over any significant category of public spending nor to relinquish the right to tax to subnational (or supranational) levels of government.

Today the financial control of central government over local government takes essentially three forms. Firstly, local government revenue expenditure is supported – that is, controlled – to the tune of about 50 per cent on a national average basis by the Aggregate Exchequer Grant paid to each local authority according to its needs and its population. Secondly, about 25 per cent of all local authority spending is financed by the proceeds of the Uniform Business Rate which is set by central government at a level which should not rise by more than the rate of inflation and which might be held below that. This should have the effect of eliminating the excessive rises in business rates which were previously imposed by high-spending local authorities, but it has also eliminated any incentive to local authorities to set their business rates at a relatively low level in order to attract mobile business investment. Thirdly, local authority capital expenditure is tightly controlled by Treasury loan sanctions, since local authorities are not encouraged to borrow directly (and more expensively) from the markets and not allowed by the Treasury to spend more than 20 per cent of their retained capital receipts in any one year. Ever since 1979 the Conservative Government has been as keen to control local government capital expenditure as it is to control local government revenue expenditure. Initially this was part of its campaign to reduce and then eliminate all public borrowing, but more recently it has been motivated principally by a desire to curb the revenue implications of all capital projects.

The only way in which central government has relaxed its direct financial grip over local authorities has been to introduce the Community Charge in April 1990 to replace the domestic rates. By doing this it has passed control over about 25 per cent of total local authority spending from an awkward combination of domestic ratepayers and Whitehall officials (brought in to monitor and limit the extent to which local authorities raised the rates) to the enlarged local electorate of Community Charge payers (mitigated, however, by charge-capping to inhibit excessive local spending) all of whom are supposed to pay at least something towards the cost of local services in their local authority area. In other words, the idea behind the new system is to substitute voter accountability at the local level for direct financial control from the centre over at any rate one-quarter of local authority expenditure. Thus, for any marginal increase in local authority expenditure, there is a deliberately painful gearing involved in the Community Charge which should mean that for every extra pound of local authority expenditure it is necessary to raise the Community Charge by four pounds in order to pay for it. In this way local voters are supposed to exert financial control on local authorities via the ballot box every few years.

16.6 Whither Local Government?

With common sense and goodwill on both sides it should be possible to achieve fruitful co-operation between local and central government. There appear to be three basic conditions for this. Firstly, it must be generally accepted that there are certain minimum national standards for the national services provided by local authorities. Secondly, it must be accepted that local authorities are best placed to co-ordinate, if not necessarily provide, many of the public services which people expect. Thirdly, it must be accepted that the relationship between local and central government can only work satisfactorily on a basis of trust and mutual respect. Alas, the second and third of these conditions proved difficult, if not impossible, to fulfil in the 1980s, because the Conservatives at Westminster were conducting something close to a vendetta against Labour-controlled local government and Labour politicians in local government were fiercely opposed to nearly all aspects of Conservative national policy.

The Politicisation of Local Government

Local government in Britain is now in a state of flux. The present Conservative Government seems likely to exert continuing pressure towards centralisation. On the other hand, Labour and the other opposition parties seem committed to varying degrees of decentralisation and devolution of power to the localities. In the extreme case, the Scottish National party is committed to an independent Scotland within the European Community. In considering the future of local government in the United Kingdom, a great deal will therefore depend upon the outcome of the next General Election.

If the Conservatives are returned to power at Westminster, it seems likely that a tight rein upon three-quarters of local authority spending will be maintained via the mechanism of central government grants and the Uniform Business Rate. Conservatives may hope that the Community Charge will have a similar restraining effect upon the remaining quarter of local authority spending, but that would be to underestimate the risk that central government as the initiator of the new mechanism of democratic accountability will get the blame for any public disappointments rather than local government which may seek to portray itself as the victim of the new system. It is hard to imagine that the Conservatives, if victorious at the next General Election, will be very keen to introduce more legislation designed to curb or emasculate local government, although the wide-ranging review of finance and functions announced in November 1990 by Michael Heseltine, once more Secretary of State for the Environment, may lead to further reforms in the next Parliament.

If the Labour party is returned to power at Westminster, it seems likely that it will take legislative steps to introduce a measure of regional government with the creation of perhaps 10 regional assemblies in England, to which would be allocated some of the strategic planning responsibilities of the Counties as well as the regional responsibilities of central government Departments. This means that a new Labour Government would abolish the existing County Councils and pass their most significant responsibilities – for example, education or social services – down to enlarged and strengthened 'most purpose' District Councils.[12] The Community Charge would be scrapped and replaced with a reformed system of domestic rates based on capital values and income, the Uniform Business Rate would be scrapped and replaced with the old system of business rates, and presumably the system of financial support from central government would continue much as before.

Scotland would be given a directly elected Scottish Assembly with substantial, devolved legislative powers, with the result that most decisions affecting Scotland would be taken in Scotland. The Assembly would have a substantial budget of its own comparable in size to all the money now allocated to Scotland under the auspices of the Scottish Office. Beneath the Assembly the Labour party sees a strong case for establishing a single tier of all-purpose local authorities which would presumably signal the demise of the existing regional authorities.

In Wales it seems likely that an incoming Labour Government would abolish the present County and District Councils and replace them with between 17 and 25 all-purpose local authorities. There would also be an elected body for Wales responsible for Welsh Office functions and the work of nominated bodies in the Principality.

In Northern Ireland, the Labour party is more cautious about structural change, saying simply that it will work with the political parties there to establish a devolved, power-sharing administration in Belfast. It is not clear what fate the party has in store for the 26 District Councils, but presumably it would leave them in place as the basis of local government in the Province.

It seems most unlikely at this stage that any of the minor parties will win, or even share, power at Westminster after the next General Election, so there is not much point in spending too much time examining their ideas for the future of local government. Suffice it to say that the Scottish Nationalists remain dedicated to the idea of an independent Scotland within a united Europe, while Plaid Cymru favours at least full cultural autonomy for Wales, if not full Welsh independence. The Liberal Democrats are drawn to the idea of regional government as a means of diminishing what they have long seen as excessive Westminster power and as one of the institutional building-blocks in a new constitutional settlement for the United Kingdom. They too appear to favour greater devolution of power to Scotland and Wales, essentially to separate assemblies in each of those parts of the United Kingdom.

Among the more far-reaching ideas of political reform which have been put forward by academics and others is the proposal that the electoral system for local elections should be changed from the present arrangements to those of proportional representation, so that local government would reflect more fully the range of political opinion in the country, and in order to diminish the risk of abrupt changes of local policy when one party succeeds another in control of a local authority. Another far-reaching idea which has been canvassed from time to time is that the democratic organisation of the larger towns should be changed from the present basis of functional committees to one based upon directly elected chief executives, as happens in France or the United States. The introduction of any such ideas would involve further fundamental reform of local government, which would have limited appeal, at any rate for those who have unhappy memories of previous attempts at ambitious reform.

Local Autonomy or Further Centralisation

The relationship between local and central government also has to be considered in the light of broader arguments for greater local autonomy on the one hand and further centralisation on the other. The arguments in favour of greater local autonomy include the need to diminish the remoteness of government from ordinary people, the desirability of enhancing democratic accountability at local level, the opportunities which could be created for greater public participation, the improved efficiency of smaller units in public administration, and the reduced financial burden upon the Exchequer. The arguments in favour of further centralisation include the need for common national standards of public provision, the uniformity of public expectations as to what government should provide, and the attractions for Ministers and civil servants of a more direct and reliable form of control over local authorities.

With so many tendencies in British society moving in favour of greater homogeneity and even uniformity, there is obviously a strong case for more local autonomy. As Professors Jones and Stewart have argued, greater autonomy should be encouraged 'not to let loose rampant and uncontrolled localism and the sharpening of geographical inequalities, but to maintain a more balanced array of pressures in public policy making'.[13]

With the increasing politicisation of local government, central government has been drawn to interfere more and more with the activities of local authorities. The present Conservative Government has taken this tendency almost to its limit by imposing the unpopular Community Charge to finance one-quarter of all local government spending, reducing still further the Aggregate Exchequer Grant to local authorities as a proportion of their total finance, and introducing the Uniform Business Rate which has the effect of removing local incentives to attract new business investment to a given local authority area with business rates at an attractively low level.

The present Conservative Government seems to believe in the value of increasing central control over local government spending, while simultaneously reducing the capacity of local authorities to interfere with business or individual decisions – for example, on local planning issues. On the other hand, Labour and the other opposition parties seem to have espoused the cause of devolution once again, whether to national assemblies in Scotland and Wales or to regional assemblies and other local institutions in England. Only a new constitutional settlement, guaranteed by a new Bill of Rights and interpreted by an independent Supreme Court, would be able to safeguard local government against the fashions and prejudices of politicians with majority power at Westminster. For the foreseeable future, such constitutional protection for local government seems unlikely to be achieved.

16.7 Conclusion

It should be clear from this chapter that the position of local government in Britain is neither immutable nor easy to describe. However it can be assessed in terms of its efficiency, vitality, adaptability and capacity for genuine partnership with central government. Let us conclude by considering each of these aspects in turn.

With regard to the efficiency of local government, it seems clear that the present division of functions is fairly sensible and does not put such a high premium upon the interests of local democracy that the interests of efficiency are unduly compromised. For example, the emphasis upon techniques of corporate management within local authorities and the discipline of tough financial limits set by central government seem to have had a positive effect upon the efficiency of local government.

With regard to the vitality of local government, the available evidence is somewhat contradictory. On the one hand, the normal turnout at local elections is seldom more than about 40 to 50 per cent of those entitled to vote, and at local by-elections it sometimes falls below 30 per cent. This suggests rather scant public interest in the democratic process of local government. On the other hand, even a cursory glance at the columns of the local press in any part of the country reveals considerable public interest in the actual decisions of local government. For example, ratepayers were very interested (and Community Charge payers should be) in seeing that value for money is secured in local authority spending, whereas beneficiary groups usually favoured the expansion of existing services or the creation of new ones. Public interest is also reflected in the volume of correspondence sent to Members of Parliament and councillors about local authority matters.

With regard to the adaptability of local government, the record over the years has been quite good. However, throughout the 1980s, when many social needs increased, the financial resources made available by central government to local government were consistently squeezed, so that the Aggregate Exchequer Grant now covers less than half of total local authority spending compared with nearly two-thirds more than 10 years ago. The response of local authorities has been one of angry criticism, epecially from Labour-controlled local authorities in inner city areas where the social problems are often greatest. Yet it is clear that local councillors of all parties resent the financial restrictions which have been imposed by central government and would like to have a system of local authority finance which enabled them to perform all their statutory duties in a more satisfactory way.

As for the ability of local government to maintain a genuine partnership with central government, this has been determined partly by the diminishing extent to which it has retained sole responsibility for providing local services. Ministers in the present Conservative Government have made determined attempts to encourage the privatisation of local services and to separate the idea of local government responsibility from local government provision – for example, in the field of community care. However the main explanation for the rather lopsided partnership between local and central government in recent years has been the failure of the former to secure any significant degree of real financial autonomy. Indeed, with the switch from local business rates to the Uniform Business Rate and with the introduction of capping for the Community Charge, the extent of local government financial autonomy has decreased still further. It is, therefore, hard to demonstrate that local government is able to maintain anything like a genuine or equal partnership with central government.

Even allowing for all these problems and shortcomings, local government in Britain still has several points in its favour. Its diversity contributes to political pluralism in our country. Its institutions offer an important sphere of political activity to a considerable number of elected councillors. It stimulates public interest in the local provision of national services. Apart from Parliament at Westminster and the European Parliament, it provides the only level of elected representation in our democracy. Such positive attributes should not be underestimated or ignored, notwithstanding the fact that they are significantly limited by the unitary nature of our political system.

Suggested Questions

1. Describe the structure of local government in the United Kingdom.
2. What are the conditions for a genuine partnership between central and local government?
3. Are the methods of central control consistent with the aspirations for local autonomy?

Notes

1. Report of the Maud Committee on local government management (London: HMSO, 1967).
2. Report of the Committee of Inquiry into the system of remuneration of members of local authorities, vol. 2, Cmnd 7010 (London: HMSO, 1977).
3. See 'The conduct of local authority business', Cmnd 9797 (London: HMSO, 1986) paras 2.23–2.31 for more information on the socioeconomic profile of modern councillors.
4. The functions transferred to the Borough and District Councils included: planning, highways and traffic management; waste regulation and disposal; housing; trading standards and related functions; support for the arts, sport and historic buildings; civil defence and emergencies; funding for Magistrates' Courts and the probation service; Coroners; school crossing patrols; building control; tourism and the licensing of places of entertainment; archives and libraries; recreation, parks and Green Belt land; safety of sports grounds; registration of common land and town or village greens; public rights of way and the registration of gipsy sites.
5. See 'Alternatives to domestic rates', Cmnd 8449 (London: HMSO, 1981) for a fuller discussion of these issues.
6. See 'Local government finance', Cmnd 6453 (London: HMSO, 1976).
7. See the Labour Government's response to the Layfield Report, Cmnd 6813 (London: HMSO, 1977).
8. Quoted in the 1987 Conservative Campaign Guide, p. 331.
9. See K. B. Smellie, *History of Local Government* (London: Allen & Unwin, 1968) for a more detailed account.
10. N. P. Hepworth, *The Finance of Local Government*, 4th edn (London: Allen & Unwin, 1978), p. 255.

11. J. A. G. Griffith, *Central Departments and Local Authorities* (London: Allen & Unwin, 1966), p. 49.
12. See 1989 Labour Policy Review, 'Meet the challenge, make the change' for a succinct and authoritative statement of Labour's approach to local government reform.
13. *The Times*, 14 August 1981.

Further Reading

Byrne, T., *Local Government in Britain* (Harmondsworth: Penguin, 1981).

Foster, C. D. *et al.*, *Local Government Finance in a Unitary State* (London: Allen & Unwin, 1980).

Hepworth, N. P., *The Finance of Local Government*, 7th edn (London: Allen & Unwin, 1984).

Jones, G. and Stewart, J., *The Case for Local Government* (London: Allen & Unwin, 1983).

Rhodes, R. A. W., *Control and Power in Central–Local Government Relations* (Farnborough: Gower, 1981).

Rhodes, R. A. W., *The National World of Local Government* (London: Allen & Unwin, 1986).

Rhodes, R. A. W., *Beyond Westminster and Whitehall* (London: Allen & Unwin, 1988).

Richards, P. G., *The Local Government System* (London: Allen & Unwin, 1983).

Smellie, K. B., *History of Local Government* (London: Allen & Unwin, 1968).

Stewart, J. and Stoker, G., *The Future of Local Government* (London: Macmillan, 1989).

(17) The public sector

In this chapter the term 'public sector' is taken to include public corporations, non-departmental public bodies and other public bodies, such as special purpose authorities. It does not include the Departments of central government (which we dealt with in Chapters 13 and 14) or the institutions of local government which we dealt with in Chapter 16. In this chapter we concentrate upon the problems which have been posed by public corporations, but we also examine the issues involved in privatisation which were central to much of the political debate in the 1980s. The various different types of institution to be found in the public sector are shown diagrammatically in Figure 17.1.

17.1 Public Corporations

In Britain today public ownership and control is usually associated with the model of the public corporation. Yet there have been many different forms of public ownership and control which have been tried over the years. In the second half of the nineteenth century the early Socialists advocated municipal ownership and control of several commercial activities. For example, those who pressed for 'gas and water Socialism' considered local authorities to be the best institutional mechanism for controlling public utilities. Before the Second World War more

Figure 17.1 The composition of the public sector

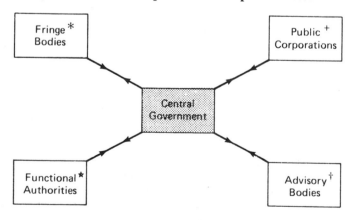

* Notably several hundred QUANGOs
+ Notably about 10 nationalised industries
* Notably the Health Authorities
† Notably Advisory and Departmental
   Committees

than two-thirds of electricity distribution and about one-third of gas distribution were under municipal control, as is still the case in some continental countries today. Over the years a number of municipal authorities also provided passenger transport services, civic amenities and other local services through their direct labour departments. It was not until after 1945 that the focus of public ownership was shifted to one of nationalisation, when the postwar Labour Government gave priority to considerations of national planning, economies of scale and distributional equity. Since that time there has been a steady decline in municipal Socialism and such attempts as there have been to revive it – for example, by Labour-controlled local authorities in the 1980s – were firmly resisted by the Conservative Government in Whitehall.

Notwithstanding the postwar triumph of nationalisation as *the* model for the public sector in Britain, there have been other forms of public ownership which have been attempted for shorter or longer periods. These have included administrative control by a Whitehall Department headed by a Minister directly responsible to Parliament, as was the case with the Post Office until 1969; financial control by a state holding company, such as the Industrial Reorganisation Corporation in the late 1960s or the National Enterprise Board in the late 1970s; and the establishment of state-owned financial institutions, such as the Post Office Giro Bank established in 1969. However, in spite of these variations, the dominant tendency has been the development of public corporations (popularly known as nationalised industries). By their peak in 1982 such institutions employed about 1 759 000 people (about 7.5 per cent of those in work at the time), they contributed about 11 per cent of gross domestic product (GDP) and accounted for about 17 per cent of total fixed investment.[1] They came to dominate four vital sectors of the economy: energy, transport, steel and communications. They included long-established institutions, such as British Rail and British Coal, as well as some relatively new institutions, such as British Telecom and the British National Oil Corporation, both of which have since been privatised by the Conservative Government. In their heyday they were important customers and suppliers of the private sector, and they had a profound and pervasive influence upon the economy and politics of Britain.[2]

Common Characteristics

Public corporations have had a number of common characteristics which have set them apart from other industrial and commercial undertakings.[3] They have been established by Acts of Parliament as statutory bodies responsible for the production of goods or the provision of services specified in the legislation. They have been publicly owned in the sense that any securities which they issue give no powers to lenders and usually pay fixed rates of interest, although in some successful cases they have paid public dividends to the Exchequer. They have been subject to government control via the indirect mechanisms of required rates of return on capital, external financial limits on spending and borrowing, and periodic ministerial appointments of their chairmen and board members. In return they have enjoyed varying degrees of day-to-day managerial independence from central government, their employees have not been civil servants (unlike their counterparts in many continental countries) and they have enjoyed at least a semi-autonomous financial status in the eyes of the Treasury.

Essential Problems

There are a number of essential problems which have bedevilled public corporations in Britain over the years. To a considerable extent these stemmed from the conflicting pressures which gave rise to their establishment in the first place, notably the Socialist impetus provided by the Labour party after 1918 and the pragmatic need for a degree of national economic planning felt by the National Government during the Depression in the early 1930s. Later on, during the Second World War, there was growing acceptance by the Coalition Government of final responsibility for the management of the economy, and by 1945 this included responsibility for the level of employment and of social security as well.

It was against this background of an emerging political consensus in favour of state responsibility for much of the economy that the postwar Labour Government took further giant strides towards public ownership and political control of the sectors which were then considered to be the 'commanding heights' of the economy. It did this principally in the cause of Socialist economic planning in an attempt to improve the chances of national recovery after the war. It did so for the sake of the employees in the industries concerned in order to relieve them of the chronic insecurity which they had experienced between the two World Wars during periods of industrial strife and chronic unemployment. It did so in fulfilment of Clause IV of the 1918 Labour party constitution which had called for the 'common ownership of the means of production, distribution and exchange'. This was the high tide of the cause of nationalisation. As time went by, it became clear to all that the idea of the public corporation was seriously flawed in practice.

To begin with, the theory of public ownership assumed that major matters of macroeconomic policy could be kept separate from the day-to-day concerns of public sector management, and that Ministers and members of nationalised industry boards could play distinct and complementary roles which would not conflict. In practice, these were soon revealed as heroic or naive assumptions, since Ministers were inevitably involved for macroeconomic and political reasons in the key decisions of public corporations. This was partly because of their economic weight and political importance in the national economy, but mainly because in a framework of attempted national planning their decisions were bound to have a significant impact upon the success or failure of government policy. Furthermore, whereas the Socialist ideal which had inspired the establishment of public corporations was intended to permit the state to take over vital industrial activities on behalf of the people, all too often the subsequent reality was characterised by public sector trade union demands for the state to rescue backward or uncompetitive undertakings mainly for the sake of keeping their employees in work. This began to diminish the attractions of public ownership, at any rate in the eyes of all those in the private sector and presented successive governments with increasingly difficult political problems.

Nor were the problems of dealing with the public corporations made any easier by their great diversity, which was clearly reflected in their very different economic fortunes. For example, at different stages during the last three decades, British Airways, British Gas and British Telecom have each had impressive records of economic performance; whereas British Rail, British Coal and London Regional Transport have each had great economic difficulties and in many aspects of their activities have never made a profit. The former group provided examples of expanding industries which proved capable of generating good economic returns on their capital and labour employed, whereas the latter group provided examples of strife-torn industries which were afflicted by economic and social problems often associated with industries in decline. However in all cases it is more useful to make observations about particular public corporations at particular times, since the fortunes of even the most hopeless have occasionally been revised, as with, for example, British Coal since the great coal strike of 1984–5.

The public corporations have also suffered over the years from the fact that their very existence has been the subject of bitter and lasting political conflict between the two main parties. In many respects, they have been treated as a political football to be kicked back and forth between two entrenched ideological positions. The old-fashioned wing of the Labour party has held that every opportunity ought to be taken by a Labour Government to extend the scope of the public sector by taking more and more industries into public ownership. The free market wing of the Conservative party, which was clearly in the ascendant in the 1980s, sought consistently to reduce the scope of the public sector by pursuing a policy of continuous privatisation. Indeed, it has been estimated that, with the successful completion of water and electricity privatisation during the present Parliament, the size of the industrial public sector will have been reduced by about two-thirds, as compared with what the Conservatives inherited from Labour in 1979. In the face of this massive and determined reduction of the public sector by the present Government, the Labour party has sought to revise its policy stance on nationalisation and its leaders now speak only of taking a few of the newly privatised industries back into 'social ownership' – for example, water and electricity by direct re-nationalisation and British Telecom by increasing the public stake to 51 per cent. This may mean that Neil Kinnock and his closest colleagues have come to terms with much of the privatisation which was done by the Conservatives in the 1980s (and, indeed, even by Socialist governments in other countries as well) and that they are unlikely to do much renationalisation if returned to power.

The central problem, however, for the public corporations has been the difficulty of establishing a satisfactory 'arm's length' relationship between the boards of the nationalised industries and the government of the day. To be successful, this always had to involve an attempt to reconcile managerial freedom for the boards with the constant temptation for Ministers to interfere with either the boundaries of the public sector or the ground-rules or, frequently, both. Traditionally the public corporations were charged with twin statutory duties: to break even taking one year with another, and to operate in the public interest. Yet these duties were often incompatible and, when they were, it was usually the latter which prevailed. This might have been acceptable if there had been a clear and lasting consensus between the two main political parties about what constituted the public interest at any one time. Yet such a consensus never existed, since there was an inherent conflict between the interests of the employees of public corporations and those of the wider community which had to support them with taxpayers' money.

A White Paper in 1961 was the first statement of government policy since the Second World War to emphasise that public corporations should not be run as if they were social services, but rather should pay their way at least over a five-year period.[4] It also restated the classic Morrisonian view that public corporations should remain at arm's length from the government of the day. This was taken to mean that Ministers in sponsoring Departments should not interfere with the decisions of the boards, any political intervention which did occur should be specified clearly in writing, and the financial requirements imposed upon the boards should be relaxed if the government of the day were to insist that a public corporation should take on additional burdens of a social character, such as subsidised pricing or regional bias in investment decisions.

Another White Paper in 1967 took this line of argument one stage further by emphasising that public corporations should be regarded as commercial undertakings and gradually eliminate all non-commercial practices, such as internal cross-subsidies and pricing according to historic rather than replacement costs.[5] Yet at the same time the then Labour Government insisted that the public corporations should comply with its prices and incomes policy, and for this purpose it allowed them to interpret their financial obligations quite flexibly. This was a clear example of the sort of political ambiguity which always made it so difficult to manage public corporations with any real degree of lasting success.

In short, experience over many years has demonstrated the great difficulties of implementing an arm's length relationship between public corporations and the government of the day. All too often the former were required by the Treasury to reduce or defer their investment programmes for the sake of national policy, notably government decisions to limit or reduce public sector borrowing. On other occasions they felt obliged to subordinate their commercial judgement to the political priorities of Ministers. For example, there have been occasions when British Coal has wanted to close non-economic pits, but the government of the day has insisted that they be kept open for social or regional reasons (but not so often under the Conservatives in the 1980s). There have been other occasions when British Steel was expected to invest too heavily in new plant and equipment at the instigation of Ministers (notably by Conservative Ministers in 1972–3) only to find that when the new plant came on stream the forecast expansion of the market had not materialised. Even under the (allegedly non-interventionist) Conservative Government in the early 1980s, the nationalised gas and electricity industries were bullied by Ministers into putting up their prices by more than their own commercial judgement suggested simply to increase the flow of revenue to the Exchequer via the mechanism of negative external financial limits. In all such cases it could be argued that the nation as a whole often got the worst of both worlds.

This unsatisfactory relationship between the public corporations and the government of the day was well summarised in a 1976 National Economic Development Office (NEDO) Report.[6] It pointed out that all too often the relationship had been characterised by 'a lack of incentives for adequate or improved performance' which then produced 'a minimising environment with few rewards for real success and negligible sanctions against failure'. In effect, Ministers tended always to pay lip-service to the idea of an arm's length relationship, but then departed from it whenever it seemed politically expedient to do so.

17.2 Regulation and Control

Since 1976 there have been some significant developments in the way in which successive governments have sought to regulate and control the public sector. In that year the Labour Government was obliged by the International Monetary Fund to introduce a system of rigorous cash limits on all forms of public spending, and this included tighter financial controls upon the public corporations. This system was refined and extended subsequently by the Conservative Government in the 1980s with the result that the boards of public corporations were affected both by the tight financial limits set by the Government and (in the early 1980s at any rate) by the adverse consequences of the down-turn in the economic cycle.

Two of the most unfortunate consequences for the public corporations were that they often had to put up their prices by more than the rate of inflation, and that their capital investment programmes had to be pruned to enable them to remain within the limits imposed upon their spending and borrowing. Although in theory the boards had the freedom to operate at arm's length from the government of the day, in practice these external constraints severely reduced their capacity to do so. In these circumstances the methods of external control fell into three categories: ministerial responsibility, parliamentary accountability and other regulatory mechanisms. We shall examine each one in turn.

Ministerial Responsibility

Ministerial responsibility has been the most orthodox method of controlling the public sector. This has taken the form of frequent consultations between Ministers and the chairmen and boards of public corporations on significant matters of policy, such as the planning of major investment, important pricing decisions, pay negotiations and significant environmental issues – for example, an airport runway extension or the siting of a new power station. In this relationship Ministers have sought to preserve a fundamental distinction between day-to-day management decisions (usually matters for the boards) and long-term strategic decisions with, inevitably, a high political content, in which they have had to take a direct interest. However such frequent and privileged contacts have often tempted Ministers to blur this important distinction, although usually it has not been possible for Ministers actually to take over the role of senior management.

When Ministers decide to intervene, they usually have the statutory right to do so by issuing a directive to the board of the public corporation concerned. In practice, however, they have often been tempted to influence board decisions in more informal ways not provided for in the original statutes. Such methods have often been known as 'lunch-time directives', since they involve informal and confidential attempts by Ministers to bring pressure to bear upon the chairmen and key board members. Techniques of this kind may well have been used to put pressure upon British Rail to keep open certain uneconomic branch lines, on the Post Office or British Airways (when the national airline was in the public sector) to buy British rather than foreign equipment, on the Central Electricity Generating Board to modify its power station ordering programme, and on British Coal in connection with the pace and scale of possible pit closures. Since 1979, under the Conservative Government, there has probably been less of this controversial practice. This is partly because more of the public corporations have been managed by new managers specially installed to pursue corporate policies in line with the objectives of Conservative industrial policy – for example, Sir Ian Macgregor at British Coal or Sir Bob Reid at British Rail – but mainly because the Government's policy of extensive privatisation has left fewer areas of potential conflict to be resolved in these ways.

When there has been serious conflict between Government and public corporations, it has often arisen because a chairman has chosen to interpret his statutory duties more narrowly (and commercially) than his sponsoring Minister would have wished. This has then faced the Minister with a choice between doing nothing about an unpopular board decision and so risking public criticism for his apparent inactivity, and intervening in a particular board decision and so breaking the conventions of their working relationship with the chairman and board concerned. On the whole, Ministers have chosen the latter course, since they have known that the general public has more clout at a General Election than any senior management of a public corporation.

Parliamentary Accountability

Another method of political control, which is really the counterpart of ministerial responsibility, has been provided by the direct or indirect accountability of public corporations to Parliament. When exercised through a Minister in the relevant sponsoring Department, it has been both indirect and imperfect, with Ministers merely assuring MPs that they will draw the matter concerned to the attention of the relevant chairman and board. Greater parliamentary accountability has, however, been achieved via the mechanism of Select Committee investigations – in the 1950s and 1960s there used to be a Select Committee on the Nationalised Industries – and via occasional debates on the floor of the House in which the annual reports or other documents produced by public corporations may be relevant. Perhaps the most powerful and effective way of exercising a degree of parliamentary accountability has always been the straightforward practice of MPs writing to senior management of public corporations whenever and wherever they have cause to do so on behalf of their constituents. Because ultimately all these undertakings depend for their continued existence upon the support and approval of Parliament and because most of them have not been able to operate without substantial support from public funds, MPs have had a clear and natural right to exercise this form of accountability and on the whole it has been rather effective.

Other Regulatory Mechanisms

From time to time other regulatory mechanisms have been used in an attempt to exercise some additional political control over institutions in the public sector. For example, the Monopolies and Mergers Commission has conducted efficiency audits of many of the public corporations under the powers provided for it in the 1980 Competition Act.[7] This has helped to sharpen up the management of a number of public corporations, such as the Post Office or British Rail, which seem more likely than others to remain within the public sector for the foreseeable future.

Occasionally Ministers have decided to establish a Royal Commission or Committee of Inquiry to conduct a full-scale review of a public corporation when its current activities or future prospects have caused an unusual degree of political and public concern. For example, in 1985 the Conservative Government established the Peacock Committee to look into the future financing of the BBC.[8] Its controversial report (which was nevertheless a disappointment to the more radical elements) subsequently triggered the far-reaching 1990 Broadcasting Act, which has set the legislative framework for the future of broadcasting in the 1990s and beyond. However it is noteworthy that, during Margaret Thatcher's time as Prime Minister, the Government seemed allergic to the establishment of Royal Commissions, presumably in view of their previous reputation as mechanisms for gathering the opinions of 'the great and the good' and then conveying them in an elegant manner back to Ministers. This rather circular process was usually more conducive to the postponement than to the taking of radical decisions, which was of course one of its attractions for previous governments of a less radical disposition.

Some of the public corporations were provided from the outset with statutory Consumer Councils to monitor their activities from the consumer point of view. The Electricity Consumer Council and the Post Office Users National Council were both examples of this institutional device, which invariably turned out to be a disappointment for those who had sought the creation of watch-dogs with real teeth. As is often the case in arrangements of this kind, the habits of regular monitoring can lead to what is known as 'agency capture', which is what happens when a watch-dog is tamed and eventually rendered largely ineffective by the very institution it is supposed to watch.

17.3 Privatisation

We have seen in the previous sections of this chapter some of the intractable problems which were caused for all governments since 1945 by the constant attempt to maintain a satisfactory arm's length relationship between Ministers and public corporations. By 1979 the lesson of experience was that the public corporations were bound to pose serious problems for any government in that their commercial performance was almost universally disappointing and their impact upon taxpayers and the rest of the economy invariably adverse.

Some senior figures in the incoming Conservative Government in 1979 would have liked to embark upon a policy of radical privatisation, but at that time they were still inhibited by the influence of the postwar industrial settlement which had meant that on the whole the Conservatives did not seek to undo much of the nationalisation done by the radical Attlee Government from 1945 to 1950. Thus, for 30 years or more, nationalised industries were regarded by both major parties as an inevitable, but not always desirable, part of the national economy on grounds of strategic necessity and public interest. Indeed, although the Heath Government came to office in 1970 pledged to begin the process of denationalisation, it soon felt itself impelled, in 1971 and 1972, to do some further nationalisation of its own – of Rolls Royce and Upper Clyde Shipbuilders – in order to stave off bankruptcy and large-scale unemployment in the aerospace and shipbuilding industries. Thus it was in no way surprising that against this background even an incoming Conservative Government with a radical programme and a comfortable parliamentary majority felt initially disinclined to do too much too fast in this direction.

In the event, the 1979–83 Conservative Government returned six major public corporations to the private sector, although only two (British Aerospace and Amersham International) were sold to the investing public in one go. However we should not forget that this period also saw the passage onto the Statute Book of the 1980 Housing Act, whose most important feature was the introduction of a statutory right for all council tenants to buy (at generous discounts) the properties in which they had lived as council tenants. This momentous shift of wealth and ownership from the public to the private sectors was a very significant measure of privatisation. It had resulted by 1989 in the creation of more than 1 million new owner–occupiers and the raising of over £10 000 million for public funds.

Having won another General Election victory in 1983, Margaret Thatcher and her senior ministerial colleagues felt more confident about extending the principle of privatisation to more parts of the public sector. Accordingly the 1983–7 Parliament saw the return to the private sector of a larger number of state-owned industries, including two giant public utilities, British Telecom and British Gas. The gross proceeds of these two sales alone, in 1984 and 1986, amounted to nearly £9000 million, and in each case the shares were extensively bought by first-time shareholders and employee shareholders. By the mid-1980s, therefore, the policy of privatisation had gathered considerable momentum. Truly it seemed to be a big idea whose time had come, both in Britain and increasingly around the world.

Meaning and Extent

It should be apparent from the foregoing paragraphs that the full meaning of privatisation is really the withdrawal of the state from the production of goods and services and, one might add, from a range of activities which previously it was considered only the state or its agencies – such as local government – could or should perform.[9] Seen in this light and bearing in mind how far the policy has since been taken, it is not an exaggeration to argue that this policy has succeeded in redefining a long-standing national consensus.

Thus the definition of privatisation includes everything from the sale of state-owned enterprises to private investors (previously known as denationalisation) to the sale of public assets, such as public land or council housing, to the contracting-out of public services, such as rubbish collection or cleaning, to the most radical ideas for the provision of individual vouchers for education and health services as an alternative to the exiting forms of tax-financed state provision. However, under Mrs Thatcher's determined leadership, the drive to privatise in order to reduce the size and burden of the public sector did not stop there, but was supplemented with aggressive liberalisation in such sectors as bus and coach services, cable television and telecommunications. It could also be said to have included the policy of deliberately reducing the size of the civil service by cutting the total number of civil servants and transferring some governmental functions to the new executive Agencies whose staff are not necessarily within the public sector, and the policy of abolishing 'unnecessary tiers' of local government, such as the Greater London Council and the other Metropolitan Counties.

In all these different ways the policy of privatisation has involved redefining and limiting the role of the state, while encouraging and extending the role of the market in the areas from which the state has been withdrawn. 'Thatcherism' and privatisation in this sense were indisputably linked: indeed, in many respects they were effectively synonymous.

At the time of writing, it is hard to be sure exactly how far the policy will eventually be taken. It was carried forward decisively with the privatisation of the Water Authorities and the electricity Area Boards. Ministers plan to follow up with the privatisation of the electricity supply industry (minus the nuclear component) which seems likely to be the largest ever flotation of privatisation stock. Much will depend upon whether the Conservative Government is able to maintain the momentum of its policy. If so, it has been estimated that by the end of the present Parliament no less than two-thirds of the state industrial sector of 1979 will have been returned to the private sector. If the Conservatives are returned to power for a fourth term of office in the 1990s, the policy could be extended further to include British Coal, British Rail and some other public bodies such as the Forestry Commission.

If the Labour party wins the next election, it is by no means certain that there will be a great deal of renationalisation. According to the relevant section of the 1989 Labour Policy Review, the party is determined to increase the public stake in British Telecom to 51 per cent (the minimum necessary for legal public ownership) and to adopt a similar approach to the challenge of renationalising the water companies and the electricity utilities. The party is equally determined to learn the lessons from the experience of Morrisonian state corporations. In the words of the Review, 'we shall determine the best way of proceeding on a case by case basis in the light of the situation we shall inherit in each instance'.[10] Whatever happens at the next election, there was a secular change in political attitudes to public ownership in the 1980s, which means that in the 1990s, no British government is likely to embark upon large-scale renationalisation in the old style.

Arguments For and Against

The arguments for privatisation were originally based upon the view that the public sector had become too large and burdensome on the rest of the economy and that, in the absence of effective reforms within the public sector, there was no sensible alternative to denationalisation. They were also inspired in the minds of radical, Thatcherite Conservatives by the strongly held belief that free enterprise was a good thing, with a beneficial effect upon political freedom, while state enterprise was almost exactly the opposite and hence undesirable on both economic and political grounds.

However, by the time that the policy had been refined in the light of experience in the mid-1980s, a fuller range of more intellectual arguments were adduced in its support.[11] Firstly, it serves to reduce government involvement in the decision making of industry. Secondly, it permits the industries concerned to raise funds for investment from the private capital markets without feeling inhibited by public borrowing limits. Thirdly, it raises extra revenue for the Exchequer which can be used either to cut taxes or to increase public expenditure or to repay public debt, or a combination of these. Fourthly, it helps to promote wider share ownership both by inducing more people to purchase privatisation issues and by encouraging employee share ownership on favourable terms. Fifthly, it is held to increase economic efficiency and performance in the sectors concerned, as has been evidenced by the dramatically improved performance in the private sector of some firms which were previously public corporations, such as Cable & Wireless or the National Freight Corporation. Sixthly, it replaces regulation and control via public ownership with a more satisfactory and legalistic system based upon independent regulatory agencies, such as the Office of Telecommunications or the Office of Gas Supplies. Finally and more generally, it is seen as support for the drive to create more of an enterprise culture in this country by replacing state industries which cannot go bankrupt with private industries which can and which therefore have to exert themselves more in order to survive in a free market.

Apart from those old-fashioned Socialists who prefer state ownership on simple ideological grounds, the arguments against privatisation have come essentially from those who believe that the costs outweigh the benefits in terms of consumers' and taxpayers' interests. Such people usually adduce the following arguments. Firstly, they argue that, when public corporations have been sold, the flotations have been either undersubscribed or underpriced. In the former case – as with Britoil and Cable & Wireless in 1983 or Enterprise Oil in 1984 – the sales were by tender and hence the market was permitted to set the price. This led to situations in which not all the shares were initially taken up, with the result that the underwriters were called upon to take the balance of unsold shares. In the latter case – as with British Telecom in 1984, British Airways in 1987 or the Water Authorities in 1989 – the sales were by fixed price directly to the institutions and the public. This led to situations in which the shares were initially underpriced and were therefore traded at a premium by the end of their first day on the market. The critics have argued that such premia – which by 1987 had totalled more than £4000 million – represented a loss to taxpayers and the nation of that large amount.

Secondly, they argue that the Conservative Government has simply been 'selling off the family silver', as Harold Macmillan put it in a memorable phrase, in order more easily to finance either tax cuts or public expenditure or a combination of the two. The burden of this charge has been the argument that privatisation has amounted to little more than public asset-stripping which brings windfall gains to some at the expense of substantial losses to the nation as a whole over the longer term. Certainly there is some powerful evidence for this argument in cases such as the sale of the Royal Ordnance in 1987 to the previously privatised British Aerospace and the sale of the Water Authorities in 1989 to a variety of private interests which had coveted their valuable land and property assets.

Thirdly, they argue that there is no real benefit to consumers and to the public at large if privatisation involves simply the transformation of a public monopoly into a private monopoly, which can subsequently exploit its privileged position to the disadvantage of its customers. Of course there are good reasons why the Conservative Government has laid itself open to this charge. Some of the most favoured candidates for privatisation (for example, British Gas or the Water Authorities) were natural monopolies. It has always been much easier to privatise a public corporation with the active support of its senior management and this has tended to be less forthcoming if it seemed to involve the break-up of such large and powerful monoliths. The sale of a monopoly always provides more money for the Exchequer than the sale of an enterprise which has been broken up and hence is likely to face more real competition and lower profits after privatisation.

Finally, some critics on the ideological Right have argued that the Conservative Government seemed to stumble into the policy of privatisation and had no coherent strategy or set of consistent priorities to guide it. For example, such people have asked whether the prime purpose of the policy is simply to sell all that which can be sold to fickle and volatile stock markets, or whether there are some other intellectually more respectable criteria for selecting the candidates for privatisation – perhaps those industries, such as British Rail or British Coal, whose poor performance in the public sector might actually be improved by an invigorating dose of free market competition in the private sector.

Problems and Consequences

We have seen how privatisation was regarded in the 1980s both as a blessing and as a curse, depending upon the political point of view of the observer. It is clear, however, that even in the eyes of its most enthusiastic proponents, there are some real problems posed by privatisation which in many ways loom as large as the problems of public ownership which we discussed in an earlier part of this chapter. It is therefore to the problems and consequences of privatisation that we now turn.

Perhaps the key problem posed by privatisation is a paradox, namely that its main purpose is to give the industries concerned much more commercial freedom than was available to them in the public sector, yet if consumers are to be adequately protected from monopoly or predatory practices it is necessary to circumscribe their market freedom with elaborate arrangements of independent regulation. The main point here is that, whereas in dealing with a public corporation it is often necessary for Ministers to intervene to protect the interests of taxpayers against any abuse of power by the management and other employees, in dealing with privatised undertakings it is necessary for independent legal regulators, such as OfTel, OfGas or OfWat, to intervene to protect consumers against any abuse which might be perpetrated by the exploitation of their newly acquired market power. For example, without such regulatory intervention, it would be possible for British Telecom to charge very high prices for services of which it is the sole supplier – such as domestic phone calls – to the detriment of the consumer interest and, indeed, that of the Government too, if such action had an adverse impact upon the Retail Price Index. It is for this reason that complicated formulae have been set by the regulatory agencies to control the prices charged to different categories of consumers by the now private 'public utilities'. For example, the recently privatised water companies are only allowed to increase their prices by the rate of inflation plus an X factor to allow for a decent rate of return on their assets in order to enable them to finance the necessary new investment. Without these external limits set by the independent regulatory agency, the companies would have been in a position to charge virtually anything they liked for the essential services which they supply, since there is no effective competition and no obvious substitute.

A more general problem posed by privatisation is that the new, more explicit forms of regulation have to be both cost-effective and publicly acceptable. This is a difficult balance to achieve, not least because the new forms of regulation have yet to establish much of a track record upon which to base durable principles. One thing seems clear already and that is that, the more genuine competition there is, the less need there ought to be for elaborate regulation. This is because real competition should ensure that most customer requirements are met at the lowest cost consistent with the need to make sufficient profits to reward shareholders, pay employees and finance future investment. However if effective regulation is necessary – as it is in all cases – it seems that it ought to contain the following key characteristics: it should be cost-effective for the privatised undertakings concerned; it should contain the least and simplest restrictions consistent with an adequate defence of the public interest; it should bring benefits to consumers which outweigh the compliance costs that will, invariably, be passed on in prices; and, as far as possible, it should be immune from 'agency capture' – that is, when a regulatory agency becomes the servant rather than the master of the industry which it is supposed to regulate.

A final and potentially very significant consequence of the drive towards privatisation and liberalisation in the 1980s has been the move to a more legalistic relationship between the private sector and the state. This has been brought about by a combination of market-led developments (especially in financial services) and the political necessity for a liberalising government which cannot afford to be justifiably accused of allowing its friends and supporters to profit too flagrantly at the expense of the wider public interest. This has resulted both in a deliberate strengthening of established regulatory agencies, such as the Office of Fair Trading or the Monopolies and Mergers Commission, and in a growing readiness to create new regulatory agencies, such as the Office of Telecommunications, the Office of Water Supplies or the Securities and Investment Board with its subordinate self-regulatory organisations. In essence, what has happened under the present Conservative Government is that the state has largely withdrawn from its previous role as both producer and regulator of public goods and services to a new role in which it has sought to ensure, via the mechanism of independent regulatory agencies, that the private sector abides by the legal rules of the game.

17.4   Non-departmental Public Bodies

In one of the earliest surveys of non-departmental public bodies (henceforth NDPBs), Geoffrey Bowen identified 252 such institutions which he defined as 'organisations which have been set up or adopted by Departments and provided with public funds to perform some function which the Government wishes to have performed, but which it does not wish to be the direct responsibility of a Minister or a Department'.[12] Such bodies were also often known as QUANGOs, or quasi-autonomous non-governmental organisations, to give them their full title. These were generally divided into three categories: executive bodies, advisory bodies and administrative tribunals. They therefore included a wide range of very different institutions, such as the British Library, the Equal Opportunities Commission, the Gaming Board, Trinity House, the Wales Tourist Board, the White Fish Authority and the Supplementary Benefits Appeal Tribunals.

When this part of the public sector was reviewed again in the 1980 Pliatzky Report, it became clear that there were as many as 2167 such institutions, employing about 217 000 people and responsible for a range of activities involving about £6150 million of public expenditure.[13] By April 1988 the number of institutions which satisfied this definition had declined to 1648, of which the greater part (1066) were advisory bodies, while only 390 were executive bodies and 65 were tribunals. This lower net figure represented the difference between the 937 such bodies which had been abolished since 1979 and the 417 which had been created. Most of the reduction had occurred between 1979 and 1983 when the QUANGO hunt had been at its height. Since then the enthusiasm of the Conservative Government for this particular sport has waned and in April 1990 there were still 1539 such bodies in existence, costing a total of £8.6 billion in public funds.[14]

Common Characteristics

On closer inspection it is clear that NDPBs have a number of characteristics in common. They derive their existence from ministerial decisions and are therefore answerable to Ministers. Their creation normally requires legislative approval by Parliament, and most of them produce annual reports which have to be laid before Parliament and can be debated there. They are usually financed by grants in aid, but may sometimes be given the power to raise their own statutory levies. Each chairman and board is appointed by a Minister for a fixed term of office and can be dismissed by the Minister at the end of such a term. NDPBs recruit their own staff, who are not normally employed as civil servants, although pay and conditions are often comparable with the civil service. Their annual accounts are audited either commercially or by the National Audit Commission. In short, they represent an identifiable sub-species of public administration in Britain.

Advantages and Disadvantages

Those who have investigated this grey area of the public sector have identified a number of advantages and disadvantages in the existence of such bodies. On the positive side, the following points can be made. They permit certain activities of importance to the state to be conducted outside the confines of government Departments, yet within the Whitehall sphere of influence. They permit such activities to be conducted free from direct or frequent oversight by Parliament and therefore largely insulated from the party battle at Westminster. They enable Parliament to pass what is essentially framework legislation in some areas of public administration with confidence that any practical problems which may arise can be solved in a satisfactory manner. They make it easier to achieve a broad continuity in certain areas of public administration and to resolve any conflicts in a largely apolitical way. They relieve civil servants of many tiresome administrative burdens and so enable the Departments of central government to be smaller than they would otherwise need to be. They provide useful opportunities for the dispensation of political patronage in a way which does not usually involve any real corruption.

On the other hand, the following negative points have been made about NDPBs.[15] There has been a lack of clarity or agreement about how many such bodies there really are and whether all those which have been identified should be included in the standard definition. The growth of such bodies has produced an institutional proliferation which has proved expensive to administer and difficult to control. The appointments to such bodies have provided scope for political patronage which has been regarded by some as unhealthy and undesirable. There has been a lack of effective democratic control over these bodies and a lack of adequate financial control over the public funds for which they are responsible. In short, they have been seen by their critics as an example of unelected and unaccountable public administration.

It was against this background of controversy that in November 1984 Margaret Thatcher announced a comprehensive review of NDPBs which later led to a systematic report, the results of which were revealed to Parliament in January 1988.[16] This showed that, during the review period which had ended in April 1987, Departments reported total savings of about £30 million in the public funding of NDPBs and a total reduction of 1830 staff as a result of the closure of

150 such bodies, the rationalisation of others and various financial management initiatives. At that time Ministers planned to eliminate a further 290 posts in NDPBs, leading to continued financial savings of about £33 million a year. For the future Mrs Thatcher made clear that such bodies would be subjected to further comprehensive reviews, at least every five years, which would consider the continued need for each and every one, its administrative objectives and its financial and other management systems.

It is clear that the present Government recognises, however reluctantly, that NDPBs can be an appropriate and cost-effective solution for some of the problems of public administration. Yet at the same time it will continue to resist proposals for new NDPBs unless their need can be clearly demonstrated within a framework of strict financial and management controls. Henceforth any legislation involving the establishment of such bodies will normally contain powers to permit their winding-up at a later date – that is, if a fixed lifetime is not established at the outset.

17.5 **Other Public Bodies**

In considering the rest of the public sector, we shall refer briefly to Royal Commissions and Departmental Committees of Inquiry, as well as the myriad of advisory committees which is to be found within the orbit of Whitehall. We shall also make brief mention of special purpose authorities, such as the Health Authorities.

Royal Commissions and Other Committees of Inquiry

The appointment of a Royal Commission or a Departmental Committee of Inquiry is an act of the Executive which requires no prior parliamentary approval, although it is often a ministerial response to political pressures. As Lord Benson and Lord Rothschild put it in an article reviewing this aspect of public administration, the purpose of such a body is 'first to ascertain all the relevant facts, next to assemble them fairly and impartially, and finally to form balanced conclusions'.[17] Once established, a body of this kind usually calls for written and oral evidence from all interested parties both inside and outside the web of central government. It may also undertake or sponsor research of its own into the problems which it has to consider. When the work is complete, a report and record of the evidence submitted is normally published for the benefit of Parliament and public. However, in matters of national security and other highly confidential areas, the report may be published with certain omissions or occasionally it may be withheld from publication altogether.

Over the period 1954–69 reviewed by Lords Benson and Rothschild, 24 Royal Commissions and more than 600 Departmental Inquiries were appointed. Most of them were disbanded when their tasks were complete, although a few were appointed on a permanent basis – for example, the Royal Commission on Environmental Pollution or the Law Commission. Among the most significant commissions or committees since that time have been the Fulton Committee on the Civil Service 1966–8, the Redcliffe–Maud Commission on Local Government 1966–9, the Kilbrandon Commission on the Constitution 1969–73, the Bullock Committee on Industrial Democracy 1975–7, the Wilson Committee on Financial Institutions 1977–80 and the Scarman Committee on the Brixton Disorders in

1981. When such bodies make their reports it is usually for the senior Minister in the Department concerned or occasionally for the Government as a whole to decide whether any or all of the recommendations should be accepted and, if so, how they should be put into effect. Sometimes this has led to ministerial decisions, sometimes to new legislation. In many cases it has turned out to be little more than a convenient device for putting off decisions on particularly vexed or difficult matters on which there may be no political agreement. Sometimes it has been a way of burying an awkward issue altogether. Perhaps this is why Margaret Thatcher, as a self-styled conviction politician, had such obvious contempt for them during her long period as Prime Minister.

Departmental Advisory Committees

As for the many advisory committees which assist Departments in the course of their day-to-day administration, we have here a clear illustration of the extent to which regular consultation, whether formal or informal, has become a characteristic part of modern central government. As we noted in Chapter 6, such advisory committees can meet the needs of Departments for expert information and advice, while satisfying the claims of sectional interest groups for access to central government and influence upon policy. They also provide one means by which any government can seek to gain and retain the consent of the governed, at least those who may be most directly concerned with the consequences of government policy.

Such advisory committees are particularly useful to Departments in the detailed preparation of technical Statutory Instruments. The need for their advice arises because Acts of Parliament often put statutory responsibilities upon Ministers to consult specified advisory bodies when drawing up such detailed legislation. For example, under the 1964 Police Act the Home Secretary must consult the Police Council which was set up to advise on regulations concerning the administration and conditions of service in police forces throughout the country. Equally, under the 1975 Social Security Act the Secretary of State must consult the National Insurance Advisory Committee on regulations to do with National Insurance.

There are also examples of such consultations which have taken place on a non-statutory basis – for example, within the framework of the National Economic Development Council originally established in 1962. Until the late 1980s this provided a forum for regular meetings between the Government and what were traditionally known as 'the two sides of industry'. In many cases mutual benefit was derived from such consultations. However the present Conservative Government became increasingly disenchanted with such meetings and saw them as an undesirable legacy of the corporatism of earlier times. It was therefore not entirely surprising when they fell into virtual abeyance after the third Conservative victory at the 1987 General Election.

Special Purpose Authorities

Until quite recently the 10 Water Authorities were responsible in the public sector for about three-quarters of the water supply, water treatment and sewerage services in England and Wales. They were a prominent example of special purpose authorities, because they had been set up in 1974 by parliamentary statute with the clear task of providing comprehensive water services within hydrologically determined areas. However in the late 1980s they were privatised by the Conservative Government and their shares were sold to the financial institutions and to the general public in a successful flotation in November 1989. This left the Health Authorities as the last prominent example of this genre of public administration in Britain.

The Health Authorities are based upon a public sector institutional structure which was originally established by the postwar Labour Government in 1948 and then subsequently reorganised in 1974 and again in 1982. Today in England this structure is composed of a National Management Board in London led by a Chief Executive who is answerable to the Secretary of State at the Department of Health; 14 Regional Health Authorities responsible for strategic management and resource allocation within their large geographic areas; and 206 District Health Authorities responsible at more local level for the day-to-day management of the service. Together these different administrative layers make up the bureaucratic side of the National Health Service.

In January 1988 Margaret Thatcher announced in the course of an interview on the BBC programme *Panorama* that the Government intended to establish a comprehensive review of the National Health Service as a basis for future reforms. The review was conducted confidentially by a group of senior Ministers and a White Paper setting out their conclusions and proposals for reform was published in early 1989.[18] The proposals involved the introduction of an internal market for medical services within the NHS in which the District Health Authorities (DHAs) could become informed purchasers, but not necessarily remain the sole providers, of health services in their localities. Services could then be purchased either from their own hospitals (as before), or from other DHAs, or from private sector facilities, or from so-called Independent Hospital Trusts which would be self-administered hospitals established under the aegis of the 1990 Health Service Reform Act. This model of an enabling and purchasing public authority has become a clear favourite of Ministers in the present Conservative Government. This is because it offers a clear alternative to the traditional Morrisonian idea that public goods and services should be provided, as well as managed and financed, solely by statutory public bodies. It offers a pattern of institutional development in the public sector which is thought to be equally applicable to health authorities, local authorities and public corporations. It is entirely consistent with the drive towards privatisation which was one of the main thrusts of policy under Margaret Thatcher. In the case of the National Health Service, it remains to be seen whether it will work without a loss of service quality or patient confidence.

17.6 Future Prospects

None of the familiar problems of the public sector has been made any easier to solve by the various myths which have permeated the political debate over the years. For example, there has been the myth that in dealing with public corporations it is possible to draw a clear and effective distinction between political and commercial considerations. There has been the myth that these hybrid institutions can act both as public institutions for promoting the national interest and as profit-maximising commercial undertakings. There has been the myth that there can be either full ministerial control or complete managerial autonomy for those who have to run such institutions.

The reality, of course, has always been rather different. It is that all governments have been condemned to relationships of inherent ambiguity with public corporations and, indeed, with all public sector institutions. This was certainly true as long as Ministers felt inhibited from moving decisively either towards tighter political control (as formerly in the Soviet bloc) or towards the clear alternative of privatisation of the state and para-state sector. In so far as some of the problems of cost and public accountability seem to have diminished in the late 1980s, this is because the Thatcher Government was so successful in pushing through its programme of privatisation.

Future Guidelines

Against this controversial and dynamic background, it is difficult to be sure about the future of the public sector in Britain. The present Conservative Government has been strongly committed to its policy of extensive privatisation, although there are now some doubts about its future momentum. On the other hand, a future Labour Government now seems likely to adopt a more cautious and limited approach towards renationalisation for electoral reasons, largely because the privatisation at any rate of the state industrial sector seems to have been quite popular with the public and a radical policy of renationalisation would threaten newly acquired vested interests, such as new home owners or shareholders in privatised undertakings. In these circumstances a few guidelines for the future of the public sector might be helpful, even if they are now quite difficult to discern.

Firstly, it would seem that in our mixed economy there are certain goods and services which probably are best provided by the public sector if they are to be provided at all, such as loss-making postal services to outlying communities or uneconomic commuter rail services to and from the suburbs of London. Yet it may be that a viable alternative in future could be the private provision of even these marginal services, as long as their cost could be subsidised by general taxation and their quality could be assured by new forms of regulation.

Secondly, there are considerations of national security which, at least in the past, have made it seem virtually essential that the public sector should undertake certain large and expensive technological projects, such as civilian nuclear power, because the financial institutions in the private sector have seemed unwilling or unable to take the necessary commercial risks in order to do so. Yet it may be that a viable alternative is offered by the model of the Channel Tunnel which, at any rate on the English side of the venture, has had to be supported entirely without public funds by private sector financial institutions.

Thirdly, there will continue to be a good deal of political argument about whether public goods and services have to be provided by the public sector or whether there are other ways in which they can be provided more cost-effectively, as long as there is adequate supervision and regulation of the private sector when it is involved. For example, some on the free market wing of the Conservative party have argued that even uneconomic rural transport services can best be provided by new private sector undertakings brought into existence by the liberalisation of public vehicle licensing, and this doctrine has been applied under the aegis of the 1982 Transport Act. Others have suggested the merits of public service flexibility, as when postmen in sparsely populated areas have been encouraged to provide a small rural transport service for the benefit of isolated communities. The real problem, of course, is that such services are usually not profitable, so they have to be run at a loss if they are to be run at all. The awkward choice then lies between realistic (but prohibitive) pricing or public subsidy from local or national sources. In short, public service and commercial profit have often been difficult to reconcile, at any rate in marginal cases. In the past both central and local government have invariably decided in favour of the former. In the future the outlook and the choice do not seem so certain.

17.7 Conclusion

In this chapter we have seen that the most notable characteristics of the public sector in Britain have been its considerable size and diversity, as well as the fierce political argument which has raged over its scope and its obligations. The problems have been thrown into sharpest relief by the history of the public corporations, although the rest of the public sector has not been without its operational and political difficulties as well.

In political and constitutional terms, the main significance of the public sector has been evident in the problems which it has posed for governments of the Left and Right alike. Manifestly, the Morrisonian model of the public corporation has not proved to be a satisfactory solution. Few people seem to have derived any worthwhile benefit from it, with the possible exception of some bureaucrats in the sponsoring Departments and some public sector employees in those trade unions with disproportionate bargaining power. Everyone else seems to have been frustrated or thwarted by this hybrid institution and it has caused real problems for Ministers and managers alike. Normally there has not been sufficient trust between Ministers and managers, continuity of policy has been prejudiced by incessant party battles over the scope and ground-rules of the public sector, and real public accountability seems to have eluded every genuine attempt to achieve it.

Faced with this sort of evidence, the Conservative Government decided to reduce the size and influence of the public sector by a policy of privatisation sustained over many years. On the other hand, the Labour party has seemed less certain about its traditional political commitment to the nationalisation or renationalisation of large parts of the private sector. It is impossible to be sure of the outcome of this particular political debate, but there is now more than a strong suspicion that the two main parties may be converging upon a new zone of political consensus based upon the idea of a smaller, but stronger state.

Suggested Questions

1. Assess the contribution of public corporations to Britain in the twentieth century.
2. To what extent can or should public corporations be controlled by Ministers?
3. Has privatisation changed everything?

Notes

1. See various publications of the Central Statistical Office, notably *National Income and Expenditure, 1983*, Tables 1.10 and 10.3; and *Economic Trends*, February 1983, Appendix 1, Table 1.
2. For example, in 1982 public sector purchases from the private sector amounted to about £9 billion, while sales to the private sector amounted to about £11 billion.
3. These generalisations refer essentially to the nationalised industries and not to all

public corporations, some of which – such as the BBC – were created by Royal Charter for very different purposes.

4. See 'The financial and economic obligations of the nationalised industries', Cmnd 1337 (London: HMSO, 1961).
5. See 'Nationalised industries, a review of economic and financial objectives', Cmnd 3437 (London: HMSO, 1967).
6. See 'A study of UK nationalised industries' (London: NEDO, 1976), p. 40.
7. Examples have included efficiency audits of the London letter post, the Severn–Trent Water Authority, the Central Electricity Generating Board, and British Rail commuter services in London and the South-East.
8. See Report of the Committee on financing the BBC, Cmnd 9824 (London: HMSO, 1986).
9. See C. Veljanovsky, *Selling the State* (London: Weidenfeld & Nicolson, 1987) for further elaboration of this point.
10. See 1989 Labour Policy Review, 'Meet the challenge, make the change', p. 15.
11. See, for example, J. Moore, *Privatisation in the UK* (London: Aims of Industry, 1986).
12. G. Bowen, *Survey of Fringe Bodies* (London: CSD, 1978).
13. L. Pliatzky, Report on non-departmental public bodies, Cmnd 7797 (London: HMSO, 1980).
14. See *Public Bodies 1990* (London: HMSO, 1990).
15. See *What's wrong with QUANGOs?* (London: Outer Circle Policy Unit, 1979).
16. See Written Answer in *Hansard*, 28 January 1988, Cols 313–314.
17. Lord Benson and Lord Rothschild, 'Royal Commissions: a memorial', in *Public Administration*, Autumn 1982.
18. See 'Working for Patients', Cm 555 (London: HMSO, 1989).

Further Reading

Ascher, K., *The Politics of Privatisation* (London: Macmillan Education, 1987).

Barker, A. (ed.), *Quangos in Britain* (London: Macmillan, 1982).

Cartwright, T. J., *Royal Commissions and Departmental Committees in Britain* (London: Hodder & Stoughton, 1975).

Glynn, J., *Public Sector Financial Control and Accounting* (Oxford: Basil Blackwell, 1987).

Pirie, M., *Privatisation, Theory, Practice and Choice* (London: Wildwood, 1988).

Prosser, T., *Nationalised Industries and Public Control* (Oxford: Basil Blackwell, 1986).

Pryke, R., *The Nationalised Industries, Policies and Performance since 1968* (Oxford: Martin Robertson, 1981).

Redwood, J., *Popular Capitalism* (London: Routledge, 1988).

Rhodes, G., *Committees of Inquiry* (London: Allen & Unwin, 1975).

Veljanovsky, C., *Selling the State* (London: Weidenfeld & Nicolson, 1987).

18 The legal system

There are five main aspects of the legal system in Britain. There is the sphere of criminal justice which involves the application of the criminal law to cases brought to court by the Crown Prosecution Service. There is the sphere of civil justice which involves the application of the civil law to cases brought by various plaintiffs, including individuals, corporate bodies and the law officers of the Crown. There is the process of judicial appeal which allows those who are dissatisfied with the verdicts of lower courts or tribunals to seek redress or reversal of judgement in the higher courts of appeal. There is the important sphere of civil rights and duties which determines the complex legal relationship between citizens and the state. There is the sphere of administrative law which involves the quasi-judicial procedures of the various administrative tribunals and the judicial review of administrative action. We shall review each of these aspects in this chapter, but we shall also touch upon the package of legal services reform introduced by the present Conservative Government.

18.1 Criminal Justice

Machinery and Procedure

The majority of criminal cases are disposed of in Magistrates' Courts and only a minority are tried in the higher courts. Trial in a Magistrates' Court is summary (that is, without a jury) and takes place before a bench of two or more Justices of the Peace or one legally qualified Stipendiary Magistrate. Most cases are brought by the Crown Prosecution Service which prefers charges against the defendants on the basis of police evidence and legal advice. Magistrates' Courts have original jurisdiction to inquire into all matters triable on indictment and, if they deem the evidence sufficient, to commit the defendant for subsequent trial at a Crown Court.

In the minority of cases which go to Crown Courts the procedure is one of trial by jury before a High Court Judge, a Circuit Judge or a Recorder (that is, a practising barrister or solicitor sitting in a judicial capacity). Most of the more serious cases are committed automatically to the Crown Courts, although even in less serious cases the defendant can opt for trial by jury in a Crown Court rather than summary trial in a Magistrates' Court – and many do, in the hope and expectation that they will stand a better chance of getting off in front of a jury. In only a few rare cases is the old-fashioned practice still used whereby magistrates commit a case to the Crown Court after they have conducted a preliminary examination of the evidence to see whether such a step is justified.

The most serious cases (for example, murder, rape or armed robbery) must be tried by a High Court Judge. Other serious cases (for example, manslaughter or serious assault) are usually tried by a High Court judge, but sometimes released to a Circuit Judge or a Recorder. Cases which involve lesser indictable offences or

Figure 18.1 The system of criminal courts

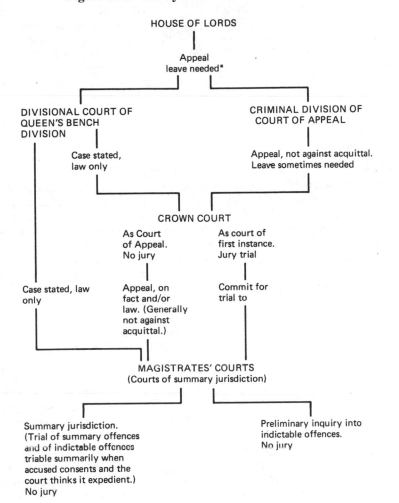

HOUSE OF LORDS

Appeal
leave needed*

DIVISIONAL COURT OF
QUEEN'S BENCH
DIVISION

CRIMINAL DIVISION OF
COURT OF APPEAL

Case stated,
law only

Appeal, not against acquittal.
Leave sometimes needed

CROWN COURT

As Court
of Appeal.
No jury

As court of
first instance.
Jury trial

Case stated, law
only

Appeal, on
fact and/or
law. (Generally
not against
acquittal.)

Commit for
trial to

MAGISTRATES' COURTS
(Courts of summary jurisdiction)

Summary jurisdiction.
(Trial of summary offences
and of indictable offences
triable summarily when
accused consents and the
court thinks it expedient.)
No jury

Preliminary inquiry into
indictable offences.
No jury

*Administration of Justice Act 1960 s. 1 provides:
(1) Subject to the provisions of this section, an appeal shall lie to the House of
Lords, at the instance of the defendant or the prosecutor
  (a) from any decision of a Divisional Court of the Queen's Bench Division in a
    criminal case or matter;
  (b) from any decision of the Court of Criminal Appeal on an appeal to that court.
(2) No appeal shall lie under this section except with the leave of the court below
or of the House of Lords; and such leave shall not be granted unless it is certified by
the court below that a point of law of general public importance is involved in the
decision and it appears to that court or to the House of Lords, as the case may be that
the point is one which ought to be considered by that House.

Source: R. M. Jackson, *The Machinery of Justice in England*,
7th edition (London: Cambridge University Press, 1977).

those in which the defendant has opted for trial by jury are usually tried by Circuit Judges or Recorders. In all these cases the most important role of the judge is directing the jury on matters of law. Yet the passing of sentence on convicted defendants has become increasingly significant, at any rate in very serious cases, since judges have tended increasingly to make specific recommendations about the length of prison sentence which should be served, largely to pacify public opinion which has become increasingly vexed by the practice of granting parole or remission of sentence, sometimes when as little as a third or a half of the sentence has been served.

Controversial Issues

There are many controversial issues in the criminal law. Most of them were carefully considered by the Royal Commission on Criminal Procedure which reported to Parliament in 1981.[1] The issues include the right of silence for criminal suspects, the exclusion of evidence which has been improperly obtained, the definition of arrestable offences, the extent of police powers to stop and search, the limits on detention in police custody, and the use of tape-recordings in interviews of criminal suspects. All these issues were debated, if not finally resolved, when the 1984 Police and Criminal Evidence Act was first discussed in Parliament in 1982–3. They were then further debated in the first year of the 1983–7 Parliament, because the original Bill had been lost when Parliament was dissolved at fairly short notice in May 1983 for the General Election in June 1983. They continue to be areas of controversy, because there is always considerable tension between the rather reactionary views and prejudices of the general public and the more enlightened, often pragmatic, views of judges, magistrates, police and prison service.

One of the difficulties in reaching balanced and lasting conclusions in this sphere of the law is that many of the issues raise important questions to do with the relationship between the police and the public, especially in some inner city areas where the relationship can be very strained between police officers and members of the coloured community.[2] Problems have arisen particularly in the area of police powers to stop and search people for offensive weapons, such as knives and other sharp instruments. There have also been intermittent complaints from suspects that they have not been able to consult a solicitor before being charged or that they have been 'fitted up' by the police with fabricated evidence and induced to make false confessions. Such problems are likely to persist as long as there are shortcomings in police practice, great public pressures upon the police to catch and charge someone for offences of a particularly heinous character, and a lasting mistrust of all law-enforcement agencies among certain sections of disaffected minority communities.

A more general problem is caused by the constant need to strike a fair and effective balance between the interests of the law-abiding majority, which wants the police and the courts to maintain law and order in a strong, even draconian way, and those of certain vociferous minorities who are often more concerned with the protection of civil liberties and the maintenance of civil rights. Since it is always difficult to strike an appropriate balance between such strongly conflicting interests, the solution has typically involved attempts to balance increased powers for the police and the courts with more effective legal safeguards for the

Figure 18.2 The system of civil courts

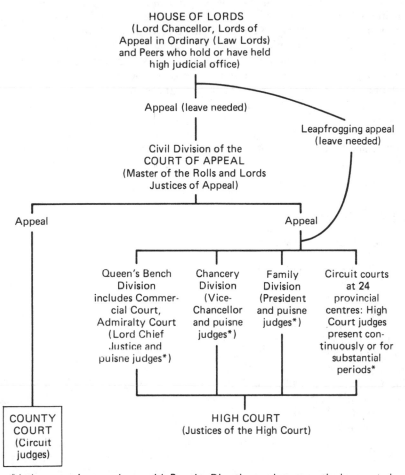

*Judges may, in accordance with Practice Directions, release a particular case to be tried by a Circuit Judge or a Recorder: these remain High Court cases.

Source: R. M. Jackson, *The Machinery of Justice in England*, 7th edition (London: Cambridge University Press, 1977).

law-abiding community. This was precisely the approach adopted in the 1984 Police and Criminal Evidence Act.

Those who are strongly committed to the maintenance of law and order have invariably argued for changes in the criminal law – for example, the return of capital punishment – which they believe would enable the police and the courts to deal more decisively with the current levels of crime and lawlessness. Indeed very few people have argued for a more permissive attitude towards crime – except those who wish to decriminalise the purchase and use of soft drugs – or more lenient procedures for dealing with convicted criminals. However growing concern has been expressed, not only by liberal-minded opinion-formers, about the large and growing number of people sent to prison in Britain compared with other advanced countries, so much so that even Conservative Home Secretaries in the 1980s looked for ways of keeping certain categories of people, such as drunks, prostitutes and the mentally defective, out of prison altogether. Others have argued the need for improved procedures to deal with complaints against the police, since a growing number of people no longer accept that there should not be at least a genuinely independent element in any body established to investigate claims of police malpractice. Finally, there is a section of largely intellectual, left-wing opinion which is disturbed by what it sees as alarming tendencies for our society to develop in an authoritarian direction wholly at variance with our liberal–democratic traditions. Such people usually cite as evidence of their concern the occasional tendency for the police, the security services and the paramilitary units of the modern state to overstep the traditional bounds in rare instances of brutality, excessive surveillance and democratically unacceptable uses of force.

18.2 Civil Justice

Machinery and Procedure

Most civil cases are heard initially either in County Courts by Circuit Judges or in one of the three civil divisions of the High Court by High Court judges. Magistrates' Courts have original jurisdiction in some cases involving the summary recovery of certain kinds of debt and some domestic proceedings, such as separation and maintenance, guardianship or adoption.

In the County Courts the jurisdiction is both local and limited. Such courts deal with actions founded on the law of contract and tort where the claim of the plaintiff does not exceed a small sum (currently £5000); equity cases up to a higher value (currently £30 000) which affects trusts, mortgages and the dissolution of partnerships; most bankruptcy proceedings outside London; and actions concerning land or buildings in which the rateable value does not exceed a small sum (currently £1000 a year). They also deal with matters arising from social legislation, such as the adoption of children, the validity of hire purchase agreements and disputes arising from the various Rent Acts. Since 1968 all undefended divorce cases (about 90 per cent of the total) have been heard in courts specially designated as Divorce Courts, while complaints of racial discrimination are heard in other courts specially designated for the purpose. While both barristers and solicitors may appear on behalf of those who come before these courts, the judge often has to hear the case on the basis of submissions made without the benefit of lawyers. In none of these cases is there call for a jury.

In the High Court the Queen's Bench division deals principally with actions founded upon the law of contract and tort.[3] It also deals with actions on bills of exchange, insurance claims, shipping actions and some landlord and tenant actions. Only a small proportion of the actions actually come to court and fewer than 2 per cent of all the cases are fought to a conclusion, since those involved are usually keen to avoid the high legal costs associated with fighting such cases. Either party may request a trial by jury in cases involving defamation of character, malicious prosecution, false imprisonment, fraud or seduction. The final decision as to whether or not a jury shall try such a case rests with the judge concerned. In general the use of juries in this division has declined, to the extent that they are now summoned only in an estimated 4 per cent of all cases. Another important function performed by this division is the supervision of the lower courts and tribunals. This is done by issuing prerogative orders, such as a prohibition, *mandamus* or *certiorari*, as well as an order of *habeas corpus*.[4] Whereas in former times these rights were available only to the Monarch, they can now be issued by the High Court upon application from an ordinary plaintiff.

The Chancery division of the High Court, which was established in London in 1873, has effective jurisdiction over the estates of deceased persons, the execution of trusts, the dissolution of partnerships, disputes in private companies and the redemption or foreclosure of mortgages. In 1921 bankruptcy jurisdiction was added to its various responsibilities, and breach of contract can be investigated here or in the Queen's Bench division.

The Family division of the High Court dates from 1971, when cases to do with wills and wives were separated from those to do with shipwrecks, with which they had been incongruously lumped since 1873 when the Probate, Divorce and Admiralty division was established.[5] Today the division deals with all domestic and matrimonial cases, guardianship and probate. Most of its work is concerned with divorce proceedings in an age when one in three of all marriages ends this way.

Controversial Issues

The main controversial issues in the civil law today are connected with the public image of the law and lawyers, and with the costs and delays in the processes of the law. We shall therefore look briefly at each of these issues in turn.

It is a widely held view among laymen that the attitudes of lawyers and the processes of the law are distinctly old-fashioned and middle-class. This view has been held especially by trade unionists and those active in Labour-controlled local government. Indeed, ever since the notorious Taff Vale case in 1901, most leading trade unionists have believed that the judiciary is biased against trade unions, and the development of judge-made case law over the years has not done much to dispel that belief. As Gavin Drewry has pointed out, 'most of the really telling criticism of lawyers centres upon their failure to win the confidence of working-class people and their inability to achieve an image of independence from the Establishment'.[6]

When hearing cases, judges are supposed to be strictly impartial. This means not only that they must not show any personal bias or prejudice, but also that they must exclude from their judgements any political or moral views which they may hold as individuals. Naturally this is difficult or impossible for anyone to achieve, so there have been times when judges have appeared to be far from impartial in the eyes of those who come before them. There is at least circumstantial evidence for these misgivings. Firstly, judges have tended to be drawn disproportionately from the ranks of the upper and middle classes, and inevitably they tend to be quite elderly by the time that they reach the bench. As J.A.G. Griffith has argued, 'they have by their education and training and the pursuit of their profession as barristers acquired a strikingly homogeneous collection of attitudes, beliefs and principles which to them represents the public interest'.[7] Secondly, Griffith and others have argued that the judicial conception of the public interest has invariably been based upon the interests of the state, notably the preservation of law and order, the protection of property and the promotion of certain other political views normally associated with the Conservative party. In so far as this may be so (and in some ways it would be surprising if it were not) it is almost inevitable that there are some people, especially among minority groups and other embattled sections of the community, who believe that judges are inherently biased against them and their interests.

Thirdly there is a widely-held view that access to the law, for those who want to have it, is not equally available to people from all classes and walks of life. Indeed, it is commonly said that only the very rich (who can afford it) and the very poor (who qualify for legal aid from the state) can now afford to go to law. In the latter category, the extent of legal aid available to any litigant has been limited by two tests: whether a solicitor, apart from the consideration of costs, would advise going to court in the particular case; and whether the applicant falls within the prescribed means-tested limits for legal aid. Over the years the effect of these two provisions has been to exclude quite a large number of fairly poor people from qualifying for legal aid, to penalise those who might otherwise want legal representation when appearing before administrative tribunals, and to put at a disadvantage litigants with a strong case who are not legally aided when their opposing parties are. Of course, there are other forms of free legal advice available to people, from, for example, Citizens' Advice Bureaux, neighbourhood law centres and even Members of Parliament. Yet there still remains a large potential demand for legally-aided litigation which probably goes unsatisfied, largely because of Treasury opposition to the mounting public expenditure cost.[8]

Fourthly, there is the deterrent of the delays in the legal system. It is not just in Dickens's novels that characters sometimes die before their legal case is over. In Britain the problems of delay can be ascribed to the rising demand for litigation, the relative shortage of judges to hear cases, the time taken in amassing all the relevant evidence for use in court in a convincing way, and the traditional commitment to an adversary procedure in court which involves the very time-consuming business of hearing and cross-examining witnesses testifying on oath. Some of the problems have been mitigated by improvements in the procedure of small claims courts, which have served to speed up that particular kind of justice. Yet further progress could undoubtedly be made if more judges could be appointed and if more use could be made of written evidence in court, at any rate in all those cases where the facts of the matter are not seriously contested by the various parties.

Finally, some have argued that the middle-class image of the law and lawyers deters many poor or inarticulate people from seeking the benefit of legal advice or legal services. To many people traditional legal procedures seem very off-putting, not to say alarming, with all the wigs and processions and general mumbo-jumbo. No doubt this is why some of the procedures have been simplified and made more 'user-friendly' in recent years, notably in cases involving families and children.

18.3 Legal Services Reform

As might have been expected, the legal system in Britain was not immune from the drive for reform which was a characteristic of the Thatcher Government from 1979 to 1990. Admittedly legal services reform was not the highest priority for that radical Administration: policies such as trade union reform and privatisation were tackled first. A strong move in this direction also had to await the retirement of Lord Hailsham from the position of Lord Chancellor and his replacement following the 1987 General Election by Lord Mackay, a more radical Scot who had previously made his name as the senior legal officer in Scotland (where there is a separate legal system).

Following the 1987 General Election, the Government went ahead with its legal reform in a measured and evolutionary way. In January 1989 three Green Papers were published on the work and organisation of the legal profession, the idea of contingency fees and conveyancing by authorised practitioners.[9] The ideas in these documents were widely discussed and gave rise to over 2000 responses, of which over half came from solicitors and over a quarter from consumer interests and members of the general public. A White Paper setting out the Government's firm proposals for reform was published in July 1989.[10] The legislation which it had foreshadowed (the Courts and Legal Services Bill) was published in December 1989 and became the law of the land in 1990.

The Aims of Reform

In the words of the Lord Chancellor, the Government's aim was 'to make the legal system of this country more straightforward, more flexible and above all more responsive to the citizen's choices and needs, while at the same time maintaining the standards necessary to achieve justice'.[11] The proposals contained in the 1989 White Paper were concerned with one part of that overall objective. Other measures were also carried forward in related areas to complete the overall strategy of legal reform.

For example, arrangements for improving the administration of legal aid under the 1988 Legal Aid Act are being put into effect. The Government is equally committed to changes designed to speed up, simplify and reduce the cost of legal proceedings via a major programme of reform based upon the recommendations of the Civil Justice Review published in June 1988.[12] The 1990 Courts and Legal Services Act has allowed redistribution of civil cases between the High Court and the County Courts, so that the former can be reserved for judicial review and other specialist or important cases, thus releasing to the latter the great bulk of more minor cases which have produced disproportionate delay and cost. Initially this should benefit plaintiffs in personal injury cases, but later on the principle will be extended to debt and housing cases. In general, the Government is seeking to tailor court procedures to the weight, importance and complexity of each case, for example by increasing the small claims jurisdiction, while making procedural improvements to protect unrepresented litigants and to encourage individuals to participate fully in cases which affect them.

The Components of Reform

There are a number of principal components in the Government's legal reforms. Firstly, a single statutory framework is being introduced to replace the previously complex arrangements for rights of audience in the courts. This will end the previous preponderance of barristers as advocates in the courts and their monopoly of audience in the High Court. In practice, it may not make much difference at first, but it does establish the principle that others who are suitably qualified may appear as advocates in court up to the highest level. Secondly, the

Law Society (the solicitors' representative and disciplinary body) and possibly other professional bodies are to be entitled by statute to grant their members the right to conduct litigation in the courts, subject to their being able to satisfy the Lord Chancellor and the judiciary on the maintenance of appropriate standards of competence and conduct. In theory, this will make it possible for a range of suitably qualified professionals (as well as laymen representing themselves) to act as 'litigators' in the courts.[13] Thirdly, the qualifications for judicial appointments to the bench are to be revised to make all suitably qualified lawyers eligible for judicial appointments. At present a few solicitors sit as Recorders (the lowest level of the professional judiciary), but they have to serve for at least three years in this capacity before becoming eligible for appointment to the Circuit Bench (the next rung up the judicial ladder). This restrictive stipulation on solicitors' progress will now be removed.

Fourthly, banks, building societies and other authorised practitioners are to be allowed, subject to certain important conditions designed to safeguard their clients against the danger of professional exploitation, to offer conveyancing services when people buy and sell houses. This will further reduce the preponderant position of solicitors in this lucrative activity – there are already so-called 'licensed conveyancers' who do some of this work – and it is yet another measure designed to subject the legal profession to greater competition. Of course what may happen in practice is that banks and building societies may simply employ more trained lawyers to do this work for them 'in house' rather than suggesting to their clients that they should go to an independent firm of solicitors for this particular service, as has been the traditional practice. Fifthly, the statutory prohibition on the formation of partnerships between solicitors and other professionals (for example, accountants or financial advisers) is to be removed, as are the barriers to the formation of partnerships between lawyers in this country and lawyers or other professionals abroad. This should enable British lawyers to compete more effectively with, for example, American firms which are already allowed this kind of multiple capacity, and it will be in line with the liberalisation of professional services throughout the European Community which is scheduled to take place as part of the progress towards the single European market by the end of 1992.

Sixthly, the rules and practices of all British lawyers will be open to investigation under proposed legislation on restrictive practices, although there will be the safeguard for the legal profession that rules approved by the Lord Chancellor will be exempt from prohibition. Finally, a new Legal Services Ombudsman is to be created, who will have powers to examine the way in which public complaints against legal practitioners are investigated by the professional bodies and to investigate such complaints himself, where appropriate, with the subsequent ability to recommend payment of compensation if a complainant has been demonstrably wronged by a member of the legal profession. This should give the public the welcome reassurance that it will no longer be necessary to rely simply upon the Bar Council and the Lay Observer to investigate and rectify complaints against barristers and solicitors.

In two areas of potential reform, however, the Government retreated in the face of strong representations from the legal profession during the consultation period on the Government's proposals in early 1989. The original proposal for a new Advisory Committee on Legal Education and Conduct with strong executive powers to supervise and discipline the profession was replaced by a weaker committee whose role is to be purely advisory in relation to the Lord Chancellor and the profession. Indeed the cherished principle of professional self-regulation, for which the lawyers, like the City institutions, fought so hard, is to be reinforced by leaving it to the professional bodies – that is, the Bar Council and the Lay Observer – to prepare their own regulations and codes (admittedly after advice from the Advisory Committee and with the concurrence of the Lord Chancellor) which will set qualification standards and practice requirements for advocacy and litigation.

It is possible that the Lord Chancellor's retreat on this point of cardinal importance to all lawyers, especially the judiciary, may be outweighed by the incremental role of the Advisory Committee in relation to legal education. After all, the advice of the new body will be designed to ensure that schemes of professional selection and recognition do not create unnecessary barriers either to new practitioners (whether lawyers or non-lawyers) entering areas of legal work or to general practitioners continuing legal work. In the long term, this leverage of the Advisory Committee should enable it to prevent the lawyers from continuing with their traditional arrangements of legal training and entry to the profession which have created what is effectively a closed shop for a privileged elite.

Another proposal, for the introduction of contingency fees which would have permitted clients to offer their lawyers a percentage of any damages awarded in their favour, was also rejected by Ministers following consultation. This, largely American, practice was strongly opposed by all those who wanted to prevent the development of an unnecessarily litigious society in this country, although it should be added that a milder version of conditional fees is to be allowed, as it is in Scotland. It is not without significance that the present Lord Chancellor is a Scot.

It is too soon to tell what will be the full consequences of these various reforms in the English legal system. However, from a political of view, these reforms constitute an important part of the present Government's commitment to freer competition in most areas of our national life. They have also been seen by senior Ministers as a token of their determination to carry on the crusade against all restrictive practices, no matter how respectable or established the interests which seek to defend them.

18.4 **Judicial Appeal**

Machinery and Procedure

The process of judicial appeal in Britain can be applied equally to cases of criminal and civil law. Most of the criminal appeals are heard by the criminal division of the Court of Appeal. This is presided over by the Lord Chief Justice or a Lord Justice of Appeal. Queen's Bench judges sit with Appeal Court judges and there are usually three judges on the bench for any hearing. When a case raises an issue of general public importance, a further appeal may be made to the House of Lords, but in criminal cases such appeals are rare.

Most of the civil appeals are heard by the Master of the Rolls and the Lord Justices of Appeal, although the Lord Chancellor, the Lord Chief Justice and a few other very senior legal figures may sit *ex officio* (by dint of their offices) in exceptional circumstances. An odd number of judges (usually three) hears the appeal and decisions of the Court are taken by majority.

On important points of law with wider legal application there is the possibility of further appeal to the House of Lords. Such appeals are made to the Appellate Committee, which is the final court of appeal and which can only be overruled by Parliament as a whole passing new legislation. The work of the Appellate Committee is done by the Lord Chancellor, 10 Law Lords and a few other very senior legal figures who may sit by virtue of having previously held high judicial office. The committee is usually made up of five Law Lords and their judgements take the form of motions, with each judge expressing his judicial opinion on the matter in question. Until 1966 it was customary for the committee to reach its decisions entirely on the basis of judicial precedents, but since then it has occasionally departed from this principle when it appears right to do so.

Mention should also be made of the Judicial Committee of the Privy Council which was established by statute in 1833. This hears appeals on cases authorised by the courts in the Isle of Man and the Channel Islands, in Britain's remaining colonial Dependencies (for example, Hong Kong) and in those member states of the Commonwealth which have chosen to retain the right of legal appeal to it.[14] It also hears appeals from Admiralty courts, ecclesiastical courts, and the disciplinary committees of the General Medical Council and the Dental Council. The Lord Chancellor is nominally its president, but in practice nearly all the work is done by Lords of Appeal. It hears about 20 appeals each year and is the final arbiter of constitutional issues in the various territories and jurisdictions concerned.

The Judicial Committee has been available as a source of advisory opinion for the Crown on matters of public concern or legal difficulty which cannot otherwise be brought conveniently before the courts, for example cases relating to disqualification from the House of Commons or those to do with parliamentary privilege. It had a role under Section 5 of the 1920 Government of Ireland Act in that, until Stormont was dissolved in 1972, the Government in London was empowered to refer to it questions relating to the interpretation of the Act, notably issues of legislative competence. As things turned out, this provision was used only once, in 1936. It would also have had a similar role of constitutional arbitration if the devolution legislation of the 1974–9 Labour Government had been brought into effect. However the 1979 Scottish and Welsh Devolution Acts remained inoperative, because the referenda held in those parts of the United Kingdom did not achieve sufficient public support to trigger the legislation.

Controversial Issues

The process of judicial appeal does not normally give rise to great political controversy, except on those rare occasions when issues of wider political importance are raised in particularly contentious cases. When this happens, judgements in the House of Lords are final, except when they trigger the government of the day to introduce fresh legislation to overturn or confirm the previous legal position.

Early examples of this process were provided by the 1906 Trade Disputes Act, which overturned the House of Lords judgement in the 1901 Taff Vale case, or the 1913 Trade Union Act, which overturned the House of Lords judgement in the 1910 Osborne case. A later well known example was the 1965 War Damage

Act, which overturned the 1965 House of Lords judgement in the case of Burmah Oil. A notable example in more recent times was the 1983 Transport Act, which took account of the 1982 House of Lords judgement in the case of *Bromley Borough Council* v. *the Greater London Council* on the politically contentious issue of passenger transport subsidies in Greater London on the bus and underground services. In all such cases, when matters of political importance have been involved, the government of the day has felt obliged to introduce legislation either to overturn or to take account of the legal position as defined by the House of Lords. Such examples demonstrate that in Britain judicial intervention at the highest level is by no means always conclusive on matters of the highest political or constitutional importance.

Over the years there have been periods of judicial activism and creativity, and periods when the behaviour of the judiciary has been characterised by conservatism and a determination to defend the established legal order. On the whole judicial conservatism has been the more prevalent. This is partly a reflection of the inherently conservative background and outlook of the judiciary in Britain, to which reference has already been made. Yet it also reflects the well-established constitutional attitude held by the judiciary over many years and most succinctly expressed by Lord Reid on several occasions. In 1961, in *Shaw* v. *the Director of Public Prosecutions*, he observed that 'where Parliament fears to tread, it is not for the courts to rush in', and in 1972 he maintained that cases which raised political issues should be decided 'on the preponderance of existing authority'.[15]

In these matters much has depended upon whether the judiciary construes the law passed by Parliament literally and narrowly or contextually and broadly. For example, Lord Denning in his many years as Master of the Rolls and chairman of the Court of Appeal was usually inclined to interpret the law in a way which was well-disposed towards the underdog. Naturally this did not endear him to those organisations which he deemed oppressive (for example, trade unions) or indeed to the Law Lords, who often had to review his judgements on further appeal. Much has also depended upon the extent to which the judiciary has thought it proper or prudent to flex its muscles in defiance of the government of the day. On the whole Labour governments have found themselves in conflict with the judiciary more often than their Conservative counterparts, although in the 1980s the judiciary was something of a brake upon the radical intentions of the Thatcher Government. On the other hand, it can be argued that such cases demonstrate not really judicial hostility to Labour governments but rather the simple reality that there is always likely to be a conflict between the judiciary, with its invariable commitment to the preservation of the existing legal order, and any radical government, whether of the Left or the Right. Like the civil service, the judiciary is one of the most significant stabilisers in the British political system.

18.5 Citizens and the State

In the modern world the complex relationship between citizens and the state raises political and legal issues of great importance. Citizens expect to enjoy certain inalienable rights, including freedoms of both a positive and negative kind. There are the freedoms *to* do certain things, and the freedoms *from* having certain things done to you. Each category of freedom is equally valuable. Yet in every case the rights concerned have to be qualified or counterbalanced by certain rights of the state or its agencies to act on behalf of the community as a whole. It is in holding this balance between the rights of citizens and the interests of the state that the legal system in Britain has had to try to resolve some of the most difficult problems of modern society. Furthermore the basis of civil rights in Britain is to some extent precarious, since we do not have a codified constitution or an effective Bill of Rights with which to constrain the possibility of parliamentary tyranny, by which one means the tyranny of any transient parliamentary majority in the House of Commons. It is therefore as well to be circumspect when pronouncing upon the important issues which are raised in this section.

Citizenship and Free Movement

There are issues which arise from rights of citizenship and free movement. Under the 1981 British Nationality Act all British citizens have the same legal rights and status, although this applies only to those with full British citizenship. The position of others resident in this country is limited by the various legal provisions governing the control of immigration. The position is qualified to some extent by the free movement provisions in European Community law by which this country is also bound.

Under the 1981 British Nationality Act anyone who is legally a British citizen has the right of abode in this country, and hence the right to enter the United Kingdom and to remain here as long as he likes. Such a person cannot legally be deported. On the other hand, the right to leave this country can be vitiated if a person is without a British passport (or at any rate a temporary British visitors' passport) if he wishes to take up legal residence outside the United Kingdom. Of course, under the provisions of European Community law, all citizens of the 12 member states are supposed to have the right to take up residence in any part of the European Community. Yet in practice there is still some way to go before this 'right' is completely and easily enforceable throughout the European Community.

Personal Liberty and Property

There are issues which arise from rights of personal liberty and property. Although British citizens are free people, in certain circumstances they can lawfully be detained – for example, after arrest and pending trial on a criminal charge (assuming bail is refused by a Magistrates' Court) or when a local authority decides within its statutory rights to take a child into care. Any such departure from the principle of personal liberty can raise issues of considerable controversy and has sometimes led to investigations by a Royal Commission or the passage of new legislation. Powers of arrest, which are normally exercised by the police (but legally available to any citizen) are regulated principally by the 1967 Criminal Law Act, although the 1984 Police and Criminal Evidence Act had a powerful bearing upon these matters as well.

As for property rights in Britain, these have never been regarded in this country as absolute or sacrosanct. Parliament has legislated on many occasions to limit such rights when they have conflicted with what is deemed by Ministers to be the public interest, for example in the spheres of public health, nationalisation or compulsory purchase. As a general rule there has not been as much determination to use the law to defend economic or property rights as there has been to defend rights of personal liberty. This must be right and it is in accordance with the European Convention on Human Rights, which has a similar bias.

Wrongful interference with the rights of personal liberty and property can be countered by the use of various legal remedies. These include civil action for damages, prosecution for assault, exercise of the right of self-defence, use of the police complaints procedure, and even the invocation of *habeas corpus*. Yet there are no final or definitive solutions to these problems, since the law governing these aspects of civil rights can be changed from time to time by Act of Parliament.

Freedom of Expression

There are issues which arise from rights of free expression and their necessary limitation. In this sphere our law has usually relied upon the principle that anything which is not prohibited is permitted. Yet the extent to which restrictions have been imposed in civil or criminal law has varied from time to time. For example, the law of defamation protects individuals from slander and libel, or rather it provides a form of legal redress if the person concerned can afford to fight a case. Substantial damages may be awarded for injury to a person's reputation, and in some cases even the threat of such legal action can be sufficient to secure a retraction or to get a newspaper to publish a (usually inadequate) note of correction. In some cases those accused of defamation can plead absolute privilege (typically in judicial or parliamentary proceedings) or qualified privilege (typically in fair and accurate reports of such proceedings). The defence of 'fair comment' can also protect expressions of opinion on matters of public interest, even if someone thinks that what has been said is defamatory. In the criminal law there are the offences of sedition, blasphemy, obscenity and criminal libel which theoretically protect society from some of the excesses of free expression. Yet in practice actions are rare and of dubious utility, since it is difficult to get juries to convict on the basis of such ancient laws. Furthermore, as we saw in the much-publicised instance of Salman Rushdie's *Satanic Verses*, the law (in this case the law of blasphemy) does not always apply. In this instance an alleged blasphemy against the prophet Mohammed fell outside the terms of the statute, which concerns itself only with blasphemy in a Christian context.

Freedom of expression in the media has traditionally been controlled to some extent by a combination of self-discipline on the part of the more responsible journalists and the intervention of certain statutory bodies whose task it has been to maintain proper standards. In the case of newspapers, the Press Council has had an unimpressive record in preventing and an even less impressive record in punishing severe lapses of taste or decency or unacceptable invasions of privacy. In the case of broadcasting, the BBC and the IBA have had greater powers over the broadcasters in radio and television, but have had few opportunities and not much inclination to use their powers, especially if urged to do so by politicians in the government of the day. In certain respects the situation may become more unrestrained with the liberalisation of the airwaves in the 1990s and the present Government's reluctance to employ more than regulation with a light touch. Yet, paradoxically, in the sensitive areas of television portrayal of violence and pornography, the recently established Broadcasting Standards Council seems likely to wield its new statutory powers with almost alarming enthusiasm, which may seriously inhibit even legitimate expressions of artistic freedom. In the world of advertising (which is likely to become even more influential with the spread of satellite and other forms of commercial television) standards of public taste and decency have been monitored in the past by the Advertising Standards Authority, with rather little obvious effect. These standards may be made more rigorous by the newly established Independent Television Commission, but it will obviously be more difficult to regulate effectively in this area once the reach of the new technologies becomes truly global.[16]

Meetings, Procession and Protest

There are issues which arise from rights to meet, process and protest freely, subject only to various necessary restraints in the interest of public order. In modern times, however, this has been a particularly difficult balance to strike, since it is bound to involve constant adjustment and compromise between conflicting interests. In principle people are free to associate for political or other purposes. In practice such freedom is not extended to the civil service, the armed services, the police or registered charities. However the civil service is heavily unionised at all levels and the police of lower ranks have powerful representation from the Police Federation. More recently the provisions of the 1986 Public Order Act curtailed what may lawfully be done on the streets and in public places by providing the police with stronger powers to avert public disorder and by introducing a new offence of disorderly conduct to deal with some forms of modern hooliganism.

Public and private meetings for any purpose are constrained not so much by the law as by the need to secure prior permission from the owners of suitable halls or open spaces. However public meetings may not lawfully be held on the public highway and any such obstruction is an offence under the 1959 Highways Act. This has special relevance to the right to picket, which is supposed to be confined under the 1980 Employment Act to peaceful persuasion in contemplation or furtherance of a trade dispute by people attending either at their own place of work or that of so-called 'first customers' and 'first suppliers'.[17] Legal protection against disorderly conduct at a meeting is still based upon the 1908 Public Meeting Act, although in modern conditions this has little practical bearing upon such matters.

In general the preservation of public order in processions and public meetings depends upon the police, who can exercise considerable discretion. Among the powers available to Chief Officers of Police under the 1986 Public Order Act are the power to specify routes for marches and demonstrations, the power to restrict the display of flags and banners, and the power to apply to the relevant Police Authority for a ban lasting not more than three months on any category of public procession and occasionally on all public processions.

Emergency Powers and State Security

There are issues which arise from the use of emergency powers by the Government and its agencies, together with the related problems of state security. In most serious emergencies the police, fire and ambulance services can cope with any problems which arise. Yet there are some occasions when the military has to be called in to assist the civilian power or to deal with particularly serious threats to the life and well-being of the community. In recent times the most notable example has been the need to keep thousands of British troops in Northern Ireland in order to help the civil authorities preserve peace and public order. Other examples have included the need to counter the action of terrorists by calling in the Special Air Service (SAS) and other special military units to assist the police and security services. The legal position on all such occasions is that military personnel have a duty to support the civil power when requested by the latter to do so. Since such emergencies usually involve sensitive and difficult issues of public safety, they require ministerial supervision and control at the highest level.

During peacetime a state of emergency may be declared under the authority of the 1920 and 1964 Emergency Powers Acts. These statutes permit the government of the day to make use of wide-ranging temporary powers designed to ensure the maintenance of essential services, subject to parliamentary approval at least every seven days. During wartime even more far-reaching powers were available to the government of the day in the shape of the 1914 and 1915 Defence of the Realm Acts and the 1939 and 1940 Emergency Powers Acts. These statutes, which were later repealed, gave the government of the day almost unlimited powers, including detention without trial for indefinite periods and the seizure of private property without compensation. Again the legislation was subject to parliamentary approval at least every 28 days.

In the case of special measures to deal with terrorism, Parliament passed some draconian statutes in 1973 and 1975 to deal with the threat in Northern Ireland from the IRA and other terrorist organisations, and in 1974 and 1976 to deal with terrorist offences anywhere in the United Kingdom. This legislation conferred very extensive powers upon the government of the day, which enabled it to take almost any measures deemed necessary to counter such dire threats to national security, including detention without charge for up to seven days (subsequently reduced to three days with the endorsement of a court in more recent legislation) and the power to exclude undesirable people from the country.

The interests of state security have also been invoked to justify the passage of the 1989 Official Secrets Act, the retention of the D Notice system and the interception of private communications by telephone-tapping and other techniques of electronic surveillance. These practices have continued on the basis of rather tenuous legal authority, subject to no more than indirect control by Ministers and virtually no control by Parliament. Admittedly security matters of this kind are kept under review by the Security Commission, a small supervisory body of Privy Councillors chaired by a Law Lord, which reports regularly to the Prime Minister and occasionally to Parliament.

In these circumstances it is not surprising that there has been continuing pressure for reform and for the replacement of the existing law with new legislation which would put more emphasis upon the rights of ordinary citizens and less on the needs of national security (which are sometimes a euphemism for ministerial convenience). There has been an active, all-party campaign for freedom of information throughout the sphere of government and the public sector, which has had some success in relation to local government and the release of environmental information. The problems of striking an appropriate balance between the needs of official secrecy (and commercial confidentiality) on the one hand and the rights of the citizen on the other have been very great and, some would say, insoluble. The difficulties have been exacerbated by the growing use of computers throughout the public sector and by the recent development of what is known as the Government Data Network. Public concern about the possible misuse of personal information kept on official files led to the 1984 Data Protection Act, which provided some safeguards against malpractice in relation to nearly all official information which is mechanically processed and stored – but not simple card-index systems.

International Conventions

There are issues which arise from the wide range of civil rights declared in international Conventions and in many cases subsequently embodied in British law by Parliament at Westminster. For example, the principle that all citizens should be equal before the law is a worthy aspiration in Britain as in other countries, but in our constitutional arrangements it is not enshrined in a codified constitution. In the last three decades Parliament has legislated against racial discrimination (in 1965, 1968 and 1976) and against sexual discrimination (in 1975). Attempts have been made to counter and eventually eradicate such discrimination from all public behaviour, with public sector institutions, such as the civil service, often required to set an example to the private sector. Many of the initiatives in these spheres have been taken by the Commission for Racial Equality and the Equal Opportunities Commission, both of which were established by a Labour Government to act as watch-dogs and agenda-setters in these areas of policy. Thus, if individual citizens feel aggrieved on racial or sexual grounds, they can use the law, often with the help of these bodies, to take cases to court in order to seek redress or reinstatement.

The protection of civil rights is a matter of wide international concern. Indeed pressure groups, such as Amnesty International, have been established, often with their base in Britain, to draw attention to human rights abuses and to campaign world-wide against such practices. National governments have been prepared to make purposeful moves in this direction at least since the 1948 UN Declaration of Human Rights and the 1950 European Convention on Human Rights. The latter, which was ratified by the British Parliament in 1951, provides judicial procedures by which alleged infringements of civil rights in Britain may be examined at international level. The European Convention provides an overt constraint upon the legislative supremacy of Parliament in that successive British governments have not wished to be found in breach of its provisions. However the Convention has not been incorporated within our national law, on the somewhat complacent grounds that civil rights in this country are adequately protected by British law and that such incorporation would be inconsistent with our traditional claim to legal supremacy for Parliament at Westminster. It was not until 1966 that the United Kingdom formally recognised the right of individual petition to the European Commission on Human Rights or the compulsory jurisdiction in this country of the European Court of Human Rights. Since then various proceedings under the Convention have helped to bring about changes in British law and legal practice, for example the introduction of immigration appeal tribunals or revised rules on access to lawyers for prisoners.

18.6 Administrative Law

From a political point of view it is administrative law which is probably the most important aspect of the legal system in Britain. H.W.R. Wade has defined this area of the law as 'the body of general principles which govern the exercise of powers and duties by public authorities'.[18] Since the end of the nineteenth century there has been a great expansion of parliamentary legislation and hence a notable multiplication of administrative bodies created by statute. This has led to growing judicial and quasi-judicial intervention in the field of public administration. Ordinary people have felt the need to appeal to tribunals and ultimately to the courts on many points of administrative law. For its part the judiciary has attempted to compensate for the failure of Parliament adequately to protect ordinary citizens from the shortcomings or injustices which can be perpetrated by the public administration.

Administrative Tribunals

In the modern British political system there is a bewildering array of administrative tribunals which have been created by Acts of Parliament. Some, such as the National Insurance tribunals which decide disputed claims to benefits, were established as a function of the Welfare State. Some, such as the industrial tribunals which adjudicate on claims of industrial injury, unfair dismissal and other employment disputes, are related to the problems of industrial relations. Some deal with housing disputes, some with pensions or unemployment, some with immigration, some with the National Health Service and some with education disputes. All exist in order to provide simpler, cheaper, quicker and more accessible forms of justice than are available in the courts.

The main characteristics of administrative tribunals are as follows. They are normally established by Act of Parliament. Their decisions are quasi-judicial in the sense that they investigate the facts of the case and then apply certain legal principles in an impartial manner. They are independent in the sense that their decisions are in no way subject to political or administrative interference. Their membership varies, but they usually consist of a legally qualified chairman and two lay members representing relevant interests. They are assisted by clerks who are usually civil servants from the relevant Department. Appeals against their decisions can be made in various ways, since Parliament has laid down no consistent procedures. Appeals may lie to a Minister, a superior tribunal, a superior court, or there may be no provision for appeal, as is the case with the National Insurance Commissioners or the National Health Service tribunal.

The main advantage of administrative tribunals is that they offer relatively quick, cheap and accessible procedures which are essential in, for example, the administration of welfare schemes involving large numbers of small claims. Another advantage is that they are well suited to deal expertly with highly technical matters, such as those referred to the Income Tax Commissioners or the Medical Appeal tribunals. On the other hand, the main disadvantage of administrative tribunals is their institutional proliferation and jurisdictional complexity. Over the years the growth of these bodies has produced over 50 different types of tribunal, all of which fall within the definition laid down in the 1971 Tribunals and Inquiries Act. They range from those which are very active, for example Supplementary Benefit or Rent tribunals, to those which have heard no cases at all, such as the Mines and Quarries tribunals.

In such a complex structure there are inevitable problems of overlapping and competing jurisdictions, and little has been done so far to amalgamate or group tribunals according to their various functions. Considerable attention has also been paid to the search for effective ways of controlling and supervising this part of the legal system. None of the existing methods has proved wholly satisfactory, which is why some have looked to practice on the Continent and others to overall constitutional reform for appropriate answers. We shall now consider each of the various solutions in turn.

Ministerial Control

The traditional view of the problems of administrative law is that the public interest can best be safeguarded by Ministers responsible to Parliament. Yet this idea has been something of a constitutional fiction ever since its mythical properties were first revealed by Lord Hewart and Professor Robson nearly 60 years ago.[19] The criticism then, and even more so today, is that no Minister can possibly be well informed about, still less truly accountable for everything which happens (or fails to happen) within all the various administrative tribunals and other quasi-judicial bodies for which he may be nominally responsible.

Even before the Second World War it was recognised that parliamentary control of Ministers was vitiated by the growth of delegated legislation, just as the purity of judge-made law was threatened by the growth of quasi-judicial powers exercised by civil servants in the name of Ministers and by administrative tribunals. Yet for many years little was done to tackle these problems, since the pressing challenges of war and reconstruction had to be given a higher priority. It was not until after the notorious Crichel Down affair in the early 1950s that some effective action began to be taken.[20] A committee chaired by Sir Oliver Franks was established to look at all these matters and in 1957 it produced a report which was broadly acceptable to the Conservative Government of the day. This led to the 1958 Tribunals and Inquiries Act which provided for the creation of the Council on Tribunals to oversee the whole sphere of administrative law. Subsequently the legislation was consolidated and brought up-to-date in the 1971 Tribunals and Inquiries Act.

In general, ministerial control has not been an adequate response to the problems of overseeing and reviewing this type of law. In effect, it has sought to deny the significance of the problems by assuming that public administration is bound to reflect the public interest as long as in each departmental area it is headed by a Minister responsible to Parliament. Such an idea is obviously defective in contemporary conditions, now that the whole process of government has become so large and complex. In circumstances in which few Ministers achieve complete control over their Departments and Parliament has even less effective control over Ministers, it is naive to pretend that the ministerial principle provides a satisfactory answer.

The Ombudsman

Another approach to solving the problem has been the creation of an independent institution specifically designed to limit serious abuses of administrative power and to deal firmly with any which arise. In Britain, as in other countries, such as New Zealand and Scandinavia, this has been achieved by the Parliamentary Commissioner for Administration, commonly known as the Ombudsman.[21] The institution was created by Act of Parliament in 1967 in a further attempt to ensure that the administrative procedures of central government and its agencies are correctly followed and that any allegations of maladministration are investigated and, if possible, acted upon.

The Ombudsman, who is usually a former lawyer or civil servant, is appointed by the Crown on the advice of the Lord Chancellor. His constitutional status is similar to that of a High Court judge, which is to say that he is completely independent of government. Like a judge, his salary is fixed by statute and charged automatically to the Consolidated Fund. He can only be removed from office by the Crown after addresses by both Houses of Parliament; in other words, he is effectively unsackable during his five-year tenure of office. He appoints his own staff who are usually drawn from the ranks of the civil service. His jurisdiction is confined to the Departments of central government and the National Health Service. It excludes the police, the public corporations and local authorities (which have their own Local Authority Ombudsman). He can investigate complaints about the way in which Departments have discharged their functions, although his jurisdiction does not extend to international relations, court proceedings, employment issues in the civil service or the commercial transactions of central government. Furthermore he has no right to investigate cases where the complainant has a right of recourse to an administrative tribunal or a remedy in the courts. Nor can he investigate complaints made more than one year after the date when the complainant first had notice of the matter. In short, Parliament did not exactly give the institution *carte blanche*, largely because at the outset it was seen by many MPs as an interloper in their territory.

It is essentially for this reason that to this day most complaints are made to the Ombudsman via a Member of Parliament. Once the complaint has been officially received, it is first for the Ombudsman to decide whether or not it properly falls within his jurisdiction. In fact, fewer than half the complaints received fall within his jurisdiction and can therefore be investigated. Of those which do, evidence of maladministration has been found in about one-third of all cases. All official documents, except Cabinet papers, have to be produced for inspection at his request and he has the same powers as a High Court judge to compel any witness to give evidence. When an investigation is complete, he normally sends his report to the MP concerned, who then sends it on to the complainant.

The Ombudsman has no executive powers, but his reports often suggest appropriate remedies upon which the Department concerned normally takes action. The remedies may include financial compensation from public funds, remission of taxation, administrative review of earlier decisions, or revised administrative procedures. For example, in the 1989 Barlow Clowes report the Ombudsman recommended that the private investors who had lost all their money to two investment funds which were not properly supervised by the Department of Trade and Industry should receive substantial financial compensation for their losses on a diminishing scale as the amounts increased. This reflected implied culpability on the part of the supervisory Department concerned and, following a lengthy parliamentary campaign by back-benchers for recompense for their constituents, led Ministers to offer taxpayers' money for the purpose. MPs work quite happily in partnership with the Ombudsman in joint efforts to secure redress for their constituents. In formal terms this relationship has been cemented by the work of a Select Committee which supervises the work of the Ombudsman and takes evidence, where appropriate, from Departments which are the subject of such investigations. This all helps to ensure that the recommendations are carried out.

Judicial Review

Another way of dealing with injustices or abuses which are perpetrated by the public administration is judicial review. The basic leverage for the judiciary is provided by the doctrine of *ultra vires*, which holds that acts of public administration can be unlawful if they go beyond interpretations of the statutes which reasonable people could reasonably accept. It is this doctrine which enables the High Court to set aside administrative decisions which, although perhaps within the literal scope of the statutes, are plainly unreasonable. The issues involved are inevitably controversial, since the nub of the argument is usually the degree of discretionary power which can properly be exercised by a public body. The judiciary has the difficult responsibility of interpreting the meaning of statutes on the basis of what reasonable people would reasonably decide. This can be approached in a narrow and literal sense or a broad and contextual sense, and the outcome of such a case will often depend upon which of the two approaches is adopted.

When a complaint against the public administration is brought before the High Court, several legal remedies are available to the plaintiffs. There are the traditional prerogative remedies which were originally vested in the Monarch, but which are now available to ordinary citizens. These are *certiorari* to quash an administrative decision already made; *prohibition* to prevent a public authority from considering a matter which it has no statutory right to consider; and *mandamus* to compel a public body to perform a public duty. Then there are the two non-prerogative remedies which are often more useful nowadays. These are an *injunction* to prohibit a public body from doing something which would be illegal and a *declaration*, which is simply a statement by the Court clarifying the legal position, so that the powers and duties of a public body can be defined more precisely.[22]

Judicial review is impartial in the sense that it is in no way influenced by the position of the complainant or the power of the public body about which the complaint has been made. Yet there are weaknesses in such procedures. For example, the Court can only intervene if a plaintiff starts legal proceedings; it can only deal with the case before it; it usually lacks the detailed expertise of the public administration which it seeks to control; it cannot oversee the way in which its remedial orders are carried out; and it proceeds so slowly and expensively that many would-be plaintiffs are deterred from going to law in the first place.

In conducting the process of judicial review, the judges tend to be guided essentially by the principles of natural justice. These are the right of the complainant to be heard before the relevant decision is taken and the absence of prejudice on the part of the Court, or other public body charged with the duty of adjudication. The problem is complicated by the fact that these principles are not presumed to apply to ministerial decisions where the relevant legislation permits a degree of administrative discretion or where it entails subsequent secondary legislation. This emphasises the difficult balance which has to be struck by the courts between the interests of the plaintiff and those of the general public as represented by the decisions of public bodies. The balance has shifted back and forth over the years. But as Hartley and Griffith have pointed out, the courts have tended to be guided 'more by policy than by precedent, more by what they think is fair and reasonable than by rigid rules'.[23] Judicial review is therefore a more than usually political form of justice.

Since about the mid-1960s the judiciary in Britain has taken more account of the principles of natural justice and has been prepared to play a more active part in arguments of political principle.[24] This has been evident especially in cases which bear upon the definition of individual rights, such as personal property, liberty, freedom of movement, retention of office and access to employment. It could also be argued that over these years the tide of judicial opinion turned against some unpopular groups of which the rest of society tended to disapprove, such as trade unionists or students. Notwithstanding the fluctuations in both judicial and public opinion on these and other questions, the judiciary has shown a growing willingness to use the process of judicial review to deal definitively with disputes which can arise in the sphere of public administration.

Continental Solutions

There are some who argue that we should look further afield to find the most effective ways of supervising and controlling the public administration. Specifically they maintain that the best solution would be to establish in Britain a new administrative division of the High Court (similar to that which exists in France) or a new administrative appeals tribunal (along the lines of that which exists in Sweden). Such approaches have been advocated by those members of the judiciary who would like to see the process of judicial review extended into all corners of the public administration.

Such a solution would almost certainly be opposed by those who already harbour a deep suspicion of the judiciary and hence a strong unwillingness to allow them a more influential political role. Certainly many of those on the Left of British politics would oppose any extension of the powers and competence of the judiciary unless and until they could feel satisfied that the judiciary had ceased to be drawn from such a deeply conservative section of the population. At the same time many of those on the Right would resist it on the ground that it is always undesirable to import foreign judicial practices into this country. Yet, as Britain becomes more deeply drawn into the process of European integration over the years leading up to 1992 and beyond, it seems almost certain that the impact of European Community law and especially the influence of the European Court will be increasingly felt in both the public and private sectors.[25]

Constitutional Reform

Finally, there are some eminent legal figures, such as Lord Scarman and Lord Hailsham, who have argued the case for comprehensive constitutional reform entailing a new Bill of Rights and the introduction of an entrenched and codified constitution which would be interpreted and protected by a newly established and completely independent Supreme Court.[26] Those who favour this response to the problems of administrative law have to contend with the traditional British view that our civil rights and political liberties are most secure if founded upon the established custom and practice of common law. Of course they would probably point out in their turn that the traditional view has become obsolete in view of the scope and complexity of public administration in contemporary political circumstances. This would then lead them to the conclusion that the new Bill of Rights should include a formal statement of civil rights and public duties.

Whatever the attractions of this grand idea, there would be several considerable difficulties with such an approach in Britain. There would need to be a codified constitution which anyone, however poor or humble, could invoke in the event of a dispute with the public authorities. There would need to be a wholly new Supreme Court quite independent from the political influence which inevitably colours the judgements of the Law Lords. There would need to be public acceptance of a very different and more distinctive role for the senior members of the judiciary. Above all, Members of Parliament would have to be willing to acknowledge that Parliament itself could no longer claim its traditional political and constitutional supremacy. Of course the irony here is that the idea of parliamentary supremacy is already rather dated, with Britain's membership of the European Community, and is likely to be further eroded as more and more national sovereignty is pooled in the process of shared decision making in the Council of Ministers and democratic power sharing between Westminster and the European Parliament.

Among those who favour such all-embracing changes, Nevil Johnson has argued that 'the challenge is to construct a different relationship between law and politics and in so doing to give law . . . a new and wider part in the regulation of the affairs of society'.[27] We have seen in Chapter 17 how this is already happening in response to the new regulatory needs highlighted by the policy of privatisation. It may yet be taken further if politicians in all parties can get used to the idea of playing second fiddle to judges in the determination of the really big legal and constitutional issues in society. Experience from the United States and West Germany in particular suggests that this may be possible.

18.7 Conclusion

It remains to be seen whether the legal system in Britain will develop in a more creative and independent direction, or whether it will remain fundamentally conservative and obedient to the idea of parliamentary supremacy. There are clearly major implications for the traditional doctrines of ministerial responsibility and parliamentary accountability if the judiciary does develop more independent and creative powers. Yet it must be said that such a development is likely to depend essentially upon the government of the day voluntarily agreeing to be limited by the courts rather than upon any inclination of the judges to strike more heroic postures. Such a condition seems unlikely to be met in the future, even under a Labour Government.

The Deputy Leader of the Labour party, Roy Hattersley, has put forward proposals for a 'Charter of Rights' which, together with his party's proposals for an elected chamber to replace the present House of Lords and the establishment of new assemblies in Scotland, Wales and the regions of England, are claimed to add up to the greatest package of legal and constitutional reform this century.[28] Such a Charter would include a Freedom of Information Act, a Right to Privacy Act and a Security Services Act, as well as proposals for the diminution of ministerial patronage in the sphere of QUANGOs and more generous legal aid for those deterred by the cost from exercising their legal rights. However competition for legislative time in Parliament is invariably fierce and of all Labour's constitutional proposals, only the plan to establish a Scottish Assembly has been promised for the first session of Parliament under a new Labour government. Thus it would be wise to suspend judgement on not only the practicality but also possibly the sincerity of such proposals, since students of these matters can recall their disappointment on previous occasions when politicians appeared to lose sight of their impressive constitutional commitments once in office.

It seems that one of the main reasons why Labour's proposals would fall short of a constitutionally guaranteed Bill of Rights or even the simple enactment into British law of the European Convention on Human Rights is that the Labour party (and indeed many politicians in other parties as well) have not overcome their traditional antipathy towards the judiciary. Obviously there is not a great deal which the judges can do about this in the short term at least – even if they were minded to do so – because of their chastening experience of traditional subordination to the governing majority in the House of Commons at any time. As H. W. R. Wade was right to point out 'if they fly too high, Parliament may clip their wings'.[29] In other words, constitutional reform of this kind is unlikely to come about unless the judiciary and the legislature make common cause against the executive, and that day seems as far off as ever.

It is well to remember that there never has been a truly effective separation of powers in Britain. Such a triangular balance nearly came about in the eighteenth century, when central government was at its weakest. Yet in more modern times the politicians in government have definitely asserted their position and the judiciary has been careful not to step too far out of line with the government of the day. This is because in the last resort the politicians in office can always use their whipped majority in the House of Commons to trump any judicial challenge.

Of course relations between the judiciary, the executive and the legislature may change in future in response to more demanding public attitudes or different constitutional arrangements. For example, the public may come to expect more from the courts by way of judicial protection and redress against over-mighty or unrepresentative government. Already there is an influential, all-party lobby group, Charter 88, which has pressed for the incorporation into British law of certain, fundamental constitutional principles long since enshrined in the European Convention on Human Rights. Its pressure may prove successful in the longer term if it can become more of a popular movement. Equally the supremacy of European law over British law, at least in the areas of expanding European Community competence, may hasten the day when the traditional doctrine of parliamentary supremacy (which really means the temporary supremacy of the political majority in the House of Commons for the time being) can no longer be sustained as the corner-stone of our constitution. Yet the strong suspicion remains that it will be only in the event of there being a significant measure of electoral reform that the door may really be unlocked to comprehensive constitutional reform in Britain.

Suggested Questions

1. Describe the structure and problems of either criminal justice or civil justice in Britain today.
2. What are the main issues in the legal relations between citizens and the state?
3. How appropriate and effective are the arrangements for applying and reviewing administrative law in Britain?

Notes

1. See Report of the Royal Commission on Criminal Procedure, Cmnd 8092 (London: HMSO, 1981).
2. For a fuller discussion of these issues see the Scarman Report on the Brixton disorders, Cmnd 8487 (London: HMSO, 1981).
3. These are breaches of duty leading to liability for damages, but non-contractual in the case of tort.
4. *Prohibition* prevents a public authority from considering a matter which it has no statutory right to consider. *Mandamus* enables the High Court to compel a public body to perform a public duty which it is statutorily obliged to perform. *Certiorari* enables the High Court to quash an administrative decision already made by a public body. A writ of *Habeas Corpus* is supposed to prevent the police from detaining without charge for more than 24 hours those suspected of non-serious offences, although in the case of suspected terrorists there is statutory provision for this time limit to be extended to 3 days inland and 7 days at a port of entry.
5. The reason for this incongruous grouping was simply that all these jurisdictions had a common basis in Roman law.
6. G. Drewry, *Law, Justice and Politics* (London: Longman, 1975), p. 128.
7. J. A. G. Griffith, *The Politics of the Judiciary* (London: Fontana, 1977), p. 193.
8. In 1989–90 £282 million was spent on criminal legal aid, £166 million on civil legal aid, and £79 million on legal assistance and advice.
9. See 'The work and organisation of the legal profession', Cm 570; 'Contingency fees', Cm 571; and 'Conveyancing by authorised practitioners', Cm 572 (London: HMSO, 1989).
10. See 'Legal services, a framework for the future', Cm 740 (London: HMSO, 1989).
11. Introduction to 'Legal services, a framework for the future', Cm 740 (London: HMSO, 1989), p. 5.
12. See Report of the Review Body on Civil Justice, Cm 394 (London: HMSO, 1988).
13. However, by the time the Bill got its Second Reading in the Commons, the Bar Council acting on behalf of all practising barristers had been successful in persuading the Government to accept an amendment originally proposed by Lord Alexander of Weedon which extended to all those professional bodies seeking to exercise rights of audience in the superior courts the requirement that their advocates should be bound by rules similar to the 'cab-rank' rule at the Bar – i.e. a principle of non-discrimination by barristers in the acceptance of instructions or briefs. Indeed, the Attorney-General, Sir Patrick Mayhew, was prepared to provide for wider application of the principle in the Bill by applying it to all rights of audience granted by a professional body in any court or proceedings. Such a principle of non-discrimination seeks to ensure that any individual, company or country with a case before a court is able to find an advocate of suitable expertise to represent them.
14. These are Trinidad and Tobago, Singapore, Dominica, Kiribati and The Gambia.
15. Both quoted in J. A. G. Griffith, *The Politics of the Judiciary*, p. 179 and p. 183. See also *Journal of the Society of Public Teachers of Law* (1972), vol. 12, p. 22.
16. This problem has been addressed in attempts to reach agreement between the 23 nations in the Council of Europe. However, no international broadcasting agreement is likely to be completely effective in an increasingly de-regulated, global media market.
17. This restricted legal immunity from civil action in the courts to the employees of the firm in dispute or the employees of a direct supplier or customer of the firm in dispute, thus theoretically limiting the scope for 'blacking' or sympathy strikes.
18. H. W. R. Wade, *Administrative Law*, 4th edn (Oxford: Clarendon Press, 1979), pp. 5–6.
19. See Lord Hewart, *The New Despotism*, 2nd edn (West Point: Greenwood, 1945) and W. Robson, *Justice and Administrative Law*, 3rd edn (London: Stevens, 1951).
20. The Crichel Down affair involved an area of farm land in Dorset about which

misleading replies and false assurances were given by a junior civil servant in the Ministry of Agriculture. Subsequent inquiries established that there had been muddle, bias, inefficiency and bad faith on the part of a few officials, as well as weak organisation in the Department. This led eventually to the resignation of the Minister, Sir Thomas Dugdale.

21. See C. M. Clothier, *Ombudsman: jurisdiction, powers and practice* (Manchester: Manchester Statistical Society, 1981) for a fuller description of the role of the Ombudsman in Britain.
22. An *injunction* and a *declaration* are two of the legal remedies generally available to litigants and they are not confined to cases in which citizens seek to challenge public authorities.
23. T. C. Hartley and J. A. G. Griffith, *Government and Law* (London: Weidenfeld & Nicolson, 1975), p. 320.
24. Notably in the Court of Appeal where Lord Denning had a long and active period as Master of the Rolls from 1962 to 1982.
25. See Chapter 19, pp. 319–24, for more on the European Court of Justice and its role in European integration.
26. See Lord Scarman, *English Law, the New Dimension* (London: Stevens, 1974) and Lord Hailsham, *The Dilemma of Democracy* (London: Collins, 1978).
27. N. Johnson, *In Search of the Constitution* (London: Methuen, 1980), p. 149.
28. See 'The Charter of Rights – guaranteeing individual liberty in a free society', (London: Labour party, 1991).
29. H. W. R. Wade, *Administrative Law*, p. 30.

Further Reading

Clothier, C. M., *Ombudsman: jurisdiction, powers and practice* (Manchester: Manchester Statistical Society, 1981).
Griffith, J. A. G., *The Politics of the Judiciary*, 3rd edn (London: Fontana, 1985).
Jackson, R. M. *et al.*, *The Machinery of Justice in England*, 8th edn (Cambridge University Press, 1989).
Stainsby, P., *Tribunal Practice and Procedure* (London: Law Society, 1988).
Wade, H. W. R., *Administrative Law*, 6th edn (Oxford: Clarendon Press, 1988).
Wade, E. C. S. and Phillips, G. G., *Constitutional and Administrative Law*, 10th edn (London: Longman, 1985).
Walker, R. J. (ed.), *The English Legal System*, 6th edn (London: Butterworths, 1985).
Zander, M., *The Law Making Process*, 2nd edn (London: Weidenfeld & Nicolson, 1985).
Zander, M., *A Matter of Justice*, revised edition (Oxford University Press, 1989).

Part VI
Democracy in Britain

⟨19⟩ Britain in Europe

No modern textbook on the British political system should ignore Britain's membership of the European Community. The vast network of economic and political relationships which this involves, especially the legal and constitutional issues which it raises, are essential to a proper understanding of contemporary British politics. Things have not been the same for this country since Britain joined the European Community in January 1973. They are likely to change even more significantly in future under the aegis of the 1986 Single European Act and the development of a single European market scheduled for completion by the end of 1992. It is, therefore, essential to include in this book a chapter on Britain in Europe.

19.1 Historical Background

The origin of the European Community can be found in the decision of the six original member states – France, West Germany, Italy, Holland, Belgium and Luxembourg – to establish the European Coal and Steel Community in 1950. This experiment in supranationalism, from which Britain decided to stand aside, involved the pooling of national economic sovereignties in the two vital sectors of coal mining and steel making. These sectors of heavy industry were chosen quite deliberately by the founding fathers of the European Community, Jean Monnet, Robert Schuman, Konrad Adenauer, Alcide de Gasperi and Paul-Henri Spaak, because they had been at the heart of national war-making capacities for the previous hundred years or so. By pooling these national resources irrevocably and then having them managed by a new supranational High Authority, it was confidently expected that war in Europe between European nations would thenceforth be rendered impossible.

Although Britain had participated in all the *international* organisations which had been established after the Second World War, such as the Brussels Treaty Organisation in 1948, the Council of Europe and the North Atlantic Alliance in 1949, the political leaders in Britain at that time could not bring themselves to participate in *supranational* organisations of which the European Coal and Steel Community was the first example. There were various reasons for this, but the principal explanation was that the realities of Britain's weakened position in the postwar world had been masked by our wartime achievements and our postwar preoccupations. After all, Britain had stood alone against Hitler's Germany in 1940, she had been acknowledged as one of the three victorious Powers in 1945, and British politicians and people alike tended to look to Britain's relations with the United States and with the Empire and Commonwealth before they looked to relations with the continent of Europe. Of the famous 'three circles' – the American, Commonwealth and European connections – of which Winston Churchill spoke so eloquently at the time, there was little doubt in British minds about the order of our national priorities. The other European nations generally came third in the British world-view. In Churchill's words, Britain was 'with them, but not of them'.

During the 1950s Britain was drawn closer towards involvement with continental Europe as her so-called 'special relationship' with the United States suffered a series of blows and disappointments, notably at the time of the ill-fated British and French invasion of the Suez Canal Zone in 1956, and as the expanding Commonwealth came to be seen in Britain as much as a liability as an asset. With the collapse of the attempt to form a European Defence Community in 1954, Britain moved swiftly to sign the 1955 Paris Accords which established the Western European Union, brought West Germany into conventional (but not nuclear) defence arrangements with her West European partners, and committed Britain to keep more than 50 000 troops on the mainland of Europe for 50 years. However when the Six took the process of European integration one stage further by signing in 1957 the Rome Treaties, which established the European Economic Community (EEC) and Euratom in the following year, Britain once again stood aside after having sent only observers to the seminal Messina Conference in 1956. The British Government then made a futile attempt to negotiate a wider European Free Trade Area with the Six in 1957–8. When this was understandably rebuffed by the Six, Britain and several other excluded European nations (Austria, Denmark, Norway, Portugal, Sweden and Switzerland) decided to establish the European Free Trade Association (EFTA) as a partial counterweight to their exclusion from the mainstream of European economic integration.

It was not long before the Conservative Government, then led by Harold Macmillan, realised the error of its ways in having stood aside from the mainstream of European integration. Accordingly, in July 1961, the Government initiated negotiations with the European Communities to see whether a basis existed for future British membership which would be consistent with the needs of Britain, the Commonwealth and EFTA. The subsequent formal statement introducing the application declared that the Government's decision had been reached 'not on any narrow or short-term grounds, but as a result of a thorough assessment over a considerable period of the needs of our own country, Europe and the free world as a whole'.[1] At last Britain seemed set on a course to bring her into full membership of the European Community. Yet in spite of the considerable progress which was later made in resolving many of the difficulties, the negotiations between Britain and the Six had to be broken off following President De Gaulle's veto, delivered at a famous press conference in Paris on 29 January 1963.

Throughout the 1960s successive British governments, both Conservative and Labour, sought to keep alive the possibility of Britain's membership of the European Community. In May 1967 the Wilson Labour Government made another formal application for Britain to join the European Community, but once again this was baulked by French opposition. However, two years later, in April 1969, President De Gaulle staked his position upon the result of a constitutional referendum and lost, thus leaving himself with no choice but to resign. This had the effect of opening the way for Britain to renew its application to join the European Community, which was duly done by the Heath Government immediately after the Conservatives returned to power in June 1970.

The detailed negotiations with the Six took little more than one year and were brought to a satisfactory conclusion. Both Houses of Parliament debated and voted upon the principle of British entry in October 1971. The House of Commons voted in favour by 356 to 244, a majority of 112, in which 69 Labour MPs defied a three-line whip to vote for the government motion; and on the same day the House of Lords approved the same motion by a majority of 393. On 22 January 1972 Edward Heath, as Prime Minister, signed the Treaty of Accession in Brussels on behalf of Britain. Parliament then proceeded to legislate to bring UK law into line with European Community law and the resulting Westminster statute was the 1972 European Communities Act. This cleared the way for full British membership of the Community from 1 January 1973, when Denmark and Ireland also joined (although Norway had earlier decided not to join, following a public referendum).

Because the Labour party had been split on the European issue, at least since the vote of principle in October 1971, Labour fought the two General Elections in 1974 pledged to a policy of renegotiating what it described as the unacceptable terms of entry. The process of renegotiation which followed was backed by the implicit threat that the renegotiated terms would be put to the British people in a consultative referendum and, if membership on such terms were rejected, then the Government would take the necessary steps for British withdrawal. When the referendum was held in 1975, the British people voted by a two to one majority in favour of Britain remaining in the European Community and this verdict was accepted by both Government and Parliament.

Since that time Britain's membership of the European Community has not been seriously in doubt. However there have been long-lasting battles by the British Government – especially during Margaret Thatcher's first Administration from 1979 to 1983 – further to improve the terms of membership, notably in relation to the working of the Common Agricultural Policy (CAP) and the size of Britain's net contribution to the Community Budget. By the mid-1980s the 'British question' seemed to have been more or less resolved, although Mrs Thatcher and other British Ministers were always prepared to fight Britain's corner in the process of Community decision making. Nevertheless it was Margaret Thatcher who agreed to an extensive revision of the Community Treaties in the 1986 Single European Act, and it is the present Conservative Government which has been foremost among those in the Community of Twelve pressing for the fullest possible progress towards the achievement of a single European market by the end of 1992.

19.2 Legal and Constitutional Implications

Britain's membership of the European Community has profound legal and constitutional implications which are becoming increasingly apparent as the Community enhances its degree of integration. Yet it is also fair to say that the problems posed by Community law in Britain should have been clear from the very beginning, when Parliament debated British entry into the Community in 1971 and 1972.

Section 2 (1) of the 1972 European Communities Act made provision for the direct effect of Community law in the United Kingdom.[2] This provided for the Community Treaties and Community legislation under the Treaties to take direct effect in this country. It explicitly included *future* Community law and it made clear that Community law would determine whether or not a particular provision was directly effective. Section 2 (2) of the Act made provision for the implementation of Community law by means of subordinate legislation at Westminster. However, in accordance with Section 2 (1), such Statutory Instruments could not be used in four specified areas: the imposition of new or increased taxation, retrospective legislation, sub-delegated legislative power and the creation of serious criminal offences. If it is necessary to do any of these things in order to implement Community law in Britain, an Act of Parliament (primary legislation) has to be passed. Section 2 (4) provided that past and future Acts of Parliament should be subordinate to Community law (in those areas where there may be a conflict) and this was reinforced by Section 3 (1) which declared that any question about the effect of Community law should be decided in accordance with the principles of any relevant decision of the European Court, the most notable of which is the supremacy of Community law. Thus all these interlocking and mutually reinforcing sections of the 1972 European Communities Act served to establish the supremacy of Community law over national law, even though it was an Act of the national Parliament which did this in Britain.

Important Features

The most important features of the relationship between Community law and British national law are the direct effect of Community law in our national courts, the supremacy of Community law over national law (if and when the two conflict), and the procedures by which Community law is enforced in this country and the other member states. It is important to be clear about the meaning of each of these key features.

The concept of direct effect means that a provision of Community law grants individual rights to citizens in Britain and the other member states which must be upheld by the national courts. This issue was clarified for the first time in the Van Gend en Loos case in 1962, when it was established that the European Court may legitimately determine that a given provision of Community law is directly effective.[3] This principle may sound relatively straightforward, but, as enunciated by the European Court ever since 1962, it has not accorded very easily with the traditional British view of the matter. In the Van Gend en Loos case the European Court held that the institutions of the Community are 'endowed with sovereign rights, the exercise of which affects member states and also their citizens'. It also declared that member states had 'limited their sovereign rights, albeit within limited fields' and that Community law can confer rights on individuals 'which become part of their legal heritage'. This was a bold assertion on the part of the European Court which the passage of time has since done nothing to dispel. Yet it is a long way removed from the theoretical principle of British law which is that Community legislation is applicable in this country only because the 1972 European Communities Act delegated powers to the European Community to legislate for the United Kingdom in certain designated areas covered by the Community Treaties.

The supremacy of Community law means that a directly effective provision of Community law always prevails over a provision of national law, irrespective of whether the former was agreed before or after the latter. The Simmenthal case in 1977 provides a good example.[4] In this case the Italian authorities had argued that Italian national law should prevail because it had been passed *after* the two relevant Community regulations, and further that the Italian law should stand until such time as its conflict with Community law had been declared unconstitutional by the Italian Constitutional Court. When the matter was referred to the European Court, it held that the national court had a duty to give full effect to Community law and not to apply any conflicting national provisions, even if these were adopted subsequently. It also held that there should be no question of waiting for the national law to be set aside by a national constitutional court or a national legislature before accepting the supremacy of Community law. However the European Court's ruling was limited to Treaty provisions and directly applicable measures of the Community institutions. It did not state that conflicting national provisions were void, but merely that they were inapplicable. And its ruling was concerned not just with conflicting national law, but also with national laws which 'encroach upon the field within which the Community exercises its legislative power'.

It can be seen from this and other judgements of the European Court that Community law prevails over national law in all cases where the former has direct effect, provided the right contained in the Community instrument is invoked against a member state. Indeed the French Merchant Seamen case in 1973 had demonstrated that there is a positive obligation upon member states to repeal national legislation which conflicts with Community law, even if the former is considered inapplicable by the national authorities.[5] Experience in the Community has also shown that the powers of the member states can be limited or removed even where the conflict with Community law is only indirect or potential. For example, under Articles 113 and 238 of the Rome Treaty the member states have lost the power to enter into commercial or association agreements with third countries, since these are powers explicitly reserved to the Commission acting on behalf of the Community as a whole. Equally, the Pigs Marketing Board case in 1978 demonstrated that in the field of agriculture, if the Community has introduced a common market regime for a given product, the member states are precluded from adopting any national measures which might undermine or create exceptions to it.[6]

The enforcement procedures for Community law are the third important feature of the relationship between Community law and national law. There are two ways in which Community law can be enforced against national governments. The first is through action taken by private individuals or firms in the national courts which seeks to apply the doctrine of direct effect. For example, when the Irish Government imposed restrictions upon fishing in Irish waters which were contrary to Community law under the common fisheries policy, a Dutch fisherman was able to invoke Community law as a defence to a charge of illegal fishing.[7] Equally, when in 1977 the Ministry of Agriculture in Britain imposed a ban upon the import of main crop potatoes, this was challenged by a Dutch potato exporter as contrary to Community law.[8] The case was referred to the European Court, which upheld the position of the plaintiff and the ban was then lifted by the British Government.

The second way in which Community law can be enforced against national governments is by direct legal proceedings against the member state concerned. This can be done under Article 88 of the ECSC Treaty, Articles 169–71 of the EEC Treaty and Articles 141–3 of the Euratom Treaty. The procedure is divided into two stages. In the first stage, the Commission either delivers a 'decision' under the ECSC Treaty which is binding and conclusive (unless the member state wishes to challenge it in proceedings before the European Court) or it merely delivers an 'opinion' under the EEC and Euratom Treaties which is not binding, so that, if the member state concerned fails to abide by it, the Commission has to bring the matter before the European Court. In the second stage, the court proceedings are not a review of the Commission's decision or opinion, but rather a consideration of the case afresh to establish whether or not a violation of the treaties has occurred. If the Court finds that the allegations are proved, it will give its judgement against the offending member state. Under the ECSC Treaty this has the effect of confirming the Commission's decision which is binding and it opens the way for the imposition of sanctions. Under the EEC and Euratom Treaties this takes the form of a declaration specifying how and why the offending member state has failed to fulfil its obligation under the treaty. Although the Court has no power to order a member state to take or not to take a particular course of action and it cannot declare invalid any national legislation (as can the US Supreme Court in relation to laws passed by the states of the United States) the member state is obliged to terminate the violation found by the Court.

Such enforcement procedures are effective in most cases, even when member states are indulging only in deliberate delaying tactics. This is largely because, in the so-called Pig Producers case in 1978, the European Court upheld the Commission's application for an interim injunction to terminate the British Government's subsidy scheme which had been designed to help British pig producers to compete against imports subsidised by the Community. This and a similar case at about the same time brought by the Commission against Ireland for introducing fisheries conservation measures which were regarded as contrary to the Treaty have meant that the use of interim measures against offending member states now seems to be established.[9] It is evidence of the *political* nature of European Community jurisdiction, in that, when deciding whether to grant an interim injunction, the Court takes into account, firstly, the likelihood of the proceedings being successful; secondly, the need for urgency; and thirdly, the evidence which there may be that irreparable damage will be done to the Community if the order is not granted. Furthermore, in those rare cases where a member state has sought to break the Community rules and even to defy the European Court, the issues have only been capable of resolution on a political basis, because it is upon the will to co-operate that the continued success of the Community finally depends.

Principal Problems

In joining the European Community in 1973, Britain laid itself open to three principal legal and constitutional problems. The dilemma was vividly put by Lord Denning, Master of the Rolls, when he observed in 1979 that 'the flowing tide of Community law is coming in fast. It has not stopped at high water mark. It has broken the dykes and banks. It has submerged the surrounding land, so much so that we have to learn to become amphibious if we wish to keep our heads above water'.[10] In other words, as long as successive British governments and Parliaments take the view that Britain's membership of the European Community is on balance beneficial to the interests of this country, we shall find ourselves increasingly woven into the fabric of evolving Community law. As this body of law is extended by agreement in the Council of Ministers into more and more areas of economic and social activity, and as the supranational institutions of the Community – notably the European Court – create a larger body of European case law on the basis of the treaties, the real scope for autonomous action by

Britain or any other member state will gradually diminish and the hallowed British principle of parliamentary supremacy will count for less and less.

The first problem is that legal provision for Britain's membership of the European Community could not be made by means of a constitutional amendment (as in the case of the Republic of Ireland) but had to be made by passing an Act of Parliament – the 1972 European Communities Act. This entailed the paradox that the legal means of providing for Britain's permanent membership of the European Community was the impermanent mechanism of an Act of Parliament which, by its very nature, could be amended or repealed by a future British Parliament.

The second problem is that the British attitude towards international law is essentially dualist, which means that in this country national and international law are regarded as two quite different things. There never has been a general rule of law in this country which allows treaties to take effect in our legal system without the essential enabling mechanism of an Act of Parliament – in this case the 1972 European Communities Act. In other Community countries which have codified constitutional systems, such as France or Italy, international treaties take precedence over national law and have direct effect without any requirement for prior enabling legislation in their respective national jurisdictions.

The third, and most fundamental, problem is the hallowed British constitutional principle of parliamentary supremacy. This means that there is no legal authority superior to Parliament in the United Kingdom and any Parliament can override the laws of its predecessors or, in other words, no Parliament can bind its successors. *In theory*, this peculiarity of the British constitution has meant that parliamentary supremacy and the primacy of European Community law over national law are fundamentally incompatible. *In practice*, the circle has been squared by the doctrine contained in the 1972 European Communities Act which holds that, in passing that Act (Section 2 (1) in particular), Parliament evidently intended that all Acts of Parliament, whether before or after that Act, *should* be subordinate to Community law in those areas of jurisdiction covered by the Community Treaties and subsequently defined by the European Court.

On the face of it, this resolution of the problem is inconsistent with the rule that no British Parliament can bind its successors and the theoretical possibility that a future British Parliament might wish to pass an Act which defied Community law. Yet in reality such an acute constitutional difficulty is most unlikely to arise. On the one hand, if a future Westminster Parliament were determined to pass a new law which flouted established Community law, it would probably do so only as a precursor to British withdrawal from the Community – a step which this country remains free to take, but which seems increasingly unlikely the longer British membership continues and the more deeply the interests of this country become integrated with those of the other member states. On the other hand, as long as the government of the day, with the support of a majority in the House of Commons, values continued British membership more than withdrawal, then Parliament and the courts will honour Britain's legal obligations to the Community or face the consequences before the European Court which, as we have seen, is capable of enforcing those obligations. Indeed, section 2 (4) of the 1972 European Communities Act makes it clear that Parliament at Westminster is presumed *not* to intend any future statute to conflict with, still less override, Community law. In other words, as long as Britain chooses to remain in the European Community, priority will be given *in practice* to Community law over national law whenever there may be a conflict. Any other interpretation of the legal and constitutional position would make a nonsense of the whole idea of Britain's Community membership.

19.3 Political and Institutional Impact

The political and institutional impact of Britain's membership of the European Community has already been significant and could become even more significant in future. Ever since Britain's entry in 1973, this country has been involved to an increasing extent in the process of European integration. This has been well described by Sir Michael Butler, a former UK Permanent Representative at the Community in Brussels, as 'primarily about solving detailed, complicated and usually technical problems by consensus in a political framework which makes it extremely difficult for Governments to do other than agree in the end'.[11] It is this apparent irreversibility of European integration which is both the secret of the European Community's success so far and the main cause of concern among those in Britain and elsewhere who wish to limit the process in future. As we shall see in this section, the drive towards ever closer European unity poses greater political and institutional problems for Britain than for other member states.

Impact upon Ministers

The impact of Britain's membership of the European Community has been felt first and foremost in the sphere of central government. Ministers in both Conservative and Labour administrations have had to play their part in the process of Community decision making. Initially this involved departmental Ministers representing Britain and defending our national interests in the Council of Ministers, whether the General Affairs Council composed of Foreign Ministers or the specific Councils of departmental Ministers, such as Agriculture, Transport or the Environment, depending upon the particular policy area under discussion. Since 1974 it has also involved the Prime Minister of the day participating in what has come to be known as the European Council with the other heads of government. Such 'summit' meetings are now held twice a year under the chairmanship of whichever country holds the presidency of the Community for the relevant six-month period. They are supposed to provide renewed impetus for the development of the Community at the highest political level.

The immediate and most obvious consequence for Ministers has been the growing amount of time which they have had to devote to preparing for and attending such meetings as the sphere of Community competence has been extended (by agreement between the member states) into more and more areas of policy. For example, there was no mention of environmental policy in the 1957 Treaty of Rome, since at that time there was no general recognition of the importance of environmental problems for the member states; whereas nowadays these matters are central to Community concerns. The traditional method of decision making in the Council of Ministers has been to continue the discussion of difficult policy issues, such as the reform of the Common Agricultural Policy or Britain's net contributions to the Community Budget, until the combined influence of physical exhaustion and the spirit of compromise emerges to make a Community decision possible. Thus the so-called Community method has imposed great strains upon Ministers and those involved could not have been indifferent to it.

Figure 19.1 The EEC decision making process

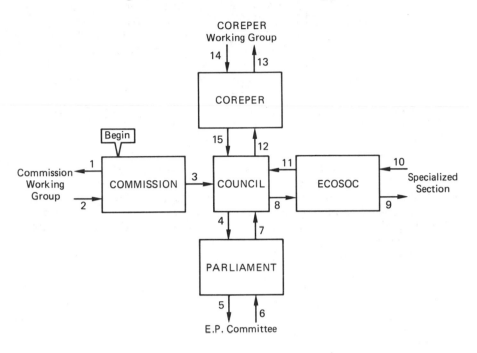

Furthermore there has been a significant change in the rules of the game since 1986, when the Single European Act became law in all the member states. This significant advance in Community decision-making procedures has involved the introduction of qualified majority voting in the Council of Ministers on all issues to do with the realisation of the Single European Market, with the exception of taxation, immigration and workers' rights, which have been reserved for unanimous decision making. This means that British Ministers can now find themselves outvoted when the Council of Ministers takes decisions by qualified majority and that a blocking minority of 23 votes out of 76 can only be assembled if two of the big countries combine with one of the smaller ones (apart from tiny Luxembourg).[12] On the other hand, qualified majority voting can and often has worked in Britain's favour (for example, in making progress on the Single Market), so the new rules of the game cut both ways. Although there is nearly always considerable pressure to find a compromise, a national government sometimes finds it politically convenient to be outvoted, so that it can argue at home that it fought its corner – even if it actually recognises the validity and good sense of the majority decision.

Impact upon Civil Servants

The impact upon civil servants has, if anything, been greater than the impact upon Ministers. Britain's membership of the European Community has spawned a vast network of new bureaucratic relationships between Whitehall and the

Community institutions in Brussels, as well as on a bilateral basis between the various national capitals. Within Whitehall itself it has been necessary for the Foreign Office and (to a lesser extent) the Cabinet Office to co-ordinate the work of all the various Departments involved in the Community policy-making process. National civil servants involved with issues of Community policy, or potential Community policy, spend a good deal of their time commuting to and from Brussels by air. A sizeable group of them from all the relevant Departments are also stationed at the UK Permanent Delegation to the Community (UKREP for short). This body, which is headed by a Foreign Office official of senior ambassadorial rank, has an essential role in preparing the Government's position at meetings of the Council of Ministers, assisting Ministers at those meetings, and carrying forward the process of permanent dialogue between the Community institutions and the British Government. Indeed the European Community would have made very little progress at all during the phase of its development when it was effectively bound by a complete unanimity rule (1966–86) if it had not been for the tireless work and continuous negotiation carried out in Brussels by the respective national delegations working within the framework of the Committee of Permanent Representatives (COREPER in French).

In view of the increasing volume of European Community legislation, civil servants in those Departments particularly involved have found themselves spending an increasing amount of their time upon the administration and implementation of Community law in the United Kingdom. For example, the Ministry of Agriculture now spends probably three-quarters of its time on the negotiation and enforcement of the Common Agricultural Policy in this country, and the Departments of Transport, Trade and Industry and Employment are increasingly busy with the administration of European regulations and directives. Even such traditionally proud and independent Departments as the Treasury, the Home Office and the Law Officers' Departments find themselves increasingly drawn into the process of Community policy making and law enforcement, with the result that few parts of the machinery of central government are now unaffected. In addition, a growing proportion of the issues considered by the Cabinet and its committees has a Community dimension of one kind or another, while the Whitehall preparation for meetings of the European Council every six months can involve the most strenuous work for 10 Downing Street, the Cabinet Office, the Foreign Office and many other Departments. Indeed it is possible to argue that large parts of the British civil service have been more affected by the Community process than any other parts of the British political system.

Impact upon Parliament

The impact upon Parliament of Britain's membership of the European Community has long been pinpointed by the so-called 'anti-Marketeers' as perhaps the most serious and adverse of all the negative consequences which they believe flow from the original decision to enter the European Community. Yet it is quite hard to find much objective evidence for their most doom-laden forecasts that Parliament at Westminster will be reduced to the status of a mere County Council in the united Europe of the future. The suspicion arises, therefore, that the anti-Marketeers believe that, by drawing attention to the threat to parliamentary supremacy posed by European Community law and especially by the growth of unaccountable judicial and bureaucratic power in the Community institutions, they will be able to scare British public opinion away from its growing support for the process of European integration.

However both the proponents and the opponents of Britain's destiny within the European Community have agreed that there are a number of real problems, both procedural and political, which face the House of Commons as it tries to come to terms with the institutional developments taking place in the European Community. The fundamental dilemmas were well expressed in the Procedure Committee Report when it reminded the House that 'European legislation is initiated almost exclusively by an executive organisation (the Commission) with which the UK Parliament has no formal relationship and over which it has no direct control'.[13] This means, as the Report went on to explain, that, 'while the House may, by changes in its own internal procedures, find ways of bringing to bear more efficiently such authority as it retains over European legislation, it cannot by such means increase that authority nor seek to claw back powers which have been ceded by Treaty'. The authors of the Report concluded that 'the House has never realistically expected to exercise total accountability in relation to Ministers' prospective actions in the Council of Ministers, though it has always demanded explanations and justifications after the event'.

Of course the real answer to these rather bleak observations is that Ministers have long been able to conclude treaties without prior parliamentary approval by their exercise of prerogative powers on behalf of the Crown – it is, after all, still 'Her Majesty's Government'. The largely retrospective nature of parliamentary control over what Ministers do or do not do in European Community decision making is no different in this respect from the power exercised by MPs in their attempts to control the activities of Ministers in their national decision making. The real difference is that, whereas Parliament at Westminster has long claimed to have supreme and exclusive jurisdiction over national legislation, it has had to share jurisdiction with the European Parliament in the control of Community legislation and, in many respects, accept a subordinate role not only in all those areas of legislation where Community law takes direct effect but also now in those areas where the European Parliament (but not the national Parliaments) has some powers of joint decision at certain stages of the European legislative process.[14]

The main procedural problems for Parliament at Westminster, which were identified by the Procedure Committee in its Report, are widely recognised by pundits and practitioners alike. Firstly, the volume of Community legislation is considerable and hard for the House of Commons to deal with within the confines of its present legislative timetable. For example, the number of European documents coming before the House of Commons and considered by the Scrutiny Committee in recent years has increased from an average of 650 a year in the period 1983–5 to an average of 840 a year between 1986 and 1988.[15] Secondly, some important European documents have been adopted by the Community institutions before the process of Westminster scrutiny and control was complete. Recent figures show that this undesirable situation occurred in relation to European documents raising matters of legal or political importance in as few as 5 out of 191 cases in 1984–5 but as many as 25 out of 362 cases in 1987–8.[16] Thirdly, there is a widespread complaint from all sides of the House that too many of the debates which are held on European legislation take place after 10 p.m. in a sterile and unproductive parliamentary atmosphere. This problem has arisen principally because there are already too many calls upon the available parliamentary time, but it is exacerbated by the unwillingness of the anti-Market MPs to acknowledge the increased scope and importance of Community law.

The fourth and most important problem, which has arisen since the passage of the 1986 Single European Act (implemented in this country via the 1986 European Communities Amendment Act), is that the introduction of qualified majority voting in the Council of Ministers on nearly all matters to do with the completion of the Single Market has further reduced the areas in which a member state can veto Community decisions or a national Parliament can refuse to enact agreed Community legislation. The fear among many MPs at Westminster is that this erosion of their parliamentary rights will continue as long as Britain remains in the European Community and the process of Community decision making moves inexorably towards majority voting on more and more policy issues.

At the same time the European Parliament has come to wield extra powers in the European legislative process via the so-called 'co-operation procedure' which was introduced as part of the Single European Act. This enables the European Parliament to play a more constructive legislative role than before. Once the Council of Ministers has reached a common position by qualified majority, the European Parliament can reject the common position or propose amendments to it which, if adopted by the Commission, can only be amended unanimously by the Council. So far the effect of this strengthening of the European Parliament's position in the Community legislative process has been to cause the Commission to change direction on perhaps one-third of all substantial amendments. In these circumstances the Procedure Committee had to admit that 'the European Parliament has already established itself as a useful additional channel for attempts to influence the final shape of Community legislation in certain closely defined areas, *over and above the traditional avenue open to the House of bringing pressure to bear directly on UK Ministers*'.[17] In other words, the European Parliament has been gaining power, while the Westminster Parliament has been losing it.

Impact upon the Rest of the Political System

It is clear that Britain's membership of the European Community has also had an impact upon the rest of the political system. This is manifest in virtually all areas to a greater or lesser extent. It can truly be said that the evolving European Community now provides the economic, political and institutional context within which more and more of our national life takes place. Unless a future British Government backed by a future British Parliament decides to take Britain out of the European Community (and such a decision would probably have to be put to a national referendum) our Community membership is likely to become an increasingly important part of life for the British people.

In the first place, the political parties are now considerably affected by the growing need to conduct their politics not just at local and national level, but also at Community level in the European Parliament and in the respective transnational political groupings. For example, the two most powerful political groupings in Europe, the Socialists and the Christian Democrats, not only dominate the proceedings of the European Parliament, but also exert considerable influence upon their affiliated national parties via the Socialist International and the European Peoples' Party respectively. It is also perhaps significant for the future development of British politics that, whereas the Labour party is now an active component of its transnational political grouping, the Conservative party is excluded from the Christian Democratic Group in the European Parliament and plays only a limited role in the wider grouping of like-minded parties of the Centre Right. Thus in some ways the Labour party now seems more 'European' than the Conservative party, which is an odd reversal of roles compared with the situation two or three decades ago.

Secondly, the development of the European Community is having its influence upon pressure groups in this country and, increasingly, upon the private sector in general. As more and more key decisions of interest to the private sector are taken by the Community institutions in Brussels rather than by national governments and Parliaments in the national capitals, power has levitated increasingly to the Community level. This has meant, for example, that British farmers are now at least as interested to lobby the Commission in Brussels and the European Parliament in Strasbourg via their transnational European organisation COPA (Comité d'Organisations de Producteurs Agricoles) as they are to lobby the Ministry of Agriculture and Parliament at Westminster via the National Farmers' Union and other national pressure groups. This is because they realise that most of the key decisions which affect their livelihood – for example, on guaranteed farm prices, agricultural levies or the rate for the 'green pound' – are taken at Community rather than national level. Similar conclusions are also being drawn in the industrial and financial sectors of our economy as further substantial progress is made towards the creation of a Single European Market based upon common rules and regulations for the entire Community.

Thirdly, the working of the European Community is having a growing impact upon local or subnational government in Britain and, indeed, all the other member states. Increasingly, local authorities in Britain are looking to the Community institutions for financial assistance and political support. In the case of the large conurbations and outlying regions of the United Kingdom there is now a widespread assumption that the Community Regional and Social Funds can be of benefit to them. They therefore lobby hard to get their fair share of such Community expenditure. Furthermore the nationalist parties in Scotland, Wales and Northern Ireland see in the European Community their best chance of developing a political counterweight to the influence of Whitehall and Westminster which, they feel, is usually insufficiently sympathetic to their claims. It is therefore not too surprising that these parties have taken a position of favouring independence from London for their respective parts of the United Kingdom, but an independence based upon the idea of national or regional autonomy within the European Community.

Fourthly, it is becoming increasingly true to say that the media, and hence public opinion, in Britain are affected by our membership of the European Community. Obviously the extent of this influence fluctuates with the course of events. Sometimes there is intense media and public interest, as there has been when the British Government has been at odds with its Community partners or when developments in central and eastern Europe have held people riveted to their television screens. More often Community affairs have taken second place to apparently more pressing domestic preoccupations. Yet, as the world has become seemingly smaller and as decisions taken in the Community framework or by the Community institutions have come to affect our lives more and more, public awareness of the costs and benefits of Britain's membership seems to have risen and the whole context of British politics seems to have been enlarged compared with what it was 10 or 20 years ago.

Obviously the process of Euro-consciousness raising in Britain has affected some sections of society more than others. For example, those who travel on behalf of British exporting companies, those who need to be in frequent touch with their professional counterparts on the Continent and a significant proportion of the internationally mobile younger generation all seem to take Britain's membership of the European Community increasingly for granted and to look upon themselves as 'Europeans' almost as much as English, Scottish or Welsh. On the other hand, it must be admitted that many of the older and less fortunate sections of the population are still pretty insular, even chauvinistic, as can be seen in the deplorable behaviour of some British football fans or tourists abroad. It will clearly take some time before the vast majority of the largely monoglot British population genuinely feels at home anywhere else in Europe.

19.4 **Possible Future Developments**

It is difficult to foresee precisely how the European Community will develop in the years ahead and to predict how Britain and its political institutions will respond to the challenges ahead. However there are a few developments which can be discerned that seem likely to be among and main driving forces of the Community as it evolves in the 1990s and beyond.

Main Driving Forces

The most obvious driving force in the European Community both now and in the future is the determination of firms and individuals in the private sector to take advantage of the economic and commercial opportunities provided by the increasingly unified single market of at least 320 million people. In this sense it seems clear that the private sector will lead the public sector in further progress towards closer European integration and that national authorities may lag behind, usually seeking to validate but sometimes actually to obstruct further developments in private sector integration.

The best examples of this process of private sector integration are to be found in the activities of large multinational companies, whether based in the Community or outside, which exert pressure in their own interests upon the Community institutions to reach agreement upon a growing number of common rules, standards and regulations that will enable them to exploit the full potential of the market. We are therefore likely to find that the real pace-setters of the single market and hence of the whole process of European economic integration in the future will be IBM and General Motors, Siemens and GEC, Nomura and Deutschebank, Toyota and Renault, Philips and Fiat – to name but some of the most prominent examples.

A second and equally significant driving force in the European Community is likely to be the power of the transnational trade union confederations which are now beginning to act more effectively to advance the interests of organised labour at Community level. Powerful national trade unions, such as IG Metal in Germany, will increasingly take the lead in forging alliances with their counterparts in the other member states and in creating supranational representative bodies to maximise their influence in negotiations at Community level. Sometimes they will do this via the mechanisms of free collective bargaining with national and multinational employers. At other times they will put pressure upon the Commission, the European Parliament and the other Community institutions to encourage them to come forward with decisions which demonstrate Community solidarity.

The best current examples of this kind of pressure are the campaigns which have been waged by the trade union movement throughout the Community for a shorter working week and a statutory minimum wage. Of course such campaigns will continue to be resisted by many employers in different parts of the Community and also by those national governments which are opposed to such binding intervention both at national and at Community level. Yet it is equally clear that at the level of general principles such initiatives are likely to find favour in the Community institutions and in most of the member states. This fondness for fine declarations, which was exemplified by the 11 to one support for the Social Charter at the Strasbourg European Council in December 1989 (with Britain alone in the minority), is characteristic of the European Community. However it is equally characteristic for the member states to fight their own corners fiercely and often to drag their feet when faced with the legally binding regulations and directives drawn up by the Commission to implement such grand decisions.

A third main driving force in the European Community of the future is likely to be the power of highly mobile finance capital. Already we have seen the emergence of the City of London, and soon very likely Frankfurt, as centres of financial operations in the European time zone between New York and Tokyo. Such developments are likely to be enhanced and possibly accelerated in future as capital and currency circulates with increasing ease and rapidity around the globe. The enormous weight of these financial flows can already be illustrated by the fact that in 1989 the daily turnover in financial transactions on the New York markets was the equivalent of three times the total gold and foreign exchange reserves of Britain, and by the fact that the value of the total currency flows in the world (that is, the buying and selling of currencies for speculative or other financial purposes) is estimated at 20 times the value of all currency used to finance world trade.

Such developments will continue to have a massive influence upon the claimed 'autonomy' of each of the Community member states and will probably drive the Community as a whole towards economic and monetary union, not only as a vital corollary of the Single European Market but also as the best available way of exercising (albeit in common) some real economic sovereignty. We see here another example of a Community imperative which will gradually drive the member states to pool more and more of their alleged national sovereignties in order to retain some real power jointly to control their common economic destiny.

A final driving force for the future of the European Community, which we have already discussed earlier in this chapter, is obviously the incremental development of European law. As we have seen in section 19.2 above, Britain and the other member states have been and will be affected by the invasion of European Community law into more and more areas of activity which were previously subject only to national competence and jurisdiction. This is happening every time that the member states resolve to make a further move towards closer integration, as they did, for example, in the 1986 Single European Act. However, in future, the further development of Community law is likely to stem at least as much from the case work of the European Court as from the political decisions of the member states to break fresh ground. Of course both sources of supranational impetus will make themselves felt in the Community, but the significance of the former is increasingly likely to outweigh the significance of the latter in what is rapidly becoming a Community of law as much as a Community of politics.

Main Divisive Issues

Since the very beginning of the European Community, there have been a number of divisive issues which have caused difficulty for the member states. Yet when the Community has been plunged into crisis, it has always emerged intact and very often strengthened by the experience. It seems clear from present evidence that this will continue to be the case in the Community of Twelve, especially because of the tension between those who wish to 'deepen' the process of integration before widening the membership still further and those who would like to see the Community enlarged to include new member states in Scandinavia, central and eastern Europe in order to dilute its supranational characteristics. This almost theological dispute, which may well be resolved by the use of pragmatic parallelism, is really the age-old dispute over national sovereignty in a new form. It is therefore worth devoting a few paragraphs to this most fundamental of all the divisive issues in the Community.

The essential problem in the debate about sovereignty in the Community is that people disagree about what constitutes 'sovereignty'. The word has different meanings and elicits different reactions in the various member states. Everywhere on the Continent, except perhaps in Denmark and Greece, the idea of pooling national sovereignties for the common good does not cause many difficulties for politicians or lawyers. This is partly because in most cases the idea of the nation state has a chequered, even disreputable history and partly because – in the case of the original Six at any rate – they were committed to the European idea from the beginning in 1950. In Britain, on the other hand, the idea of pooling our national sovereignty with that of other nations in an apparently irreversible, supranational arrangement such as the European Community has raised all sorts of fears and misgivings, since it has tended to be (wilfully) confused with the erosion of parliamentary supremacy and the blurring of national identity.

In the case of the supremacy of Parliament at Westminster, we have already seen in earlier sections of this chapter that those who have always been hostile to Britain's membership of the European Community – especially its supranational aspects – deeply resent the fact that the 1972 European Communities Act and the 1986 European Communities Amendment Act effectively provide for the supremacy of European law over national law in those areas covered by the Community treaties. As for the preservation of our national identity, there are those who worry that, as the European Community develops and as the member states become more closely integrated, the British people will in some way lose their distinctive identity in a sort of multinational *minestrone*. Such misgivings cannot be entirely banished or disproved, but we can observe with some clarity that the French do not seem any less French, the Germans any less German or the Italians any less Italian as a result of their relatively longer period within the European Community. It is therefore fair to conclude that this aspect of the sovereignty debate is little more than an emotional red herring.

The substantial aspect of the debate about national sovereignty within the European Community concerns issues of political and governmental competence.

It raises important questions about whether or not the member states have *a legal right* to act in the spheres covered by the Community treaties (which they would appear to have retained at least in theory) and further questions about whether or not they have *the capacity* to act effectively now that they are no more than medium-sized nation states in the modern world. On the former point, no one seriously denies that each member state retains the right to act in defiance of European Community law (at the risk of being found guilty before the European Court) and the ultimate right to adopt an 'empty chair' policy, as Gaullist France did for a time in the mid-1960s. Yet this is a somewhat empty definition of national sovereignty in the modern world, since it probably leaves the member states less rather than more able to protect their national interests. On the latter point, we come immediately to the very heart of the argument for membership of the European Community in the first place – that, by freely pooling national sovereignties in certain agreed areas of activity, the member states have all discovered that collectively they have a capacity to act effectively which is superior in the modern world to anything which they could have achieved on their own. In short, this is the very *raison d'être* of the European Community in its present form.

Since not all political and public opinion in Britain is prepared to accept this argument, an arcane discussion has developed in recent times about governmental functions and the most appropriate levels at which these should be exercised in each case. This is the debate about the doctrine of *subsidiarity*, a notion widely canvassed by the President of the European Commission, Jacques Delors.[18] It is based upon the contention that the loss of national power to the European level can be limited by the fact that the member states and the Community institutions are said to agree that no functions should be exercised at supranational level which could more appropriately and effectively be exercised at national level and, it should be added (although this does not seem to be accepted by the present British Government), no functions should be exercised at national level which could more appropriately and effectively be exercised at subnational level, that is, regional or local government. So far this reassuring doctrine has been confined largely to the realm of Euro-rhetoric and there is nothing in the Community treaties or Community case law to guarantee that it is observed. All that can be said with any certainty is that the Community institutions will find it difficult to accrue significantly more powers and functions without the introduction of treaty amendments or the assistance of evolving case law in the European Court. Nevertheless it is likely that in practice the member states and their national political institutions will continue to lose their effective power and autonomy in the face of the growing power and influence of the Community institutions above them and, perhaps, local institutions below them.

Assuming that national powers and functions levitate upwards to the Community institutions in Brussels and gravitate downwards to the institutions of local government throughout the Community, many political practitioners and observers have identified an emerging problem of a 'democratic deficit' in the European Community. This phrase is used to describe a situation in which the transfer of such powers and functions to European Community civil servants and judges on the one hand and to local administration on the other has not yet been matched by a sufficient enhancement of the powers of the European Parliament or, indeed, of democratically elected local authorities to compensate for the loss of effective democratic powers for national Parliaments, which have found themselves increasingly less able to monitor and control national decision making and legislation, let alone policy and decision making at Community level.

As far as Parliament at Westminster is concerned, we dealt with some of these problems of democratic accountability in earlier sections of this chapter. Suffice it to say, the 'pro-Europeans' in British politics are often relatively relaxed about the idea of sharing the responsibilities of democratic control with the directly elected European Parliament, whereas the 'anti-Europeans' wish to stifle what they see as a rival institution in Strasbourg and insist that the Council of Ministers should continue to take all the important decisions and then preferably only with the prior agreement of the national Parliaments. In the longer term, it seems likely that the European Parliament (often in alliance with the European Commission) will continue to press for increased powers of democratic control at the expense of national Parliaments and that, as the areas of supranational activity in the Community grow, it will be successful.

19.5 Conclusion

We have seen in this chapter how Britain excluded herself from full participation in the mainstream of gathering European integration after the Second World War and how this country paid an economic and political price for this self-imposed exclusion. However, since joining the European Community in 1973, Britain has played a full part in nearly all Community developments, even if she has invariably been ranged on the side of those trying to slow down the pace and limit the scope of European integration. This was especially the case in recent times when Margaret Thatcher saw in developments in central and eastern Europe a chance to put the brakes on the process of ever closer European integration, notably of the kind advocated by the Commission with the strong support of the French, Italian and Benelux Governments.

The reasons for this cautious approach and scepticism about the European ideal, as we have seen, have been a widely-held British suspicion of supranationalism in all its forms and a marked preference for an international approach towards the development of the European Community based upon the sovereign rights of the member states. There is also considerable hostility at Westminster to the prospect that European law will increasingly encroach upon, and perhaps eventually dominate, the sphere of British national law and widespread resentment at the erosion of real national autonomy. In short, many of the misgivings felt in Britain about membership of the European Community stem from a nostalgic yearning for the era when Britain was a truly Great Power strong enough to stay clear of binding continental entanglements and able to throw her weight from time to time into the European balance of power on one side or the other.

No one can tell exactly how the European Community will develop over the years ahead, not least because there is now the prospect of moves towards economic and monetary union, paralleled by the further enlargement of the Community to the north and the east. The present British Government is strongly attracted by the goal of a genuinely single European market by the end of 1992, and the Labour Opposition has become reconciled to Britain's membership of the Community, indeed the leadership can now see considerable advantages in it. Consequently it seems clear that, whatever else happens, Britain is now in the

European Community to stay and our destiny is irrevocably linked with that of our Community partners.

Suggested Questions

1. Explain why it was that Britain so often and so consistently 'missed the bus' in its relations with the six original members of the European Community from 1945 to 1973.
2. How profound and far reaching are the legal and constitutional implications of Britain's membership of the European Community?
3. What seem likely to be the main driving forces and divisive issues in the European Community of the future, and how will these affect the course of British politics?

Notes

1. See 'The United Kingdom and the European Community', Cmnd 1565 (London: HMSO, 1961), para. 3.
2. Section 2(1) clearly states: 'All such rights, powers, liabilities, obligations and restrictions from time to time created or arising by or under the Treaties, and all such remedies and procedures from time to time provided for by or under the Treaties, as in accordance with the Treaties are without further enactment to be given legal effect or used in the United Kingdom shall be recognised and available in law, and be enforced, allowed and followed accordingly; and the expression 'enforceable Community right' and similar expressions shall be read as referring to one to which this sub-section applies'.
3. See Case 26/62 (1963) ECR1.
4. See Case 106/77 (1978) ECR 629.
5. See *Commission* v. *France*, Case 167/73 (1974) ECR 359.
6. See *Pigs Marketing Board* v. *Redmond*, Case 83/78 (1978) ECR 2347.
7. See *Minister for Fisheries* v *Schoenenberg*, Case 88/77 (1978) ECR 473.
8. See *Meijer* v. *Department of Trade*, Case 118/78 (1979) ECR 1387.
9. See *Commission* v. *Ireland*, Case 61/77 (1978) ECR 417.
10. See *Shields* v. *E. Coomes (Holdings) Ltd*, (1979) 1 All ER 456, 461–2.
11. M. Butler, *Europe, More Than a Continent* (London: Heinemann, 1986), p. 169.
12. 'Qualified majority voting' is defined in Article 148 (2) of the Treaty of Rome. Under this procedure the votes of each of the 12 member states are weighted as follows: Germany, France, Italy, UK 10 votes each; Spain 8 votes; Belgium, Greece, Netherlands, Portugal 5 votes each; Denmark, Ireland 3 votes each; Luxembourg 2 votes. The total number of votes is 76 and a qualified majority is 54. Where a decision is not based upon a Commission proposal, there is an additional requirement that at least 8 of the 12 member states must vote in favour. The magic figure of 54 votes required for a qualified majority means that the 5 largest member states cannot outvote the 7 smaller member states.
13. See Fourth Report from the Select Committee on Procedure 1988–89 on 'The Scrutiny of European legislation', vol. I, 622–I, 8 November 1989.
14. The limited legislative powers of the European Parliament (the so-called 'co-operation procedure') are laid down in Articles 6 and 7 of the 1986 Single European Act. This means that once the Council of Ministers has adopted what is called a 'common position' by qualified majority, the European Parliament has 3 months in which to approve, reject or amend it. If the Parliament approves or fails to act, the Council simply adopts the measure. If the Parliament rejects the common position then the Council can act only by unanimity. If the Parliament amends, the Council can either accept the Commission's reformulation of the proposal by qualified majority or it can reject or amend the Commission's reformulation (in the light of the Parliament's opinion), but only by unanimity.
15. See 1988–9 Procedure Committee Report, para. 11.

16. Ibid., para. 15.
17. Ibid., para. 108 (my emphasis).
18. The doctrine of 'subsidiarity' has its origin in a pronouncement by Pope Pius XI in 1931 in his *Rundschreiben über die gesellschaftliche Ordnung* (Encyclical on social order).

Further Reading

Butler, M., *Europe, More Than a Continent* (London: Heinemann, 1986).

Cecchini, P. *et al.*, *The European Challenge, 1992* (Aldershot: Wildwood House, 1988).

George, S., *Politics and Policy in the European Community* (Oxford University Press, 1985).

Hartley, T. C., *The Foundations of European Community Law*, 2nd edn (Oxford: Clarendon Press, 1988).

Institute of Economic Affairs, *Whose Europe? – competing visions for 1992* (London: IEA, 1989).

Neville Brown, L. and Jacobs, F. G., *The Court of Justice of the European Communities*, 3rd edn (London: Sweet & Maxwell, 1989).

Wallace, H., *Budgetary Politics: the finances of the European Communities* (London: Allen & Unwin, 1980).

20 British parliamentary democracy

British parliamentary democracy has evolved over the centuries. From Simon de Montfort's Parliament in 1265 to the outbreak of the Civil War in 1641 it was based upon the changing relations between the Monarch and the various estates of the realm. By the time of the Bill of Rights in 1689 a more explicit constitutional relationship had evolved between the Monarch and his Ministers on the one hand and the Lords and the Commons on the other. It was not until the 1832 Reform Act and the successive extensions of the franchise by subsequent Acts of Parliament from then until the present day that a recognisably modern political system evolved and the relationship between the Government and the people came to assume its familiar shape. Today both politicians and people live in a parliamentary democracy which has been formed by centuries of evolutionary development.

20.1 The Conditions of Democracy

British parliamentary democracy has a number of essential characteristics which we shall consider later in this chapter, but, before we can do so, we need to understand that there are a number of conditions which have to be met if the system is to function satisfactorily in Britain as in other comparable countries. Joseph Schumpeter described these as 'conditions for the success of the democratic method' and it may be helpful for us to recall his argument.[1]

The first condition was that the politicians active in the political system should be of sufficiently high quality. It would obviously be invidious for the author to comment in any detail upon this point, save to observe that quality is influenced by attitude, in that politicians who adopt a positive and constructive approach to the problems which confront them are often more attractive and persuasive than those whose approach is negative and destructive. Clearly high quality is a necessary but not a sufficient condition for success in a democracy, while cynicism or defeatism is usually unattractive to the voters.

The second condition was that the range of political decisions should be limited. This is obviously a salutary point to make in relation to contemporary politics, since the persistence of unrealistic public expectations, often encouraged by unscrupulous politicians at election time, leads people to suppose that governments can have a solution to every problem. Unless leading politicians show themselves capable of preaching and practising the virtues of limited government, the dangers of public disappointment are likely to increase.

The third condition was that there should be a strong and impartial bureaucracy. The importance of this condition is best illustrated by its absence – for example, in developing countries where the lack of a suitable administrative infrastructure can be a significant barrier to economic and social development. Ironically in this country the nature and quality of our civil service has sometimes been seen as an obstacle rather than an aid to our success, because of the tendency of bureaucrats to prefer established ideas and procedures to anything new or untried.

The fourth condition was that vanquished political minorities (especially the losing political parties) should acquiesce in their electoral defeat and accept the consequences of the voters' verdict. This condition is bound to be fundamental to the satisfactory functioning of a democracy and in this country the rule of the (parliamentary) majority has invariably been accepted by all parties. Of course a healthy democracy ought also to have safeguards for the defeated minorities against possible abuse of power by the majority. Yet in Britain this is bound to be difficult to achieve as long as our electoral system enables the victorious party (which is normally elected by no more than the largest minority of the votes cast) to impose its political will upon Parliament and the country simply by dint of its overall majority in the House of Commons.

The final condition was that everyone involved in politics, and especially those in the victorious party at any time, should show tolerance and magnanimity towards the interests and concerns of all those on the losing side at the previous General Election. This is a condition which was broadly fulfilled in this country during the 25 years or so after the Second World War. It ought also to appeal to any party in government which realises that its period in office will not be indefinite and that sooner or later it too will find itself licking its wounds in opposition. However there were signs in the 1980s of Conservative triumphalism and an apparent belief in political invincibility on the government side which marked a clear departure from the more prudent conventions of British politics and, incidentally, an obvious contrast with the coalition politics on the Continent. If this attitude were to dominate in the 1990s, the Conservatives would have to expect reciprocal treatment from Labour if latter were returned to power at a future General Election.

20.2 Essential Characteristics

One essential characteristic of British parliamentary democracy is that it is a representative system which is supposed to function in a democratically responsible way. This has some positive consequences for the political system. It endows the government of the day with democratic legitimacy, although a wise government will not take its authority for granted. It allows the electorate every four or five years to deliver a verdict on the record of the party in office and on the competing attractions of the other parties. It provides institutional channels of communication between the Government and the governed, although by no means the only channels in a political system in which pressure groups and the media play such an important part. It has the effect of magnifying or filtering the force of public opinion according to the nature of the issue and the political imperatives for each political party.

Notwithstanding these positive characteristics, our form of parliamentary democracy has never secured unanimous approval. This is partly because our political institutions have been subject to close scrutiny and criticism nearly every time that public expectations have been seriously disappointed. It is also because some people have been attracted to other political arrangements which they believe to have been more successful in other countries. There are significant arguments on each side of this question.

On the one hand, it is argued that the legitimacy of government in Britain is based upon the fact that the party in office is invariably the sole victor of the previous General Election and can therefore command the support of an overall majority in the House of Commons on virtually all decisive occasions. Of course this is a qualified legitimacy, in that it is usually based upon no more than a plurality of the votes cast at the previous General Election – that is to say, the largest single minority – and it lasts for no more than a single Parliament, which is a maximum of five years. This means that our politics are based upon an implicit contract between the Government and the people. Ministers accept that there are limits to the action which they can take if they are to remain within the bounds of public tolerance and acceptability. The general public accepts that the party in office should have considerable latitude in the fulfilment of its election mandate and in its day-to-day government of the country. The limits of public tolerance and acceptability vary from time to time and from government to government. Much depends upon the extent to which policy runs counter to powerful party or pressure group opinion; upon the perceived gravity or urgency of the situation; upon the possibilities of making progress by stealth without attracting too much media or public attention; and upon the likelihood of policy reversal in the event of the Opposition winning power at the ensuing General Election. In short, such limits cannot be precisely determined in advance, but only deduced from experience.

On the other hand, the power of the electorate is based upon the fact that, whatever the party in government may do during its term of office, it is the voters who have the final say at the ensuing General Election. Even so, such final power is qualified by a number of significant factors. Firstly, the voters are able to exercise no more than intermittent democratic control, in view of the relative infrequency of General Elections in Britain. At other times they can put pressure upon their elected representatives by stressing their vulnerability to rejection in the ballot box if public wishes are not met. Secondly, the voters are able to exercise their democratic choice, but only within the range of alternatives offered by the various political parties. Thus Conservative voters who may live in safe Labour seats and support the return of capital punishment are unlikely to have their point of view expressed by their own MP; just as Labour voters who live in safe Conservative seats and support further measures of nationalisation are unlikely to have their point of view expressed by their own MP. As for the supporters of minor parties, they seem doomed to cast wasted votes, at any rate at most General Elections. Thirdly, the ignorance and apathy of many voters is also a limiting factor, since people who vote with little real knowledge of the issues or who do not bother to vote at all, cannot really be said to have laid claim to an unchallengeable ascendancy in the political process.

Another essential characteristic is the great importance of the political parties as two-way channels of communication between the Government and the people. They are not flawless mechanisms of communication, but they do manage to enlist the energies of nearly all political activists in lawful and constitutional directions. This is achieved largely because party political divisions reflect real cleavages in British society, yet usually without such viciousness or intolerance that the defeated minority is led to challenge or reject the will of the majority. As long as the party system is working as it should, those who have political causes to advance or grievances to air ought to feel able to do so within one of the parties. This is one of the reasons why each of the main parties has had such a strong interest in remaining a broad church which can encompass different interpretations of its political faith. If the main political parties were ever to lose this representative quality – and each of them came close to it in the 1980s – they might be by-passed and possibly displaced by other political organisations better equipped to perform the vital functions of democratic representation in our society.

A third essential characteristic of British parliamentary democracy is the way in which the government of the day has usually sought to preserve a broad balance of political power in the country. This can serve to ensure that the general interest gets an adequate hearing above the cacophony of special interests. This is never easy for any government to achieve. Indeed the present Conservative Government has sometimes been accused of identifying the general interest with its own radical and particular view of economic and social priorities. Other governments of this type have occasionally won power in this century, but they have been the exception rather than the rule and all came unstuck in the end.

In considering this aspect of the political system, the central issue is how far any government can manage to represent the general interest, while remaining responsive to the various sectional interests which exist in modern society. Too great an emphasis upon protecting the general interest can lay a government open to the charge that it is not sufficiently pluralist in its inclinations, yet too great a willingness to rely upon understandings or deals with sectional interests can suggest an inclination to downgrade Parliament and embark upon the path of corporatism. Thus a judicious balance has to be struck and, however this is done, it is always a matter of political controversy.

20.3 **Other Significant Features**

British parliamentary democracy has some other significant features which need to be taken into consideration. Each of these has assumed different importance at different times, but all have helped to determine the character of the British political system.

Political Polarisation

The tendency towards political polarisation in Britain derives very largely from the trend in each of the main political parties in the 1970s and early 1980s to adopt notably ideological positions in the wake of political defeat at the polls. Thus the Labour Opposition moved discernibly to the Left in the early 1970s, when Harold Wilson virtually abdicated from the responsibilities of moderate parliamentary leadership, and the Conservative Opposition moved discernibly to the Right in the late 1970s, when Margaret Thatcher sought to lead the party on avowedly free market principles. The result of these matching political developments was that by the mid-1980s there was less consensus and more polarisation in British politics than at any time since the immediate postwar period.

Such polarisation was in marked contrast to the more limited party-political differences which existed during the 1950s and 1960s when each of the main parties broadly accepted the political consensus which emerged during and immediately after the Second World War. It can also be differentiated from the emerging political choices of the 1990s between the modified radicalism of John Major's Conservatism and the apparently revisionist instincts of the Labour party under Neil Kinnock. The genius of the British political system seems to be that, if one party stays in office long enough to build a new political consensus, it eventually forces a degree of accommodation with the new political realities upon the other main party sufficient to render it non-threatening and even attractive to the general electorate.

Institutional Inertia

Institutional inertia is another significant feature of the British political system which seems capable of coexisting with the political polarisation just described. Although a number of important institutional changes have been made over the past 20 years or so – for example, the reform of local government in the early 1970s or the abortive attempt to introduce devolution for Scotland and Wales in the late 1970s, or the abolition of the Greater London and other Metropolitan Councils in the mid-1980s – none has proved particularly successful and some have not worked at all. This has led the opponents of institutional change to argue that all such initiatives do more harm than good and suffer from the law of unintended consequences. They point out that institutional change is not necessarily a suitable remedy for problems which are often attitudinal or even psychological in origin. They also maintain that such institutional discontinuity is inherently unsettling and usually inimical to the interests of good government.

On the other hand, those who believe in the value of institutional change have tended to focus upon the remedy of proportional representation as the key with which to unlock many of our political problems. They argue that Britain's existing first-past-the-post electoral system is the most significant obstacle to a fair outcome at General Elections and, indeed, to the adoption of sensible, middle-of-the-road policies by any government. Yet their argument takes insufficient account of the strong vested interests within each of the main parties in favour of the existing electoral system. Furthermore, with a people as basically conservative as the British, the onus of establishing the need for radical change usually rests upon those who propose it. Only on rare occasions when the bulk of the electorate decides that it is time for a change is this normal predisposition overwhelmed by more adventurous impulses.

Elective Dictatorship

Lord Hailsham and others have argued that in certain circumstances British parliamentary democracy can be virtually an 'elective dictatorship'.[2] This is true in the sense that any British government with an effective majority in the House of Commons can usually get its way in Parliament, at any rate on all the issues which really matter. Over the last two decades or so this has been reflected in the tendency of Labour governments to impose high rates of direct taxation, to take into public ownership large sections of British industry, and to increase tax-financed welfare benefits; and the tendency of the present Conservative Government to raise rents in public sector housing, to curb the power of the trade unions by legislative means and to return to private ownership more than half of the state-owned industrial sector which it inherited in 1979.

On the other hand, it can be argued that an 'elective dictatorship' is an exaggerated description of one of the shortcomings of British parliamentary democracy which tends to be voiced by those who have lost a General Election and are bemoaning the uses to which their political opponents choose to put the power of government. The reality is that beyond the twin citadels of Whitehall and Westminster powerful vested interests have the capacity to frustrate and occasionally defeat the plans of any government. For example, in 1969 the trade unions were able to use their influence in the Parliamentary Labour party to defeat the Labour Government's proposals for trade union reform which were embodied in a White paper entitled *In Place of Strife*. Similarly, in 1983, the Stock Exchange was able to persuade the Conservative Government not to refer certain restrictive City practices to the courts and settle for a system of self-regulation within a new statutory framework. Each of these examples serves to demonstrate that Ministers have only limited and conditional power in office, which they often have to share with powerful interest groups between elections and which always depends upon endorsement or rejection by the voters at every General Election.

Limited Government

In contemporary political circumstances it may seem strange to argue that the limited power of government is one of the most significant features of the British political system. Yet this is borne out by the fact that the writ of even the most powerful Ministers does not always run without powerful challenge beyond the twin citadels of Whitehall and Westminster. One obvious reason for this is that the implementation of policy in a free society depends much more than Ministers are sometimes prepared to recognise upon the tacit acquiescence, if not the active support, of those most directly affected by it. Another reason is that many problems in the world today are not susceptible to governmental solutions, but require the active co-operation of private individuals and organisations for their solution. However perhaps the most significant reason in the 1990s is that all national governments, even the most powerful, are now vulnerable to developments and decisions elsewhere in the world over which they have limited influence and still less effective control.

The gulf between the ambitious objectives of nearly all modern governments and their modest achievements in office may have damaged the reputation of parliamentary democracy in the eyes of many British people. It seems to have undermined public faith in our national political institutions and certainly to have increased public cynicism about the promises and protestations of all politicians. In the 1970s this led to demands for extensive institutional change, for example in local government reform, the introduction of proportional representation and the use of referenda to settle vexed constitutional issues in which the very future of Parliament itself was engaged. In the 1990s we hear less of these arguments, at any rate in England, although in Scotland, Wales and Northern Ireland there are powerful pressures from nationalist quarters for more control over their own destiny and even 'national independence within the European Community' in some cases.

20.4 Some Unresolved Issues

The traditional pattern of politics in Britain since 1945 has left unresolved some very important issues. These include the extent to which there is scope for significant change in a national political system which is now no more than one important part of the increasingly significant European Community, and the extent to which it is possible to gain and retain public consent for at any rate the most controversial acts of government. In each case the experience of recent years has not been particularly encouraging.

The Scope for Change

It is a paradox that there have been few political or institutional changes of lasting significance in Britain since the Second World War, in spite of the fact that successive governments – and especially the present one since 1979 – have often sought to make a radical mark upon Britain's performance and upon attitudes in British society. On the whole any government has only three different means of bringing about change: it can introduce new policy, it can change or abolish institutions and it can seek to modify or transform public attitudes.

In the 1950s and 1960s successive governments relied upon policy adjustments within a fairly well-defined political consensus. In the 1970s the attention of governments was concentrated more upon institutional remedies to our seemingly intractable national problems. In the 1980s, under the impetus provided by Thatcherite Conservatism, the main emphasis was upon spirited attempts to bring about fundamental attitudinal changes designed to engender an entrepreneurial and cultural revolution among the British people. Great claims were made for the success of this ambitious crusade to transform first the attitudes of the British people and then the performance of the British economy. To some extent the claims were justified, in that there are now many more small businesses and self-employed than there were more than a decade ago, and all this entrepreneurial activity has helped to generate extra personal disposable income and national wealth. On the other hand, the asset price inflation which accompanied the boom years of the 1980s turned us increasingly into a nation of obsessive home-buyers and even property speculators, a development which did little or nothing to enhance our national performance in highly competitive European and world markets. Thus it is not self-evident that, even with the most determined and radical political leadership for 40 years, the mass of the British people were willing or able to make the attitudinal step-change that was expected of them.

There are various plausible explanations for this rather sobering observation. The most obvious would seem to be that radicalism was not and is not the most congenial political instinct of the vast majority of the British people, who much prefer a less strenuous approach to life and politics. Furthermore, when a determined political minority – in this case Thatcherite Conservatives – manages to establish a temporary ascendancy, it usually sows the seeds of its own destruction, either by going too far in its chosen direction or by ceasing to appear particularly relevant in changed political circumstances. When this happens the conditions are created for the revival of political alternatives which may appear more attractive or relevant in changed political circumstances. It seems, therefore, that the iron laws of British politics are not suspended even for the most determined and 'mould-breaking' politicians.

The Importance of Consent

Any modern British government ought to give a high priority to gaining and retaining public consent, if only because its attenuation or absence can fatally undermine the position of even the most powerful Administration. Of course, in many cases governments can get by with no more than the tacit acquiescence of the general public as a basis for their policies. Yet, for the most part, active consent is desirable for the fulfilment of policy and this usually implies a number of important preconditions. It requires a well-informed and influential Parliament in which all MPs not in the Government have sufficient opportunities to influence policy and control the Executive. It requires genuine and extensive consultations with a wide variety of interest and cause groups representing the full gamut of sectional interests in modern society. It requires a serious and responsible approach by the media to the discussion and interpretation of the great political issues of the day. Even if all such conditions are met, the interests of good government can be prejudiced by the complicated and uncomfortable constraints within which nearly all political decisions have to be made.

If any British government is to deal successfully with the difficult problems of our time – for example, the intractable problem of inflation, the impact of rapid technological advance, or the effect of demographic changes upon the labour market and the Welfare State – there will always be a great need for responsible and far-sighted leadership by politicians in all parties. Such leadership may well require the elaboration of convincing new formulations of many of our familiar economic and social objectives in ways which increase our chances of attaining them. For its part the general public will need to realise that many of our traditional attitudes and assumptions often obstruct rather than assist the emergence of new syntheses essential for further economic growth, social progress and enhancement of the quality of life to which we all aspire in the 1990s and beyond. Even assuming that we manage to move in such a virtuous circle, it will not be easy, and may be impossible, to avoid bouts of public disappointment and even distress, especially in today's interdependent world in which no national government or Parliament is completely master in its own house.

20.5 Conclusion

It should be clear from this book that British parliamentary democracy is easy neither to describe nor to explain. It is changing all the time, yet in many ways it remains the same. It is imbued with fascinating paradoxes and contradictions. While the system allows for and even encourages strong government, its capacity for legitimising the decisions actually taken has not always been so impressive. This may have been because some controversial decisions were not founded upon a sufficiently broad political consensus at the time when they were taken. Yet more often we must point to the essentially cautious and even complacent attitudes which imbue so many of our most influential groups and powerful institutions. This provides the real explanation for our patchy and often disappointing national performance over so many years.

There are some signs that a new political consensus did emerge in the 1980s to replace many of the received ideas which had been inherited from the 1950s and 1960s, but there are now other signs that the spirit of the 1990s may be different again and that not even the so-called Thatcherite revolution managed to put down firm and lasting roots in British society. In the future, as in the past, politicians and public alike will have to strive for continuous understanding and mutual accommodation, without which things are more likely to go wrong than right. With it there will be no guarantee of success, but it may be possible to maintain sufficient mutual trust and public consent to enable our parliamentary democracy to function satisfactorily for some time to come.

Suggested Questions

1. What is the essence of British parliamentary democracy?
2. Is the British political system successful in gaining and retaining the consent of the people?
3. Have British politics been permanently altered by Britain's membership of the European Community?

Notes

1. See J. A. Schumpeter, *Capitalism, Socialism and Democracy*, 3rd edn (New York: Harper & Row, 1962), pp. 289–96.
2. See Q. Hailsham, *The Dilemma of Democracy* (London: Collins, 1978), pp. 280–1.

Further Reading

Brittan, S., *The Role and Limits of Government* (London: Temple Smith, 1983).
Dahrendorf, R., *Life Chances* (London: Weidenfeld & Nicolson, 1979).
Hailsham, Q., *The Dilemma of Democracy* (London: Collins, 1978).
Hirsch, F., *Social Limits to Growth* (London: Routledge & Kegan Paul, 1977).
Luard, E., *The Globalisation of Politics* (London: Macmillan, 1990).
Marquand, D., *The Unprincipled Society* (London: Fontana Press, 1988).
Miliband, R., *Capitalist Democracy in Britain* (Oxford University Press, 1984).
Schumpeter, J. A., *Capitalism, Socialism and Democracy*, 3rd edn (New York: Harper & Row, 1962).

Name Index

Subject index